SPURS – THE PROGRAMME GUIDE

SPURS
THE PROGRAMME GUIDE

A GUIDE TO THE HOME AND AWAY PROGRAMMES OF TOTTENHAM HOTSPUR FC 1946 - 2020

BOB GOODWIN AND GRAHAM BETTS

ROBWIN PUBLISHING HOUSE

First published in Great Britain by
Robwin Publishing House
20 Roundcroft, West Cheshunt, Herts EN7 6DL
2020

ISBN 0-9540434-5-6

INTRODUCTION

"You can please some of the people all of the time, you can please all of the people some of the time, but you can't please all of the people all of the time". - John Lydgate

Some of you may recall that the authors recently asked, via social media, what kind of book collectors were looking for as we considered updating our earlier publication *"Away The Spurs"*. As you can imagine we got a lot of differing views on everything from the size of the book, the actual content, whether the book should serve as a checklist and what kind of price people might be prepared to pay. It also goes without saying that the two authors also held differing views on virtually all of the above! Therefore, what you are now holding is what can probably best be described as a compromise book; hopefully all the elements you had hoped to see included are present and to those who are left disappointed we can only apologise.

One of the earliest agreements we reached was that the book should containing listings of both home and away first team programmes. Avid collectors will undoubtedly recall Chris Ward and Steve Isaac's Programme & Handbook Guides that were published in 1993 and 1994. These books contained listings of every match played at White Hart Lane (and a few home games played elsewhere) and therefore covered the first team, reserves and occasionally junior and youth teams as well as representative matches played at the old stadium. Rather than merely reproduce those listings, we decided to only cover first team matches, simply because had we listed everything, we would have had to have done similar for away programmes, an altogether impossible undertaking, as we are sure you will appreciate.

This decision is not without its own drawbacks of course. The new stadium hosted a couple of games that featured the Under 18's (against Southampton Under 18's) and a legends side (against a similar Inter Milan side) while the club pursued the necessary safety certificates. They fall outside the scope of this book. Likewise, there are numerous non-footballing events that have been held at both the old and new stadium, in particular boxing and American football, which would have found their way into the Programme and Handbook Guides but are excluded from this book.

It is also worth remembering that *"Away The Spurs"* was compiled in the days when the internet was in its infancy, so our knowledge of what programmes were issued and what were not was based almost entirely on our own collections and recollections. The world wide web has proven to be a godsend in this respect, enabling collectors from around the globe to liaise and find out relatively easily and quickly whether or not a programme had been issued for a particular game.

Which brings us to an area where the internet (and desktop publishing) has been more of a hindrance than a help. If pirate programmes were the bane of unsuspecting purchasers up until the 1970s, then they have returned with a vengeance in recent years; our UEFA Cup tie in Zimbru in 1999 saw an official programme and at least five pirates, and our more recent forays into European competition have been similarly commemorated by an abundance of pirate programmes. Some of these have actually been produced in England, others many hundreds of miles from the match venue, after the game in question purely for Spurs fans. The quality of these has varied, as you might expect. In the main it has been poor, but there have been some that pass muster. Likewise some producers have adopted the practice of labelling their efforts as 'official' when they quite clearly are nothing of the sort and simply described as such to fool the gullible. Caveat emptor, as the Romans would have said.

Many of these programmes, both official and unofficial, have enjoyed a resurgence of sales over the last twenty five or so years, fuelled almost entirely by the popularity of online sales and auction site ebay. For many ebay has been responsible for rekindling their enthusiasm for collecting football programmes and memorabilia, finding that elusive programme or ticket stub now a mere click of the mouse away. Again, however, technological progress has increased the ease with which items can be almost professionally copied and there are a myriad of sellers offering reproduction items without making it fully clear what it is exactly they are selling. Even worse than the reproduction items are those which claim to be original but are nothing more than the creation of someone sitting in front of a computer.

It was therefore to try and sort out some of the confusion over official programmes, monthly magazines issued by the clubs in question, pirates and local newspapers that we embarked on the latest listing. Once again, we reiterate that although we are confident that we have managed to identify many of the anomalies we mention above, as well as correcting some errors that appeared in the original publication, there will no doubt be readers who have details (or more importantly, actual copies) of programmes that we state don't exist. The beauty of print on demand means we will be able to correct these errors in subsequent editions! So, if know of any programmes we have omitted, or if you notice any mistakes, please do let us know.

Finally, we could not have produced this book without the help and input of others – John Matthews, Daren Burney, Nick Manning, Steve Martin, John Davies deserve special thanks.

Bob and Graham.
October 2020

SEASON BY SEASON REVIEW

The programmes, handbooks, tickets, and other publications featured in these listings and which provide the many illustrations throughout this book showcase the mixed fortunes of Tottenham Hotspur Football Club over the last seventy four years. The matches covered represent the very heights of achievement as well as the depths of despair (Spurs fans of almost any age will fully understand these variables), and no doubt the mere glimpse of a programme cover will invoke instant memories, good and bad, among collectors and supporters alike.

As we stated in the introduction, this book (or at least the listings section) only covers recognised first team matches, with boxes provided if you want to indicate you have the programme, ticket stub, teamsheet or whatever, or even went to the match. There are some matches where we know there was no official programme issued so have lightly shaded the first box to show that, allowing those who accept a press sheet, pirate programme or newspaper as an alternative to utilise it. We have also provided boxes for those who collect handbooks and/or season tickets to use.

Again, we also know of instances where there was more than one official programme issued (the European Cup-Winners' Cup Final against Atletico Madrid being one such example) and we have allowed for this should you collect all the available editions.

As you may recall, Steve Isaac and Graham provided relatively extensive season-by-season reviews in *'The Programme & Handbook Guide*'s and *'Away The Spurs '* respectively, so apologies if some of the information has appeared before. It does, however, give us an opportunity to highlight some of the changes that have occurred over the ensuing years, such as the availability of certain programmes, the confirmation of others that were previously thought not to exist and, perhaps more worryingly for avid collectors, the sudden appearance of a programme or two that relatively few people knew about previously.

The names of the opposition throughout these listings are as they were at the time of the match, so Leyton Orient of the First Division in 1962-63 subsequently became Orient for the Second Division clashes in 1977-78 and were back to Leyton Orient for the friendly fixtures in 1997-98 and onwards.

The dates listed refer to the date of the match; if the match was postponed and the same programme utilised, this has been noted. Unless otherwise stated, all away matches took place on the opposition's recognised home ground.

1946-47

The resumption of the Football League in 1946-47 brought with it a major change at Tottenham, a switch of printer for the club programme. Crusha & Son, a company based in Tottenham High Road and part of the local community since 1861 (they also published the *'Tottenham & Edmonton Weekly Herald*') had produced both the programme and handbook since 1935 (succeeding C Coventry who had been the club printer since at least 1897), both of which were instantly recognisable by their salmon pink colour. Supporters who arrived for the first of two public trial matches in August were greeted with a familiar four page programme (basically a large sheet folded in half) that featured blue print on white paper and was printed by Thomas Knight & Co of Hoddesdon in Hertfordshire. This company would print virtually every official programme, handbook, ticket, and document issued by the club until the early 1980s. Not helped by paper rationing that was still in force following the Second World War, programmes both home and away, were somewhat sparse compared with current issues. The rarities from this season are undoubtedly the home fixtures against Southampton, Newport County and Swansea Town in the League and the friendly against Arsenal and the away League fixtures at Newport and Swansea, the FA Cup replay at Stoke and end of season visit to Norwich for the Norwich Hospital Charity Cup. It is not known whether programmes were produced for the end of season tour games in France.

1947-48

There are two programmes for the visit to Saltergate to play Chesterfield in the Second Division on 27 December. The first is an official edition published by the club, but following something of a dispute between the football club and the Supporters Club, the latter (The Spire-Ites') had taken to producing their own programme! By all accounts it was an extremely professional production too, with a recent visiting chairman expressing his envy. The dispute, whatever it may have been, had obviously led the club to believe the Spire-Ites' version would not last long; the Spurs edition was their tenth. Finally, we have managed to confirm that there was a team sheet that served as a basic programme for our first match in the Channel Islands at the end of the season.

1948-49

The Official Handbook, last published in 1939, returned for the 1948-49 season. Whereas the pre-war handbook had retained the same salmon colour as the programme and the same cover design for virtually every issue, the new handbook cover was blue with a dark blue cockerel in the centre (this design would itself be retained for three seasons) as well as being a slighter larger size booklet. The programmes identified as being rare twenty five years ago, away to Chelmsford City and Cornwall, continue to prove elusive.

1949-50

The season the Second Division championship and with it promotion to the First Division was won features a significant number of important programmes, with the home match against Grimsby Town issued as an eight page commemorative edition. It is not known whether a programme was produced for the final end of season tour match against Royal Beerschot, but just to remind collectors, there are two programmes for the match against Tennis Borussia; one issued by the club and written in German and a second written in English and issued by the British Army.

1950-51

Considering the club produced a special edition to commemorate winning the Second Division it is surprising nothing was done to acknowledge winning the First Division for the first time. The major rarity from this season is the friendly against Lovells Athletic on a late Monday afternoon in September, which attracted a crowd of just 3,124. Copies of the programme do turn up from time to time, but invariably they are auctioned off by the big auctioneers rather than appearing on eBay! It is not known whether programmes were produced for the visits to Liege or Paris. Racing Club de Paris are known to have issued in the 1950s for visits by another club from north London, but nothing has surfaced for any of Spurs' several visits during the same decade. We are now able to confirm that there was a publication for the end of season trip to Copenhagen, although it is unclear whether it covered one or all three games.

1951-52

There could be as many as four different versions of the programme for the home League match against Huddersfield Town. The match was originally scheduled for 29 March but postponed for two days as White Hart Lane was chosen as the venue for the FA Cup semi-final between Arsenal and Chelsea. Snow caused both matches to be postponed (the semi-final to 5 April), with Spurs and Huddersfield being moved to 2 April. Three versions of the programme are known – a) 31 March outside and 2 April inside, b) 2 April outside but 31 March inside, c) 2 April both outside and inside! It begs the question of whether there are examples with 31 March both inside and out? Rarities this season are undoubtedly the FA Charity Shield against Newcastle United and the friendly against a Copenhagen Combination XI.

1952-53

As well as a club issued standard programme, the FA Cup-tie away at Preston in January saw the Lancashire Evening Post produce a 16 page brochure for the game. Although primarily concerned with Preston's history in the FA Cup, it did feature pen pics and photographs of the two teams. After overcoming Preston, Spurs required three attempts at beating Birmingham City, finally winning at Molineux. The rarities this season however are the cup tie at Halifax Town, the Coronation Cup tie against Hibernian and the League match at Old Trafford against Manchester United, with the latter played on a Wednesday afternoon. Despite the match featuring the last two sides to have won the League title, a crowd of a little over 20,000 attended the match!

1953-54

Another extended FA Cup run saw Spurs venture as far as the sixth round, with the away third round match at Leeds United the real domestic rarity from this season. An end of season tour of Austria and West Germany was undertaken, with all four programmes somewhat elusive.

1954-55

This season contains at least three home and one away domestic programme that are in seriously short supply and therefore attract premium prices. The four programmes are all friendlies, against Finchley, Arsenal and FC Servette at White Hart Lane and the abandoned match at Accrington Stanley. Equally difficult to source are any end of season tour match programmes in Austria, Hungary, and France, if any were produced.

1955-56

Spurs enjoyed another extended FA Cup run, again reaching the semi-final before the Villa Park curse dealt a third consecutive blow. The previously elusive away cup tie at Doncaster Rovers has fallen sharply in price in recent years, meaning the most sought after item is the away friendly at Aarhus.

1956-57

Six matches against Scottish opposition, home and away against Hibernian, Partick Thistle and Hearts, were to have been in an Anglo-Scottish Floodlit Tournament (see the cover to the Hibernian away match), but both the FA and the Scottish FA refused to sanction such a competition. Since the games had all been scheduled it was decided to play them all officially as friendlies. At the end of the season Spurs undertook an extensive tour of the USA and Canada, where further Scottish opposition in Celtic was met on no fewer than four occasions. The programme for the match in New York was an edition of the American Soccer League News. Programmes are not known for the match with a Hartford XI or the two games in Mexico.

1957-58

The three foreign friendlies during the course of the season (in Stuttgart, Basel, and Rotterdam) are the elusive items from this season, combined with the obligatory scarcity of the Leeds United and Burnley away matches.

1958-59

In recent years, the three Russian tour programmes have become more readily available, although they still command high purchase prices. One anomaly for the season is the London Challenge Cup Final against West Ham United played at White Hart Lane on 1 December; although the match was scheduled as a reserve team fixture, both sides agreed to field as close to a full XI as was possible, attracting a crowd in excess of 18,000 in the process. The original home programme guide upgraded this fixture to a first team match (based on the wording in the following home programme, which stated the match had been 'a preview of the Boxing Day encounter'). We have omitted this fixture from our listing as it was officially a reserve team match.

1959-60

The two cup ties against Crewe have become popular in recent years, the home tie entirely because it represents Spurs record winning score. There was no programme for the end of season friendly in Turin against Juventus, though the '*Tutto Sport*' paper featured the team line-ups.

1960-61

The Double season contains several highly sought after programmes, including Bolton (the most expensive), Preston, Newcastle, and Burnley in particular, but every programme has a value in excess of normal programmes from the era. The final home game also saw the production of a special twelve page edition and thus marked the end of the old four page format. At the end of the season Spurs played two friendly matches in Holland for which there are programmes, two for the fixture against an Amsterdam XI.

1961-62

The first foray into the European Cup saw Spurs travel behind the Iron Curtain to meet Gornik Zabrze in Poland, with the programme continuing to be an expensive item. The final away trip in the competition to Benfica saw no programmes issued, although in recent years edition 1008 of '*O Benfica* ' (an official weekly club newspaper) has almost attained programme status. Finally, we can confirm that there were no programmes issued for two post-season friendlies in Israel.

1962-63

As far as the compilers of this book are concerned, there was no official programme issued for the first and reserve team friendly matches against Arsenal on 26 January. What was available (reputedly to those in the press and directors' boxes and about forty in total) was a hastily typed up team sheet covering both games copied onto A4 paper. Photocopies have turned up in abundance; copies of the originals invariably sell for vast sums at auction. By comparison three programmes were issued for the European Cup-Winners' Cup Final in Rotterdam. Two were issued by UEFA, one of 20 pages, the other of 28 pages (both including the four page cover wrap), while the third was issued by the stadium authorities at host club Feijenoord. For the end of season tour of South Africa an identical programme differing only in the centre spread line-up pages was issued for all three matches with a large giveaway poster of Spurs included in the first of them.

1963-64

This season (and the next) saw a brief return of the public trial as a curtain raiser, although these programmes are infinitely easier to locate than those from the three previous decades. Little else from this season should present too many problems with the possible exception of the Burnley postponed and end of season friendly at Coventry City.

1964-65

Not for the first nor last time, it is the away friendlies that prove to be the most difficult programmes to obtain, in particular those from the end of season tour of Israel that included competing for the John White Cup against Maccabi Tel Aviv.

1965-66

As if to prove the above point, the American tour programmes are pretty elusive. Two editions of the *'American League Soccer News* ' (publication dates 6 and 13 March) preview the forthcoming visit by Spurs and Celtic for those wanting an overview of the tour. The programme issued for the match against Bologna on 29 May also covered the fixture between Bologna and Celtic two days previously, while the issue for Celtic on 1 June also covered Celtic's match against Bayern Munich a week later. Aside from the tour programmes, the real rarity from this season is that for the match due to be played at Arsenal on 26 February that was postponed owing to a waterlogged pitch.

1966-67

As well as the programme that covered all matches in the Costa Del Sol Tournament in August, it may be of interest to pick up a copy of the 4 August edition of the Barcelona based sports newspaper *'Dicen'*, which as well as containing a full page preview of the tournament also carried full details of the World Cup finals in England! While programmes from the first and last matches of the end of season Swiss tour are known, the same cannot be said of the match against BSC Young Boys.

1967-68

The return to European competition should not present too many problems for collectors, leaving the post-season tour of Greece and Cyprus as the difficult items. No programme appears to have been issued for the match against Panathinaikos while a tour brochure covered the four matches in Cyprus. The real rarity for this season is the home programme for the postponed match against Burnley that was due to take place on 6 January, perhaps the rarest of all Spurs home programmes since the Second World War.

1968-69

Closely following the above Burnley programme for scarcity is the similarly postponed issue against Queens Park Rangers on 30 November. Programmes for postponed fixtures against Ipswich Town and Southampton are readily available. At the end of the season Spurs returned to North America to compete in the Toronto Cup. Apart from the centre line-up pages, the programme content for Spurs' matches was identical save that the Rangers issue contained a feature on Colin Stein that was replaced with one on Jimmy Greaves for the Fiorentina game. The Rangers issue was printed in black, the Fiorentina one in blue.

1969-70

As well as three individual programmes being issued for the visit to Malta post season, Sliema Wanderers produced a souvenir edition of their club magazine *'Blue Review'* for the trip while Spurs Malta Supporters Club produced a welcome magazine and club history supplement. At home, the two postponements and one abandonment are all easy to obtain.

1970-71

Hardest programme from the campaign to obtain is undoubtedly the away Ipswich Town postponed issue from Boxing Day. It was originally believed that there was a single brochure to cover the three matches against All-Japan XIs. It now transpires that there was an identical programme issued for all three games with the line-up page left blank for spectators to complete, plus a locally produced issue for the first match.

1971-72

Before we look at the rarities from European competition, a note about the League fixture at Derby County. While the host club had taken to producing a newspaper style programme, there was a "Complimentary Programme (for internal use only)" that was reportedly only given to directors and VIPs. This was a simple four page wraparound that covered the regular newspaper issue, although it did contain the team line-ups. In Europe we have located two teamsheets for the fixture at Rapid Bucharest, one on official Rapid paper and the other (apparently a press sheet) on plain paper. The programme, such as it was, for the UT Arad match, was printed in red and white; the readily available black and white copies are just that, copies. Finally (or perhaps semi finally), although there was no programme for the match against AC Milan, the April edition of the Milan club magazine, Forza, does contain coverage of Spurs' success.

1972-73

Although Red Star Belgrade did not issue a standard programme for Spurs' UEFA Cup visit, the club's monthly magazine has always been hugely collectable as a viable alternative. The match at Olympiakos Piraeus saw only a teamsheet on flimsy paper being issued.

1973-74

Just as the European Cup-Winners' Cup Final in 1963 in Rotterdam saw three programmes being issued, so there are four for the UEFA Cup Final second leg against Feyenoord. According to legend, the original programme (with a colour cover) was produced but a fire at the warehouse/printing company saw all available copies destroyed. A hastily printed replacement (with a black and white cover) was produced and sold on the night, along with a De Sportgids club newspaper and Sportblad Feyenoord supporters edition. After the match, the original programme was reprinted with the colour cover!

1974-75

We can now confirm that there was a programme produced for the cancelled Rod Smithson testimonial at Oxford in November, resulting in it being probable that only the away friendly against Red Star Belgrade was without a programme.

1975-76

There are numerous uncertainties from this particular campaign, commencing with the pre-season tour of West Germany and Holland and early season trip to France to play Stade Rennais. No programmes are known for any of those games. A cancelled trip to Norway has produced a programme for only one of the two matches that were to be played, while the programme for a testimonial against non-League opposition at Stevenage has proved as difficult to obtain as those for the end of season tour of Fiji, New Zealand, and Australia by way of Canada. While programmes of some description have surfaced for most of the games, nothing was produced for that in Fiji and nothing is known for that against Victoria.

1976-77

A disastrous season began with a five game tour of West Germany, with three opponents issuing programmes. Nothing is known from the mid-campaign visit to Napredec Krusevac in Yugoslavia, or the two matches in Norway that followed relegation. The previously expensive Peter Simpson testimonial and League match at Manchester City have fallen rapidly in price.

1977-78

The sojourn in the Second Division saw a major change in home programmes, with an increase in size and the cover now being in full colour, although the same picture was invariably used for three or four programmes in a row. Away from home pre-season began with three matches in Sweden, with a brochure covering the Nolia Cup matches. At the end of a successful season, Spurs made a short trip to Syria, followed by one to Sweden and Norway. Programmes were issued for the Scandinavian matches while it appears there was nothing from the two in Syria.

1978-79

While the cover design of the handbook had continually altered since its re-appearance in 1948, it had remained the same size, able to fit in a hand. A slightly larger size was now introduced that was to last for three years before another increase. Further changes in the home programme saw colour being introduced inside each edition and a changing image on the front cover for what would be the final season for Thomas Knight & Co. It was also the first season for Argentinian imports Ossie Ardiles and Ricky Villa, resulting in Spurs being a big draw the world over. Programmes (some more in the form of a teamsheet) were issued for matches in Belgium, Sweden, and Dubai, while nothing more than a teamsheet has surfaced for the game in Holland and nothing at all is known for matches in Saudi Arabia, Kuwait, Malaysia and Bermuda. Although one brochure covers all five matches in the Japan Cup, there were single sheet supplements showing the Thai and Burmese national squads, late additions to the tournament. There is also a Japanese football magazine – *'Soccer Magazine '* - published after the tournament that gave excellent coverage to the competition. For Ian Gillard's Testimonial QPR's usual programme became a brochure with a single sheet programme also issued. The home FA Cup tie against Altrincham, scheduled for 6 January was played four days later owing to the arctic conditions on the original match day.

1979-80

Maybank Press took over printing the programme, expanding the content by four pages, increasing the cover price, and introducing advertisements throughout. In comparison with previous years, only one excursion across the channel took place, neither of the two end of season friendlies in Austria producing a programme.

1980-81

A further increase in page content brought about another increase in cover price, but the general consensus was that the home programme was beginning to represent value for money. Away from home there were programmes for every match during the regular season, which included a trip to Jersey for a friendly against Rothmans Combination (still difficult to obtain) and culminated in winning the FA Cup. No programmes are known for the end of season trips to Bahrain, Kuwait, and Turkey.

1981-82

Although Maybank Press had been printing the home programmes for two years, it was only now that they replaced Thomas Knight in producing the handbook, slightly increasing the size beyond that of most hands. The home programme settled on the previous season's size and pricing, with the exception of a special edition for the visit of Wolverhampton Wanderers, which saw the new West Stand officially opened by Sir Stanley Rous. This edition cost 50p (as opposed to the usual 30p) but it did include a 16 page supplement. Another trip to Jersey saw a difficult to obtain newspaper supplement programme while it appears nothing was produced for the visit to Sporting Lisbon. Neither the Israeli XI friendly in Jaffa nor Barcelona in the European Cup-Winners' Cup produced programmes, although the Barcelona magazine for 6 April advertised Spurs visit on its cover. Sadly, the inside reveals just two pages of coverage.

1982-83

Although we previously listed the Lausanne friendly as having no programme, there was a teamsheet that was well distributed around the stadium. There were no programmes for the two friendlies in Israel, while a brochure covered the two matches in the Amsterdam 707 Tournament at the start of the campaign. At home, in what was Spurs Centenary Season, there appears to have been a missed opportunity – no special edition and errors in the first three issues (wrong season on the cover)! The end of season trip to Swaziland produced a brochure covering Spurs two matches against Manchester United and a combined Spurs/United team meeting with the Swazi national side.

1983-84

A hectic but hugely successful season, culminating in winning the UEFA Cup. At home, the season began and ended with testimonials for Spurs two most successful managers, Bill Nicholson and Keith Burkinshaw, with the visit of West Ham United on a Sunday for the former also seeing a teamsheet issued. The other Sunday fixture, the first televised match against Nottingham Forest, also featured a teamsheet, although of special interest was the four page wraparound that gave details of the forthcoming flotation of Tottenham Hotspur Plc on the stock market. The programme for the second leg of the UEFA Cup final saw a 40 page edition produced, costing a then astronomical £1! Away from home one oddity is the two matches played on the same day (against Aylesbury and Brentford). Strong teams were fielded in both games and as there will always be debate as to whether both could be classed as "first team" games, they are both included. Other oddities are a programme and newspaper for the UEFA Cup-tie against Bayern Munich and no programme but a club magazine for the semi-final against Hajduk Split. Spurs ended the campaign with a return to Swaziland, with a brochure covering the two matches against Liverpool and a combined Spurs/Liverpool team against the national side.

1984-85

Two visits were made to Real Madrid during the course of the season. In the first Spurs provided the opposition for Goyo Benito's testimonial, for which there is no programme though a teamsheet can be found. For the second, a UEFA Cup tie later in the campaign, there was a free programme and an official club magazine. One other away UEFA Cup tie failed to produce a programme, that against Braga, although the local newspaper *'Jornal de Noticias '* gave good coverage in its Desporto section. Other matches for which there were no known programmes are OGC Nice, a Kuwait XI and Seiko, although there was a Seiko Sports magazine. The season ended with the Australian $200,000 Tournament, although Spurs participation was in doubt up until the last minute owing to the blanket ban on English clubs playing abroad following the Heysel Stadium disaster.

1985-86

Only two matches failed to produce a programme during the course of the season; a friendly against Wycombe Wanderers at Bisham Abbey and a Jersey Select XI in St Helier, the only trip outside the mainland. The hastily arranged Screen Sport Super Cup saw six matches played home and away, with probably the lowest print runs of any Spurs programmes of the era, although all six are readily available. The season also saw Ossie Ardiles granted a testimonial (with Diego Maradona guesting for Spurs), the first of the large (A4) size programmes being issued.

1986-87

Although there was no programme for Barcelona's Joan Gamper tournament, the leading Catalan sports paper *'Sport '* did produce a 12 page pre-tournament supplement prior to the usual excellent daily coverage so well-known of Spanish papers. Midway through the campaign Spurs travelled to Bermuda to play the national XI; programmes from this match have continued to increase in value. We now know there was no programme for the match against Millonarios in Miami, although the local Spanish Language sports paper *'Golaz '* featured the fixture. At home there were three matches for which a teamsheet was also issued, the fixtures against Arsenal and Liverpool in the League and Arsenal in the Littlewoods Cup. The League meeting with Arsenal was the 100th such match and the programme contained a reprint of the Woolwich Arsenal programme from the first League meeting in 1910. Spurs also produced a commemorative magazine to record the occasion. One other programme has recently come to light – a postponed issue for the away match originally scheduled against Newcastle United for 17th January.

1987-88

Although production of the home programme remained with Maybank Press, Valentine Press now took on responsibility for the handbook that increased in size if not content. At home, the season kicked off with an oversize programme for the visit of Arsenal for Chris Hughton's testimonial, while there were two Sunday matches for which a teamsheet was issued, against Arsenal and Charlton Athletic. Away, there was only one match that did not see a programme issued, that being against Euskadi (Basque Country), though a teamsheet was obtainable.

1988-89

After a pre-season in Sweden (programmes issued for all four matches), four away testimonials and a Wembley International Tournament (one programme covering both days of football), attention turned to the start of the new season. Unfortunately, the ground was not quite ready, meaning the home fixture against Coventry City was postponed on the morning of the game! The programme, the first designed and printed by Valentine Press, is relatively easy to get hold of. There was a cancelled match too, a friendly against Portsmouth being called off owing to a heavy downpour on the morning of the game; the programme is readily available. There were teamsheets issued for two matches during the course of the season, at West Ham United for Alvin Martin's Testimonial and the home League fixture with Nottingham Forest. There were also two home friendlies that attracted low crowds, AS Monaco and Bordeaux, but programmes from both fixtures are easy to obtain.

1989-90

As well as a programme for the away friendly against Viking there is a club magazine, with the August edition of '*Viking Innkast* ' featuring a decent spread on the game. Paul Ramsey's testimonial at Leicester City saw both a single sheet programme (effectively an A4 sheet printed on cardboard) and an official numbered teamsheet. There were no programmes issued for the two matches in the Trofeo Villa De Madrid, nor the friendly against Caen in Cherbourg.

1990-91

Edmonton's Total Graphics took on the job of printing the home programmes, designed by CDC of Watford. As well as a standard issue for the home League match against Liverpool, there was a special '*The Match* ' edition produced by ITV for their live coverage. This was a standard programme with a four page wraparound. Similar editions were produced for the away fixtures with Everton (which also saw two standard issues containing programme notes by outgoing manager Jimmy Gabriel and returning manager Howard Kendall) and Derby County. Away from home the August edition of the Viking magazine '*Viking Innkast* ' covered the game though not as well as the previous year. At the end of the season Spurs participated in the Kirin Cup in Japan. As well as a tour brochure covering all three games there was a magazine of which half was given over to Spurs.

1991-92

As M Press (Sales) took over production of the handbook, Total Graphics assumed the design of home programmes as well as printing them. There were editions of '*The Match* ' for both the home European Cup-Winners' Cup tie against Feyenoord and the League fixture at Arsenal, but unlike previous seasons these were magazines produced by ITV not just the standard programme with a wraparound. There were no programmes for the European Cup-Winners' Cup ties against Hajduk Split (played in Linz, Austria) or Porto, although there was a club magazine covering the latter fixture. The only other no show programme wise was Brann in pre-season. A single programme covers the two matches played in the Nicola Ceravolo Memorial Tournament. Grimsby produced a souvenir brochure for Spurs' Rumbelows Cup visit.

1992-93

Real Madrid and Internazionale were Spurs' guests in the Fiorucci Cup, which saw three games of 45 minutes played at White Hart Lane, Spurs losing to both before Real beat Inter 2-1. One programme covers all three games. While teamsheets are known, there were no programmes issued for the away Capital Cup fixture against Lazio or the friendly against Real Zaragoza.

1993-94

For the Makita International Tournament at the start of the season one programme was issued covering all four matches played over two days. Away from home Spurs provided the opposition for Tom Sundby's testimonial, with Lyn Oslo producing a four page newspaper featuring the game as well as a programme. There were no programmes for the matches against Brann or Atletico Madrid (played in Jerez). The League fixture at Oldham

Athletic proved to be something of a nightmare. Originally scheduled for 16 March it was postponed a few hours before kick-off – programmes were released. Re-scheduled for 20 April, it was postponed again a few hours before kick-off, again with programmes released. It finally took place at the third attempt on 5 May, with the 20 April issue used for the occasion, albeit sold at lower than the cover price! M Press (Sales) continued printing the handbook, but production of it passed to Wolff Evans.

1994-95

The season that saw Spurs become a big draw again, thanks largely to the arrival of Jurgen Klinsmann. Total Graphics added the handbook design and production to their programme responsibilities. Programmes exist for all matches played throughout the season, and there are two postponed issues, away at Newcastle (considerably easier to get hold of than the 1986-87 issue) and home against Manchester City. At the end of the season Spurs headed to the Far East for three matches, which proved a difficult journey for programme collectors. There was a programme for the Euro-Asia Challenge match against Eastern/Kitchee Select in Hong Kong, but this was not available to the general public; copies were only to be found in the VIP and press area of the ground. There were no programmes for the match against Guangzhou (teamsheets were almost impossible to obtain) or Singapore Lions (a team sheet was only produced at half-time following complaints from the press box).

1995-96

The large size programme made a re-appearance for Gary Mabbutt's testimonial against Newcastle United at the start of the season. Although played on consecutive days Rangers produced separate programmes for the Ibrox tournament. The FA Cup tie at Nottingham Forest was abandoned after some six minutes owing to the heaviest snow fall anyone could remember. A new slimmed down (eight instead of forty page) programme was issued for the replayed match on 28 February, although the original tickets were used to gain admittance. And then the match ended a draw, requiring a further replay! Although programmes exist for all four Intertoto Cup matches played (two at "home" in Brighton and two away) we have not included them. While UEFA may consider them 'official', they are not regarded as "first team" matches. When a mix of youth and specially signed players was losing 0-8 in Cologne (a result UEFA likes to regard as Spurs' heaviest European defeat), the first team was in action in Silkeborg.

1996-97

Programmes exist for all our matches played during the course of the season. Unlike at Raufoss where a teamsheet was handed out at the turnstiles, the friendly against Ham-Kam at Hamar Stadion saw a black and white teamsheet made available to VIPs and the press only. This was subsequently copied onto green Ham-Kam paper the day after the match at the request of a visiting supporter! Although the programme for the following match against Odd Greenland is date 27 July, the match was played on 25 July. How odd. There was a programme for the postponed League fixture at Leicester City that is easy to obtain.

1997-98

Handbook and programme production/design was now assumed by Wolff Evans, with both being printed by Security Printers. Programmes exist for every game played this season, which began with four friendlies in Scandinavia and ended with Spurs having flirted with relegation. The return of Jurgen Klinsmann saw Spurs pull out of the danger area, as probably be-fitted the winners of the inaugural Bill Halsey Memorial Trophy!

1998-99

There was further silverware to celebrate this season, with Spurs proving triumphant in the only competition not won by Manchester United (who were beaten on the way to lifting the trophy), the Worthington Cup. The run also resulted in five matches against Wimbledon in one month – two Worthington Cup semi-finals, an FA Cup tie and replay and a League match, a run that is probably unique. The League fixture against Leeds United saw the Yorkshire Evening Post produce a 'Special Publication' covering the match and Leeds Rhinos Silk Cut Challenge Cup game with Wigan Warriors.

1999-2000

After so many years with Crusha & Son, C Coventry, and Thomas Knight, changing handbook and programme producers was now a constant event. For this season Peterhurst Limited arrived on the scene to produce both. Pre-season found Spurs back in Scandinavia for three matches, with the fixture against GAIS seeing three different editions of the one programme available - light green, dark green and black and white! There was equally an abundance of programmes for the UEFA Cup tie against Zimbru Chișinău in Moldova, for as well as one official programme there were at least five pirate issues and three local newspapers that made their way back to Britain.

2000-01

The new century brought renewed optimism and, midway through the season, a new manager steeped in Tottenham's traditions. Despite the year ending in one all hopes of a trophy in the cabinet came to a halt at Old Trafford with defeat in the FA Cup semi-final. Peterhurst continued to produce and print the handbook and programme though 'shoot the moon ' designed the handbook. On the programme front, the only matter of note came with the Worthington Cup fixture at Brentford on 19 September. For some reason, the Bees programme was issued in a sealed bag, although there were no inserts or additions to justify the packaging. How many have never been opened?

2001-02

The pre-season friendly away against AEK Athens saw three separate editions of the teamsheet readily available in the main stand, being issued in Greek and English with both club badges present and a Greek edition without the Spurs badge. There was a programme for the postponed home FA Cup tie against Bolton Wanderers; this is easy to obtain. Bill Nicholson was afforded a second testimonial at the start of the season, the issue for this game being one of the larger sized programmes. There was a similarly large sized programme for the Worthington Cup final against Blackburn Rovers, played at the Millennium Stadium in Cardiff as Wembley was being rebuilt.

2002-03

Programmes exist for all matches played during the course of the season, although the 'issue' for the curtain falling match against DC United on 14 May is little more than an oversized team card. Spurs had met the American side in a charity match at White Hart Lane in aid of the Tottenham Trust, with a large sized programme being issued.

2003-04

Creative Print Group took over production of the home programme, while Sidan Press' appointment to produce the handbook resulted not only in a totally new design, but the publication no longer being called "Handbook". Chunky and with a hardback cover, it was now entitled "Yearbook". After an absence of forty years a return to South Africa was made with Spurs playing local sides Orlando Pirates (in Durban) and Kaiser Chiefs (in Cape Town) in matches that were part of South Africa's bid to host the forthcoming 2010 FIFA World Cup. Programmes exist for both matches played. Indeed, programmes exist for all fifty three matches played during the course of the season, with no postponements.

2004-05

The season began with three friendlies in Scandinavia followed by five matches in Britain, with programmes being issued for all eight games. Spurs then journeyed to Seville to take part in the Kappa Cup, with neither match producing a programme. The local paper *'Estadio Deportivo '* produced an 8 page pull-out supplement covering the tournament, and Real Betis, the fourth team in the competition, referred to it in its *'Mundo Berico '* pre-season magazine. At the end of the season Spurs travelled to Mauritius to face Club M. A programme that was only available in the VIP area was reprinted after the match at the request of a programme dealer. The reprint differed from the original in that it featured the Spurs badge on the front cover in place of the Mauritius FA badge. At home, the death of Spurs great Bill Nicholson was announced on the morning of 23 October, shortly before the fixture against Bolton Wanderers. Bill graced the cover of the next home match programme against Charlton Athletic, with a Memorial Service being held at White Hart Lane the following morning.

2005-06

After two years of being a yearbook, the handbook returned with Creative Print Group taking on its production. No longer hardback, a major revamp left it rectangular and coil bound. Pre-season saw Spurs win the Peace Cup tournament in Korea. Apart from the tournament programme there was also a small tournament guide. At home, the earliest possible exits from both domestic cup competitions, left Spurs free to concentrate on securing European competition for the following season.

2006-07

Only two of six pre-season matches saw official programmes issued - Birmingham City and Stevenage Borough. Although there was nothing produced by Borussia Dortmund there were two pirates available. There was a similar abundance of pirate programmes for the away UEFA Cup ties, including Slavia Prague and Bayer 04 Leverkusen, the only two ties to have official programmes. For the matches against Besiktas, Braga and Sevilla there were only pirate issues, with Inferno Braga being considered the best of the two produced for the match there. For Sevilla there was an "Official Souvenir Match Magazine", but since this was written entirely in English it was clearly a pirate produced for sale to visiting fans. There was even a pirate produced for a match that never was – the away tie with Feyenoord, cancelled when the Dutch club was expelled from the competition. Tickets for the game were also released before the expulsion became final.

2007-08

While the format remained the same, handbook design was taken over by CRE8 who also took on production of the home programme. Pre-season began with what had become a traditional match at Stevenage Borough before Spurs journeyed to Ireland to play St Patrick's Athletic, the programme misprinted with a date of 12 June instead of 12 July when the match was actually played! This was followed by a return to South Africa to participate in the Vodacom Challenge, with a brochure covering Spurs three matches. The local South African magazine *''Kickoff '* featured the competition, as did Kaizer Chiefs' official magazine *'Amakhosi* '. There was no programme for the UEFA Cup tie at Anderlecht, although a pirate that called itself "The Matchprogramme of Royal Sporting Club Anderlecht" did appear, all in English and nothing to do with the home club. At home there was a special edition for the fixture against Aston Villa to celebrate Spurs 125th anniversary, the programme being one of the larger sized issues.

2008-09

The handbook designers were now known as Cre8 Publishing. Spurs began pre-season with a friendly against Hercules; there was no official programme, but a pirate was produced, and the sport paper AS featured the game. This was followed, after a couple of domestic friendlies, by a visit to Rotterdam for the Feyenoord Jubileum Toernooi. As well as an official programme covering all the matches, there was a *'Stadion Sports Nieuws '* featuring the tournament. There were also two programmes produced for our League fixture at Middlesbrough, with different covers appearing respectively on red and white issues. There were three "programmes" to collect for the UEFA Cup tie against Udinese, a small black issue, a newspaper edition, and a fold-out issue. Spartak Moscow produced a programme to cover their four group matches. There are two handbooks for this season. Juande Ramos and the management team were sacked just as the first was to be released. It was quickly withdrawn and later replaced by one featuring Harry Redknapp and his team. A few of the originals escaped destruction.

2009-10

Spurs took part in two pre-season tournaments, the Wembley Cup (one programme covering all the matches) and the Barclays Asia Trophy (again, one programme covering all matches). A teamsheet is all that was, with considerable difficulty, available for the match against South China. Programmes for the postponed League fixture at Liverpool have proved easy to obtain despite early stories all copies were to be pulped, while there were two issues for the final League match against Burnley, a standard issue, and a limited edition.

2010-11

Another new name came on the Spurs' handbook and programme production scene - Programmemaster. While the coil bound format of the handbook remained, the increase to 100 pages in the programme led to the programme becoming a paperback. Pre-season saw Spurs visiting North America, playing a friendly in San Jose and then competing in the Barclays New York Challenge, with one programme covering all matches in the competition. Closer to home, Benfica's *'O Benfica '* newspaper made little reference to Spurs visit for the Eusebio Cup and few copies of the teamsheet were available. Spurs first venture into the UEFA Champions League saw a mixed bag of programmes. All six home programmes were issued as larger sized (and priced) editions, while away from home there were no official programmes for the matches against Werder Bremen, Internazionale, AC Milan or Real Madrid, only BSC Young Boys (a small issue) and FC Twente issuing. What there was for the other four games was an abundance of pirate and newspaper editions, varying in size and content. Inter, for example, saw one of the most ridiculously sized programmes (especially when compared against the mini issue by Young Boys) alongside the newspaper styled Interista. There was a similar newspaper – *'Milanista '* for the game against AC Milan, while for Real Madrid the best issue was that of *'Media Punta '*.

2011-12

Spurs began pre-season competing in the Vodacom Challenge in South Africa, where apart from a programme covering all three matches there was the *'Soccer Laduuuuma!'* newspaper, Kickoff magazine and the official Kaizer Chiefs magazine *'Amakhosi '* that covered the competition. The only fixture for which there was no programme was PAOK in the Europa League, although the club magazine and sports papers provided coverage. At home, the FA Cup tie with Bolton Wanderers has a special significance. Abandoned after the visitor's Fabrice Muamba collapsed and nearly died.

2012-13

Spurs played three games in America ahead of the season, with a variety of issues being seen; a four page card for the match against LA Galaxy, an oversized issue that was more of a poster for the game against Liverpool in Baltimore, and little more than a teamsheet for the New York Red Bulls. There was similarly nothing more than a teamsheet for the friendly match against Valencia, although newspapers *'Super Deporte '* and *'AS '* provided decent coverage of the game. The return to the Europa League was barren where away programmes were concerned, with NK Maribor and FC Basel the only clubs to issue anything resembling a programme (the Maribor issue was a club magazine covering all the group matches). The earlier tie against Panathinaikos produced two pirates, the better quality in English, the poorer in Greek, with both available at the ground. For Lazio there was *'Metro Stadio '* and *'Magazin Cittaceleste.it '*, the latter not a club publication but a free Lazio oriented newspaper distributed at the ground. The other ties against Inter and Lyon were also programme-less, but there was a pirate edition at Inter and an eight page *'La Tribune OL2 '* pull-out from the local *'Direct Matin '* newspaper in Lyon. The season ended in the Bahamas with a friendly against the Jamaica Reggae Boys, for which there was a programme.

2013-14

Programmemaster were replaced as producers of both the handbook and home programme by Sport Media, though there was little substantial difference. Only one game failed to produce a programme this season, the away Europa League match against Benfica. The club's *'O Benfica '* weekly newspaper covered the match. There were two programmes for both Anzhi and Dnipro, with the former providing an A3 programme and A4 brochure and the latter issuing programmes in B3 and A4 (although this was little more than a four page effort with pictures of both sides' players and written in English). Far more interesting was a Ukrainian football magazine that featured a detailed Spurs history across fourteen of the 50 pages. A short-lived free football magazine, *'Halftime Whistle '* appeared in August 2013, with the second issue featuring a 32 page special on the forthcoming North London derby.

2014-15

A return to North America saw two programmes for the match against Seattle Sounders - Soccer Seattle and Matchday and a programme and player card for the meeting with Toronto. After a final friendly against Chicago, Spurs travelled to Finland to face Celtic, for which there was a programme. There were no programmes for our Europa League ties against AEL (the island's main paper *'Phileleftheros '* contained a pull-out supplement entitled *'Goal News '*), Besiktas (the local paper *'Fanatik '* contained plenty of information on the game) or Fiorentina (there was a small *'tutto-viola '* programme and *'il Brivido Sportivo '* paper available at the ground). The away programme highlight of the season was Burnley in the FA Cup, with the cover reminiscent of the 1962 final. The home highlight, a special large issue for Newcastle United's visit remembering Bill Nicholson ten years after his passing and with the increased sale proceeds going to the Tottenham Tribute Trust. The season finished with two matches, both for an AIA Cup, in Malaysia and Australia, with programmes issued for both fixtures. That in Kuala Lumpur only made it to the VIP area minutes before kick-off having been left in an official's car!

2015-16

Once again Spurs faced Fiorentina in the Europa League, and once again there was no official programme but *'tutto-viola "* was available at the ground, with the only difference to last year being that it had now grown into a newspaper. The season had started with another friendly in America, against the MLS All-Stars; a glorified teamsheet being available. Spurs then journeyed to Munich to participate in the Audi Cup, with programmes available for both matches.

2016-17

With White Hart Lane scheduled for demolition at the end of the season and part of the old stadium carved out for preparatory work, Spurs moved their Champions League home ties to Wembley, producing large size programmes for each game. All their opponents also produced official programmes. The drop into the Europa League saw a return to the standard size issue for the home game with KAA Gent, while the Belgians produced an official 28 page programme in English for the first leg, when a 16 page pirate in Belgian was also available. For the home EFL Cup game against Gillingham, the visitors produced a 100 limited edition commemorative shirt boxset that included their own eight page programme for the game. The final home game of the season, against Manchester United, saw a bumper programme and a four page booklet entitled The Finale (Farewell Ceremony), with the latter difficult to get hold of on the day. Away from home the season began in Australia in the International Champions Cup against Juventus and Atletico Madrid, with one programme covering both matches. The League campaign ended at Hull, with the home club issuing a programme with a double cover. There was a programme for the final game of the season, against Kitchee in Hong Kong.

2017-18

The three matches played in the International Champions Cup in America, where Spurs faced PSG, AS Roma and Manchester City, feature the same programme contents for each, with only the covers being different. Neither Real Madrid nor Juventus, Champions League opponents, issued programmes, although the pirate *'Inferno Blanco '* appeared for the Real Madrid match describing itself as official. For Juventus, the *'JuveToro '* paper found at the ground along with *'Metro Stadio '* were among those collected by attendees.

2018-19

A momentous season, both home and away. Spurs began by again competing in the International Champions Cup, though this time there were no programmes or even a tournament brochure. No programme was produced for the Trofeu Costa Brava game against Girona, although the sports paper *'L'Esportiu '* gave over two pages to the game. With the new stadium still under construction, Spurs opened the season back at Wembley though the national stadium was not available for the Carabao Cup tie against Watford, so the match was moved to Milton Keynes. Following two test events (against Southampton Under-18s and an Inter Milan Legends XI), Crystal Palace were the visitors for the first team's debut at the new stadium, a special edition programme being produced. The story of the season, new stadium notwithstanding, was the run to the Champions League final. Neither Inter nor Barcelona, faced in the group stages, issued programmes, although there were pirates at both and the Metro Stadio available in Milan. There was no official programme as such for the semi-final second leg against Ajax, but a regular Ajax production was available in the home areas of the ground, so all but impossible to get hold of on the day. A bumper programme was produced for the final, complete with two double sided shirt posters depicting the two finalists, with a plethora of magazines appearing throughout Europe.

2019-20

Quite the most unusual season in living memory began with Spurs again participating in the International Champions Cup. No programmes were issued for the matches against Juventus or Manchester United played in Singapore and Shanghai. Likewise with the Audi Cup fixtures against Real Madrid and Bayern Munich in Munich, although there was coverage in the local paper. Spurs, with a new publisher in Reach Sport, did produce a programme for the ICC match at home to Internazionale. Reach also took over the handbook, retaining the oblong shape but jettisoning the coil binding. Bayern also failed to produce one for the Champions League group match, although pirates were available. In the first knock out stage Red Bull Leipzig produced both German and English language editions of their programme. On 13th March, the season was brought to an abrupt halt owing to the growing Covid 19 pandemic, with the scheduled visit of Manchester United two days later, Spurs first victim of the suspension. After a brief delay and much interest from collectors, Spurs released the programme for the postponed match. When football resumed without supporters in attendance Spurs produced truncated editions for their five remaining home fixtures, 68 pages instead of the normal 100. The four away fixtures produced a mixed response. Sheffield United produced one programme to cover all four of their remaining matches, although they later allowed individual programmes to be published. Newcastle United, perhaps a sign of things to come, decided to only produce an online version of their programme, but quickly allowed hard copies to be printed. Having decided not to produce a programme, Bournemouth willingly provided their standard teamsheet to anyone who asked. The final match, at Crystal Palace, saw a standard issue programme.

THE SEASON BY SEASON LISTINGS

1946-47

HOME

17 August	Whites v Blue & White Hoops	Public Trial
24 August	Whites v Blue & White Hoops	Public Trial
31 August	Birmingham City	Football League
9 September	Southampton	Football League
14 September	Newcastle United	Football League
28 September	Manchester City	Football League
5 October	Burnley	Football League
7 October	Newport County	Football League
26 October	Sheffield Wednesday	Football League
9 November	Bury	Football League
23 November	Plymouth Argyle	Football League
7 December	Chesterfield	Football League
21 December	Bradford	Football League
26 December	Coventry City	Football League
4 January	West Bromwich Albion	Football League
11 January	Stoke City	FA Cup
25 January	Arsenal	Friendly
27 January	Swansea Town	Football League
8 March	Fulham	Football League
22 March	Luton Town	Football League
4 April	Nottingham Forest	Football League
5 April	Leicester City	Football League
19 April	Millwall	Football League
17 May	West Ham United	Football League
7 June	Barnsley	Football League

☐ Handbook ☐ Season Ticket

Season Ticket

17 August
Public Trial

24 August
Public Trial

31 August
Birmingham City

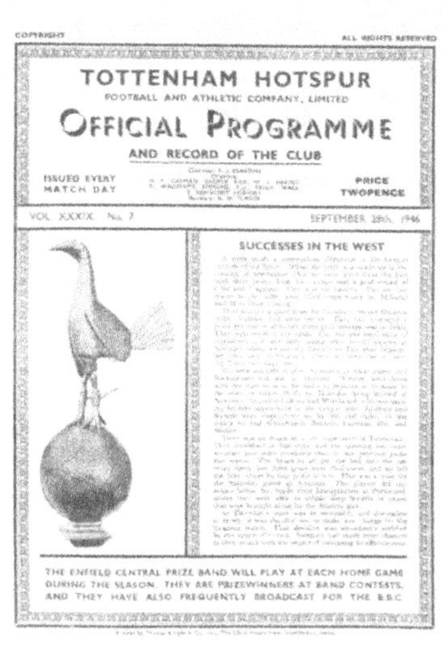

28 September
Manchester City

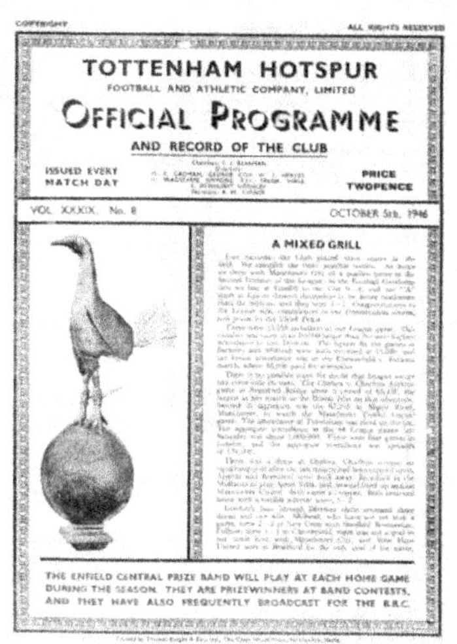

5 October
Burnley

23 November
Plymouth Argyle

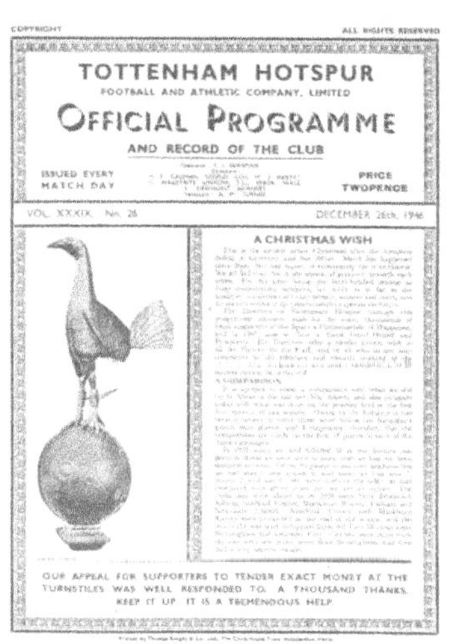

26 December
Coventry City

27 January
Swansea Town

22 March
Luton Town

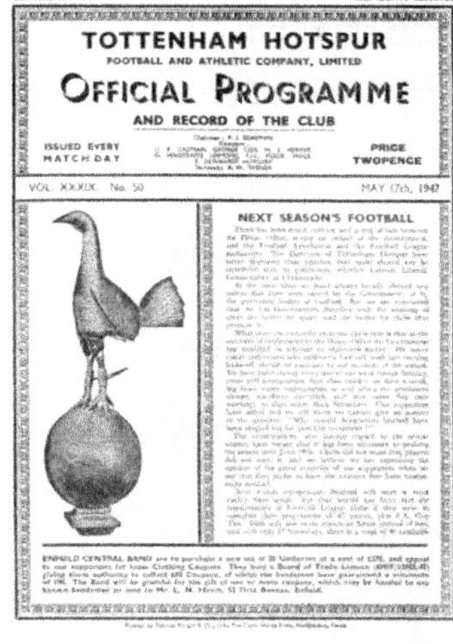

17 May
West Ham United

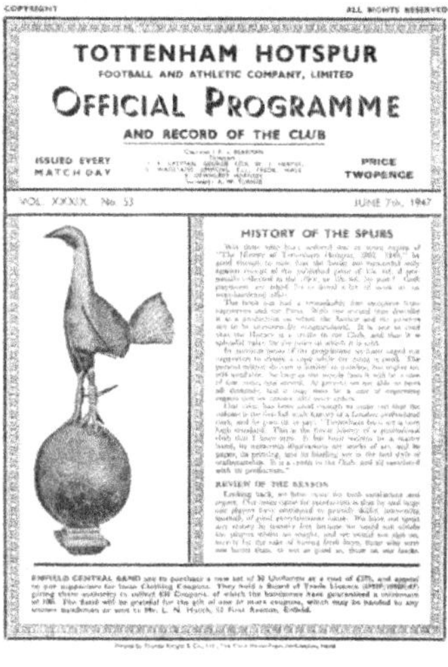

7 June
Barnsley

1946-47

AWAY

		7 September	West Bromwich Albion	Football League
		19 September	Newport County	Football League
		21 September	Swansea Town	Football League
		12 October	Barnsley	Football League
		19 October	West Ham United	Football League
		2 November	Fulham	Football League
		16 November	Luton Town	Football League
		30 November	Leicester City	Football League
		14 December	Millwall	Football League
		25 December	Coventry City	Football League
		28 December	Birmingham City	Football League
		15 January	Stoke City	FA Cup
		18 January	Newcastle United	Football League
		1 February	Manchester City	Football League
		18 February	Burnley	Football League
		1 March	Sheffield Wednesday	Football League
		29 March	Plymouth Argyle	Football League
		7 April	Nottingham Forest	Football League
		12 April	Chesterfield	Football League
		26 April	Bradford	Football League
		3 May	Bury	Football League
		10 May	Southampton	Football League
		12 May	Norwich City	Norwich Hospital Charity Cup
		13 June	Olympique de Marseilles	Friendly
		15 June	Toulouse	Friendly
		19 June	Olympique de Montpellier	Friendly
		21 June	Saint-Etienne	Friendly

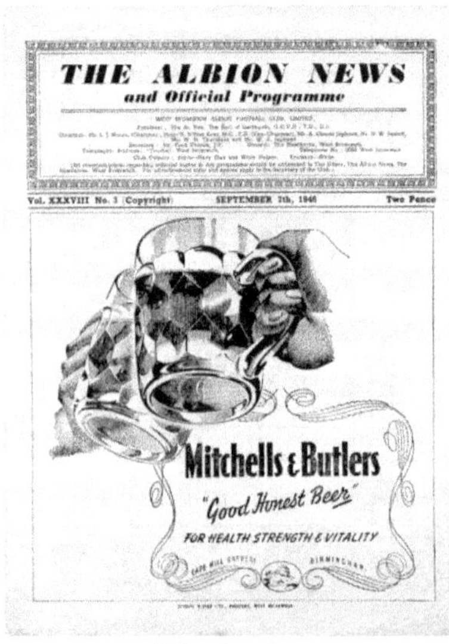

7 September
West Bromwich Albion

19 September
Newport County

2 November
Fulham

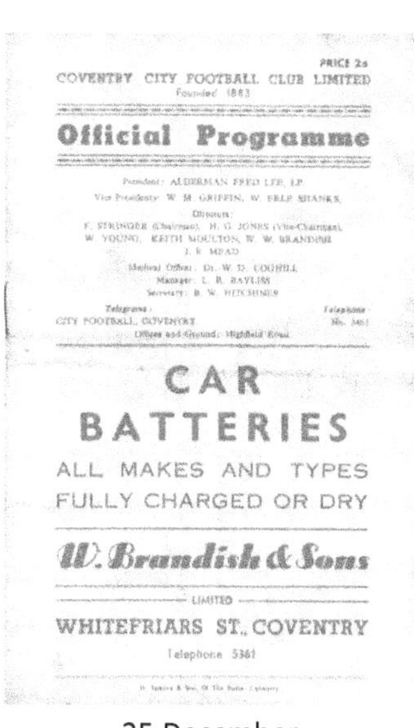

25 December
Coventry City

28 December
Birmingham City

15 January
Stoke City

18 February
Burnley

12 April
Chesterfield

26 April
Bradford

3 May
Bury

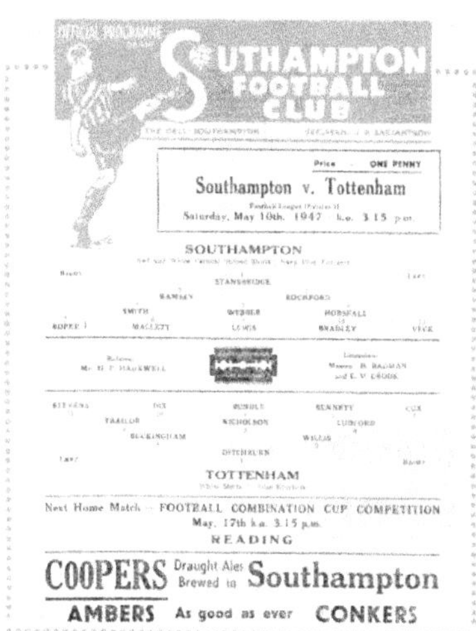

10 May
Southampton

12 May
Norwich City

1947-48

HOME

9 August	Whites v Reds	Public Trial
16 August	Whites v Reds	Public Trial
30 August	Sheffield Wednesday	Football League
1 September	Bury	Football League
13 September	Bradford	Football League
15 September	West Ham United	Football League
27 September	Doncaster Rovers	Football League
18 October	Plymouth Argyle	Football League
1 November	Brentford	Football League
15 November	Leeds United	Football League
29 November	Coventry City	Football League
13 December	Birmingham City	Football League
20 December	West Bromwich Albion	Football League
25 December	Chesterfield	Football League
17 January	Cardiff City	Football League
24 January	West Bromwich Albion	FA Cup
7 February	Leicester City	FA Cup
21 February	Southampton	Football League
15 March	Barnsley	Football League
27 March	Leicester City	Football League
29 March	Millwall	Football League
5 April	Luton Town	Football League
10 April	Fulham	Football League
12 April	Nottingham Forest	Football League
24 April	Newcastle United	Football League

Handbook

Season Ticket

Season Ticket

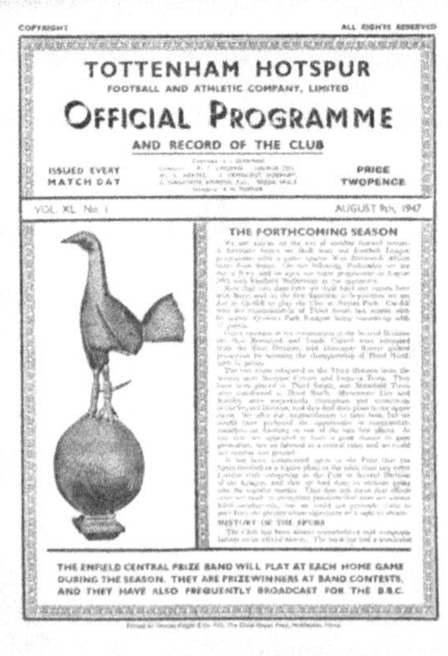

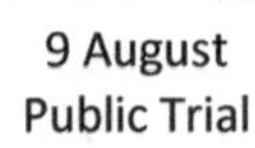

9 August
Public Trial

30 August
Sheffield Wednesday

COPYRIGHT ALL RIGHTS RESERVED

TOTTENHAM HOTSPUR
FOOTBALL AND ATHLETIC COMPANY, LIMITED
OFFICIAL PROGRAMME
AND RECORD OF THE CLUB
ISSUED EVERY MATCH DAY
PRICE TWOPENCE
VOL. XL. No. 9 SEPTEMBER 13th, 1947

THE CLUB'S FINANCES

THE ENFIELD CENTRAL PRIZE BAND WILL PLAY AT EACH HOME GAME DURING THE SEASON. THEY ARE PRIZEWINNERS AT BAND CONTESTS, AND THEY HAVE ALSO FREQUENTLY BROADCAST FOR THE B.B.C.

13 September
Bradford

COPYRIGHT ALL RIGHTS RESERVED

TOTTENHAM HOTSPUR
FOOTBALL AND ATHLETIC COMPANY, LIMITED
OFFICIAL PROGRAMME
AND RECORD OF THE CLUB
ISSUED EVERY MATCH DAY
PRICE TWOPENCE
SEPTEMBER 27th, 1947

PLAYERS AND ESSENTIAL WORKS ORDER

SUPPORT THE NATIONAL SAVINGS 'SILVER LINING' CAMPAIGN AND TURN WISHING INTO HAVING.
Join a Savings Group and become a Regular Saver.

27 September
Doncaster Rovers

COPYRIGHT ALL RIGHTS RESERVED

TOTTENHAM HOTSPUR
FOOTBALL AND ATHLETIC COMPANY, LIMITED
OFFICIAL PROGRAMME
AND RECORD OF THE CLUB
ISSUED EVERY MATCH DAY
PRICE TWOPENCE
VOL. XL. No. 15 OCTOBER 18th, 1947

BOARD ROOM NEWS

THE ENFIELD CENTRAL PRIZE BAND WILL PLAY AT EACH HOME GAME DURING THE SEASON. THEY ARE PRIZEWINNERS AT BAND CONTESTS, AND THEY HAVE ALSO FREQUENTLY BROADCAST FOR THE B.B.C.

18 October
Plymouth Argyle

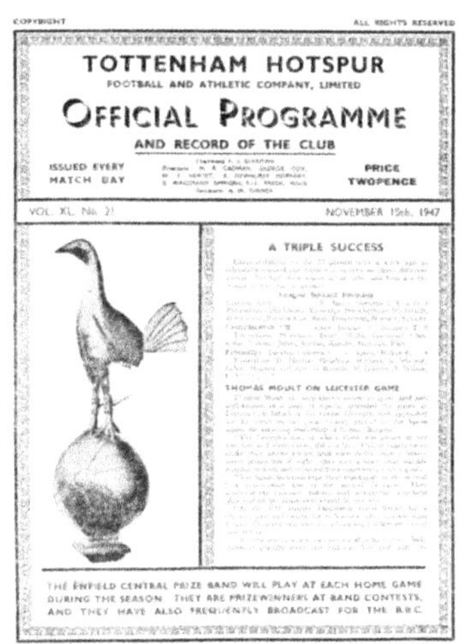
COPYRIGHT ALL RIGHTS RESERVED

TOTTENHAM HOTSPUR
FOOTBALL AND ATHLETIC COMPANY, LIMITED
OFFICIAL PROGRAMME
AND RECORD OF THE CLUB
ISSUED EVERY MATCH DAY
PRICE TWOPENCE
NOVEMBER 15th, 1947

A TRIPLE SUCCESS

THE ENFIELD CENTRAL PRIZE BAND WILL PLAY AT EACH HOME GAME DURING THE SEASON. THEY ARE PRIZEWINNERS AT BAND CONTESTS, AND THEY HAVE ALSO FREQUENTLY BROADCAST FOR THE B.B.C.

1 November
Brentford

COPYRIGHT ALL RIGHTS RESERVED

TOTTENHAM HOTSPUR
FOOTBALL AND ATHLETIC COMPANY, LIMITED
OFFICIAL PROGRAMME
AND RECORD OF THE CLUB
ISSUED EVERY MATCH DAY
PRICE TWOPENCE
NOVEMBER 15th, 1947

A TRIPLE SUCCESS

THE ENFIELD CENTRAL PRIZE BAND WILL PLAY AT EACH HOME GAME DURING THE SEASON. THEY ARE PRIZEWINNERS AT BAND CONTESTS, AND THEY HAVE ALSO FREQUENTLY BROADCAST FOR THE B.B.C.

15 November
Leeds United

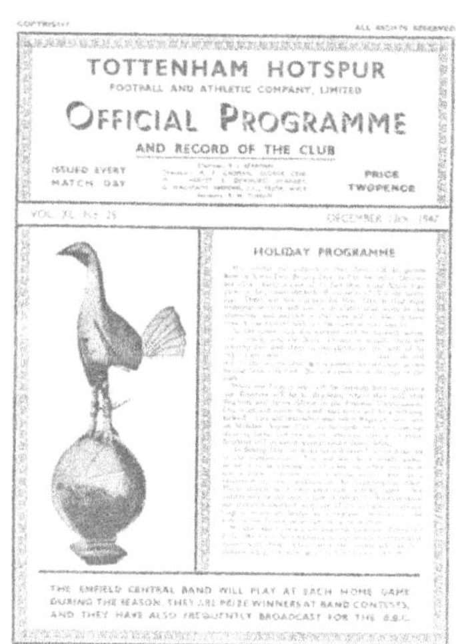
COPYRIGHT ALL RIGHTS RESERVED

TOTTENHAM HOTSPUR
FOOTBALL AND ATHLETIC COMPANY, LIMITED
OFFICIAL PROGRAMME
AND RECORD OF THE CLUB
ISSUED EVERY MATCH DAY
PRICE TWOPENCE

HOLIDAY PROGRAMME

THE ENFIELD CENTRAL BAND WILL PLAY AT EACH HOME GAME DURING THE SEASON. THEY ARE PRIZE WINNERS AT BAND CONTESTS, AND THEY HAVE ALSO FREQUENTLY BROADCAST FOR THE B.B.C.

13 December
Birmingham City

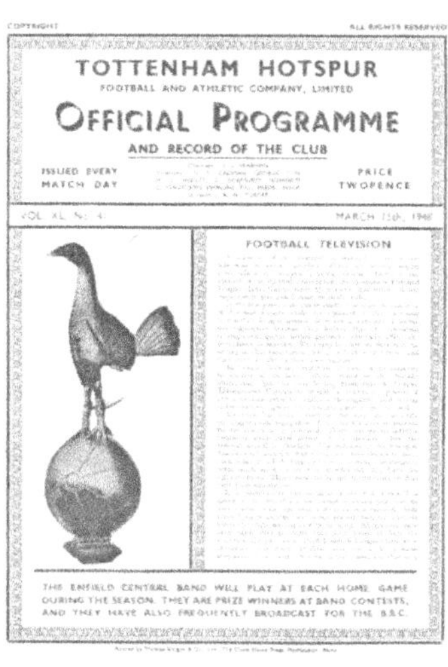
COPYRIGHT ALL RIGHTS RESERVED

TOTTENHAM HOTSPUR
FOOTBALL AND ATHLETIC COMPANY, LIMITED
OFFICIAL PROGRAMME
AND RECORD OF THE CLUB
ISSUED EVERY MATCH DAY
PRICE TWOPENCE

FOOTBALL TELEVISION

THE ENFIELD CENTRAL BAND WILL PLAY AT EACH HOME GAME DURING THE SEASON. THEY ARE PRIZE WINNERS AT BAND CONTESTS, AND THEY HAVE ALSO FREQUENTLY BROADCAST FOR THE B.B.C.

15 March
Barnsley

COPYRIGHT ALL RIGHTS RESERVED

TOTTENHAM HOTSPUR
FOOTBALL AND ATHLETIC COMPANY, LIMITED
OFFICIAL PROGRAMME
AND RECORD OF THE CLUB
ISSUED EVERY MATCH DAY
PRICE TWOPENCE

INTERNATIONAL YOUTHS' TOURNAMENT

THE ENFIELD CENTRAL BAND WILL PLAY AT EACH HOME GAME DURING THE SEASON. THEY ARE PRIZE WINNERS AT BAND CONTESTS, AND THEY HAVE ALSO FREQUENTLY BROADCAST FOR THE B.B.C.

10 April
Fulham

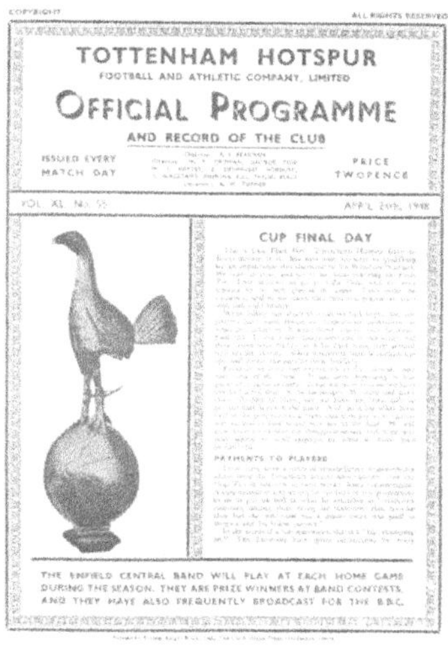
COPYRIGHT ALL RIGHTS RESERVED

TOTTENHAM HOTSPUR
FOOTBALL AND ATHLETIC COMPANY, LIMITED
OFFICIAL PROGRAMME
AND RECORD OF THE CLUB
ISSUED EVERY MATCH DAY
PRICE TWOPENCE

CUP FINAL DAY

PAYMENTS TO PLAYERS

THE ENFIELD CENTRAL BAND WILL PLAY AT EACH HOME GAME DURING THE SEASON. THEY ARE PRIZE WINNERS AT BAND CONTESTS, AND THEY HAVE ALSO FREQUENTLY BROADCAST FOR THE B.B.C.

24 April
Newcastle United

1947-48

AWAY

		23 August	West Bromwich Albion	Football League
		27 August	Bury	Football League
		6 September	Cardiff City	Football League
		8 September	West Ham United	Football League
		20 September	Nottingham Forest	Football League
		4 October	Southampton	Football League
		11 October	Barnsley	Football League
		25 October	Luton Town	Football League
		8 November	Leicester City	Football League
		22 November	Fulham	Football League
		6 December	Newcastle United	Football League
		27 December	Chesterfield	Football League
			- Supporters' Club issue	
		3 January	Sheffield Wednesday	Football League
		10 January	Bolton Wanderers	FA Cup
		31 January	Bradford	Football League
		14 February	Doncaster Rovers	Football League
		28 February	Southampton	FA Cup
		6 March	Plymouth Argyle	Football League
		13 March	Blackpool (Villa Park)	FA Cup
		20 March	Brentford	Football League
		26 March	Millwall	Football League
		3 April	Leeds United	Football League
		17 April	Coventry City	Football League
		1 May	Birmingham City	Football League
		8 May	Jersey	Friendly
		12 May	Guernsey Island XI	Friendly

6 September
Cardiff City

11 October
Barnsley

25 October
Luton Town

6 December
Newcastle United

27 December
Chesterfield - Official issue

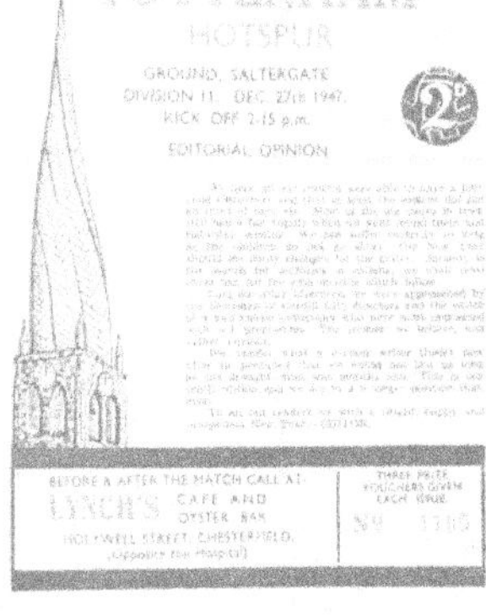

27 December
Chesterfield - Supporters Club issue

3 January
Sheffield Wednesday

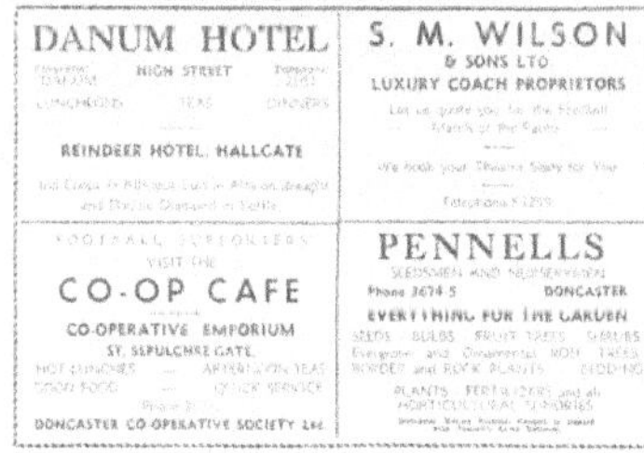

14 February
Doncaster Rovers

20 March
Brentford

3 April
Leeds United

Liberation Day, Saturday, May, 8th, 1948.

JERSEY
(Red and White)

1 G. ARTHUR

2 D. CROWELL — 3 P. POINGDESTRE

4 J. SHERRY — 5 R. JONES — 6 D. PITMAN

7 J. OLLIVIER — 8 R. HART — 9 G. LE MAISTRE (Captain) — 10 R. PAMPLIN — 11 J. DREW

11 E. JONES — 10 L. BENNETT — 9 L. DUQUEMIN — 8 E. BAILY — 7 C. JORDAN

6 R. BURGESS — 5 M. J. WOODWARD — 4 G. LUDFORD

3 V. F. BUCKINGHAM — 2 S. TICKRIDGE

1 E. DITCHBURN

TOTTENHAM HOTSPURS
(Blue and White)

8 May
Jersey

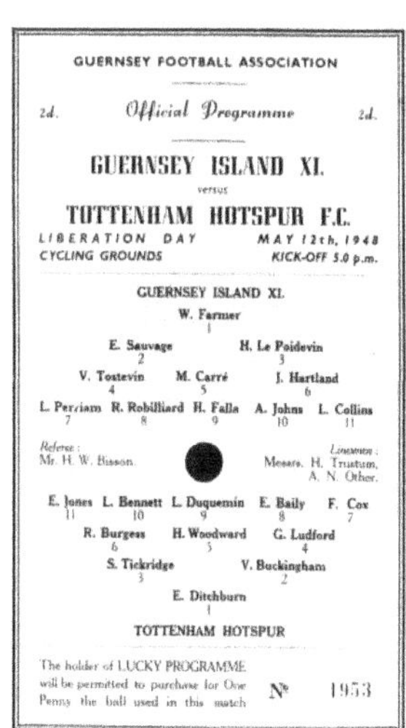

GUERNSEY FOOTBALL ASSOCIATION

2d. *Official Programme* 2d.

GUERNSEY ISLAND XI.
versus
TOTTENHAM HOTSPUR F.C.

LIBERATION DAY — MAY 12th, 1948
CYCLING GROUNDS — KICK-OFF 5.0 p.m.

GUERNSEY ISLAND XI.

W. Farmer 1

E. Sauvage 2 — H. Le Poidevin 3

V. Tostevin 4 — M. Carré 5 — J. Hartland 6

L. Perriam 7 — R. Robilliard 8 — H. Falla 9 — A. Johns 10 — L. Collins 11

Referee: Mr. H. W. Bisson.

Linesmen: Messrs. H. Trustum, A. N. Other.

E. Jones 11 — L. Bennett 10 — L. Duquemin 9 — E. Baily 8 — F. Cox 7

R. Burgess 6 — H. Woodward 5 — G. Ludford 4

S. Tickridge 3 — V. Buckingham 2

E. Ditchburn 1

TOTTENHAM HOTSPUR

The holder of LUCKY PROGRAMME will be permitted to purchase for One Penny the ball used in this match — № 1953

12 May
Guernsey Island XI

1948-49

HOME

☐	☐	7 August	Whites v Reds	Public Trial
☐	☐	14 August	Whites v Reds	Public Trial
☐	☐	21 August	Sheffield Wednesday	Football League
☐	☐	30 August	Coventry City	Football League
☐	☐	4 September	Chesterfield	Football League
☐	☐	13 September	Leeds United	Football League
☐	☐	18 September	Bury	Football League
☐	☐	2 October	Blackburn Rovers	Football League
☐	☐	16 October	Queens Park Rangers	Football League
☐	☐	30 October	Bradford	Football League
☐	☐	13 November	Barnsley	Football League
☐	☐	27 November	Nottingham Forest - abandoned	Football League
☐	☐	11 December	Plymouth Argyle	Football League
☐	☐	27 December	Leicester City	Football League
☐	☐	1 January	Lincoln City	Football League
☐	☐	22 January	West Bromwich Albion	Football League
☐	☐	29 January	Middlesbrough	Friendly
☐	☐	12 February	Nottingham Forest	Football League
☐	☐	19 February	West Ham United	Football League
☐	☐	5 March	Cardiff City	Football League
☐	☐	19 March	Luton Town	Football League
☐	☐	2 April	Southampton	Football League
☐	☐	15 April	Brentford	Football League
☐	☐	16 April	Grimsby Town	Football League
☐	☐	25 April	Hibernian	Friendly
☐	☐	30 April	Fulham	Football League

☐ Handbook ☐ Season Ticket

Season Ticket

Handbook

7 August
Public Trial

COPYRIGHT ALL RIGHTS RESERVED

TOTTENHAM HOTSPUR
FOOTBALL AND ATHLETIC COMPANY, LIMITED
OFFICIAL PROGRAMME
AND RECORD OF THE CLUB
ISSUED EVERY MATCH DAY PRICE TWOPENCE

THE SEASON OPENS

DO YOU KNOW?

THE ENFIELD CENTRAL BAND WILL PLAY AT EACH HOME GAME DURING THE SEASON. THEY ARE PRIZE WINNERS AT BAND CONTESTS, AND THEY HAVE ALSO FREQUENTLY BROADCAST FOR THE B.B.C.

21 August
Sheffield Wednesday

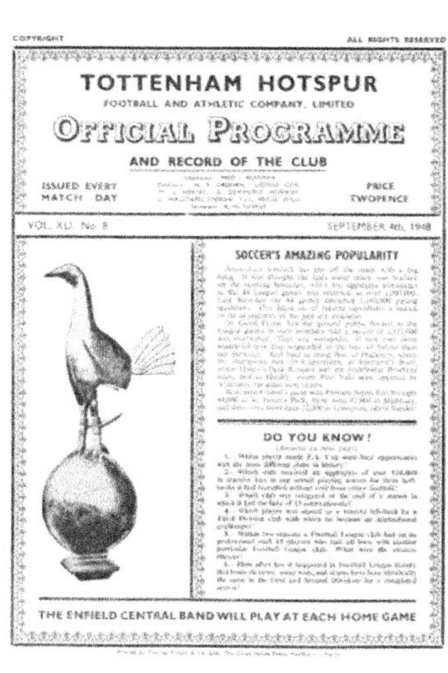
COPYRIGHT ALL RIGHTS RESERVED

TOTTENHAM HOTSPUR
FOOTBALL AND ATHLETIC COMPANY, LIMITED
OFFICIAL PROGRAMME
AND RECORD OF THE CLUB
ISSUED EVERY MATCH DAY PRICE TWOPENCE

SOCCER'S AMAZING POPULARITY

DO YOU KNOW?

THE ENFIELD CENTRAL BAND WILL PLAY AT EACH HOME GAME

4 September
Chesterfield

COPYRIGHT ALL RIGHTS RESERVED

TOTTENHAM HOTSPUR
FOOTBALL AND ATHLETIC COMPANY, LIMITED
OFFICIAL PROGRAMME
AND RECORD OF THE CLUB
ISSUED EVERY MATCH DAY PRICE TWOPENCE

SPURS AGAIN UNDEFEATED

OUR FOOTBALL QUIZ

THE ENFIELD CENTRAL BAND WILL PLAY AT EACH HOME GAME

30 October
Bradford

COPYRIGHT ALL RIGHTS RESERVED

TOTTENHAM HOTSPUR
FOOTBALL AND ATHLETIC COMPANY, LIMITED
OFFICIAL PROGRAMME
AND RECORD OF THE CLUB
ISSUED EVERY MATCH DAY PRICE TWOPENCE

A DISAPPOINTMENT

OUR FOOTBALL QUIZ

THE ENFIELD CENTRAL BAND WILL PLAY AT EACH HOME GAME

13 November
Barnsley

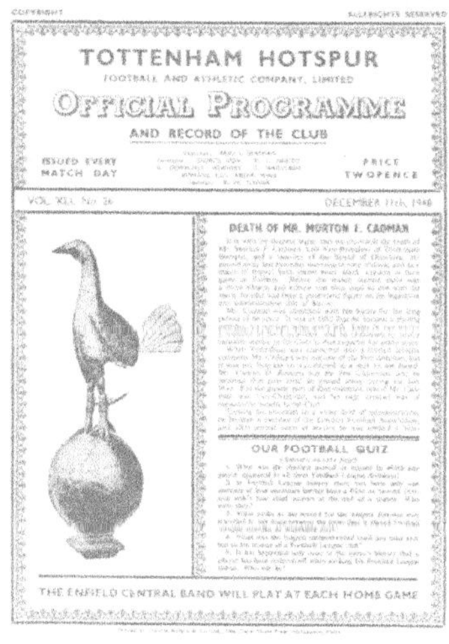
COPYRIGHT ALL RIGHTS RESERVED

TOTTENHAM HOTSPUR
FOOTBALL AND ATHLETIC COMPANY, LIMITED
OFFICIAL PROGRAMME
AND RECORD OF THE CLUB
ISSUED EVERY MATCH DAY PRICE TWOPENCE

DEATH OF MR. MORTON F. CADMAN

OUR FOOTBALL QUIZ

THE ENFIELD CENTRAL BAND WILL PLAY AT EACH HOME GAME

11 December
Plymouth Argyle

COPYRIGHT ALL RIGHTS RESERVED

TOTTENHAM HOTSPUR
FOOTBALL AND ATHLETIC COMPANY, LIMITED
OFFICIAL PROGRAMME
AND RECORD OF THE CLUB
ISSUED EVERY MATCH DAY PRICE TWOPENCE

THE SEASON'S GREETINGS

OUR FOOTBALL QUIZ

THE ENFIELD CENTRAL BAND WILL PLAY AT EACH HOME GAME

27 December
Leicester City

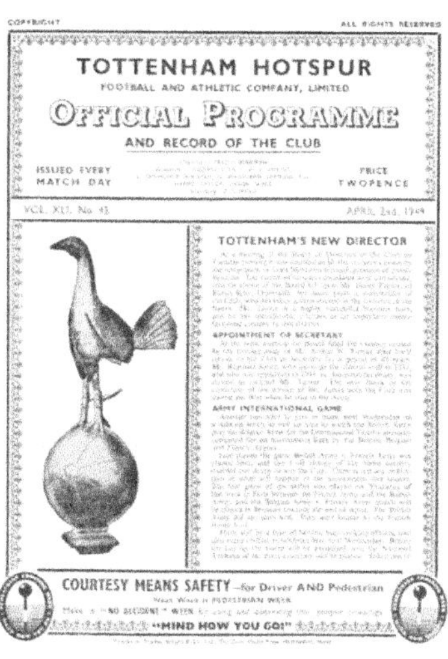
COPYRIGHT ALL RIGHTS RESERVED

TOTTENHAM HOTSPUR
FOOTBALL AND ATHLETIC COMPANY, LIMITED
OFFICIAL PROGRAMME
AND RECORD OF THE CLUB
ISSUED EVERY MATCH DAY PRICE TWOPENCE

TOTTENHAM'S NEW DIRECTOR

COURTESY MEANS SAFETY —for Driver AND Pedestrian
"MIND HOW YOU GO!"

2 April
Southampton

COPYRIGHT ALL RIGHTS RESERVED

TOTTENHAM HOTSPUR
FOOTBALL AND ATHLETIC COMPANY, LIMITED
OFFICIAL PROGRAMME
AND RECORD OF THE CLUB
ISSUED EVERY MATCH DAY PRICE TWOPENCE

WELCOME TO HIBERNIAN

OUR FOOTBALL QUIZ

THE ENFIELD CENTRAL BAND WILL PLAY AT EACH HOME GAME

25 April
Hibernian

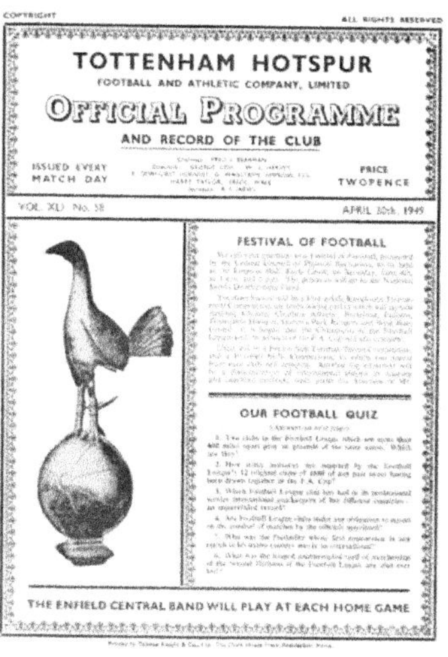
COPYRIGHT ALL RIGHTS RESERVED

TOTTENHAM HOTSPUR
FOOTBALL AND ATHLETIC COMPANY, LIMITED
OFFICIAL PROGRAMME
AND RECORD OF THE CLUB
ISSUED EVERY MATCH DAY PRICE TWOPENCE

FESTIVAL OF FOOTBALL

OUR FOOTBALL QUIZ

THE ENFIELD CENTRAL BAND WILL PLAY AT EACH HOME GAME

30 April
Fulham

1948-49

AWAY

Date	Opponent	Competition
23 August	Coventry City	Football League
28 August	Lincoln City	Football League
8 September	Leeds United	Football League
11 September	West Bromwich Albion	Football League
20 September	Chelmsford City	Fred Sargent Memorial
25 September	West Ham United	Football League
9 October	Cardiff City	Football League
23 October	Luton Town	Football League
6 November	Southampton	Football League
20 November	Grimsby Town	Football League
4 December	Fulham	Football League
18 December	Sheffield Wednesday	Football League
25 December	Leicester City	Football League
8 January	Arsenal	FA Cup
15 January	Chesterfield	Football League
5 February	Bury	Football League
26 February	Blackburn Rovers	Football League
12 March	Queens Park Rangers	Football League
26 March	Bradford	Football League
9 April	Barnsley	Football League
18 April	Brentford	Football League
23 April	Nottingham Forest	Football League
7 May	Plymouth Argyle	Football League
9 May	Cornwall County XI (Penzance)	Friendly

28 August
Lincoln City

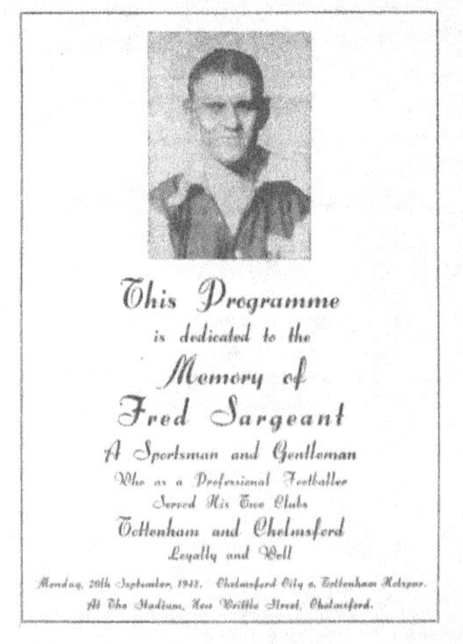

20 September
Chelmsford City

25 September
West Ham United

9 October
Cardiff City

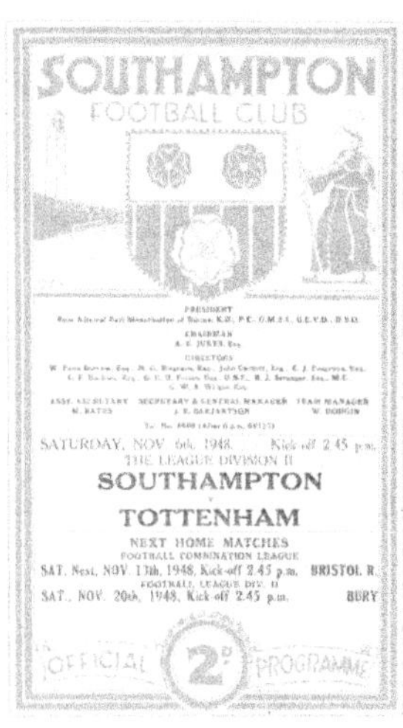

6 November
Southampton

18 December
Sheffield Wednesday

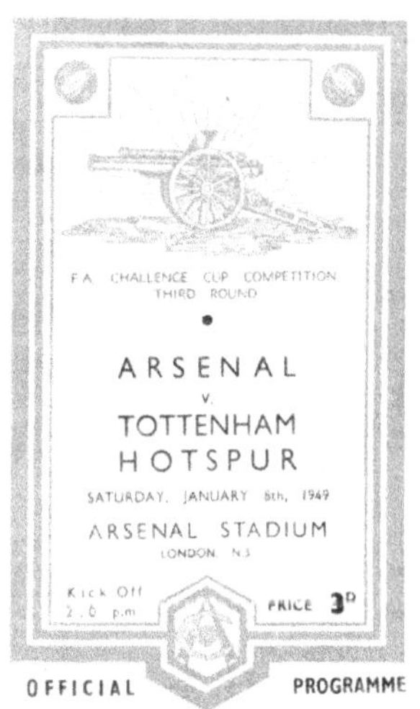

8 January
Arsenal

26 February
Blackburn Rovers

12 March
Queens Park Rangers

23 April
Nottingham Forest

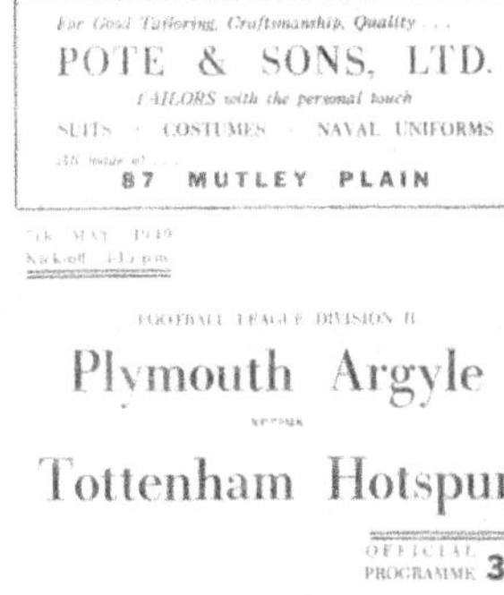

7 May
Plymouth Argyle

9 May
Cornwall

1949-50

HOME

Date	Opponent	Competition
6 August	Whites v Reds	Public Trial
13 August	Whites v Reds	Public Trial
22 August	Plymouth Argyle	Football League
27 August	Blackburn Rovers	Football League
5 September	Sheffield Wednesday	Football League
10 September	Leeds United	Football League
17 September	Bury	Football League
1 October	Bradford	Football League
15 October	Coventry City	Football League
29 October	Barnsley	Football League
12 November	Sheffield United	Football League
26 November	Queens Park Rangers	Football League
10 December	Swansea Town	Football League
17 December	Brentford	Football League
26 December	Chesterfield	Football League
31 December	Cardiff City	Football League
28 January	Sunderland	FA Cup
4 February	Leicester City	Football League
25 February	Southampton	Football League
11 March	Luton Town	Football League
25 March	West Ham United	Football League
7 April	Hull City	Football League
8 April	Preston North End	Football League
22 April	Grimsby Town	Football League
1 May	Hibernian	Friendly

☐ Handbook ☐ Season Ticket

Season Ticket

Handbook

6 August
Public Trial

TOTTENHAM HOTSPUR
FOOTBALL AND ATHLETIC COMPANY, LIMITED
Official Programme
AND RECORD OF THE CLUB
ISSUED EVERY MATCH DAY
PRICE TWOPENCE
MONDAY, AUGUST 22nd, 1949
WELCOME TO PLYMOUTH ARGYLE
THE ENFIELD CENTRAL BAND WILL PLAY AT EACH HOME GAME

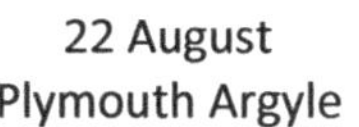
22 August
Plymouth Argyle

TOTTENHAM HOTSPUR
FOOTBALL AND ATHLETIC COMPANY, LIMITED
Official Programme
AND RECORD OF THE CLUB
ISSUED EVERY MATCH DAY
PRICE TWOPENCE
SATURDAY, SEPTEMBER 10th, 1949
ANOTHER TREBLE WIN
THE ENFIELD CENTRAL BAND WILL PLAY AT EACH HOME GAME

10 September
Leeds United

TOTTENHAM HOTSPUR
FOOTBALL AND ATHLETIC COMPANY, LIMITED
Official Programme
AND RECORD OF THE CLUB
ISSUED EVERY MATCH DAY
PRICE TWOPENCE
SATURDAY, OCTOBER 15th, 1949
AWAY RECORD LOST
THE ENFIELD CENTRAL BAND WILL PLAY AT EACH HOME GAME

15 October
Coventry City

TOTTENHAM HOTSPUR
FOOTBALL AND ATHLETIC COMPANY, LIMITED
Official Programme
AND RECORD OF THE CLUB
ISSUED EVERY MATCH DAY
PRICE TWOPENCE
SATURDAY, OCTOBER 29th, 1949
STILL UNBEATEN AWAY
"SAVE FOR BRITAIN AND A HAPPY FUTURE"
YOU MUST SAVE
TO GET THOSE THINGS THAT YOU WANT

29 October
Barnsley

TOTTENHAM HOTSPUR
FOOTBALL AND ATHLETIC COMPANY, LIMITED
Official Programme
AND RECORD OF THE CLUB
ISSUED EVERY MATCH DAY
PRICE TWOPENCE
MONDAY, DECEMBER 26th, 1949
SEASONABLE GREETINGS
A Happy Christmas and a Prosperous 1950
THE ENFIELD CENTRAL BAND WILL PLAY AT EACH HOME GAME

26 December
Chesterfield

TOTTENHAM HOTSPUR
FOOTBALL AND ATHLETIC COMPANY, LIMITED
Official Programme
AND RECORD OF THE CLUB
PRICE TWOPENCE
SATURDAY, JANUARY 28th, 1950
FIGHT FOR THE CUP
THE ENFIELD CENTRAL BAND WILL PLAY AT EACH HOME GAME

28 January
Sunderland

TOTTENHAM HOTSPUR
FOOTBALL AND ATHLETIC COMPANY, LIMITED
Official Programme
AND RECORD OF THE CLUB
PRICE TWOPENCE
SATURDAY, APRIL 8th, 1950
FIRST DIVISION NEXT SEASON
THE ENFIELD CENTRAL BAND WILL PLAY AT EACH HOME GAME

8 April
Preston North End

TOTTENHAM HOTSPUR
FOOTBALL AND ATHLETIC COMPANY, LIMITED
Souvenir Programme
PRICE TWOPENCE
SATURDAY, APRIL 22nd, 1950
A Message from the President
TOTTENHAM HOTSPUR F.C.—FIRST TEAM 1949-50

22 April
Grimsby Town

TOTTENHAM HOTSPUR
FOOTBALL AND ATHLETIC COMPANY, LIMITED
Official Programme
AND RECORD OF THE CLUB
PRICE TWOPENCE
MONDAY, MAY 1st, 1950
WELCOME TO HIBERNIAN F.C.
THE ENFIELD CENTRAL BAND WILL PLAY AT EACH HOME GAME

1 May
Hibernian

1949-50

AWAY

Date	Opponent	Competition
20 August	Brentford	Football League
31 August	Plymouth Argyle	Football League
3 September	Cardiff City	Football League
24 September	Leicester City	Football League
8 October	Southampton	Football League
22 October	Luton Town	Football League
5 November	West Ham United	Football League
19 November	Grimsby Town	Football League
3 December	Preston North End	Football League
24 December	Blackburn Rovers	Football League
27 December	Chesterfield	Football League
7 January	Stoke City	FA Cup
14 January	Leeds United	Football League
21 January	Bury	Football League
11 February	Everton	FA Cup
18 February	Bradford	Football League
4 March	Coventry City	Football League
18 March	Barnsley	Football League
1 April	Queens Park Rangers	Football League
10 April	Hull City	Football League
15 April	Sheffield United	Football League
24 April	Chelmsford City	Les Pyle Benefit
29 April	Swansea Town	Football League
6 May	Sheffield Wednesday	Football League
8 May	Norwich City	Norwich and Norwich Charities' Cup
14 May	Hanover Arminia	Friendly
18 May	Tennis-Borussia	Friendly
	- BAOR issue	
21 May	Wacker Club	Friendly
24 May	Borussia Dortmund	Friendly
27 May	Royal Beerschot	Friendly

19 November
Grimsby Town

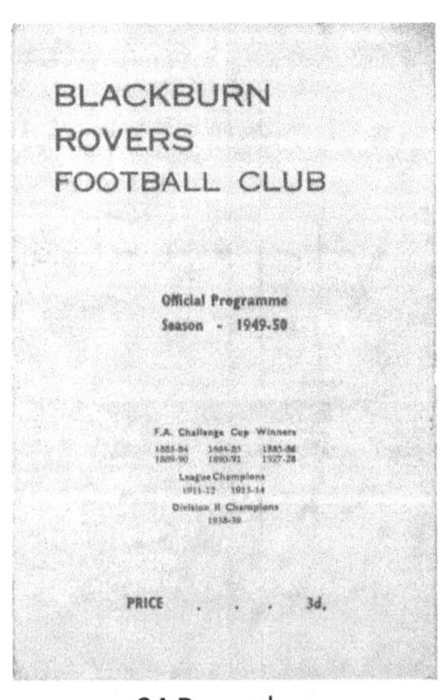

24 December
Blackburn Rovers

18 February
Bradford

10 April
Hull City

15 April
Sheffield United

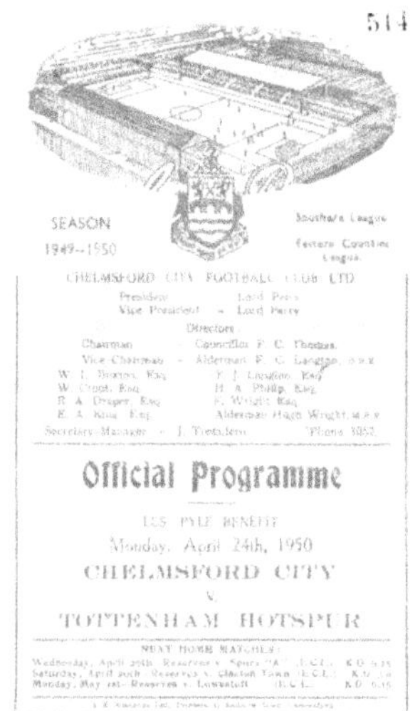

24 April
Chelmsford City

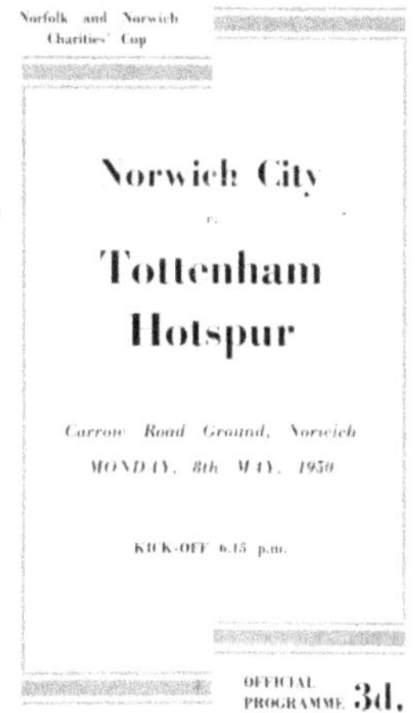

8 May
Norwich City

14 May
Arminia Hannover

18 May
Tennis Borussia

FOOTBALL

TOTTENHAM HOTSPUR

versus

TENNIS BORUSSIA

OLYMPIC STADIUM
THURSDAY 18 MAY 1950
KICK OFF 15[30] HRS

A Football Match between University West-Berlin and University Kiel will be played at 13[30] hrs

18 May
Tennis Borussia - BAOR issue

21 May
Wacker Club

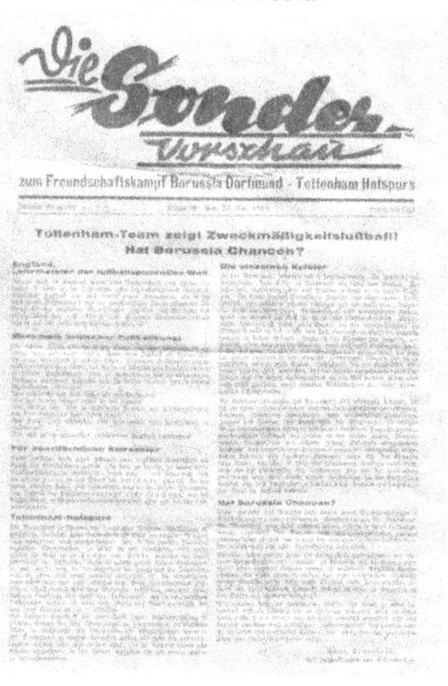

24 May
Borussia Dortmund

1950-51

HOME

		Date	Opponent	Competition
☐	☐	12 August	Whites v Reds	Public Trial
☐	☐	19 August	Blackpool	Football League
☐	☐	28 August	Bolton Wanderers	Football League
☐	☐	9 September	Manchester United	Football League
☐	☐	18 September	Lovell's Athletic	Friendly
☐	☐	23 September	Sunderland	Football League
☐	☐	7 October	Burnley	Football League
☐	☐	21 October	Stoke City	Football League
☐	☐	4 November	Portsmouth	Football League
☐	☐	18 November	Newcastle United	Football League
☐	☐	2 December	Middlesbrough	Football League
☐	☐	23 December	Arsenal	Football League
☐	☐	26 December	Derby County	Football League
☐	☐	30 December	Charlton Athletic	Football League
☐	☐	20 January	Wolverhampton Wanderers	Football League
☐	☐	17 February	Aston Villa	Football League
☐	☐	3 March	Chelsea	Football League
☐	☐	17 March	West Bromwich Albion	Football League
☐	☐	26 March	Fulham	Football League
☐	☐	31 March	Everton	Football League
☐	☐	14 April	Huddersfield Town	Football League
☐	☐	28 April	Sheffield Wednesday	Football League
☐	☐	5 May	Liverpool	Football League
☐	☐	7 May	FC Austria	Festival of Britain
☐	☐	12 May	Borussia Dortmund	Festival of Britain

☐ Handbook ☐ Season Ticket

Season Ticket

Handbook

COPYRIGHT ALL RIGHTS RESERVED

TOTTENHAM HOTSPUR

FOOTBALL AND ATHLETIC COMPANY, LIMITED

Official Programme

AND RECORD OF THE CLUB

PRICE TWOPENCE

SATURDAY, AUGUST 12th, 1950

PUBLIC TRIAL MATCH

THE ENFIELD CENTRAL BAND WILL PLAY AT EACH HOME GAME

12 August
Public Trial

TOTTENHAM HOTSPUR
FOOTBALL AND ATHLETIC COMPANY, LIMITED
Official Programme
AND RECORD OF THE CLUB
PRICE TWOPENCE
SATURDAY, SEPTEMBER 9th, 1950
TO-DAY'S VISITORS
A NEW NURSERY GROUND
A POINT FROM THE VALLEY
THE ENFIELD CENTRAL BAND WILL PLAY AT EACH HOME GAME

9 September
Manchester United

TOTTENHAM HOTSPUR
FOOTBALL AND ATHLETIC COMPANY, LIMITED
Official Programme
AND RECORD OF THE CLUB
PRICE ONE PENNY
MONDAY, SEPTEMBER 18th, 1950
SUNDERLAND BRENTFORD RES.
TOTTENHAM HOTSPUR v LOVELL'S ATHLETIC
Friendly Match September 18th, 1950 Kick-off 5.45
TOTTENHAM HOTSPUR
DITCHBURN
HENTY WILLIS
NICHOLSON CLARKE (Capt.) BURGESS
WALTERS DUQUEMIN MEDLEY
BIRSDALE J. B. GRIFFITHS LEWIS WOOD HOODER
BYE EVANS I. ROBLING
EDMUNDS FISHER
LOVELL'S ATHLETIC
ANY ALTERATION WILL BE NOTED ON THE BOARD

18 September
Lovell's Athletic

TOTTENHAM HOTSPUR
FOOTBALL AND ATHLETIC COMPANY, LIMITED
Official Programme
AND RECORD OF THE CLUB
PRICE TWOPENCE
SATURDAY, OCTOBER 21st, 1950
TO-DAY'S VISITORS
DO YOU ? KNOW
THE ENFIELD CENTRAL BAND WILL PLAY AT EACH HOME GAME

21 October
Stoke City

TOTTENHAM HOTSPUR
FOOTBALL AND ATHLETIC COMPANY, LIMITED
Official Programme
AND RECORD OF THE CLUB
PRICE TWOPENCE
SATURDAY, NOVEMBER 18th, 1950
OUR WIN AT EVERTON
WELCOME TO NEWCASTLE
DO YOU ? KNOW
THE ENFIELD CENTRAL BAND WILL PLAY AT EACH HOME GAME

18 November
Newcastle United

TOTTENHAM HOTSPUR
FOOTBALL AND ATHLETIC COMPANY, LIMITED
Official Programme
AND RECORD OF THE CLUB
PRICE TWOPENCE
TUESDAY, DECEMBER 26th, 1950

We wish all our Supporters a Happy Christmas and a Prosperous New Year

26 December
Derby County

TOTTENHAM HOTSPUR
FOOTBALL AND ATHLETIC COMPANY, LIMITED
Official Programme
AND RECORD OF THE CLUB
PRICE TWOPENCE
SATURDAY, FEBRUARY 17th, 1951
WELCOME TO ASTON VILLA
DO YOU ? KNOW
THE ENFIELD CENTRAL BAND WILL PLAY AT EACH HOME GAME

17 February
Aston Villa

TOTTENHAM HOTSPUR
FOOTBALL AND ATHLETIC COMPANY, LIMITED
Official Programme
AND RECORD OF THE CLUB
PRICE TWOPENCE
SATURDAY, APRIL 14th, 1951
DOUBLE v NEWCASTLE
TO-DAY'S MATCH
DO YOU ? KNOW
THE ENFIELD CENTRAL BAND WILL PLAY AT EACH HOME GAME

14 April
Huddersfield Town

TOTTENHAM HOTSPUR
FOOTBALL AND ATHLETIC COMPANY, LIMITED
Official Programme
AND RECORD OF THE CLUB
PRICE TWOPENCE
SATURDAY, MAY 5th, 1951

THE ENFIELD CENTRAL BAND WILL PLAY AT EACH HOME GAME

5 May
Liverpool

TOTTENHAM HOTSPUR
FOOTBALL AND ATHLETIC COMPANY, LIMITED
Official Programme
AND RECORD OF THE CLUB
PRICE TWOPENCE
SATURDAY, MAY 12th, 1951
WELCOME TO DORTMUND BORUSSIA
A MEMORABLE FINISH
DO YOU ? KNOW
THE ENFIELD CENTRAL BAND WILL PLAY AT EACH HOME GAME

12 May
Borussia Dortmund

1950-51

AWAY

Date	Opponent	Competition
23 August	Bolton Wanderers	Football League
26 August	Arsenal	Football League
2 September	Charlton Athletic	Football League
6 September	Liverpool	Football League
16 September	Wolverhampton Wanderers	Football League
30 September	Aston Villa	Football League
14 October	Chelsea	Football League
28 October	West Bromwich Albion	Football League
11 November	Everton	Football League
25 November	Huddersfield Town	Football League
9 December	Sheffield Wednesday	Football League
16 December	Blackpool	Football League
25 December	Derby County	Football League
6 January	Huddersfield Town	FA Cup
13 January	Manchester United	Football League
27 January	Cardiff City	Friendly
3 February	Sunderland	Football League
6 February	Combined Liege XI	Friendly
24 February	Burnley	Football League
10 March	Stoke City	Football League
23 March	Fulham	Football League
24 March	Portsmouth	Football League
7 April	Newcastle United	Football League
21 April	Middlesbrough	Football League
23 April	Hibernian	Friendly
30 April	Chelmsford City	Denny Foreman Benefit
16 May	Racing Club de Paris	Friendly
29 May	Combined Copenhagen XI	Friendly
30 May	Combined Copenhagen XI	Friendly
31 May	Combined Copenhagen XI	Friendly

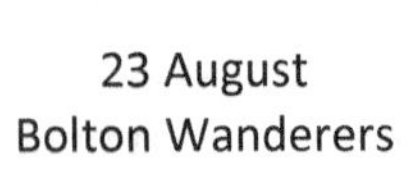
23 August
Bolton Wanderers

26 August
Arsenal

16 September
Wolverhampton Wanderers

11 November
Everton

25 November
Huddersfield Town

25 December
Derby County

13 January
Manchester United

3 February
Sunderland

24 March
Portsmouth

7 April
Newcastle United

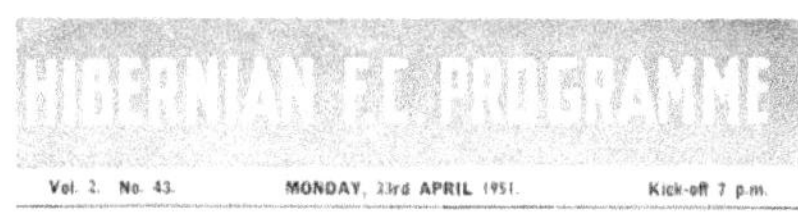

23 April
Hibernian

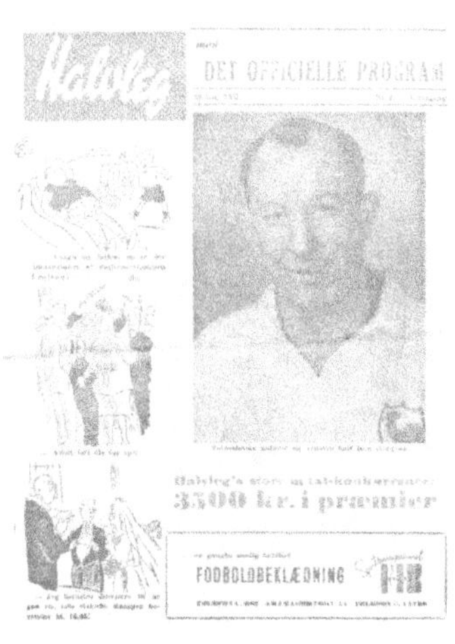

28 May (magazine date)
Combined Copenhagen XI

1951-52

HOME

		Date	Opponent	Competition
☐	☐	11 August	Whites v Colours	Public Trial
☐	☐	20 August	Fulham	Football League
☐	☐	25 August	West Bromwich Albion	Football League
☐	☐	8 September	Bolton Wanderers	Football League
☐	☐	10 September	Burnley	Football League
☐	☐	22 September	Manchester United	Football League
☐	☐	24 September	Newcastle United	FA Charity Shield
☐	☐	6 October	Manchester City	Football League
☐	☐	10 October	Copenhagen Combined XI	Friendly
☐	☐	20 October	Aston Villa	Football League
☐	☐	3 November	Wolverhampton Wanderers	Football League
☐	☐	17 November	Chelsea	Football League
☐	☐	1 December	Liverpool	Football League
☐	☐	15 December	Middlesbrough	Football League
☐	☐	26 December	Charlton Athletic	Football League
☐	☐	29 December	Newcastle United	Football League
☐	☐	19 January	Stoke City	Football League
☐	☐	2 February	Newcastle United	FA Cup
☐	☐	9 February	Arsenal	Football League
☐	☐	23 February	Preston North End	Football League
☐	☐	1 March	Derby County	Football League
☐	☐	15 March	Sunderland	Football League
☐	☐	31 March	Huddersfield Town (dated 2.4 on inside) - postponed	Football League
☐	☐	2 April	Huddersfield Town (dated 2.4 inside and outside)	Football League
☐	☐		(dated 2.4 outside, 31.3 inside)	
☐	☐	12 April	Portsmouth	Football League
☐	☐	23 April	Hibernian	Friendly
☐	☐	26 April	Blackpool	Football League

☐ Handbook ☐ Season Ticket

Season Ticket

Handbook

TOTTENHAM HOTSPUR

FOOTBALL AND ATHLETIC COMPANY, LIMITED

Official Programme

AND RECORD OF THE CLUB

PRICE TWOPENCE

WELCOME BACK!

DO YOU ? KNOW

FOUR SATURDAY TEAMS

THE ENFIELD CENTRAL BAND WILL PLAY AT EACH HOME GAME

11 August
Public Trial

25 August
West Bromwich Albion

10 October
Combined Copenhagen XI

3 November
Wolverhampton Wanderers

26 December
Charlton Athletic

9 February
Arsenal

1 March
Derby County

31 March
Huddersfield Town - postponed

2 April
Huddersfield Town

26 April
Blackpool

1951-52

AWAY

Date	Opponent	Competition
18 August	Middlesbrough	Football League
29 August	Fulham	Football League
1 September	Newcastle United	Football League
3 September	Burnley	Football League
15 September	Stoke City	Football League
29 September	Arsenal	Football League
13 October	Derby County	Football League
27 October	Sunderland	Football League
10 November	Huddersfield Town	Football League
24 November	Portsmouth	Football League
8 December	Blackpool	Football League
22 December	West Bromwich Albion	Football League
25 December	Charlton Athletic	Football League
5 January	Bolton Wanderers	Football League
12 January	Scunthorpe United	FA Cup
26 January	Manchester United	Football League
16 February	Manchester City	Football League
8 March	Aston Villa	Football League
22 March	Wolverhampton Wanderers	Football League
26 March	FC Austria (Brussels)	Le Soir Cup
14 April	Preston North End	Football League
19 April	Liverpool	Football League
30 April	Chelsea	Football League
3 May	Racing Club de Paris	Friendly
5 May	Ipswich Town	Ipswich Hospital Charity Cup
8 May	Crittall Athletic	Braintree, Witham & District Tuberculosis After-care
22 May	Ontario All-Stars (Toronto)	Friendly
28 May	Saskatchewan FA (Saskatoon)	Friendly
{ 31 May	BC Mainland All-Stars (Vancouver)	Friendly
2 June	Victoria (Victoria)	Friendly
{ 4 June	BC Mainland All-Stars (Vancouver)	Friendly
7 June	Alberta All Stars (Calgary)	Friendly
9 June	Manitoba FA (Winnipeg)	Friendly
14 June	Manchester United (Toronto)	Friendly
15 June	Manchester United (New York)	Friendly
18 June	Montreal All Stars (Montreal)	Friendly

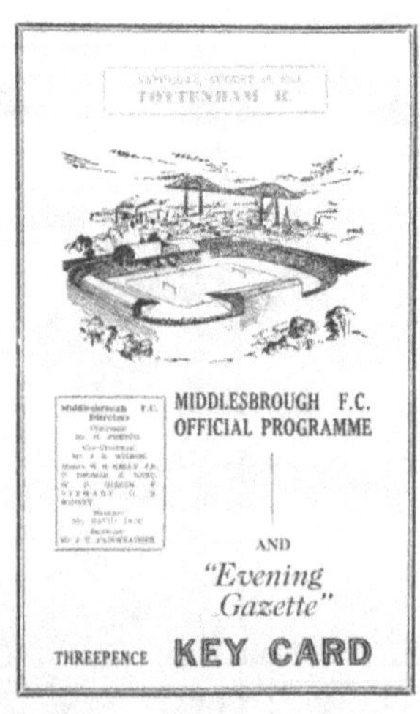

18 August
Middlesbrough

12 January
Scunthorpe United

26 March
FC Austria

5 May
Ipswich Town

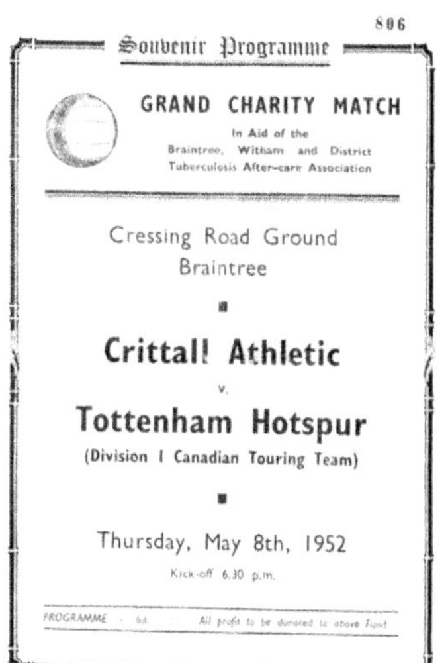

8 May
Crittall Athletic

TOTTENHAM HOTSPUR (English League, First Division)
VS.
ONTARIO ALL-STARS
THURSDAY, MAY 22nd, 1952
MUNICIPAL SPORTS STADIUM
C. N. E., TORONTO, CANADA

22 May
Ontario All-Stars

31 May & 4 June
BC Mainland All-Stars

2 June
Victoria

7 June
Alberta All-Stars

MANCHESTER UNITED
VS
TOTTENHAM HOTSPUR
SATURDAY, JUNE 14th 1952
VARSITY STADIUM, TORONTO

14 June
Manchester United

OFFICIAL 25c PROGRAM

INTERNATIONAL SOCCER MATCH

MANCHESTER UNITED
(English Champions 1951-1952)
vs.
TOTTENHAM HOTSPUR
(English Champions 1950-1951)

YANKEE STADIUM
NEW YORK

SUNDAY
JUNE 15, 1952

Preliminary game at 2 o'clock
PHILADELPHIA NATIONALS vs. NEW YORK AMERICANS
Final for the Lewis Cup

15 June
Manchester United

Souvenir Programme

INTERNATIONAL SOCCER GAME

Tottenham Hotspur
VS
MONTREAL All Stars

Sponsored by the
PROVINCE OF QUEBEC FOOTBALL ASSOCIATION

WEDNESDAY, JUNE 18th, 1952
8 p.m.
DELORIMIER STADIUM

18 June
Montreal All-Stars

1952-53

HOME

Date	Opponent	Competition
16 August	Whites v Blues	Public Trial
23 August	West Bromwich Albion	Football League
1 September	Manchester City	Football League
6 September	Cardiff City	Football League
15 September	Liverpool	Football League
20 September	Arsenal	Football League
27 September	Burnley	Football League
18 October	Blackpool	Football League
1 November	Manchester United	Football League
15 November	Bolton Wanderers	Football League
29 November	Sunderland	Football League
13 December	Charlton Athletic	Football League
25 December	Middlesbrough	Football League
3 January	Newcastle United	Football League
12 January	Tranmere Rovers	FA Cup
24 January	Sheffield Wednesday	Football League
4 February	Preston North End	FA Cup
21 February	Preston North End	Football League
4 March	Birmingham City	FA Cup
12 March	Derby County	Football League
14 March	Chelsea	Football League
28 March	Portsmouth	Football League
3 April	Stoke City	Football League
11 April	Aston Villa	Football League
25 April	Wolverhampton Wanderers	Football League

☐ Handbook ☐ Season Ticket

Season Ticket

Handbook

16 August
Public Trial

COPYRIGHT ALL RIGHTS RESERVED

TOTTENHAM HOTSPUR
FOOTBALL AND ATHLETIC COMPANY, LIMITED

Official Programme
AND RECORD OF THE CLUB

PRICE TWOPENCE

VOL. XLV. No. 11 SATURDAY, SEPTEMBER 27th, 1952

THE NORTH LONDON DERBY—1st LEG

DISTINGUISHED VISITORS

WELCOME TO BURNLEY

DO YOU ? KNOW

OUR BAND WILL PLAY AT EACH HOME GAME

27 September
Burnley

COPYRIGHT ALL RIGHTS RESERVED

TOTTENHAM HOTSPUR
FOOTBALL AND ATHLETIC COMPANY, LIMITED

Official Programme
AND RECORD OF THE CLUB

PRICE TWOPENCE

VOL. XLV. No. 16 SATURDAY, OCTOBER 18th, 1952

OUR GAME AT DERBY

BLACKPOOL HERE TO-DAY

DO YOU ? KNOW

OUR BAND WILL PLAY AT EACH HOME GAME

18 October
Blackpool

COPYRIGHT ALL RIGHTS RESERVED

TOTTENHAM HOTSPUR
FOOTBALL AND ATHLETIC COMPANY, LIMITED

Official Programme
AND RECORD OF THE CLUB

PRICE TWOPENCE

VOL. XLV. No. 21 SATURDAY, NOVEMBER 15th, 1952

BOLTON W. HERE TODAY

DISAPPOINTMENT AT TOTTENHAM

DO YOU ? KNOW

OUR BAND WILL PLAY AT EACH HOME GAME

15 November
Bolton Wanderers

COPYRIGHT ALL RIGHTS RESERVED

TOTTENHAM HOTSPUR
FOOTBALL AND ATHLETIC COMPANY, LIMITED

Official Programme
AND RECORD OF THE CLUB

PRICE TWOPENCE

VOL. XLV. No. 27 THURSDAY, DECEMBER 25th, 1952

The Season's Greetings . . .

A MERRY CHRISTMAS AND A PROSPEROUS NEW YEAR

OUR FIRST DEFEAT IN SIX WEEKS

25 December
Middlesbrough

COPYRIGHT ALL RIGHTS RESERVED

TOTTENHAM HOTSPUR
FOOTBALL AND ATHLETIC COMPANY, LIMITED

Official Programme
AND RECORD OF THE CLUB

PRICE TWOPENCE

VOL. XLV. No. 29 SATURDAY, JANUARY 3rd, 1953

REVIEWING OUR POSITION

THE DOUBLE AT MIDDLESBROUGH'S EXPENSE

DO YOU ? KNOW

OUR BAND WILL PLAY AT EACH HOME GAME

3 January
Newcastle United

COPYRIGHT ALL RIGHTS RESERVED

TOTTENHAM HOTSPUR
FOOTBALL AND ATHLETIC COMPANY, LIMITED

Official Programme
AND RECORD OF THE CLUB

PRICE TWOPENCE

VOL. XLV. No. 35 WEDNESDAY, FEBRUARY 4th, 1953

THE MAGIC OF "THE CUP"

DO YOU ? KNOW

OUR BAND WILL PLAY AT EACH HOME GAME

4 February
Preston North End

COPYRIGHT ALL RIGHTS RESERVED

TOTTENHAM HOTSPUR
FOOTBALL AND ATHLETIC COMPANY, LIMITED

Official Programme
AND RECORD OF THE CLUB

PRICE TWOPENCE

VOL. XLV. No. 45 SATURDAY, MARCH 28th, 1953

HISTORY REPEATS ITSELF AT VILLA PK.

DO YOU ? KNOW

OUR BAND WILL PLAY AT EACH HOME GAME

28 March
Portsmouth

COPYRIGHT ALL RIGHTS RESERVED

TOTTENHAM HOTSPUR
FOOTBALL AND ATHLETIC COMPANY, LIMITED

Official Programme
AND RECORD OF THE CLUB

PRICE TWOPENCE

VOL. XLV. No. 51 SATURDAY, APRIL 11th, 1953

STOKE'S VISIT

THE RETURN WITH STOKE

POINTS FROM BOLTON

TO-DAY'S RETURN WITH THE VILLA

DO YOU ? KNOW

OUR BAND WILL PLAY AT EACH HOME GAME

11 April
Aston Villa

COPYRIGHT ALL RIGHTS RESERVED

TOTTENHAM HOTSPUR
FOOTBALL AND ATHLETIC COMPANY, LIMITED

Official Programme
AND RECORD OF THE CLUB

PRICE TWOPENCE

VOL. XLV. No. 54 SATURDAY, APRIL 25th, 1953

OUR VISIT TO SUNDERLAND

WELCOME TO WOLVES

THE RESERVES

DO YOU ? KNOW

OUR BAND WILL PLAY AT EACH HOME GAME

25 April
Wolverhampton Wanderers

1952-53

AWAY

	Date	Opponent	Competition
	27 August	Manchester City	Football League
	30 August	Newcastle United	Football League
	10 September	Liverpool	Football League
	13 September	Sheffield Wednesday	Football League
	4 October	Preston North End	Football League
	11 October	Derby County	Football League
	25 October	Chelsea	Football League
	27 October	Gloucester City	Friendly
	8 November	Portsmouth	Football League
	22 November	Aston Villa	Football League
	6 December	Wolverhampton Wanderers	Football League
	20 December	West Bromwich Albion	Football League
	27 December	Middlesbrough	Football League
	10 January	Tranmere Rovers	FA Cup
	17 January	Cardiff City	Football League
	31 January	Preston North End	FA Cup
		- Lancashire Evening Post brochure	
	7 February	Arsenal	Football League
	14 February	Halifax Town	FA Cup
	17 February	Burnley	Football League
	28 February	Birmingham City	FA Cup
	7 March	Blackpool	Football League
	9 March	Birmingham City (Molineux)	FA Cup
	21 March	Blackpool (Villa Park)	FA Cup
	25 March	Manchester United	Football League
	4 April	Bolton Wanderers	Football League
	6 April	Stoke City	Football League
	16 April	West Ham United	Friendly
	18 April	Sunderland	Football League
	20 April	Reading	Stan Wicks Testimonial
	30 April	Charlton Athletic	Football League
	4 May	Arsenal	Lord Mayor of London's National Flood and Tempest Distress Fund
	11 May	Hibernian (Ibrox Park)	Coronation Cup
	12 May	Hibernian (Hampden Park)	Coronation Cup
	15 May	Heart of Midlothian	Friendly
	30 May	Racing Club de Paris	Friendly

27 August
Manchester City

25 October
Chelsea

27 October
Gloucester City

8 November
Portsmouth

10 January
Tranmere Rovers

14 February
Halifax Town

28 February
Birmingham City

25 March
Manchester United

16 April
West Ham United

20 April
Reading

11 May
Hibernian

15 May
Heart of Midlothian

1953-54

HOME

		Date	Opponent	Competition
☐	☐	15 August	Whites v Colours	Public Trial
☐	☐	19 August	Aston Villa	Football League
☐	☐	26 August	Charlton Athletic	Football League
☐	☐	29 August	Middlesbrough	Football League
☐	☐	12 September	Liverpool	Football League
☐	☐	16 September	Burnley	Football League
☐	☐	26 September	Manchester United	Football League
☐	☐	29 September	Racing Club de Paris	Friendly
☐	☐	10 October	Arsenal	Football League
☐	☐	24 October	Manchester City	Football League
☐	☐	28 October	FC Austria	Friendly
☐	☐	7 November	Chelsea	Football League
☐	☐	21 November	Huddersfield Town	Football League
☐	☐	5 December	Wolverhampton Wanderers	Football League
☐	☐	19 December	Sheffield Wednesday	Football League
☐	☐	25 December	Portsmouth	Football League
☐	☐	13 January	Leeds United	FA Cup
☐	☐	16 January	West Bromwich Albion	Football League
☐	☐	6 February	Newcastle United	Football League
☐	☐	24 February	Hull City	FA Cup
☐	☐	3 March	Bolton Wanderers	Football League
☐	☐	6 March	Cardiff City	Football League
☐	☐	20 March	Sunderland	Football League
☐	☐	3 April	Blackpool	Football League
☐	☐	5 April	Hibernian	Friendly
☐	☐	17 April	Sheffield United	Football League
☐	☐	19 April	Preston North End	Football League

☐ Handbook

☐ Season Ticket

Season Ticket

Handbook

COPYRIGHT — ALL RIGHTS RESERVED

TOTTENHAM HOTSPUR

FOOTBALL AND ATHLETIC COMPANY LIMITED

Official Programme

AND RECORD OF THE CLUB

PRICE TWOPENCE

VOL. XLVI No. 1 — SATURDAY, AUGUST 15th, 1953

WELCOME TO ANOTHER NEW SEASON!

TO-DAY'S TRIAL MATCH

THE VILLA HERE NEXT WEDNESDAY

DO YOU ? KNOW

OUR BAND WILL PLAY AT EACH HOME GAME

15 August
Public Trial

COPYRIGHT ALL RIGHTS RESERVED

TOTTENHAM HOTSPUR

FOOTBALL AND ATHLETIC COMPANY LIMITED

Official Programme

AND RECORD OF THE CLUB

PRICE TWOPENCE

OUR VISITORS TODAY

DO YOU ? KNOW

OUR BAND WILL PLAY AT EACH HOME GAME

16 September
Burnley

COPYRIGHT ALL RIGHTS RESERVED

TOTTENHAM HOTSPUR

FOOTBALL AND ATHLETIC COMPANY LIMITED

Official Programme

AND RECORD OF THE CLUB

PRICE TWOPENCE

WELCOME TO RACING CLUB DE PARIS

29 September
Racing Club de Paris

COPYRIGHT ALL RIGHTS RESERVED

TOTTENHAM HOTSPUR

FOOTBALL AND ATHLETIC COMPANY LIMITED

Official Programme

AND RECORD OF THE CLUB

PRICE TWOPENCE

WELCOME TO OUR AUSTRIAN GUESTS

28 October
FC Austria

COPYRIGHT ALL RIGHTS RESERVED

TOTTENHAM HOTSPUR

FOOTBALL AND ATHLETIC COMPANY LIMITED

Official Programme

AND RECORD OF THE CLUB

PRICE TWOPENCE

WELCOME TO HUDDERSFIELD TOWN

DO YOU ? KNOW

OUR BAND WILL PLAY AT EACH HOME GAME

21 November
Huddersfield Town

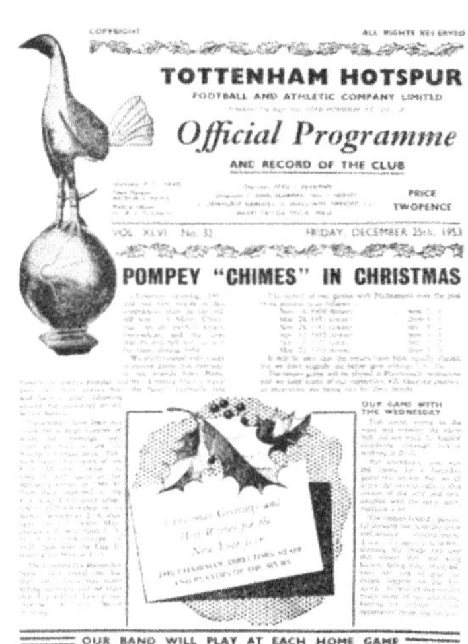
COPYRIGHT ALL RIGHTS RESERVED

TOTTENHAM HOTSPUR

FOOTBALL AND ATHLETIC COMPANY LIMITED

Official Programme

AND RECORD OF THE CLUB

PRICE TWOPENCE

POMPEY "CHIMES" IN CHRISTMAS

OUR BAND WILL PLAY AT EACH HOME GAME

25 December
Portsmouth

COPYRIGHT ALL RIGHTS RESERVED

TOTTENHAM HOTSPUR

FOOTBALL AND ATHLETIC COMPANY LIMITED

Official Programme

AND RECORD OF THE CLUB

PRICE TWOPENCE

ANOTHER GREAT LOSS TO THE CLUB

OUR BAND WILL PLAY AT EACH HOME GAME

6 February
Newcastle United

COPYRIGHT ALL RIGHTS RESERVED

TOTTENHAM HOTSPUR

FOOTBALL AND ATHLETIC COMPANY LIMITED

Official Programme

AND RECORD OF THE CLUB

PRICE TWOPENCE

VISITORS FROM WALES

DO YOU ? KNOW

OUR BAND WILL PLAY AT EACH HOME GAME

6 March
Cardiff City

COPYRIGHT ALL RIGHTS RESERVED

TOTTENHAM HOTSPUR

FOOTBALL AND ATHLETIC COMPANY LIMITED

Official Programme

AND RECORD OF THE CLUB

PRICE TWOPENCE

VISIT OF OUR SCOTTISH FRIENDS

5 April
Hibernian

COPYRIGHT ALL RIGHTS RESERVED

TOTTENHAM HOTSPUR

FOOTBALL AND ATHLETIC COMPANY LIMITED

Official Programme

AND RECORD OF THE CLUB

PRICE TWOPENCE

WELCOME TO THE CUP FINALISTS

DO YOU ? KNOW

OUR BAND WILL PLAY AT EACH HOME GAME

19 April
Preston North End

1953-54

AWAY

		Date	Opponent	Competition
		22 August	Sheffield Wednesday	Football League
		3 September	Charlton Athletic	Football League
		5 September	West Bromwich Albion	Football League
		7 September	Burnley	Football League
		19 September	Newcastle United	Football League
		21 September	Hibernian	Friendly
		3 October	Bolton Wanderers	Football League
		17 October	Cardiff City	Football League
		19 October	Millwall	Friendly
		31 October	Sunderland	Football League
		14 November	Blackpool	Football League
		28 November	Sheffield United	Football League
		12 December	Aston Villa	Football League
		26 December	Portsmouth	Football League
		2 January	Middlesbrough	Football League
		9 January	Leeds United	FA Cup
		23 January	Liverpool	Football League
		30 January	Manchester City	FA Cup
		13 February	Manchester United	Football League
		20 February	Hull City	FA Cup
		27 February	Arsenal	Football League
		13 March	West Bromwich Albion	FA Cup
		17 March	Manchester City	Football League
		27 March	Chelsea	Football League
		10 April	Huddersfield Town	Football League
		16 April	Preston North End	Football League
		24 April	Wolverhampton Wanderers	Football League
		28 April	Austrian State XI (Vienna)	Friendly
		1 May	Vfb Stuttgart	Friendly
		5 May	Eintracht Braunschweig	Friendly
		8 May	Hamburg	Friendly

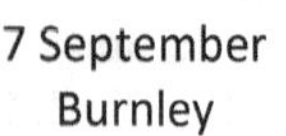

7 September
Burnley

21 September
Hibernian

19 October
Millwall

31 October
Sunderland

14 November
Blackpool

28 November
Sheffield United

20 February
Hull City

17 March
Manchester City

28 April
Austrian State XI

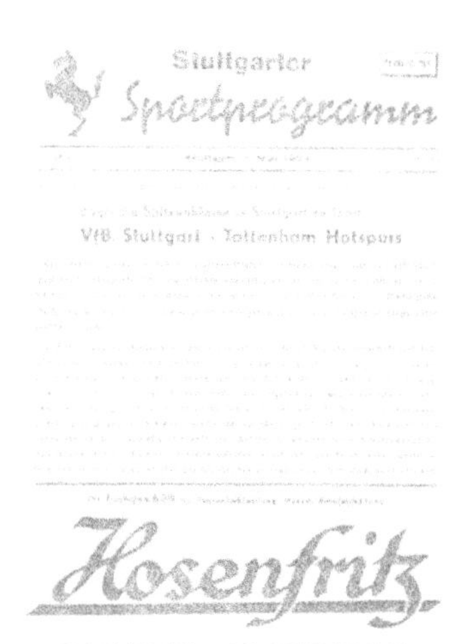

1 May
Vfb Stuttgart

5 May
Eintracht Braunschweig

8 May
Hamburg

1954-55

HOME

Date	Opponent	Competition
10 August	Blue & White Stripes v Whites	Public Trial
25 August	Wolverhampton Wanderers	Football League
28 August	Sunderland	Football League
8 September	Manchester United	Football League
18 September	Portsmouth	Football League
2 October	Charlton Athletic	Football League
9 October	West Bromwich Albion	Football League
18 October	Sportklub Wacker	Friendly
23 October	Preston North End	Football League
2 November	Rot-Weiss Essen	Friendly
6 November	Cardiff City	Football League
15 November	Finchley	Friendly
20 November	Leicester City	Football League
4 December	Everton	Football League
18 December	Aston Villa	Football League
27 December	Bolton Wanderers	Football League
15 January	Arsenal	Football League
22 January	Sheffield Wednesday	Football League
29 January	Port Vale	FA Cup
12 February	Blackpool	Football League
2 March	Arsenal	Friendly
5 March	Manchester City	Football League
9 March	Racing Club de Paris	Friendly
19 March	Sheffield United	Football League
30 March	Servette	Friendly
2 April	Chelsea	Football League
11 April	Huddersfield Town	Football League
16 April	Burnley	Football League
30 April	Newcastle United	Football League

☐ Handbook ☐ Season Ticket

Season Ticket

Handbook

TOTTENHAM HOTSPUR
FOOTBALL AND ATHLETIC COMPANY LIMITED
Official Programme
AND RECORD OF THE CLUB
PRICE TWOPENCE
TUESDAY, AUGUST 10, 1954
WELCOME TO ANOTHER NEW SEASON
OUR BAND WILL PLAY AT EACH HOME GAME

10 August
Public Trial

TOTTENHAM HOTSPUR
FOOTBALL AND ATHLETIC COMPANY LIMITED
Official Programme
AND RECORD OF THE CLUB
PRICE TWOPENCE
VOL. XLVII. No. 7 WEDNESDAY, SEPTEMBER 8th, 1954
WELCOME TO MANCHESTER UNITED
DO YOU ? KNOW
ARSENAL REVIVAL
OUR BAND WILL PLAY AT EACH HOME GAME

8 September
Manchester United

TOTTENHAM HOTSPUR
FOOTBALL AND ATHLETIC COMPANY LIMITED
Official Programme
AND RECORD OF THE CLUB
PRICE TWOPENCE
VOL. XLVII. No. 19 MONDAY, OCTOBER 18th, 1954
WELCOME TO OUR AUSTRIAN GUESTS
SPORTKLUB WACKER

18 October
Sportklub Wacker

TOTTENHAM HOTSPUR
FOOTBALL AND ATHLETIC COMPANY LIMITED
Official Programme
AND RECORD OF THE CLUB
PRICE TWOPENCE
VOL. XLVII. No. 23 TUESDAY, NOVEMBER 2nd, 1954
WELCOME TO ESSEN ROT-WEISS
ESSEN ROT-WEISS

2 November
Essen Rot-Weiss

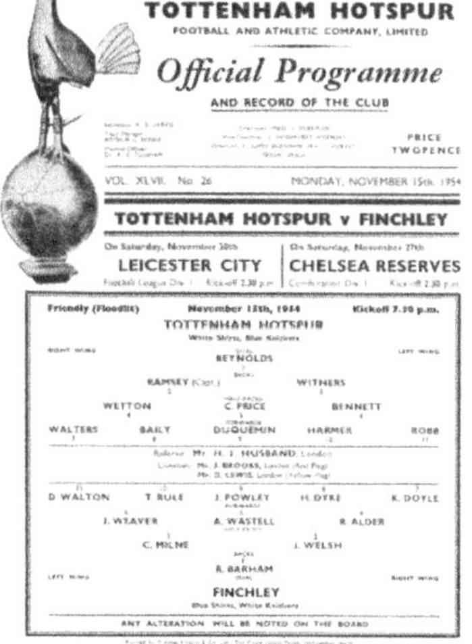
TOTTENHAM HOTSPUR
FOOTBALL AND ATHLETIC COMPANY, LIMITED
Official Programme
AND RECORD OF THE CLUB
PRICE TWOPENCE
VOL. XLVII. No. 26 MONDAY, NOVEMBER 15th, 1954
TOTTENHAM HOTSPUR v FINCHLEY
On Saturday, November 20th LEICESTER CITY
On Saturday, November 27th CHELSEA RESERVES
Friendly (Floodlit) November 15th, 1954 Kick-off 7.30 p.m.
TOTTENHAM HOTSPUR
FINCHLEY
ANY ALTERATION WILL BE NOTED ON THE BOARD

15 November
Finchley

TOTTENHAM HOTSPUR
FOOTBALL AND ATHLETIC COMPANY, LIMITED
Official Programme
AND RECORD OF THE CLUB
PRICE TWOPENCE
VOL. XLVII. No. 43 WEDNESDAY, MARCH 2nd, 1955
TOTTENHAM HOTSPUR v ARSENAL
On Saturday, March 5th MANCHESTER CITY
On Wednesday, March 9th RACING CLUB DE PARIS
Friendly (Floodlit) March 2nd, 1955 Kick-off 7.30 p.m.
TOTTENHAM HOTSPUR
ARSENAL
ANY ALTERATION WILL BE NOTED ON THE BOARD

2 March
Arsenal

TOTTENHAM HOTSPUR
FOOTBALL AND ATHLETIC COMPANY, LIMITED
Official Programme
AND RECORD OF THE CLUB
PRICE TWOPENCE
VOL. XLVII. No. 45 WEDNESDAY, MARCH 9th, 1955
TOTTENHAM HOTSPUR v RACING CLUB DE PARIS
HENDON v HOUNSLOW T.
SHEFFIELD UNITED
Friendly (Floodlit) March 9th, 1955 Kick-off 7.30 p.m.
TOTTENHAM HOTSPUR
RACING CLUB DE PARIS
ANY ALTERATION WILL BE NOTED ON THE BOARD

9 March
Racing Club de Paris

TOTTENHAM HOTSPUR
FOOTBALL AND ATHLETIC COMPANY, LIMITED
Official Programme
AND RECORD OF THE CLUB
PRICE TWOPENCE
VOL. XLVII. No. 51 WEDNESDAY, MARCH 30th, 1955
TOTTENHAM HOTSPUR v F.C. SERVETTE
On Saturday, April 2nd CHELSEA
On Monday, April 4th LUTON TOWN RESERVES
Friendly (FLOODLIT) March 30th, 1955 Kick-off 7.30 p.m.
TOTTENHAM HOTSPUR
F. C. SERVETTE
ANY ALTERATION WILL BE NOTED ON THE BOARD

30 March
Servette

TOTTENHAM HOTSPUR
FOOTBALL AND ATHLETIC COMPANY LIMITED
Official Programme
AND RECORD OF THE CLUB
PRICE TWOPENCE
VOL. XLVII. No. 52 SATURDAY, APRIL 2nd, 1955
WELCOME TO THE LEAGUE LEADERS
OUR BAND WILL PLAY AT EACH HOME GAME

2 April
Chelsea

TOTTENHAM HOTSPUR
FOOTBALL AND ATHLETIC COMPANY LIMITED
Official Programme
AND RECORD OF THE CLUB
PRICE TWOPENCE
SATURDAY, APRIL 30th, 1955
CUP FINALISTS VISIT US TO-DAY
CAR PARKING
OUR BAND WILL PLAY AT EACH HOME GAME

30 April
Newcastle United

1954-55

AWAY

		Date	Opponent	Competition
		14 August	Lille Olympique (Boulogne)	Friendly
		21 August	Aston Villa	Football League
		30 August	Wolverhampton Wanderers	Football League
		4 September	Arsenal	Football League
		11 September	Sheffield Wednesday	Football League
		15 September	Manchester United	Football League
		25 September	Blackpool	Football League
		11 October	Queens Park Rangers	Friendly
		16 October	Newcastle United	Football League
		30 October	Sheffield United	Football League
		13 November	Chelsea	Football League
		27 November	Burnley	Football League
		29 November	Accrington Stanley - abandoned	Friendly
		11 December	Manchester City	Football League
		25 December	Bolton Wanderers	Football League
		1 January	Sunderland	Football League
		8 January	Gateshead	FA Cup
		5 February	Portsmouth	Football League
		19 February	York City	FA Cup
		26 February	West Bromwich Albion - postponed	Football League
		12 March	Preston North End	Football League
		14 March	Hibernian	Friendly
		26 March	Cardiff City	Football League
		9 April	Everton	Football League
		12 April	Huddersfield Town	Football League
		23 April	Leicester City	Football League
		27 April	West Bromwich Albion	Football League
		5 May	Charlton Athletic	Football League
		11 May	FC Austria	Friendly
		15 May	Kinizsi	Friendly
		18 May	Vasas	Friendly
		20 May	Pécsi Dózsa	Friendly
		25 May	Racing Club de Paris	Friendly

14 August
Lille Olympique

4 September
Arsenal

11 October
Queens Park Rangers

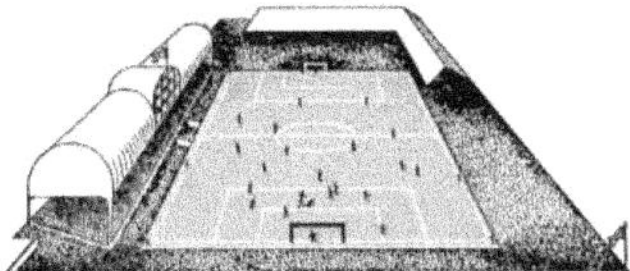

16 October
Newcastle United

29 November
Accrington Stanley - abandoned

11 December
Manchester City

GATESHEAD A.F.C.

GATESHEAD v TOTTENHAM H.

SEASON 1954-55 PRICE 3d.

BENSHAM
PICTURE HOUSE

Always a Good Show
—at Reasonable Prices

8 January
Gateshead

19 February
York City

THE
ALBION NEWS
AND OFFICIAL PROGRAMME

NOTICE

OUR VISITORS

26 February
West Bromwich Albion - postponed

14 March
Hibernian

26 March
Cardiff City

23 April
Leicester City

1955-56

HOME

	Date	Opponent	Competition
☐☐	13 August	Whites v Blues	Public Trial
☐☐	20 August	Burnley	Football League
☐☐	31 August	Manchester United	Football League
☐☐	3 September	Charlton Athletic	Football League
☐☐	10 September	Arsenal	Football League
☐☐	24 September	Newcastle United	Football League
☐☐	8 October	Bolton Wanderers	Football League
☐☐	12 October	Vasas	Friendly
☐☐	22 October	Sunderland	Football League
☐☐	5 November	Cardiff City	Football League
☐☐	19 November	Wolverhampton Wanderers	Football League
☐☐	3 December	Blackpool	Football League
☐☐	6 December	Swansea Town	Friendly
☐☐	24 December	Luton Town	Football League
☐☐	26 December	West Bromwich Albion	Football League
☐☐	7 January	Boston United	FA Cup
☐☐	21 January	Everton	Football League
☐☐	28 January	Middlesbrough	FA Cup
☐☐	11 February	Birmingham City	Football League
☐☐	25 February	Chelsea	Football League
☐☐	3 March	West Ham United	FA Cup
☐☐	10 March	Portsmouth	Football League
☐☐	24 March	Manchester City	Football League
☐☐	30 March	Preston North End	Football League
☐☐	7 April	Aston Villa	Football League
☐☐	21 April	Huddersfield Town	Football League
☐☐	28 April	Sheffield United	Football League

☐ Handbook ☐ Season Ticket

Season Ticket

Handbook

13 August
Public Trial

TOTTENHAM HOTSPUR
FOOTBALL AND ATHLETIC COMPANY LIMITED
Official Programme
AND RECORD OF THE CLUB
PRICE TWOPENCE
SATURDAY, SEPTEMBER 3rd, 1955
SPURS v CHARLTON
OUR BAND WILL PLAY AT EACH HOME GAME

3 September
Charlton Athletic

TOTTENHAM HOTSPUR
FOOTBALL AND ATHLETIC COMPANY LIMITED
Official Programme
AND RECORD OF THE CLUB
PRICE TWOPENCE
SATURDAY, OCTOBER 8th, 1955
OUR VISITORS FROM LANCASHIRE
OUR BAND WILL PLAY AT EACH HOME GAME

8 October
Bolton Wanderers

TOTTENHAM HOTSPUR
FOOTBALL AND ATHLETIC COMPANY LIMITED
Official Programme
AND RECORD OF THE CLUB
PRICE TWOPENCE
WEDNESDAY, OCTOBER 12th, 1955
OUR VISITORS FROM BUDAPEST

12 October
Vasas

TOTTENHAM HOTSPUR
FOOTBALL AND ATHLETIC COMPANY LIMITED
Official Programme
AND RECORD OF THE CLUB
PRICE TWOPENCE
SATURDAY, NOVEMBER 5th, 1955
SPURS v CARDIFF CITY
OUR BAND WILL PLAY AT EACH HOME GAME

5 November
Cardiff City

TOTTENHAM HOTSPUR
FOOTBALL AND ATHLETIC COMPANY LIMITED
Official Programme
AND RECORD OF THE CLUB
PRICE TWOPENCE
SATURDAY, DECEMBER 3rd, 1955
LEAGUE LEADERS FROM BLACKPOOL
OUR BAND WILL PLAY AT EACH HOME GAME

3 December
Blackpool

TOTTENHAM HOTSPUR
FOOTBALL AND ATHLETIC COMPANY LIMITED
Official Programme
AND RECORD OF THE CLUB
PRICE TWOPENCE
SATURDAY, DECEMBER 24th, 1955
SPURS v LUTON TOWN
THE DIRECTORS PLAYERS & STAFF
Wish all our Supporters
A HAPPY CHRISTMAS
and a
PROSPEROUS NEW YEAR
OUR BAND WILL PLAY AT EACH HOME GAME

24 December
Luton Town

TOTTENHAM HOTSPUR
FOOTBALL AND ATHLETIC COMPANY LIMITED
Official Programme
AND RECORD OF THE CLUB
PRICE TWOPENCE
SATURDAY, JANUARY 7th, 1956
BOSTON'S CUP-TIE VISIT
OUR BAND WILL PLAY AT EACH HOME GAME

7 January
Boston United

TOTTENHAM HOTSPUR
FOOTBALL AND ATHLETIC COMPANY LIMITED
Official Programme
AND RECORD OF THE CLUB
PRICE TWOPENCE
SATURDAY, MARCH 3rd, 1956
6th ROUND CUP-TIE WITH WEST HAM
OUR BAND WILL PLAY AT EACH HOME GAME

3 March
West Ham United

TOTTENHAM HOTSPUR
FOOTBALL AND ATHLETIC COMPANY LIMITED
Official Programme
AND RECORD OF THE CLUB
PRICE TWOPENCE
SATURDAY, APRIL 28th, 1956
END OF SEASON STRUGGLE
OUR BAND WILL PLAY AT EACH HOME GAME

28 April
Sheffield United

1955-56

AWAY

		Date	Opponent	Competition
		24 August	Manchester United	Football League
		27 August	Luton Town	Football League
		5 September	Sheffield United	Football League
		17 September	Everton	Football League
		25 September	Aarhus Gymnastikforening	Friendly
		1 October	Birmingham City	Football League
		15 October	Chelsea	Football League
		24 October	Plymouth Argyle	Friendly
		29 October	Portsmouth	Football League
		12 November	Manchester City	Football League
		14 November	Partick Thistle	Friendly
		26 November	Aston Villa	Football League
		10 December	Huddersfield Town	Football League
		17 December	Burnley	Football League
		27 December	West Bromwich Albion	Football League
		31 December	Charlton Athletic	Football League
		14 January	Arsenal	Football League
		4 February	Newcastle United	Football League
		18 February	Doncaster Rovers	FA Cup
		8 March	West Ham United	FA Cup
		17 March	Manchester City (Villa Park)	FA Cup
		21 March	Bolton Wanderers	Football League
		31 March	Sunderland	Football League
		2 April	Preston North End	Football League
		14 April	Blackpool	Football League
		18 April	Wolverhampton Wanderers	Football League
		23 April	Cardiff City	Football League
		3 May	Kings Lynn	Friendly

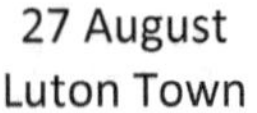

27 August
Luton Town

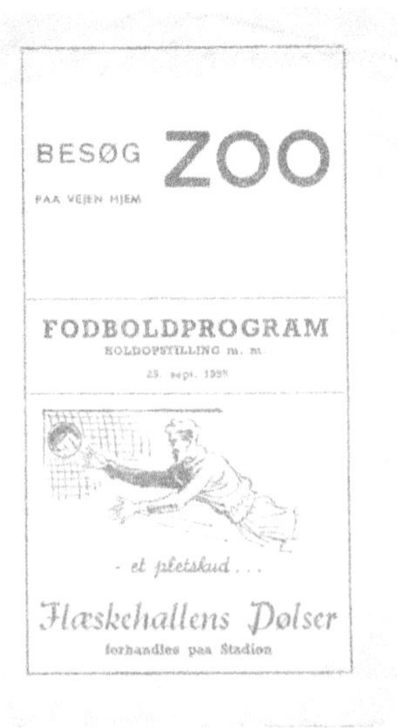

25 September
Aarhus Gymnastikforening

1 October
Birmingham City

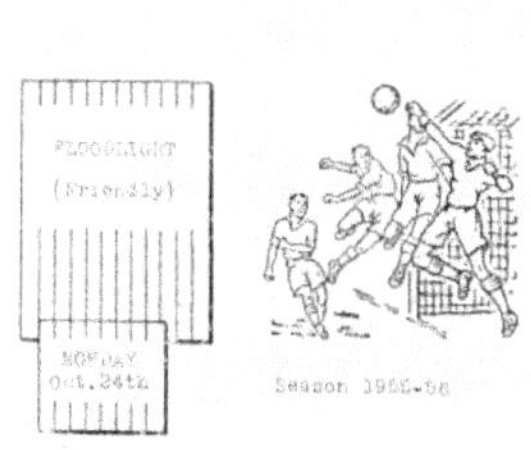

24 October
Plymouth Argyle

10 December
Huddersfield Town

17 December
Burnley

31 December
Charlton Athletic

4 February
Newcastle United

18 February
Doncaster Rovers

8 March
West Ham United

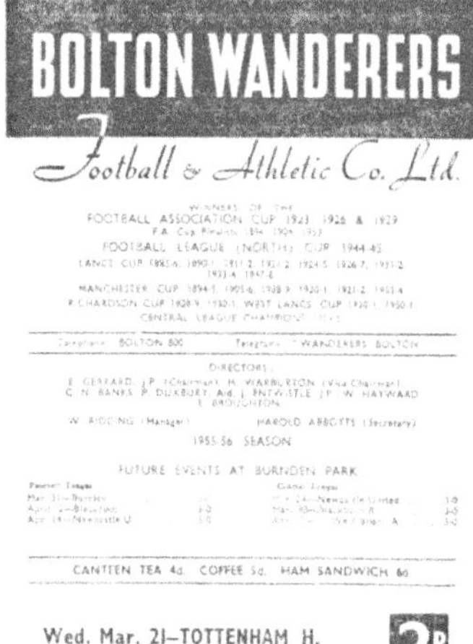

21 March
Bolton Wanderers

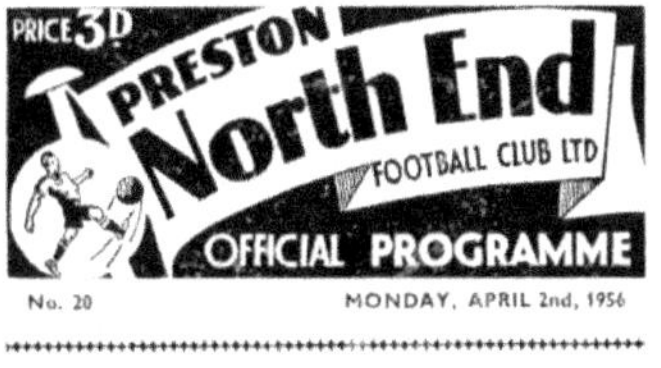

2 April
Preston North End

1956-57

HOME

Date	Opponent	Competition
11 August	Whites v Blues	Public Trial
25 August	Leeds United	Football League
29 August	Manchester City	Football League
8 September	Wolverhampton Wanderers	Football League
11 September	Racing Club de Paris	Friendly
22 September	Luton Town	Football League
26 September	Partick Thistle	Anglo-Scottish Floodlit Tournament
13 October	Cardiff City	Football League
27 October	Burnley	Football League
31 October	Hibernian	Anglo-Scottish Floodlit Tournament
10 November	Newcastle United	Football League
12 November	Heart of Midlothian	Anglo-Scottish Floodlit Tournament
24 November	Manchester United	Football League
3 December	Red Banner	Friendly
8 December	West Bromwich Albion	Football League
15 December	Preston North End	Football League
25 December	Everton	Football League
29 December	Bolton Wanderers	Football League
5 January	Leicester City	FA Cup
19 January	Aston Villa	Football League
26 January	Chelsea	FA Cup
9 February	Sunderland	Football League
20 February	Chelsea	Football League
13 March	Arsenal	Football League
16 March	Portsmouth	Football League
30 March	Sheffield Wednesday	Football League
13 April	Birmingham City	Football League
22 April	Charlton Athletic	Football League
27 April	Blackpool	Football League

☐ Handbook

☐ Season Ticket

Season Ticket

Handbook

11 August
Public Trial

11 September
Racing Club de Paris

26 September
Partick Thistle

31 October
Hibernian

12 November
Heart of Midlothian

3 December
Red Banner

24 December
Everton

20 February
Chelsea

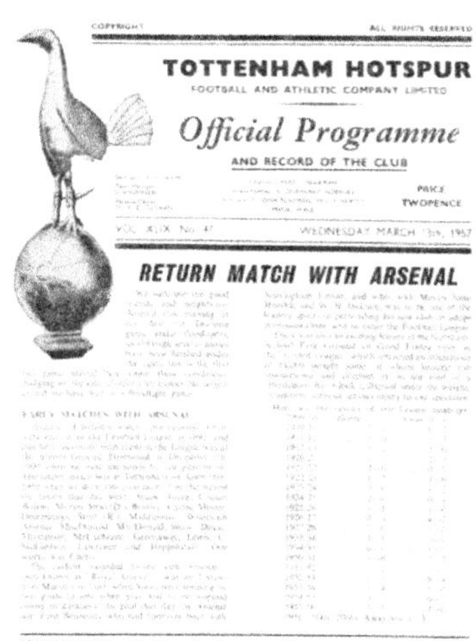

13 March
Arsenal

27 April
Blackpool

1956-57

AWAY

Date	Opponent	Competition
18 August	Preston North End	Football League
22 August	Manchester City	Football League
1 September	Bolton Wanderers	Football League
3 September	Blackpool	Football League
15 September	Aston Villa	Football League
17 September	Hibernian	Anglo-Scottish Floodlit Tournament
29 September	Sunderland	Football League
6 October	Chelsea	Football League
15 October	Heart of Midlothian	Anglo-Scottish Floodlit Tournament
20 October	Arsenal	Football League
3 November	Portsmouth	Football League
17 November	Sheffield Wednesday	Football League
26 November	Partick Thistle	Anglo-Scottish Floodlit Tournament
1 December	Birmingham City	Football League
22 December	Leeds United - postponed	Football League
26 December	Everton	Football League
12 January	Wolverhampton Wanderers	Football League
2 February	Luton Town	Football League
16 February	Bournemouth & Boscombe Athletic	FA Cup
23 February	Burnley - postponed	Football League
2 March	Leeds United	Football League
9 March	West Bromwich Albion	Football League
19 March	Combined Antwerp XI	Friendly
23 March	Newcastle United	Football League
6 April	Manchester United	Football League
19 April	Charlton Athletic	Football League
20 April	Cardiff City	Football League
29 April	Burnley	Football League
19 May	Celtic (New York)	Friendly
22 May	Essex County All Stars (Windsor)	Friendly
25 May	Ontario All-Stars (Ontario)	Friendly
29 May	Alberta All-Stars (Calgary)	Friendly
{ 1 June	Celtic (Vancouver)	Friendly
{ 3 June	British Columbia All Stars (Vancouver)	Friendly
5 June	Manitoba All-Stars (Winnipeg)	Friendly
8 June	Celtic (Toronto)	Friendly
9 June	Celtic (Montreal)	Friendly

17 September
Hibernian

15 October
Heart of Midlothian

22 December
Leeds United - postponed

16 February
Bournemouth & Boscombe Athletic

23 February
Burnley - postponed

22 May
Essex County All Stars

25 May
Ontario All-Stars

29 May
Alberta All-Stars

1 & 3 June
Celtic & British Columbia All Stars

5 June
Manitoba All-Stars

8 June
Celtic

9 June
Celtic

1957-58

HOME

Date	Opponent	Competition
17 August	Whites v Blues	Public Trial
24 August	Chelsea	Football League
4 September	Portsmouth	Football League
7 September	Burnley	Football League
18 September	Birmingham City	Football League
21 September	Sheffield Wednesday	Football League
5 October	Nottingham Forest	Football League
12 October	Arsenal	Football League
26 October	Leeds United	Football League
9 November	Everton	Football League
11 November	Vfb Stuttgart	Friendly
23 November	Luton Town	Football League
7 December	Leicester City	Football League
26 December	Wolverhampton Wanderers	Football League
28 December	Newcastle United	Football League
4 January	Leicester City	FA Cup
18 January	Preston North End	Football League
25 January	Sheffield United	FA Cup
8 February	Manchester City	Football League
1 March	Partick Thistle	Friendly
12 March	Bolton Wanderers	Football League
15 March	Sunderland	Football League
29 March	Aston Villa	Football League
4 April	West Bromwich Albion	Football League
12 April	Manchester United	Football League
14 April	Hibernian	Friendly
24 April	Canto Do Rio	Friendly
26 April	Blackpool	Football League

☐ Handbook ☐ Season Ticket

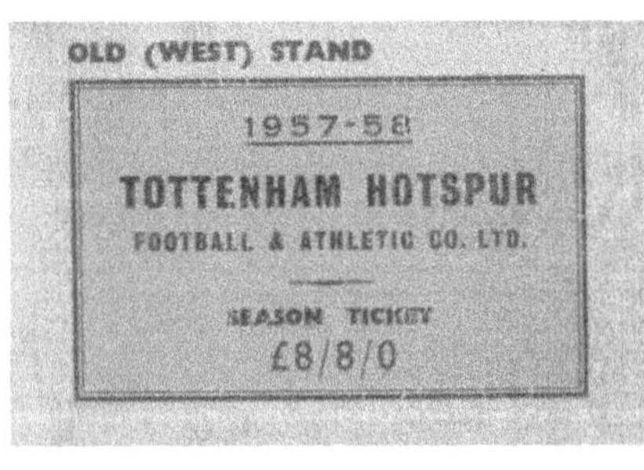

Season Ticket

Handbook

17 August
Public Trial

18 September
Birmingham City

5 October
Nottingham Forest

11 November
Vfb Stuttgart

26 December
Wolverhampton Wanderers

25 January
Sheffield United

1 March
Partick Thistle

14 April
Hibernian

24 April
Canto Do Rio

26 April
Blackpool

1957-58

AWAY

		Date	Opponent	Competition
		3 August	Vfb Stuttgart – Sportblatt issue	Friendly
			- Sportprogramm issue	
		28 August	Portsmouth	Football League
		31 August	Newcastle United	Football League
		11 September	Birmingham City	Football League
		14 September	Preston North End	Football League
		28 September	Manchester City	Football League
		2 October	Wolverhampton Wanderers	Football League
		14 October	Hibernian	Friendly
		19 October	Bolton Wanderers	Football League
		23 October	Swiss National XI (Basel)	Friendly
		2 November	Sunderland	Football League
		6 November	Bristol City	Friendly
		16 November	Aston Villa	Football League
		30 November	Manchester United	Football League
		14 December	Blackpool	Football League
		21 December	Chelsea	Football League
		11 January	Burnley	Football League
		1 February	Sheffield Wednesday	Football League
		15 February	Nottingham Forest	Football League
		22 February	Arsenal	Football League
		8 March	Leeds United	Football League
		22 March	Luton Town	Football League
		27 March	Rotterdam Select XI	Sophia's Childrens' Hospital Charity
			- Stadion Nieuws issue	
		5 April	Everton	Football League
		7 April	West Bromwich Albion	Football League
		19 April	Leicester City	Football League

3 August
Vfb Stuttgart – Sportblatt issue

3 August
Vfb Stuttgart – Sportprogramm issue

31 August
Newcastle United

2 October
Wolverhampton Wanderers

19 October
Bolton Wanderers

23 October
Swiss National XI

6 November
Bristol City

30 November
Manchester United

1 February
Sheffield Wednesday

15 February
Nottingham Forest

27 March
Rotterdam Select XI

27 March
Rotterdam Select XI – stadium issue

1958-59

HOME

Date	Opponent	Competition
16 August	Whites v Blues	Public Trial
23 August	Blackpool	Football League
3 September	Chelsea	Football League
6 September	Newcastle United	Football League
17 September	Nottingham Forest	Football League
27 September	Wolverhampton Wanderers	Football League
11 October	Everton	Football League
14 October	Bela Vista	Friendly
25 October	Leeds United	Football League
8 November	Bolton Wanderers	Football League
10 November	Hibernian	Friendly
22 November	Birmingham City	Football League
6 December	Preston North End	Football League
8 December	Bucharest Select XI	Friendly
26 December	West Ham United	Football League
3 January	Blackburn Rovers	Football League
10 January	West Ham United	FA Cup
24 January	Newport County	FA Cup
31 January	Arsenal	Football League
7 February	Manchester United	Football League
14 February	Norwich City	FA Cup
21 February	Portsmouth	Football League
7 March	Leicester City	Football League
21 March	Manchester City	Football League
27 March	Aston Villa	Football League
4 April	Luton Town	Football League
8 April	Burnley	Football League
18 April	West Bromwich Albion	Football League

☐ Handbook ☐ Season Ticket

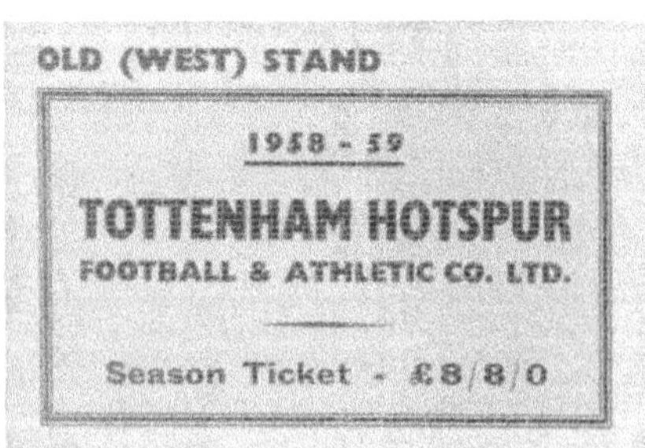

Season Ticket

Handbook

16 August
Public Trial

COPYRIGHT ALL RIGHTS RESERVED

TOTTENHAM HOTSPUR

FOOTBALL AND ATHLETIC COMPANY LIMITED

Official Programme

AND RECORD OF THE CLUB

PRICE TWOPENCE

WEDNESDAY, 3rd SEPTEMBER, 1958

RETURN MATCH WITH CHELSEA

IN THE INTERESTS OF GROUND CONDITIONS PLAYERS ON EITHER SIDE WILL NOT SIGN AUTOGRAPHS ON THE FIELD

3 September
Chelsea

COPYRIGHT ALL RIGHTS RESERVED

TOTTENHAM HOTSPUR

FOOTBALL AND ATHLETIC COMPANY LIMITED

Official Programme

AND RECORD OF THE CLUB

PRICE TWOPENCE

SATURDAY, 27th SEPTEMBER, 1958

WELCOME TO THE WOLVES

IN THE INTERESTS OF GROUND CONDITIONS, PLAYERS ON EITHER SIDE WILL NOT SIGN AUTOGRAPHS ON THE FIELD

27 September
Wolverhampton Wanderers

COPYRIGHT ALL RIGHTS RESERVED

TOTTENHAM HOTSPUR

FOOTBALL AND ATHLETIC COMPANY LIMITED

Official Programme

AND RECORD OF THE CLUB

PRICE TWOPENCE

SATURDAY, 11th OCTOBER, 1958

WELCOME TO EVERTON

IN THE INTERESTS OF GROUND CONDITIONS, PLAYERS ON EITHER SIDE WILL NOT SIGN AUTOGRAPHS ON THE FIELD

11 October
Everton

COPYRIGHT ALL RIGHTS RESERVED

TOTTENHAM HOTSPUR

FOOTBALL AND ATHLETIC COMPANY LIMITED

Official Programme

AND RECORD OF THE CLUB

PRICE TWOPENCE

TUESDAY, 14th OCTOBER, 1958

BELA VISTA F.C. (BRAZIL)

14 October
Bela Vista

COPYRIGHT ALL RIGHTS RESERVED

TOTTENHAM HOTSPUR

FOOTBALL AND ATHLETIC COMPANY LIMITED

Official Programme

AND RECORD OF THE CLUB

PRICE TWOPENCE

MONDAY, 10th NOVEMBER, 1958

VISIT OF OUR SCOTTISH FRIENDS

IN THE INTERESTS OF GROUND CONDITIONS, PLAYERS ON EITHER SIDE WILL NOT SIGN AUTOGRAPHS ON THE FIELD

10 November
Hibernian

COPYRIGHT ALL RIGHTS RESERVED

TOTTENHAM HOTSPUR

FOOTBALL AND ATHLETIC COMPANY LIMITED

Official Programme

AND RECORD OF THE CLUB

PRICE TWOPENCE

MONDAY, 8th DECEMBER, 1958

WELCOME TO OUR RUMANIAN FRIENDS

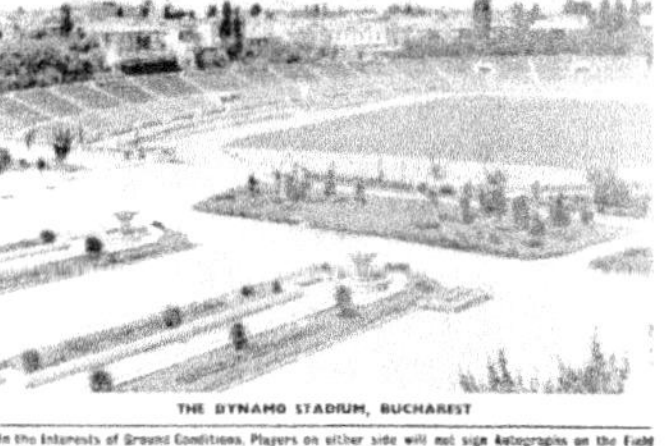
THE DYNAMO STADIUM, BUCHAREST

In the Interests of Ground Conditions, Players on either side will not sign Autographs on the Field

8 December
Bucharest Select XI

COPYRIGHT ALL RIGHTS RESERVED

TOTTENHAM HOTSPUR

FOOTBALL AND ATHLETIC COMPANY LIMITED

Official Programme

AND RECORD OF THE CLUB

PRICE TWOPENCE

SATURDAY, 24th JANUARY, 1959

CUP-TIE WITH NEWPORT COUNTY

IN THE INTERESTS OF GROUND CONDITIONS, PLAYERS ON EITHER SIDE WILL NOT SIGN AUTOGRAPHS ON THE FIELD

24 January
Newport County

COPYRIGHT ALL RIGHTS RESERVED

TOTTENHAM HOTSPUR

FOOTBALL AND ATHLETIC COMPANY LIMITED

Official Programme

AND RECORD OF THE CLUB

PRICE TWOPENCE

SATURDAY, 14th FEBRUARY, 1959

NORWICH CITY HERE FOR CUP-TIE

IN THE INTERESTS OF GROUND CONDITIONS, PLAYERS ON EITHER SIDE WILL NOT SIGN AUTOGRAPHS ON THE FIELD

16 February
Norwich City

COPYRIGHT ALL RIGHTS RESERVED

TOTTENHAM HOTSPUR

FOOTBALL AND ATHLETIC COMPANY LIMITED

Official Programme

AND RECORD OF THE CLUB

PRICE TWOPENCE

SATURDAY, 18th APRIL, 1959

VISIT OF WEST BROMWICH ALBION

IN THE INTERESTS OF GROUND CONDITIONS, PLAYERS ON EITHER SIDE WILL NOT SIGN AUTOGRAPHS ON THE FIELD

18 April
West Bromwich Albion

1958-59

AWAY

		27 August	Chelsea	Football League
		30 August	Blackburn Rovers	Football League
		10 September	Nottingham Forest	Football League
		13 September	Arsenal	Football League
		20 September	Manchester United	Football League
		4 October	Portsmouth	Football League
		18 October	Leicester City	Football League
		1 November	Manchester City	Football League
		15 November	Luton Town	Football League
		29 November	West Bromwich Albion	Football League
		13 December	Burnley	Football League
		20 December	Blackpool	Football League
		25 December	West Ham United	Football League
		17 January	Newcastle United	Football League
		18 February	Norwich City	FA Cup
		28 February	Everton	Football League
		2 March	Wolverhampton Wanderers	Football League
		14 March	Leeds United	Football League
		28 March	Bolton Wanderers	Football League
		30 March	Aston Villa	Football League
		11 April	Birmingham City	Football League
		25 April	Preston North End	Football League
		27 May	Torpedo Moscow	Friendly
		1 June	Dynamo Kiev	Friendly
		4 June	CCCP Select XI (Leningrad)	Friendly

27 August
Chelsea

30 August
Blackburn Rovers

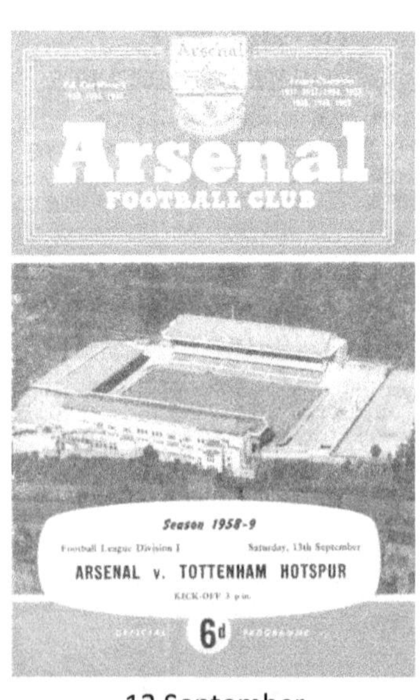

13 September
Arsenal

20 September
Manchester United

1 November
Manchester City

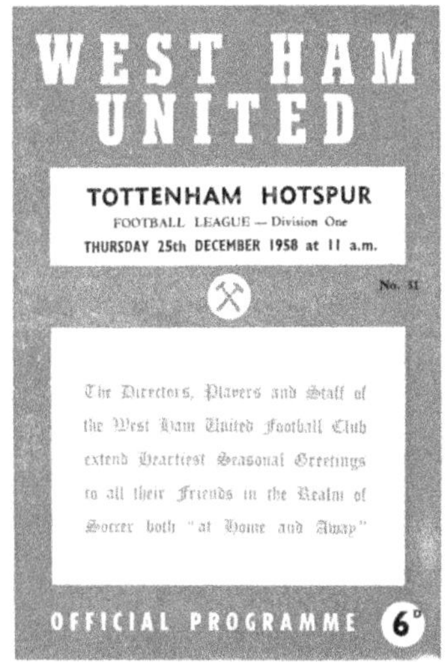

25 December
West Ham United

17 January
Newcastle United

18 February
Norwich City

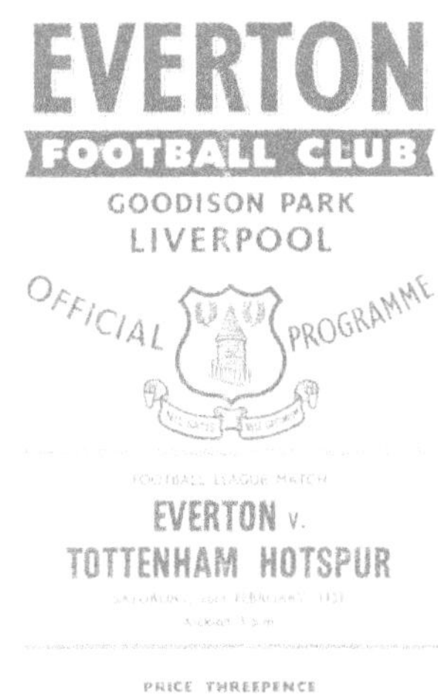

28 February
Everton

27 May
Torpedo Moscow

1 June
Dynamo Kiev

4 June
CCCP Select XI

1959-60

HOME

Date	Opponent	Competition
15 August	Whites v Blues	Public Trial
26 August	West Bromwich Albion	Football League
29 August	Birmingham City	Football League
9 September	West Ham United	Football League
19 September	Preston North End	Football League
3 October	Burnley	Football League
10 October	Wolverhampton Wanderers	Football League
24 October	Nottingham Forest	Football League
7 November	Bolton Wanderers	Football League
16 November	Torpedo Moscow	Friendly
21 November	Everton	Football League
5 December	Blackburn Rovers	Football League
19 December	Newcastle United	Football League
28 December	Leeds United	Football League
16 January	Arsenal	Football League
23 January	Manchester United	Football League
3 February	Crewe Alexandra	FA Cup
13 February	Leicester City	Football League
20 February	Blackburn Rovers	FA Cup
5 March	Sheffield Wednesday	Football League
19 March	Fulham	Football League
2 April	Luton Town	Football League
16 April	Manchester City	Football League
18 April	Chelsea	Football League
30 April	Blackpool	Football League

☐ Handbook ☐ Season Ticket

Season Ticket

Handbook

15 August
Public Trial

TOTTENHAM HOTSPUR

FOOTBALL AND ATHLETIC COMPANY LIMITED

Official Programme

AND RECORD OF THE CLUB

WELCOME TO WEST BROMWICH ALBION

In the Interests of Ground Conditions, Players on either side will not sign Autographs on the Field

PRICE TWOPENCE

26 August
West Bromwich Albion

TOTTENHAM HOTSPUR

FOOTBALL AND ATHLETIC COMPANY LIMITED

Official Programme

AND RECORD OF THE CLUB

WELCOME TO "PROUD PRESTON"

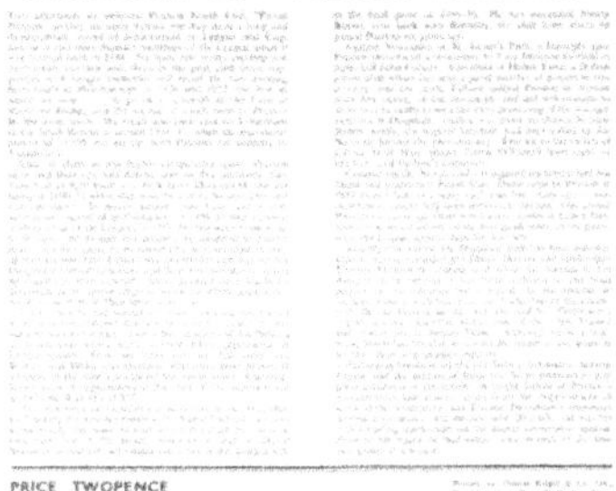

PRICE TWOPENCE

19 September
Preston North End

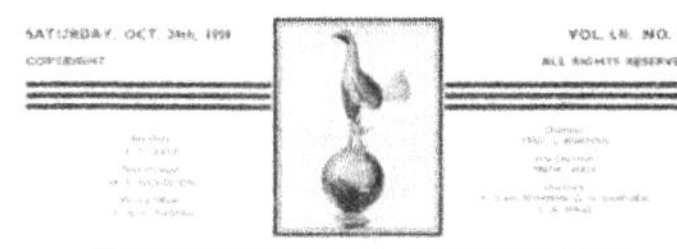

TOTTENHAM HOTSPUR

FOOTBALL AND ATHLETIC COMPANY LIMITED

Official Programme

AND RECORD OF THE CLUB

A HAPPY ANNIVERSARY

VISIT OF NOTTINGHAM FOREST

PRICE TWOPENCE

24 October
Nottingham Forest

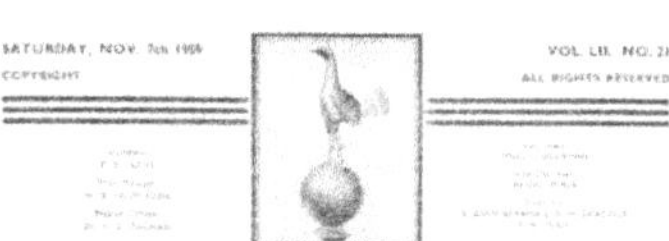

TOTTENHAM HOTSPUR

FOOTBALL AND ATHLETIC COMPANY LIMITED

Official Programme

AND RECORD OF THE CLUB

OUR VISITORS FROM BOLTON

PRICE TWOPENCE

7 November
Bolton Wanderers

TOTTENHAM HOTSPUR

FOOTBALL AND ATHLETIC COMPANY LIMITED

Official Programme

AND RECORD OF THE CLUB

WELCOME TO THE TORPEDO CLUB (MOSCOW)

PRICE TWOPENCE

16 November
Torpedo Moscow

TOTTENHAM HOTSPUR

FOOTBALL AND ATHLETIC COMPANY LIMITED

Official Programme

AND RECORD OF THE CLUB

WELCOME TO LEEDS UNITED

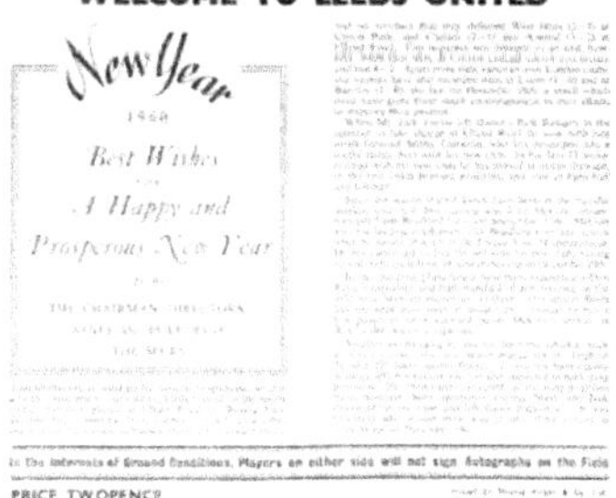

In the Interests of Ground Conditions, Players on either side will not sign Autographs on the Field

PRICE TWOPENCE

28 December
Leeds United

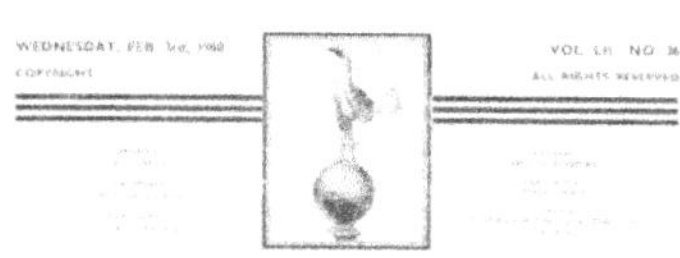

TOTTENHAM HOTSPUR

FOOTBALL AND ATHLETIC COMPANY LIMITED

Official Programme

AND RECORD OF THE CLUB

CUP REPLAY WITH CREWE ALEXANDRA

In the Interests of Ground Conditions, Players on either side will not sign Autographs on the Field

PRICE TWOPENCE

3 February
Crewe Alexandra

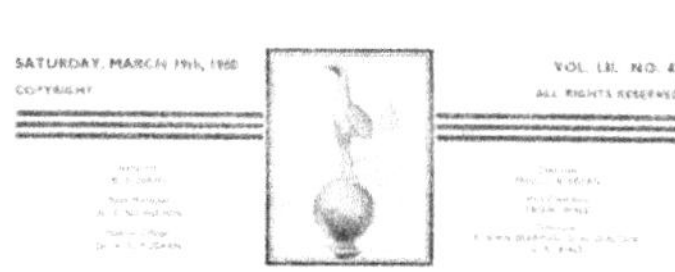

TOTTENHAM HOTSPUR

FOOTBALL AND ATHLETIC COMPANY LIMITED

Official Programme

AND RECORD OF THE CLUB

"LOCAL DERBY" WITH FULHAM

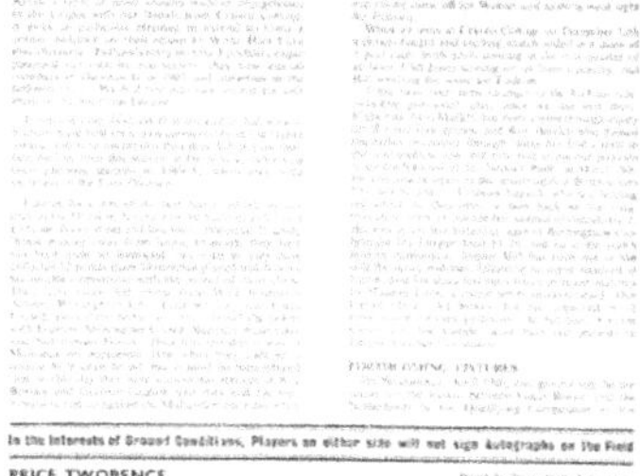

In the Interests of Ground Conditions, Players on either side will not sign Autographs on the Field

PRICE TWOPENCE

19 March
Fulham

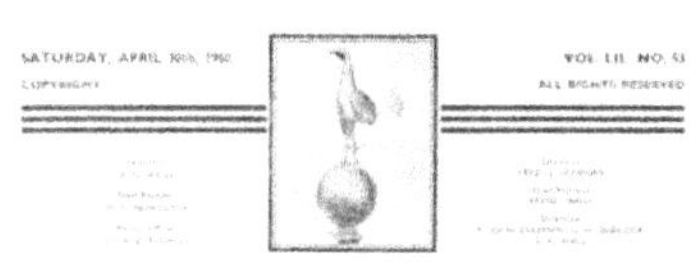

TOTTENHAM HOTSPUR

FOOTBALL AND ATHLETIC COMPANY LIMITED

Official Programme

AND RECORD OF THE CLUB

THE CLOSE OF AN EXCITING SEASON

PRICE TWOPENCE

30 April
Blackpool

1959-60

AWAY

	Date	Opponent	Competition
☐☐	22 August	Newcastle United	Football League
☐☐	2 September	West Bromwich Albion	Football League
☐☐	5 September	Arsenal	Football League
☐☐	12 September	Manchester United	Football League
☐☐	14 September	West Ham United	Football League
☐☐	26 September	Leicester City	Football League
☐☐	17 October	Sheffield Wednesday	Football League
☐☐	21 October	Reading	Campbell, Meeson & Reeves Testimonial
☐☐	31 October	Manchester City	Football League
☐☐	14 November	Luton Town	Football League
☐☐	28 November	Blackpool	Football League
☐☐	12 December	Fulham	Football League
☐☐	26 December	Leeds United	Football League
☐☐	2 January	Birmingham City	Football League
☐☐	9 January	Newport County	FA Cup
☐☐	30 January	Crewe Alexandra	FA Cup
☐☐	6 February	Preston North End	Football League
☐☐	27 February	Blackburn Rovers	Football League
☐☐	1 March	Burnley	Football League
☐☐	12 March	Nottingham Forest	Football League
☐☐	26 March	Bolton Wanderers	Football League
☐☐	9 April	Everton	Football League
☐☐	15 April	Chelsea	Football League
☐☐	23 April	Wolverhampton Wanderers	Football League
☐☐	2 May	Crystal Palace	Friendly
☐☐	25 May	Juventus	Friendly

22 August
Newcastle United

2 September
West Bromwich Albion

17 October
Sheffield Wednesday

21 October
Reading

31 October
Manchester City

14 November
Luton Town

12 December
Fulham

9 January
Newport County

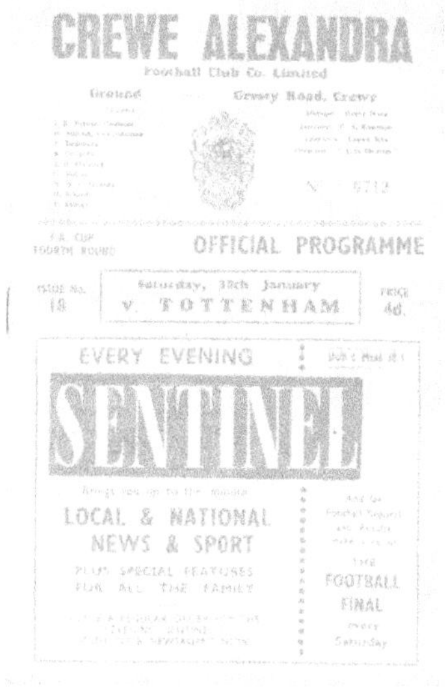

30 January
Crewe Alexandra

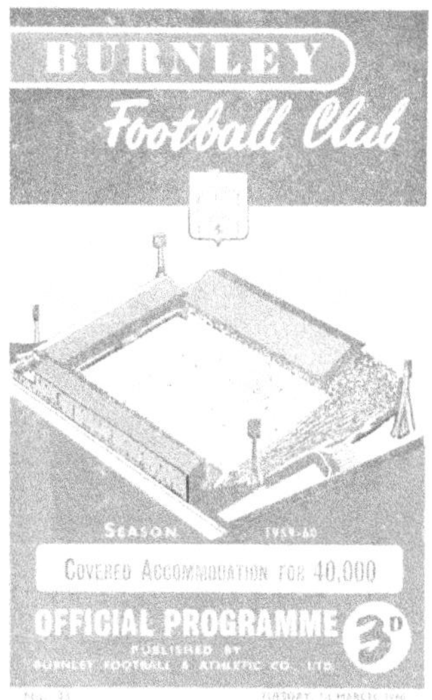

1 March
Burnley

12 March
Nottingham Forest

2 May
Crystal Palace

1960-61

HOME

Date	Opponent	Competition
13 August	Whites v Blues	Public Trial
20 August	Everton	Football League
31 August	Blackpool	Football League
3 September	Manchester United	Football League
14 September	Bolton Wanderers	Football League
24 September	Aston Villa	Football League
10 October	Manchester City	Football League
24 October	The Army	Friendly
2 November	Cardiff City	Football League
5 November	Fulham	Football League
14 November	Dinamo Tbilisi	Friendly
19 November	Birmingham City	Football League
3 December	Burnley	Football League
24 December	West Ham United	Football League
31 December	Blackburn Rovers	Football League
7 January	Charlton Athletic	FA Cup
21 January	Arsenal	Football League
28 January	Crewe Alexandra	FA Cup
4 February	Leicester City	Football League
22 February	Wolverhampton Wanderers	Football League
8 March	Sunderland	FA Cup
22 March	Newcastle United	Football League
31 March	Chelsea	Football League
1 April	Preston North End	Football League
17 April	Sheffield Wednesday	Football League
26 April	Nottingham Forest	Football League
29 April	West Bromwich Albion	Football League

☐ Handbook ☐ Season Ticket

Season Ticket

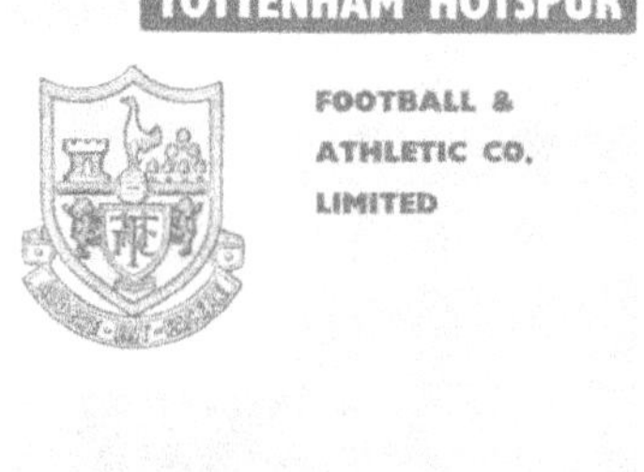

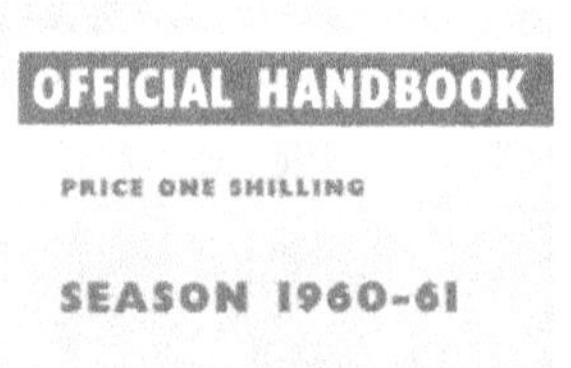

Handbook

13 August
Public Trial

SATURDAY, AUG. 20th, 1960 | VOL. LIII. No. 2

COPYRIGHT | ALL RIGHTS RESERVED

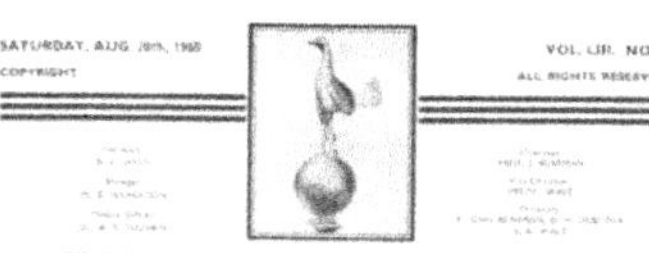

TOTTENHAM HOTSPUR

FOOTBALL AND ATHLETIC COMPANY LIMITED

Official Programme

AND RECORD OF THE CLUB

EVERTON OPEN THE SEASON

In the Interests of Ground Conditions, Players on either side will not sign Autographs on the Field

PRICE TWOPENCE

20 August
Everton

MONDAY, 24th OCT., 1960 | VOL. LIII. No. 16

COPYRIGHT | ALL RIGHTS RESERVED

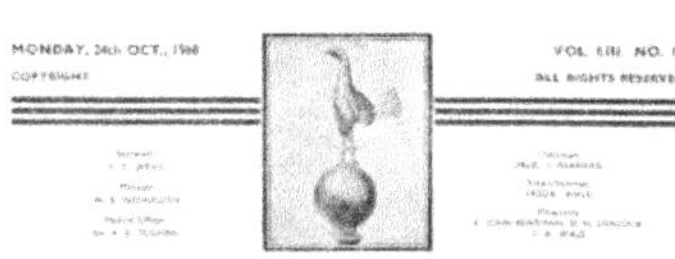

TOTTENHAM HOTSPUR

FOOTBALL AND ATHLETIC COMPANY LIMITED

Official Programme

AND RECORD OF THE CLUB

TOTTENHAM HOTSPUR v. THE ARMY

Floodlit Friendly | October 24th, 1960 | Kick-off 7.30 p.m.

TOTTENHAM HOTSPUR
White Shirts, Blue Shorts

BROWN

BAKER | HENRY

DODGE | NORMAN | MARCHI (Capt.)

JONES or AITCHISON | COLLINS | SAUL | ALLEN | DYSON

Referee: Major W. R. ECCLES, R.A.O.C.

Linesmen: C.S.M. L. PENTNEY, R.A.O.C. | Sgt. R. A. PEARSON, R.A.

Pte. J. SYDENHAM | Pte. G. STRONG | L/Cpl. J. BYRNE

Pte. C. CROWE | Pte. A. YOUNG

Pte. J. SMITH | Pte. R. YEATS | Pte. M. SCOTT

Pte. D. FERGUSON | L/Cpl. B. HILL

Sgt. J. OGSTON

THE ARMY
Red Shirts, White Shorts

ANY ALTERATION WILL BE NOTED ON THE BOARD

PRICE TWOPENCE

24 October
The Army

MONDAY, NOV. 14th, 1960 | VOL. LIII. No. 21

COPYRIGHT | ALL RIGHTS RESERVED

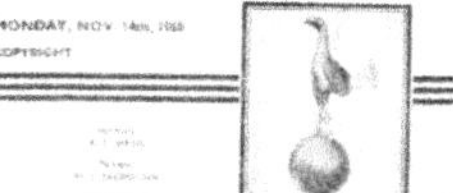

TOTTENHAM HOTSPUR

FOOTBALL AND ATHLETIC COMPANY LIMITED

Official Programme

AND RECORD OF THE CLUB

WELCOME TO TBILISI DYNAMO

In the Interests of Ground Conditions, Players on either side will not sign Autographs on the Field

PRICE TWOPENCE

14 November
Dinamo Tbilisi

SATURDAY, DEC. 24th, 1960 | VOL. LIII. No. 27

COPYRIGHT | ALL RIGHTS RESERVED

TOTTENHAM HOTSPUR

FOOTBALL AND ATHLETIC COMPANY LIMITED

Official Programme

AND RECORD OF THE CLUB

The Directors, Players and Staff wish all Supporters a Happy Christmas and a Prosperous New Year

PRICE TWOPENCE

24 December
West Ham United

SATURDAY, JAN. 21st, 1961 | VOL. LIII. No. 31

COPYRIGHT | ALL RIGHTS RESERVED

TOTTENHAM HOTSPUR

FOOTBALL AND ATHLETIC COMPANY LIMITED

Official Programme

AND RECORD OF THE CLUB

RETURN WITH THE "GUNNERS"

In the Interests of Ground Conditions, Players on either side will not sign Autographs on the Field

PRICE TWOPENCE

21 January
Arsenal

WEDNESDAY, MAR. 8th, 1961 | VOL. LIII. No. 38

COPYRIGHT | ALL RIGHTS RESERVED

TOTTENHAM HOTSPUR

FOOTBALL AND ATHLETIC COMPANY LIMITED

Official Programme

AND RECORD OF THE CLUB

CUP REPLAY WITH SUNDERLAND

In the Interests of Ground Conditions, Players on either side will not sign Autographs on the Field

PRICE TWOPENCE

8 March
Sunderland

MONDAY, APRIL 17th, 1961 | VOL. LIII.

COPYRIGHT | ALL RIGHTS RESERVED

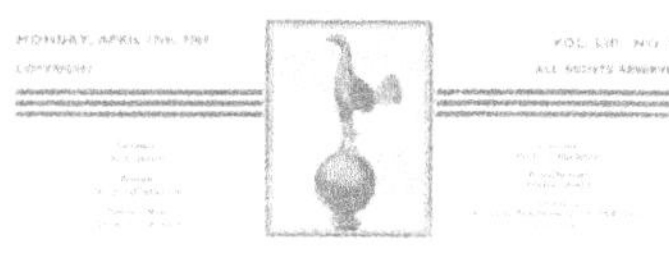

TOTTENHAM HOTSPUR

FOOTBALL AND ATHLETIC COMPANY LIMITED

Official Programme

AND RECORD OF THE CLUB

VISIT OF SHEFFIELD WEDNESDAY

In the Interests of Ground Conditions, Players on either side will not sign Autographs on the Field

PRICE TWOPENCE

17 April
Sheffield Wednesday

WEDNESDAY, APRIL 26th, 1961 | VOL. LIII.

COPYRIGHT | ALL RIGHTS RESERVED

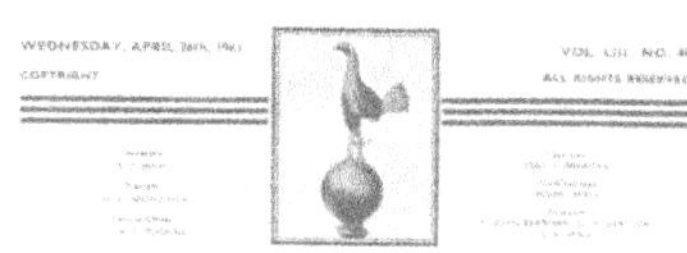

TOTTENHAM HOTSPUR

FOOTBALL AND ATHLETIC COMPANY LIMITED

Official Programme

AND RECORD OF THE CLUB

AN EVENTFUL SEASON

In the Interests of Ground Conditions, Players on either side will not sign Autographs on the Field

PRICE TWOPENCE

26 April
Nottingham Forest

TOTTENHAM HOTSPUR
FOOTBALL AND ATHLETIC
COMPANY LIMITED

SATURDAY, APRIL 29th, 1961 | PRICE TWOPENCE

A Message from the Chairman

Souvenir Programme

29 April
West Bromwich Albion

1960-61

AWAY

Date	Opponent	Competition
22 August	Blackpool	Football League
27 August	Blackburn Rovers	Football League
7 September	Bolton Wanderers	Football League
10 September	Arsenal	Football League
17 September	Leicester City	Football League
1 October	Wolverhampton Wanderers	Football League
15 October	Nottingham Forest	Football League
29 October	Newcastle United	Football League
12 November	Sheffield Wednesday	Football League
26 November	West Bromwich Albion	Football League
10 December	Preston North End	Football League
17 December	Everton	Football League
26 December	West Ham United	Football League
16 January	Manchester United (dated 14 January)	Football League
11 February	Aston Villa	Football League
18 February	Aston Villa	FA Cup
25 February	Manchester City	Football League
4 March	Sunderland	FA Cup
11 March	Cardiff City	Football League
18 March	Burnley (Villa Park)	FA Cup
25 March	Fulham	Football League
3 April	Chelsea	Football League
8 April	Birmingham City	Football League
22 April	Burnley	Football League
6 May	Leicester City (Wembley)	FA Cup
15 May	Feijenoord	Friendly
17 May	Amsterdam Select XI	Friendly
	- Stadion Nieuws issue	

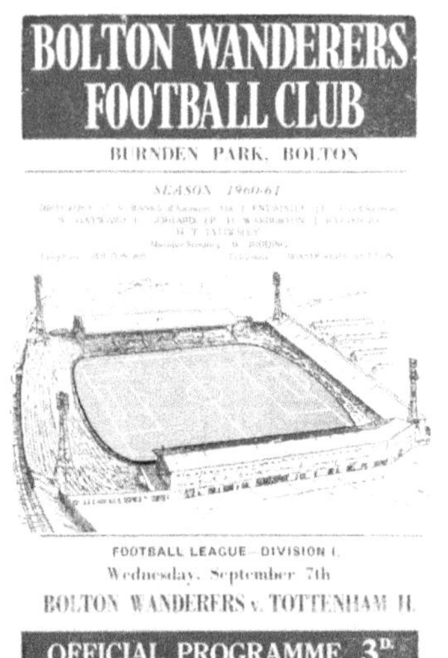

7 September
Bolton Wanderers

15 October
Nottingham Forest

29 October
Newcastle United

12 November
Sheffield Wednesday

10 December
Preston North End

18 February
Aston Villa

4 March
Sunderland

11 March
Cardiff City

22 April
Burnley

15 May
Feijenoord

17 May
Amsterdam Select XI

17 May
Amsterdam Select XI – stadium issue

1961-62

HOME

Date	Opponent	Competition
12 August	FA XI	FA Charity Shield
23 August	West Ham United	Football League
26 August	Arsenal	Football League
2 September	Cardiff City	Football League
16 September	Wolverhampton Wanderers	Football League
20 September	Gornik Zabrze	European Cup
30 September	Aston Villa	Football League
14 October	Manchester City	Football League
28 October	Burnley	Football League
11 November	Fulham	Football League
15 November	Feijenoord	European Cup
25 November	Leicester City	Football League
9 December	Birmingham City	Football League
16 December	Blackpool	Football League
30 December	Chelsea	Football League
10 January	Birmingham City	FA Cup
20 January	Manchester United	Football League
10 February	Nottingham Forest	Football League
24 February	Bolton Wanderers	Football League
26 February	Dukla Prague	European Cup
10 March	Aston Villa	FA Cup
14 March	Ipswich Town	Football League
24 March	Everton	Football League
5 April	Benfica	European Cup
7 April	Sheffield Wednesday	Football League
9 April	Sheffield United	Football League
20 April	Blackburn Rovers	Football League
21 April	West Bromwich Albion	Football League

☐ Handbook ☐ Season Ticket

Season Ticket

Handbook

12 August
Public Trial

2 September
Cardiff City

16 December
Blackpool

30 December
Chelsea

20 January
Manchester United

10 February
Nottingham Forest

10 March
Aston Villa

7 April
Sheffield Wednesday

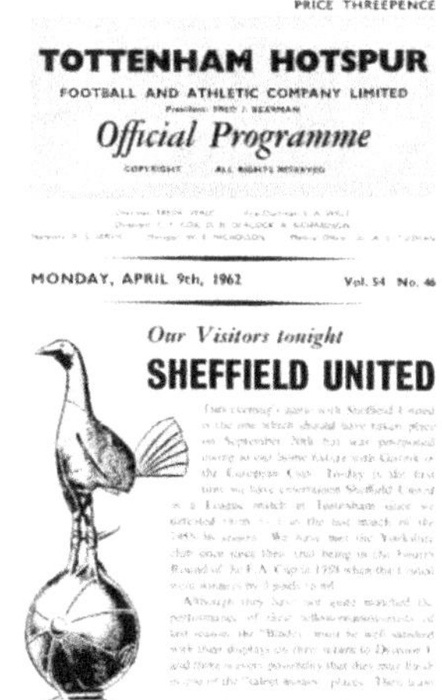

9 April
Sheffield United

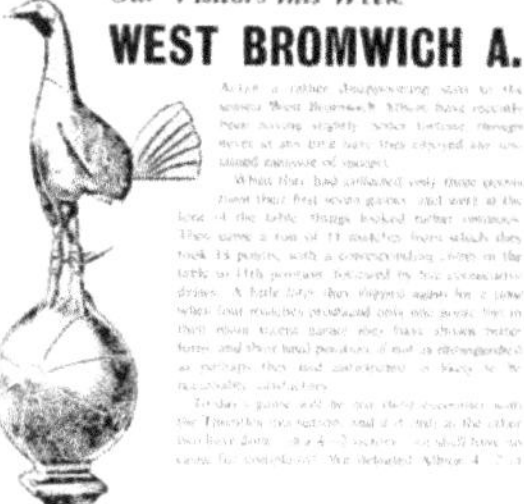

21 April
West Bromwich Albion

1961-62

AWAY

	Date	Opponent	Competition
☐☐	19 August	Blackpool	Football League
☐☐	28 August	West Ham United	Football League
☐☐	4 September	Sheffield United	Football League
☐☐	9 September	Manchester United	Football League
☐☐	13 September	Gornik Zabrze	European Champions Cup
☐☐	23 September	Nottingham Forest	Football League
☐☐	9 October	Bolton Wanderers	Football League
☐☐	21 October	Ipswich Town	Football League
☐☐	1 November	Feijenoord	European Champions Cup
☐☐	4 November	Everton	Football League
☐☐	18 November	Sheffield Wednesday	Football League
☐☐	2 December	West Bromwich Albion	Football League
☐☐	23 December	Arsenal	Football League
☐☐	26 December	Chelsea	Football League
☐☐	6 January	Birmingham City	FA Cup
☐☐	13 January	Cardiff City (dated 13 December 1962)	Football League
☐☐	27 January	Plymouth Argyle	FA Cup
☐☐	3 February	Wolverhampton Wanderers	Football League
☐☐	14 February	Dukla Prague	European Champions Cup
☐☐	17 February	West Bromwich Albion	FA Cup
☐☐	21 February	Aston Villa	Football League
☐☐	3 March	Manchester City	Football League
☐☐	17 March	Burnley	Football League
☐☐	21 March	Benfica - O Benfica newspaper	European Champions Cup
☐☐	31 March	Manchester United (Hillsborough)	FA Cup
☐☐	17 April	Fulham	Football League
☐☐	23 April	Blackburn Rovers	Football League
☐☐	28 April	Birmingham City	Football League
☐☐	30 April	Leicester City	Football League
☐☐	5 May	Burnley (Wembley)	FA Cup
☐☐	26 May	Tel Aviv Select XI	Friendly
☐☐	30 May	Haifa Select XI	Friendly

28 August
West Ham United

4 September
Sheffield United

9 September
Manchester United

9 October
Bolton Wanderers

21 October
Ipswich Town

4 November
Everton

18 November
Sheffield Wednesday

23 December
Arsenal

26 December
Chelsea

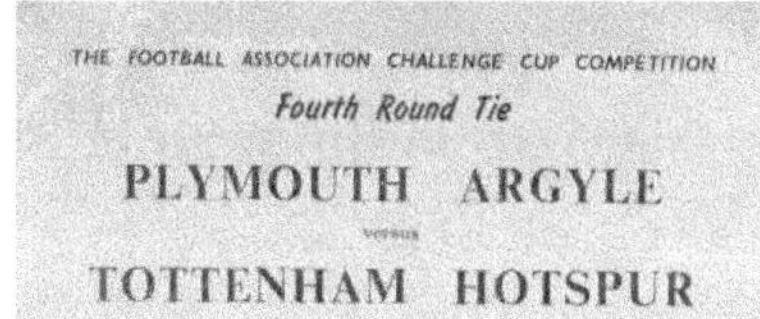

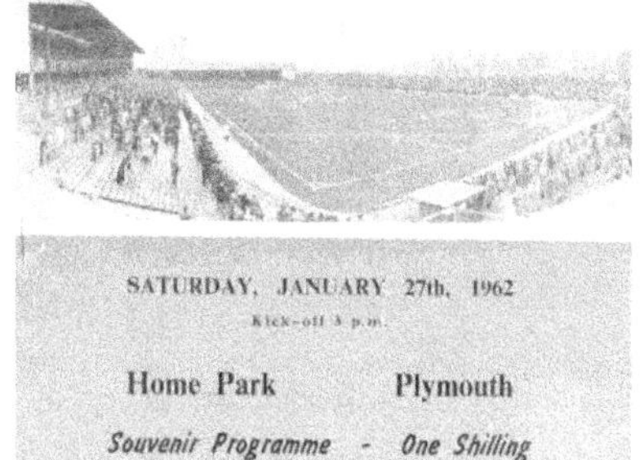

27 January
Plymouth Argyle

23 April
Blackburn Rovers

30 April
Leicester City

1962-63

HOME

Date	Opponent	Competition
18 August	Birmingham City	Football League
29 August	Aston Villa	Football League
1 September	Manchester City	Football League
12 September	Wolverhampton Wanderers	Football League
15 September	Blackburn Rovers	Football League
29 September	Nottingham Forest	Football League
6 October	Arsenal	Football League
24 October	Manchester United	Football League
31 October	Rangers	European Cup-Winners' Cup
3 November	Leicester City	Football League
17 November	Sheffield Wednesday	Football League
1 December	Everton	Football League
22 December	West Ham United	Football League
26 December	Ipswich Town	Football League
16 January	Burnley	FA Cup
19 January	Blackpool	Football League
26 January	Arsenal - teamsheet	Friendly
9 February	Sheffield United - postponed	Football League
2 March	West Bromwich Albion	Football League
14 March	Slovan Bratislava	European Cup-Winners' Cup
27 March	Leyton Orient	Football League
30 March	Burnley	Football League
13 April	Fulham	Football League
15 April	Liverpool	Football League
27 April	Bolton Wanderers	Football League
1 May	OFK Belgrade	European Cup-Winners' Cup
4 May	Sheffield United	Football League

☐ Handbook ☐ Season Ticket

Season Ticket

Handbook

18 August
Birmingham City

29 August
Aston Villa

29 September
Nottingham Forest

24 October
Manchester United

17 November
Sheffield Wednesday

26 December
Ipswich Town

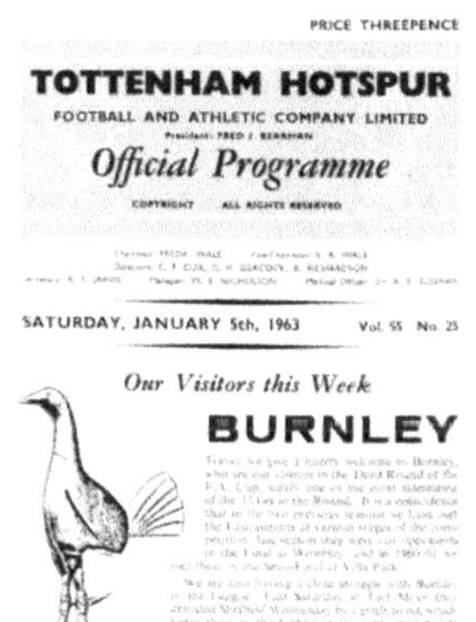

5 January
Burnley

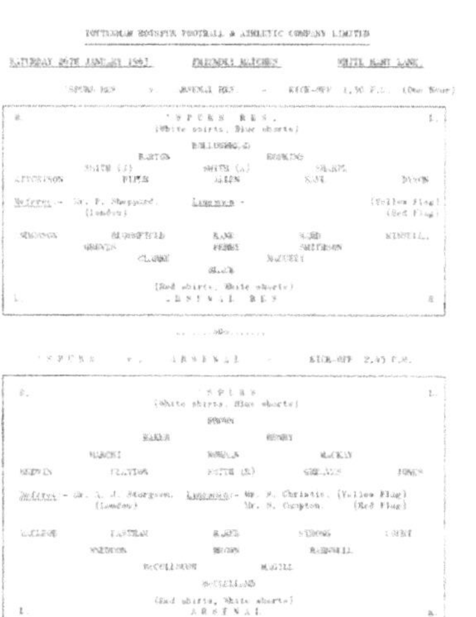

26 January
Arsenal

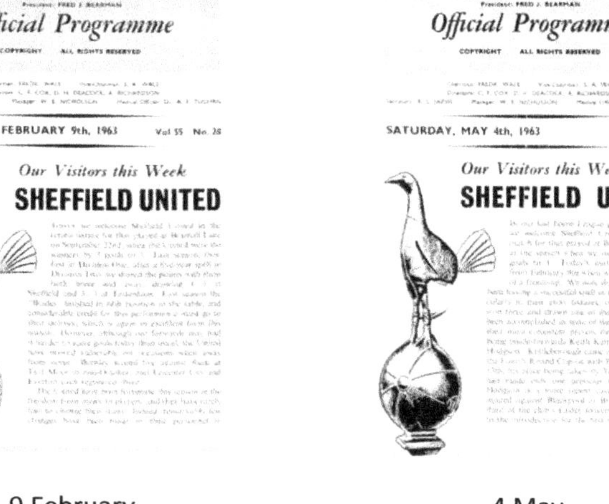

9 February
Sheffield United – postponed

4 May
Sheffield United

1962-63

AWAY

Date	Opponent	Competition
11 August	Ipswich Town	FA Charity Shield
20 August	Aston Villa	Football League
25 August	West Ham United	Football League
8 September	Blackpool	Football League
19 September	Wolverhampton Wanderers	Football League
22 September	Sheffield United	Football League
13 October	West Bromwich Albion	Football League
27 October	Leyton Orient	Football League
10 November	Fulham	Football League
14 November	Zamalek Combined XI	Friendly
24 November	Burnley	Football League
8 December	Bolton Wanderers	Football League
11 December	Rangers (dated 5 December)	European Cup-Winners' Cup
15 December	Birmingham City	Football League
29 December	Ipswich Town – postponed	Football League
2 February	Portsmouth	Friendly
16 February	Nottingham Forest - postponed	Football League
23 February	Arsenal	Football League
5 March	Slovan Bratislava	European Cup-Winners' Cup
9 March	Manchester United	Football League
16 March	Ipswich Town	Football League
23 March	Leicester City	Football League
8 April	Sheffield Wednesday	Football League
12 April	Liverpool	Football League
20 April	Everton	Football League
24 April	OFK Belgrade	European Cup-Winners' Cup
11 May	Manchester City	Football League
15 May	Atletico Madrid (Rotterdam) - 20 page issue	European Cup-Winners' Cup
	- 28 page issue	
	- Stadion Nieuws issue	
18 May	Nottingham Forest	Football League
20 May	Blackburn Rovers	Football League
31 May	NSAFL Invitation XI (Cape Town)	Friendly
8 June	NFL Select XI (Durban)	Friendly
12 June	South African XI (Johannesburg)	Friendly

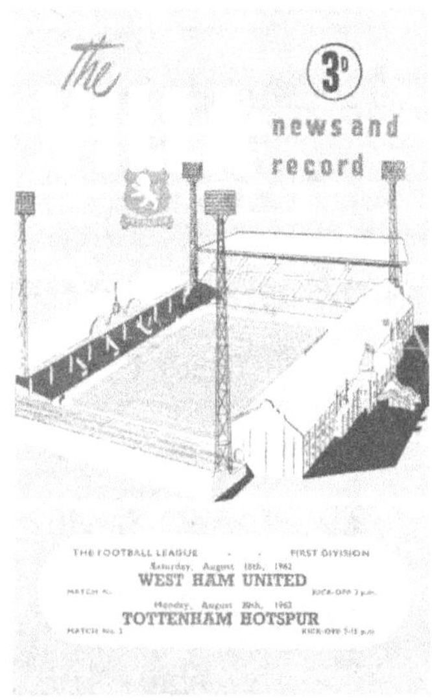

20 August
Aston Villa

8 September
Blackpool

13 October
West Bromwich Albion

27 October
Leyton Orient

10 November
Fulham

14 November
Zamalek Combined XI

29 December
Ipswich Town - postponed

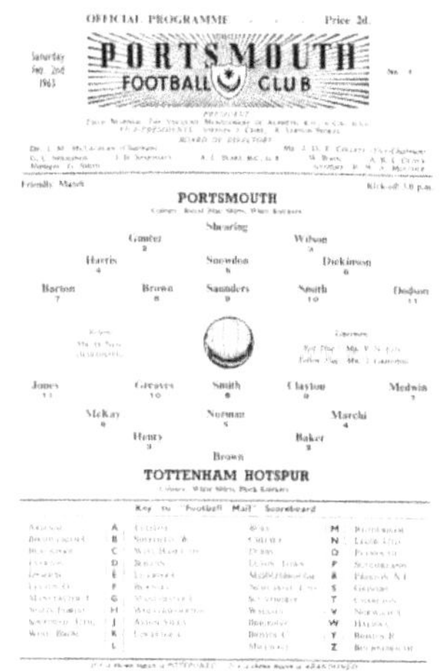

2 February
Portsmouth

16 February
Nottingham Forest - postponed

23 March
Leicester City

12 April
Liverpool

31 May
NSAFL Invitation XI

1963-64

HOME

		Date	Opponent	Competition
		17 August	Whites v Blues	Public Trial
		31 August	Nottingham Forest	Football League
		4 September	Wolverhampton Wanderers	Football League
		14 September	Blackpool	Football League
		28 September	West Ham United	Football League
		2 October	Birmingham City	Football League
		19 October	Leicester City	Football League
		2 November	Fulham	Football League
		16 November	Burnley	Football League
		27 November	Manchester United - postponed	European Cup-Winners' Cup
		30 November	Sheffield Wednesday	Football League
		3 December	Manchester United	European Cup-Winners' Cup
		14 December	Stoke City	Football League
		28 December	West Bromwich Albion	Football League
		4 January	Chelsea	FA Cup
		11 January	Blackburn Rovers	Football League
		25 January	Aston Villa	Football League
		1 February	Chelsea	Football League
		15 February	Sheffield United	Football League
		22 February	Arsenal	Football League
		7 March	Everton	Football League
		21 March	Manchester United	Football League
		27 March	Liverpool	Football League
		4 April	Ipswich Town	Football League
		18 April	Bolton Wanderers	Football League

☐ Handbook ☐ Season Ticket

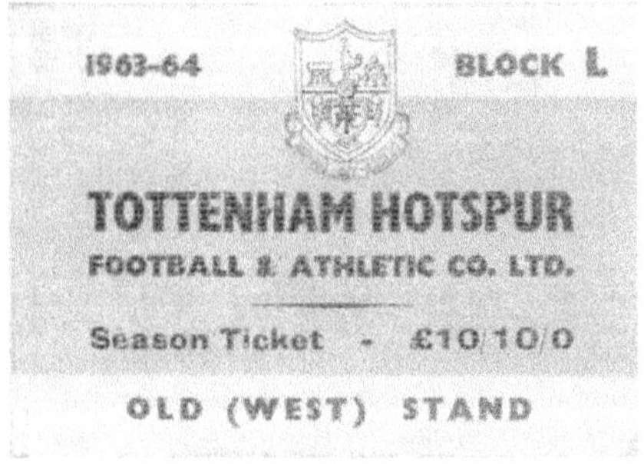

Season Ticket

Handbook

17 August
Public Trial

PRICE THREEPENCE

TOTTENHAM HOTSPUR

FOOTBALL AND ATHLETIC COMPANY LIMITED

Official Programme

SATURDAY, SEPTEMBER 14th, 1963 Vol. 56 No. 6

RECORDS

Our Visitors this week

BLACKPOOL

14 September
Blackpool

PRICE THREEPENCE

TOTTENHAM HOTSPUR

FOOTBALL AND ATHLETIC COMPANY LIMITED

Official Programme

SATURDAY, OCTOBER 19th, 1963 Vol. 56 No. 13

RECORDS

Our Visitors this week

LEICESTER CITY

19 October
Leicester City

PRICE THREEPENCE

TOTTENHAM HOTSPUR

FOOTBALL AND ATHLETIC COMPANY LIMITED

Official Programme

SATURDAY, NOVEMBER 16th, 1963 Vol. 56 No. 19

RECORDS

Our Visitors this week

BURNLEY

16 November
Burnley

PRICE THREEPENCE

TOTTENHAM HOTSPUR

FOOTBALL AND ATHLETIC COMPANY LIMITED

Official Programme

SATURDAY, DECEMBER 14th, 1963 Vol. 56 No. 25

RECORDS

Christmas Greetings to all our Supporters

FROM THE DIRECTORS PLAYERS AND STAFF OF TOTTENHAM HOTSPUR FOOTBALL CLUB

14 December
Stoke City

PRICE THREEPENCE

TOTTENHAM HOTSPUR

FOOTBALL AND ATHLETIC COMPANY LIMITED

Official Programme

SATURDAY, JANUARY 11th, 1964 Vol. 56 No. 29

RECORDS

Our Visitors this week

BLACKBURN ROVERS

11 January
Blackburn Rovers

PRICE THREEPENCE

TOTTENHAM HOTSPUR

FOOTBALL AND ATHLETIC COMPANY LIMITED

Official Programme

SATURDAY, JANUARY 25th, 1964 Vol. 56 No. 31

RECORDS

Our Visitors this week

ASTON VILLA

25 January
Aston Villa

PRICE THREEPENCE

TOTTENHAM HOTSPUR

FOOTBALL AND ATHLETIC COMPANY LIMITED

Official Programme

SATURDAY, FEBRUARY 22nd, 1964 Vol. 56 No. 35

RECORDS

Our Visitors this week

ARSENAL

22 February
Arsenal

PRICE THREEPENCE

TOTTENHAM HOTSPUR

FOOTBALL AND ATHLETIC COMPANY LIMITED

Official Programme

FRIDAY, MARCH 27th, 1964 Vol. 56 No. 42

RECORDS

Our Visitors this week

LIVERPOOL

27 March
Liverpool

PRICE THREEPENCE

TOTTENHAM HOTSPUR

FOOTBALL AND ATHLETIC COMPANY LIMITED

Official Programme

SATURDAY, APRIL 18th, 1964 Vol. 56 No. 46

RECORDS

Our Visitors this week

BOLTON WANDERERS

18 April
Bolton Wanderers

1963-64

AWAY

		24 August	Stoke City	Football League
		28 August	Wolverhampton Wanderers	Football League
		7 September	Blackburn Rovers	Football League
		16 September	Aston Villa	Football League
		21 September	Chelsea	Football League
		5 October	Sheffield United	Football League
		15 October	Arsenal	Football League
		26 October	Everton	Football League
		9 November	Manchester United	Football League
		23 November	Ipswich Town	Football League
		7 December	Bolton Wanderers	Football League
		10 December	Manchester United	European Cup-Winners' Cup
		21 December	Nottingham Forest	Football League
		26 December	West Bromwich Albion	Football League
		8 January	Chelsea	FA Cup
		18 January	Blackpool	Football League
		8 February	West Ham United	Football League
		29 February	Birmingham City	Football League
		14 March	Burnley - postponed	Football League
		28 March	Fulham	Football League
		30 March	Liverpool	Football League
		13 April	Sheffield Wednesday	Football League
		21 April	Burnley	Football League
		25 April	Leicester City	Football League
		28 April	Coventry City	Friendly

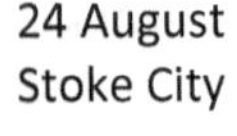

24 August
Stoke City

5 October
Sheffield United

15 October
Arsenal

9 November
Manchester United

23 November
Ipswich Town

8 January
Chelsea

18 January
Blackpool

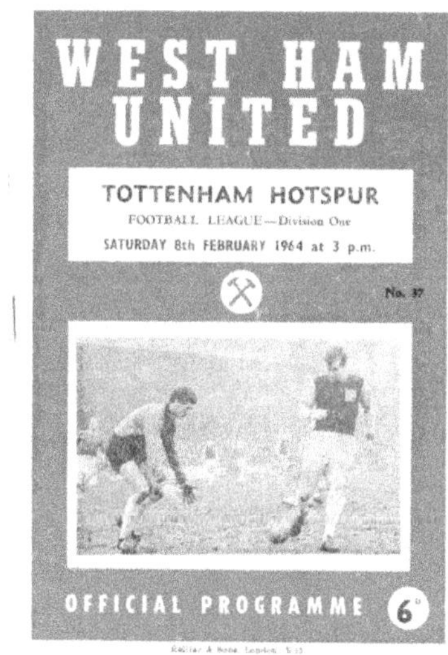

8 February
West Ham United

14 March
Burnley - postponed

28 March
Fulham

13 April
Sheffield Wednesday

OFFICIAL PROGRAMME

28 April
Coventry City

1964-65

HOME

Date	Opponent	Competition
14 August	Whites v Blues	Public Trial
22 August	Sheffield United	Football League
2 September	Burnley	Football League
5 September	Birmingham City	Football League
16 September	Stoke City	Football League
19 September	West Bromwich Albion	Football League
5 October	Fulham	Football League
10 October	Arsenal	Football League
24 October	Chelsea	Football League
7 November	Sunderland	Football League
11 November	Scotland XI (dated 10 November)	John White Memorial
21 November	Aston Villa	Football League
5 December	Sheffield Wednesday	Football League
19 December	Everton	Football League
28 December	Nottingham Forest	Football League
16 January	West Ham United	Football League
18 January	Torquay United	FA Cup
30 January	Ipswich Town	FA Cup
6 February	Manchester United	Football League
27 February	Leeds United	Football League
13 March	Blackpool	Football League
27 March	Wolverhampton Wanderers	Football League
9 April	Liverpool	Football League
16 April	Blackburn Rovers	Football League
24 April	Leicester City	Football League

☐ Handbook ☐ Season Ticket

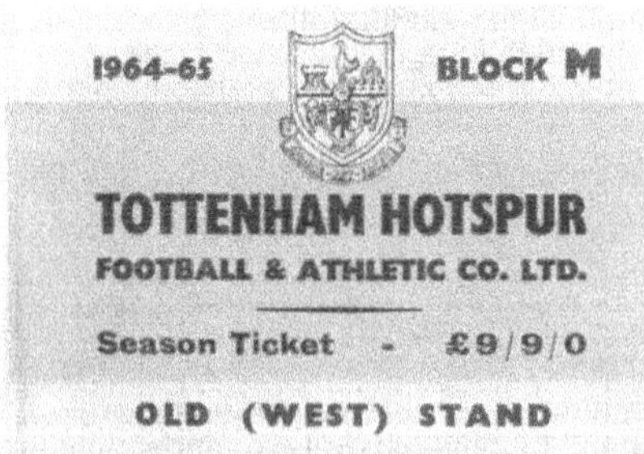

Season Ticket

Handbook

14 August
Public Trial

TOTTENHAM HOTSPUR
FOOTBALL AND ATHLETIC COMPANY LIMITED
PRICE THREEPENCE

Vol. 57 No. 4
Official Programme
WEDNESDAY, 2nd SEPT., 1964
OUR VISITORS TONIGHT
BURNLEY

2 September
Burnley

Vol. 57 No. 8
Official Programme
SATURDAY, 19th SEPT., 1964
OUR VISITORS TODAY
WEST BROMWICH

19 September
West Bromwich Albion

TOTTENHAM HOTSPUR
FOOTBALL AND ATHLETIC COMPANY LIMITED
PRICE THREEPENCE

Vol. 57 No. 12
Official Programme
SATURDAY, OCT., 10th, 1964
OUR VISITORS TODAY
ARSENAL

10 October
Arsenal

TOTTENHAM HOTSPUR
FOOTBALL AND ATHLETIC COMPANY LIMITED
PRICE SIXPENCE

JOHN WHITE MEMORIAL MATCH
Tuesday, November 10th, 1964

SPURS v. SCOTLAND XI
Souvenir Programme

11 November
Scotland XI

Vol. 57 No. 24
Official Programme
MONDAY, DEC. 28th, 1964
OUR VISITORS TODAY
NOTTINGHAM FOREST

28 December
Nottingham Forest

TOTTENHAM HOTSPUR
FOOTBALL AND ATHLETIC COMPANY LIMITED
PRICE THREEPENCE

Vol. 57 No. 26
Official Programme
WEDNESDAY, JAN. 13th, 1965
OUR VISITORS TONIGHT
TORQUAY UNITED

13 January
Torquay United

TOTTENHAM HOTSPUR
FOOTBALL AND ATHLETIC COMPANY LIMITED
PRICE THREEPENCE

Vol. 57 No. 29
Official Programme
SATURDAY, JAN. 30th, 1965
OUR VISITORS TODAY
IPSWICH TOWN

SIR WINSTON CHURCHILL

This afternoon on sports grounds and football grounds throughout the country, tribute will be paid to the memory of Sir Winston Churchill. Prior to the start of today's match there will be a one minute's silence, and we ask all supporters to join us in this tribute to a great man whose recent death has saddened us all.

30 January
Ipswich Town

TOTTENHAM HOTSPUR
FOOTBALL AND ATHLETIC COMPANY LIMITED
PRICE THREEPENCE

Vol. 57 No. 33
Official Programme
SATURDAY, FEB. 27th, 1965
OUR VISITORS TODAY
LEEDS UNITED

27 February
Leeds United

TOTTENHAM HOTSPUR
FOOTBALL AND ATHLETIC COMPANY LIMITED
PRICE THREEPENCE

Vol. 57 No. 46
Official Programme
SATURDAY, APRIL 24th, 1965
OUR VISITORS TODAY
LEICESTER CITY

24 April
Leicester City

1964-65

AWAY

		5 August	Glasgow XI (Hampden Park)	Glasgow Charity Cup
		8 August	Feijenoord	Friendly
		25 August	Burnley	Football League
		29 August	Everton	Football League
		9 September	Stoke City	Football League
		12 September	West Ham United	Football League
		23 September	Stævnet (Copenhagen Select XI)	Friendly
		26 September	Manchester United	Football League
		28 September	Blackpool	Football League
		17 October	Leeds United	Football League
		31 October	Leicester City	Football League
		14 November	Wolverhampton Wanderers	Football League
		28 November	Liverpool	Football League
		8 December	Leytonstone	Friendly
		12 December	Sheffield United	Football League
		26 December	Nottingham Forest	Football League
		2 January	Birmingham City	Football League
		9 January	Torquay United	FA Cup
		23 January	West Bromwich Albion	Football League
		13 February	Fulham	Football League
		20 February	Chelsea	FA Cup
		23 February	Arsenal	Football League
		10 March	Chelsea	Football League
		20 March	Sunderland	Football League
		3 April	Aston Villa	Football League
		17 April	Sheffield Wednesday	Football League
		19 April	Blackburn Rovers	Football League
		27 April	Anderlecht	Friendly
		29 April	Coventry City	Friendly
		18 May	DWS	Friendly
		22 May	Telstar	Friendly
		21 June	Hakoah	Friendly
		24 June	Maccabi Tel Aviv	John White Cup

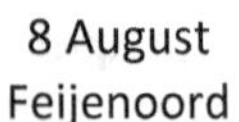

8 August
Feijenoord

9 September
Stoke City

WELCOME TO TOTTENHAM HOTSPUR

On behalf of THE COPENHAGEN FOOTBALL-COMBINATION it is a great pleasure to me to wish our outstanding guests a very hearty welcome.

It is 13 years since we had the pleasure to meet you here in our City as weel as in your city and many things has happen since that. It is a long time, too long from our point of view, but to-day we have the opportunity to renew the friendship from the field and off the field.

Danish friends of English Football, and there are quite a lot, have had the pleasure to follow Tottenham's great succes on the TV-screen during the past years, when you played in the different European-Cup competitions as well as in the English Cup. We all remember the glorius year in 1961 where you won the "impossible" Double as the first team in modern time.

I feel sure that the Danish spectators are looking forward to welcome one of the teams, which name has been on the headlines in the World's papers for a long time, and we all look forward to a good sporting game to-night.

Vilh. Skousen
Hon. Secretary.

Der bliver i pausen udtrukket 7 gevinster, et dejligt herre-armbåndsur og et smukt dame-armbåndsur, som er skænket af SCHWEIZER UR-IMPORT, samt 5 konservesæsker skænket af GLYNGØRE Fiskeindustri.

№ 1663 **Pris 50 øre**

23 September
Stævnet

17 October
Leeds United

EAT

RONALD SHORT

FATHER CHRISTMAS
still has some Toys left
Pop in quickly and don't be disappointed

"THE CAMPING SHOP"

LEYTONSTONE FOOTBALL CLUB Programme 3d.

NICHOLS & MOWBRAY
Printers and Stationers
539 HIGH ROAD
LEYTONSTONE, E.11

J. H. SANKEY & SON LTD.

YORKSHIRE GREY

8 December
Leytonstone

TORQUAY UNITED
TOTTENHAM HOTSPUR
SATURDAY 9th JANUARY, 1965
ONE SHILLING

9 January
Torquay United

13 February
Fulham

20 February
Chelsea

29 April
Coventry City

D.W.S.

Tottenham Hotspur

18 May
DWS

TELSTAR BODE

A. J. v. LENT's Automobielbedrijven

27 May
Telstar

טוטנהאם

TOTTENHAM • MACCABI T-A

מכבי תל־אביב

איצטדיון הפועל ע"ש בלומפילד
יום חמישי 24.6.65 שעה 16.30

24 June
Maccabi Tel Aviv

1965-66

HOME

		Date	Opponent	Competition
☐	☐	25 August	Leicester City	Football League
☐	☐	27 August	Blackpool	Football League
☐	☐	8 September	Leeds United	Football League
☐	☐	11 September	Arsenal	Football League
☐	☐	18 September	Liverpool	Football League
☐	☐	6 October	Sunderland	Football League
☐	☐	16 October	Manchester United	Football League
☐	☐	30 October	West Bromwich Albion	Football League
☐	☐	13 November	Sheffield Wednesday	Football League
☐	☐	18 November	Hungarian Select XI	Friendly
☐	☐	27 November	Stoke City	Football League
☐	☐	11 December	Chelsea	Football League
☐	☐	27 December	Sheffield United	Football League
☐	☐	1 January	Everton	Football League
☐	☐	15 January	Newcastle United	Football League
☐	☐	22 January	Middlesbrough	FA Cup
☐	☐	29 January	Blackburn Rovers	Football League
☐	☐	12 February	Burnley	FA Cup
☐	☐	19 February	Fulham	Football League
☐	☐	19 March	Aston Villa	Football League
☐	☐	2 April	Nottingham Forest	Football League
☐	☐	8 April	West Ham United	Football League
☐	☐	16 April	Northampton Town	Football League
☐	☐	30 April	Burnley	Football League

☐ Handbook

☐ Season Ticket

Season Ticket

Handbook

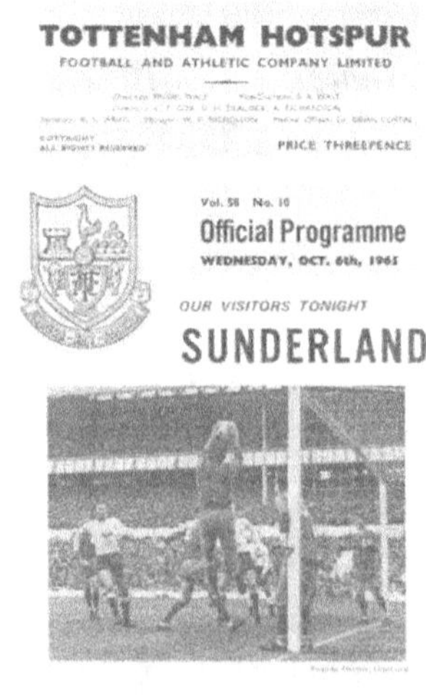

6 October
Sunderland

13 November
Sheffield Wednesday

18 November
Hungarian Select XI

27 December
Sheffield United

22 January
Middlesbrough

29 January
Blackburn Rovers

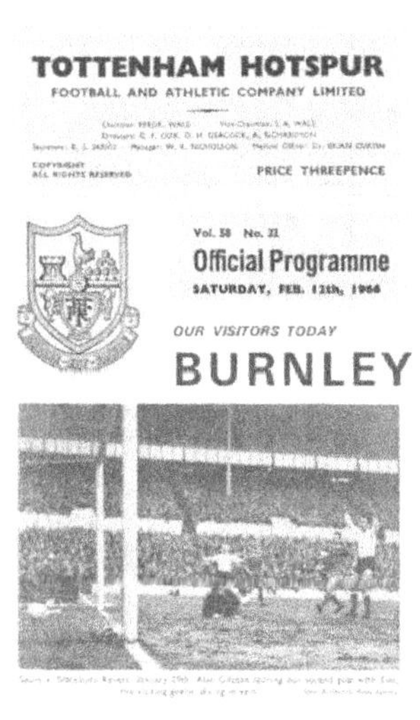

12 February
Burnley

19 February
Fulham

8 April
West Ham United

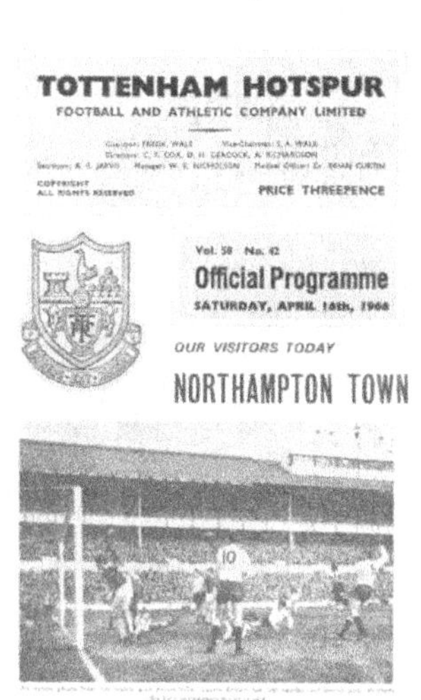

16 April
Northampton Town

1965-66

AWAY

Date	Opponent	Competition
{ 14 August	Valencia (Malaga)	Costa Del Sol Tournament
{ 15 August	Standard Liege (Malaga)	Costa Del Sol Tournament
1 September	Leicester City	Football League
4 September	Fulham	Football League
15 September	Leeds United	Football League
22 September	Walton & Hersham	Friendly
25 September	Aston Villa	Football League
9 October	Everton	Football League
23 October	Newcastle United	Football League
6 November	Nottingham Forest	Football League
20 November	Northampton Town	Football League
4 December	Burnley	Football League
18 December	Manchester United	Football League
28 December	Sheffield United	Football League
8 January	Chelsea	Football League
5 February	Blackpool	Football League
26 February	Arsenal - postponed	Football League
5 March	Preston North End	FA Cup
8 March	Arsenal	Football League
12 March	Liverpool	Football League
26 March	Sunderland	Football League
9 April	Sheffield Wednesday	Football League
23 April	Stoke City	Football League
25 April	West Ham United	Football League
3 May	WKS Legia	Friendly
7 May	West Bromwich Albion	Football League
9 May	Blackburn Rovers	Football League
15 May	Sarpsborg	Friendly
19 May	Bermuda Select XI (Hamilton)	Friendly
21 May	Celtic (Toronto)	Friendly
25 May	Hartford Select XI	Friendly
29 May	Bologna (Jersey City)	Friendly
1 June	Celtic (San Francisco)	Friendly
4 June	Celtic (Vancouver)	Friendly
8 June	British Columbia All-Stars (Vancouver)	Friendly
12 June	Mexican National XI (Mexico City)	Friendly
15 June	America Club of Mexico	Friendly
17 June	Bayern Munich (Detroit)	Friendly
19 June	Bayern Munich (Chicago)	Friendly

14 & 15 August
Costa Del Sol Tournament

22 September
Walton & Hersham

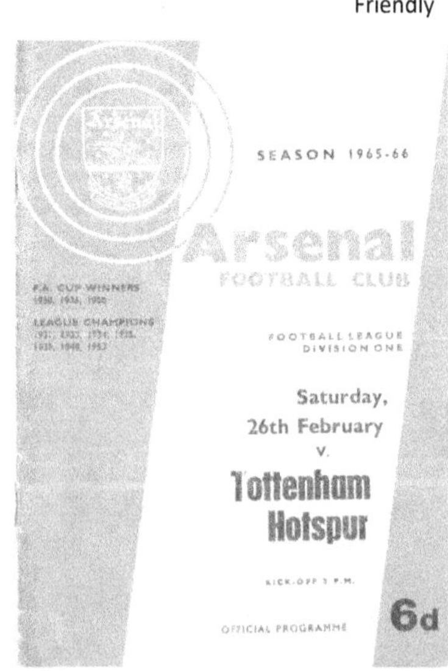

26 February
Arsenal - postponed

3 May
WKS Legia

15 May
Sarpsborg

Glasgow Celtic — Tottenham Hotspurs
SOCCER TOURS

SPONSORED BY
DEVONSHIRE RECREATION CLUB and ST. GEORGE'S CRICKET CLUB
May 11th — May 19th, 1966
PRICE 2/6

19 May
Celtic

21 May
Celtic

29 May
Bologna

INTERNATIONAL
SOCCER FOOTBALL

1 June
Celtic

8 June
British Columbia All-Stars

Official Program
TOTTENHAM HOTSPUR F.C. of England
VS.
F.C. BAYERN of Munich W. Germany

presented by INTERNATIONAL SPORTS CO.
U. of D. Stadium - Fri. June 17 8:15 pm.

17 June
Bayern Munich

INTERNATIONAL
SOCCER GAMES
25c
Sponsored by
Midwest Soccer Football Promotions

Friday, May 6	Sunday, June 19	Wed., June 22
Chicago All-Stars	Bayern Munchen	V.F.L. Schlangen-Paderborn
vs.	vs.	vs.
Hertha Berlin (ZEHLENDORF)	TOTTENHAM "Hotspurs"	Midwest S.F.P.A.

19 June
Bayern Munich

1966-67

HOME

		Date	Opponent	Competition
☐	☐	20 August	Leeds United	Football League
☐	☐	31 August	Stoke City	Football League
☐	☐	3 September	Arsenal	Football League
☐	☐	10 September	Manchester United	Football League
☐	☐	24 September	Nottingham Forest	Football League
☐	☐	15 October	Blackpool	Football League
☐	☐	29 October	Aston Villa	Football League
☐	☐	12 November	West Ham United	Football League
☐	☐	23 November	Polish Select XI	Friendly
☐	☐	26 November	Southampton	Football League
☐	☐	10 December	Leicester City	Football League
☐	☐	27 December	West Bromwich Albion	Football League
☐	☐	31 December	Newcastle United	Football League
☐	☐	21 January	Burnley	Football League
☐	☐	1 February	Millwall	FA Cup
☐	☐	11 February	Fulham	Football League
☐	☐	18 February	Portsmouth	FA Cup
☐	☐	25 February	Manchester City	Football League
☐	☐	11 March	Bristol City	FA Cup
☐	☐	18 March	Chelsea	Football League
☐	☐	27 March	Everton	Football League
☐	☐	1 April	Liverpool	Football League
☐	☐	12 April	Birmingham City	FA Cup
☐	☐	15 April	Sheffield Wednesday	Football League
☐	☐	3 May	Sunderland	Football League
☐	☐	13 May	Sheffield United	Football League

☐ Handbook ☐ Season Ticket

Season Ticket

Handbook

20 August
Leeds United

TOTTENHAM HOTSPUR
FOOTBALL AND ATHLETIC COMPANY LIMITED
PRICE THREEPENCE

Official Programme
WEDNESDAY, AUG. 31st, 1966
OUR VISITORS TONIGHT

STOKE CITY

31 August
Stoke City

TOTTENHAM HOTSPUR
FOOTBALL AND ATHLETIC COMPANY LIMITED
PRICE THREEPENCE

Official Programme
SATURDAY, NOV. 12th, 1966
WELCOME TO
WEST HAM UNITED

12 November
West Ham United

TOTTENHAM HOTSPUR
GROUND, HIGH ROAD,
Tottenham, N.17

Tottenham Hotspur
versus
Polish Select XI

WEDNESDAY
23rd NOVEMBER, 1966
Kick-off 7.30 p.m.

23 November
Polish Select XI

TOTTENHAM HOTSPUR
FOOTBALL AND ATHLETIC COMPANY LIMITED
PRICE THREEPENCE

Official Programme
SATURDAY, DEC. 10th, 1966
WELCOME TO
LEICESTER CITY

10 December
Leicester City

TOTTENHAM HOTSPUR
FOOTBALL AND ATHLETIC COMPANY LIMITED
PRICE THREEPENCE

Official Programme
TUESDAY, DEC. 27th, 1966
WELCOME TO
WEST BROMWICH

27 December
West Bromwich Albion

TOTTENHAM HOTSPUR
FOOTBALL AND ATHLETIC COMPANY LIMITED
PRICE THREEPENCE

Official Programme
SATURDAY, DEC. 31st, 1966
WELCOME TO
NEWCASTLE UTD.

31 December
Newcastle United

TOTTENHAM HOTSPUR
FOOTBALL AND ATHLETIC COMPANY LIMITED
PRICE THREEPENCE

Official Programme
SATURDAY, JAN. 21st, 1967
WELCOME TO
BURNLEY

21 January
Burnley

TOTTENHAM HOTSPUR
FOOTBALL AND ATHLETIC COMPANY LIMITED
PRICE THREEPENCE

Official Programme
SATURDAY, MAR. 11th, 1967
WELCOME TO
BRISTOL CITY

11 March
Bristol City

TOTTENHAM HOTSPUR
FOOTBALL AND ATHLETIC COMPANY LIMITED
PRICE THREEPENCE

Official Programme
SATURDAY, 13th MAY, 1967
WELCOME TO
SHEFFIELD UNITED

13 May
Sheffield United

1966-67

AWAY

Date	Opponent	Competition
{ 14 August	Malaga	Costa Del Sol Tournament
{ 15 August	Benfica (Malaga)	Costa Del Sol Tournament
24 August	Stoke City	Football League
27 August	Newcastle United	Football League
6 September	Sheffield United	Football League
14 September	West Ham United	Football League Cup
17 September	Burnley	Football League
1 October	Fulham	Football League
8 October	Manchester City	Football League
10 October	Dundee	Friendly
26 October	Chelsea	Football League
5 November	Blackpool	Football League
19 November	Sheffield Wednesday	Football League
3 December	Sunderland	Football League
17 December	Leeds United	Football League
26 December	West Bromwich Albion	Football League
7 January	Arsenal	Football League
14 January	Manchester United	Football League
28 January	Millwall	FA Cup
4 February	Nottingham Forest	Football League
4 March	Aston Villa	Football League
22 March	Everton	Football League
25 March	Leicester City	Football League
8 April	Birmingham City	FA Cup
22 April	Southampton	Football League
29 April	Nottingham Forest (Hillsborough)	FA Cup
6 May	Liverpool	Football League
9 May	West Ham United	Football League
20 May	Chelsea (Wembley)	FA Cup
30 May	FC Zurich	Friendly
1 June	BSC Young Boys	Friendly
7 June	Servette	Friendly

14 & 15 August
Costa Del Sol Tournament

27 August
Newcastle United

14 September
West Ham United

1 October
Fulham

10 October
Dundee

17 December
Leeds United

28 January
Millwall

4 March
Aston Villa

8 April
Birmingham City

22 April
Southampton

30 May
FC Zurich

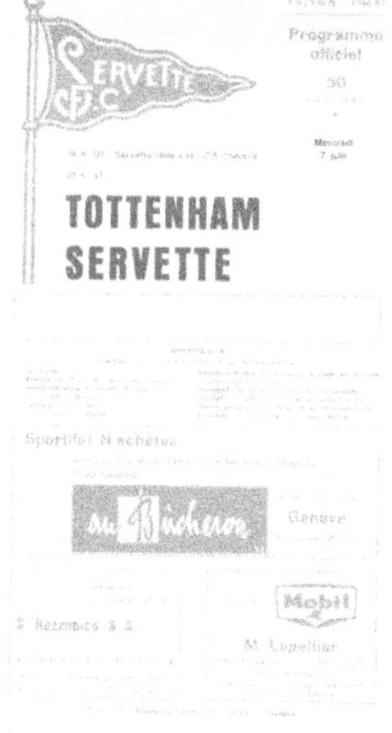

7 June
Servette

1967-68

HOME

	Date	Opponent	Competition
☐☐	23 August	Everton	Football League
☐☐	26 August	West Ham United	Football League
☐☐	6 September	Wolverhampton Wanderers	Football League
☐☐	9 September	Sheffield Wednesday	Football League
☐☐	27 September	Hajduk Split	European Cup-Winners' Cup
☐☐	30 September	Sunderland	Football League
☐☐	7 October	Sheffield United	Football League
☐☐	25 October	Nottingham Forest	Football League
☐☐	4 November	Liverpool	Football League
☐☐	18 November	Chelsea	Football League
☐☐	2 December	Newcastle United	Football League
☐☐	13 December	Olympique Lyonnais	European Cup-Winners' Cup
☐☐	16 December	Leicester City	Football League
☐☐	26 December	Fulham	Football League
☐☐	6 January	Burnley - postponed	Football League
☐☐	20 January	Arsenal	Football League
☐☐	31 January	Manchester United	FA Cup
☐☐	3 February	Manchester United	Football League
☐☐	17 February	Preston North End	FA Cup
☐☐	1 March	West Bromwich Albion	Football League
☐☐	9 March	Liverpool	FA Cup
☐☐	23 March	Stoke City	Football League
☐☐	30 March	Burnley	Football League
☐☐	6 April	Southampton	Football League
☐☐	12 April	Leeds United	Football League
☐☐	20 April	Coventry City	Football League
☐☐	4 May	Manchester City	Football League

☐ Handbook ☐ Season Ticket

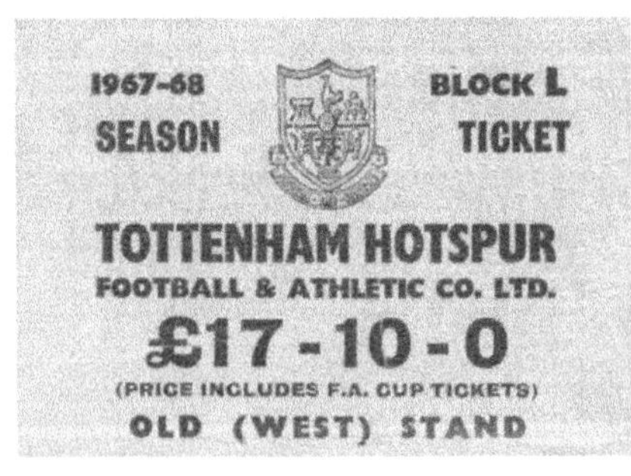

Season Ticket

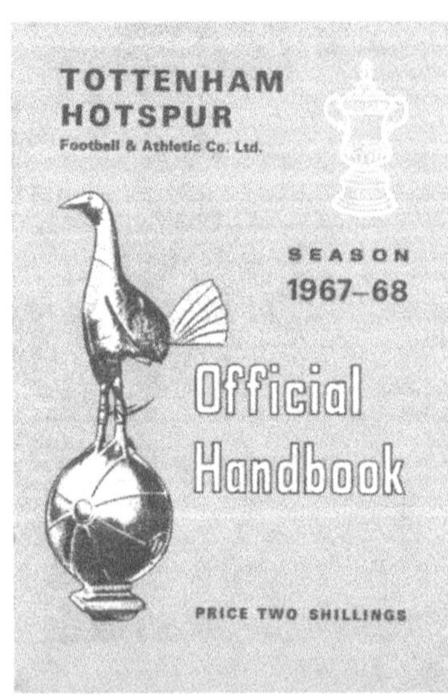

Handbook

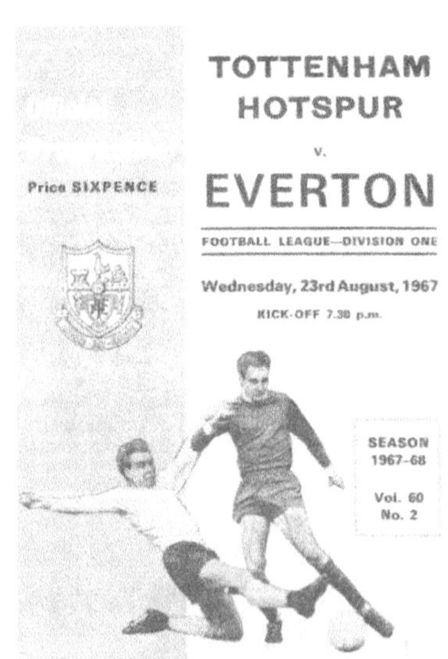

23 August
Everton

9 September
Sheffield Wednesday

30 September
Sunderland

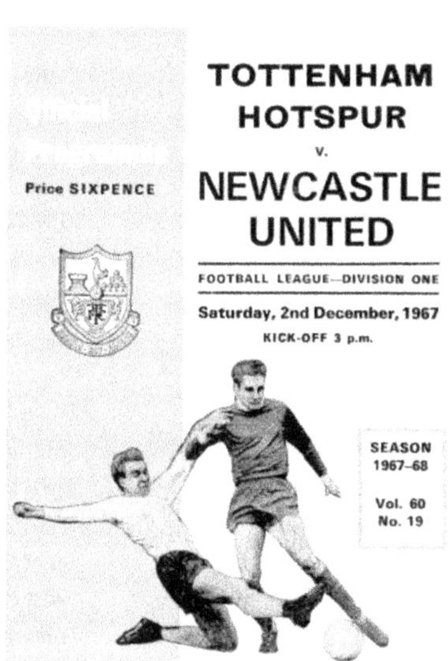

2 December
Newcastle United

26 December
Fulham

6 January
Burnley - postponed

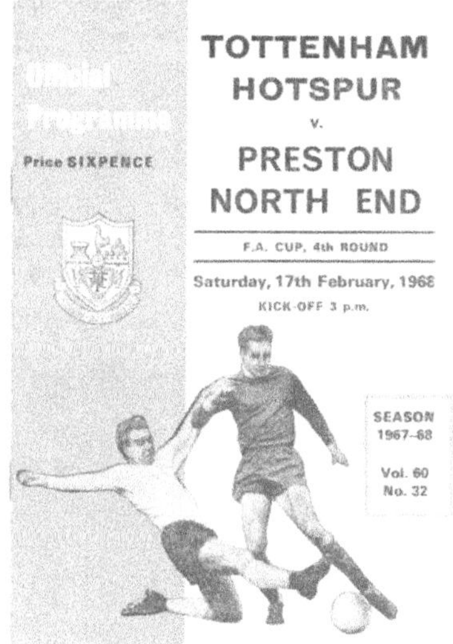

17 February
Preston North End

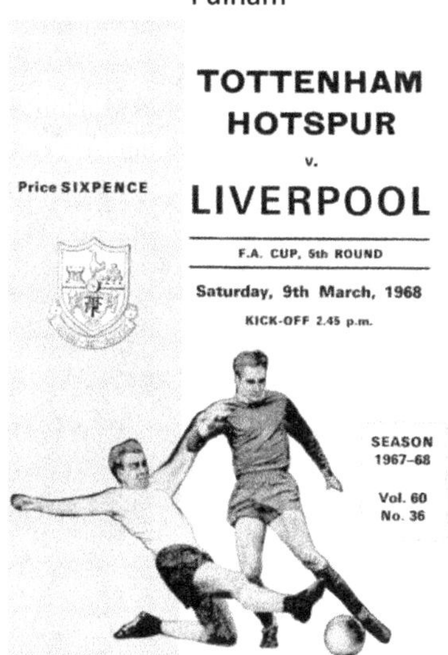

9 March
Liverpool

6 April
Southampton

4 May
Manchester City

1967-68

AWAY

Date	Opponent	Competition
5 August	Celtic (Hampden Park)	Friendly - Hampden Park
12 August	Manchester United	FA Charity Shield
19 August	Leicester City	Football League
29 August	Everton	Football League
2 September	Burnley	Football League
16 September	Arsenal	Football League
20 September	Hajduk Split	European Cup-Winners' Cup
23 September	Manchester United	Football League
14 October	Coventry City	Football League
28 October	Stoke City	Football League
11 November	Southampton	Football League
25 November	West Bromwich Albion	Football League
29 November	Olympique Lyonnais	European Cup-Winners' Cup
9 December	Manchester City	Football League
23 December	West Ham United	Football League
30 December	Fulham	Football League
17 January	Sheffield Wednesday	Football League
27 January	Manchester United	FA Cup
10 February	Sunderland	Football League
26 February	Sheffield United	Football League
12 March	Liverpool	FA Cup
16 March	Nottingham Forest	Football League
13 April	Chelsea	Football League
17 April	Leeds United	Football League
27 April	Newcastle United	Football League
29 April	Liverpool	Football League
11 May	Wolverhampton Wanderers	Football League
15 May	Panathinaikos	Friendly
{ 19 May	Anorthosis	Friendly
{ 22 May	AEL	Friendly
{ 25 May	Cyprus International XI (Nicosia)	Friendly
{ 29 May	Apoel	Friendly

5 August
Celtic

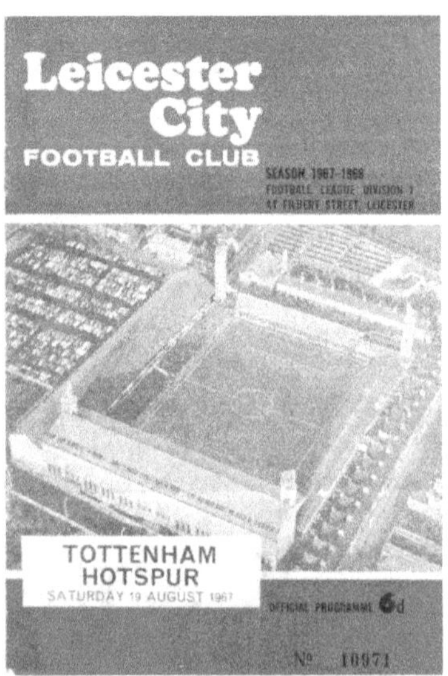

19 August
Leicester City

14 October
Coventry City

28 October
Stoke City

23 December
West Ham United

27 January
Manchester United

26 February
Sheffield United

12 March
Liverpool

16 March
Nottingham Forest

27 April
Newcastle United

11 May
Wolverhampton Wanderers

19 - 29 May
Cyprus Tour

1968-69

HOME

	Date	Opponent	Competition
☐☐	31 July	Rangers	Friendly
☐☐	10 August	Arsenal	Football League
☐☐	21 August	West Bromwich Albion	Football League
☐☐	24 August	Sheffield Wednesday	Football League
☐☐	7 September	Burnley	Football League
☐☐	21 September	Nottingham Forest	Football League
☐☐	25 September	Exeter City	Football League Cup
☐☐	5 October	Leicester City	Football League
☐☐	9 October	Manchester United	Football League
☐☐	16 October	Peterborough United	Football League Cup
☐☐	19 October	Liverpool	Football League
☐☐	30 October	Southampton	Football League Cup
☐☐	2 November	Stoke City	Football League
☐☐	16 November	Sunderland	Football League
☐☐	30 November	Queens Park Rangers - postponed	Football League
☐☐	4 December	Arsenal	Football League Cup
☐☐	14 December	Manchester City	Football League
☐☐	28 December	Ipswich Town - postponed	Football League
☐☐	18 January	Leeds United	Football League
☐☐	25 January	Wolverhampton Wanderers	FA Cup
☐☐	29 January	Queens Park Rangers	Football League
☐☐	12 February	Aston Villa (dated 8 February)	FA Cup
☐☐	19 February	Southampton - postponed	Football League
☐☐	22 February	Wolverhampton Wanderers	Football League
☐☐	8 March	Everton	Football League
☐☐	18 March	Ipswich Town	Football League
☐☐	22 March	Chelsea	Football League
☐☐	2 April	Newcastle United	Football League
☐☐	4 April	Coventry City	Football League
☐☐	19 April	West Ham United	Football League
☐☐	22 April	Southampton	Football League

☐ Handbook ☐ Season Ticket

Season Ticket

Handbook

31 July
Rangers

24 August
Sheffield Wednesday

25 September
Exeter City

16 October
Peterborough United

30 November
Queens Park Rangers - postponed

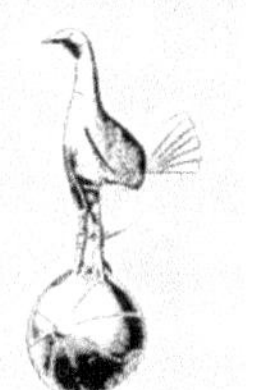

28 December
Ipswich Town - postponed

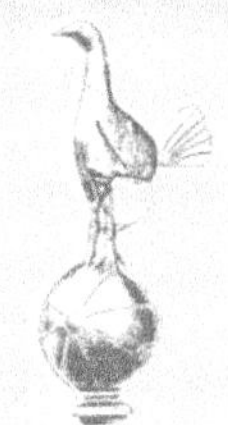

25 January
Wolverhampton Wanderers

19 February
Southampton - postponed

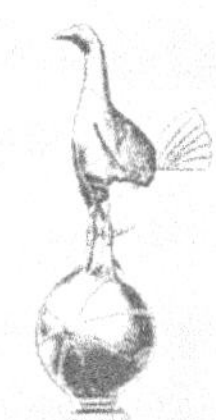

18 March
Ipswich Town

19 April
West Ham United

1968-69

AWAY

	Date	Opponent	Competition
☐☐	3 August	FK Austria	Friendly
☐☐	17 August	Everton	Football League
☐☐	28 August	Manchester United	Football League
☐☐	31 August	Chelsea	Football League
☐☐	4 September	Aston Villa	Football League Cup
☐☐	14 September	West Ham United	Football League
☐☐	17 September	Coventry City	Football League
☐☐	28 September	Newcastle United	Football League
☐☐	12 October	Manchester City	Football League
☐☐	26 October	Ipswich Town	Football League
☐☐	9 November	Leeds United	Football League
☐☐	20 November	Arsenal	Football League Cup
☐☐	23 November	Southampton	Football League
☐☐	7 December	Wolverhampton Wanderers	Football League
☐☐	21 December	Liverpool	Football League
☐☐	26 December	Leicester City - postponed	Football League
☐☐	4 January	Walsall	FA Cup
☐☐	11 January	Stoke City	Football League
☐☐	1 February	Sunderland	Football League
☐☐	15 February	Queens Park Rangers	Football League
☐☐	1 March	Manchester City	FA Cup
☐☐	24 March	Arsenal	Football League
☐☐	29 March	Burnley	Football League
☐☐	7 April	West Bromwich Albion	Football League
☐☐	12 April	Nottingham Forest	Football League
☐☐	29 April	Leicester City	Football League
☐☐	12 May	Sheffield Wednesday	Football League
☐☐	15 May	West Ham United (Baltimore)	Friendly
☐☐	17 May	Aston Villa (Atlanta)	Friendly
☐☐	28 May	Fiorentina (Toronto)	Toronto Cup
☐☐	1 June	Rangers (Toronto)	Toronto Cup

28 August
Manchester United

4 September
Aston Villa

14 September
West Ham United

28 September
Newcastle United

26 December
Leicester City - postponed

4 January
Walsall

15 February
Queens Park Rangers

1 March
Manchester City

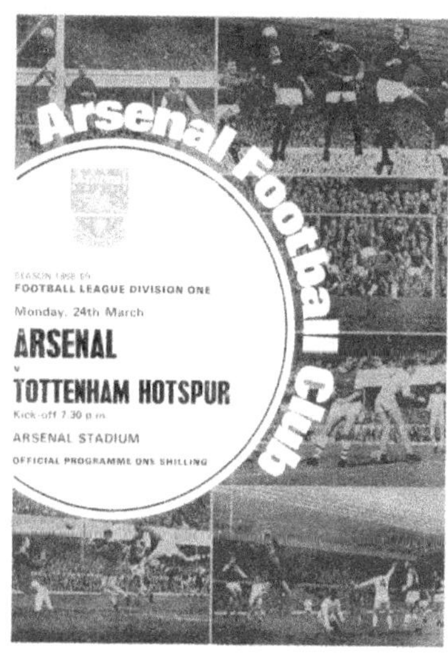

24 March
Arsenal

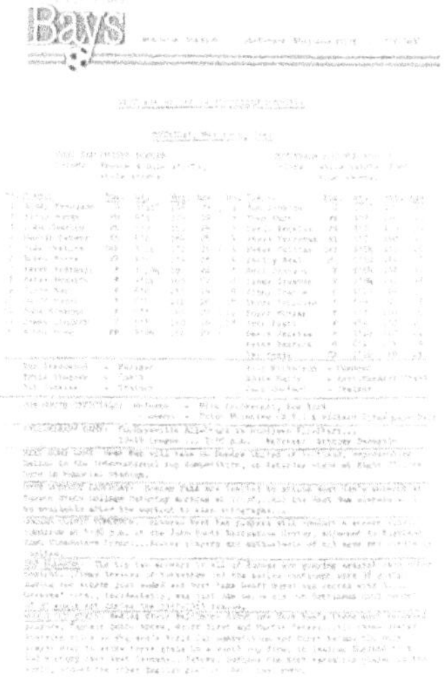
15 May
West Ham United

17 May
Aston Villa

1 June
Rangers

1969-70

HOME

	Date	Opponent	Competition
☐☐	13 August	Burnley	Football League
☐☐	16 August	Liverpool	Football League
☐☐	27 August	Chelsea	Football League
☐☐	30 August	Ipswich Town	Football League
☐☐	13 September	Manchester City	Football League
☐☐	27 September	Sunderland	Football League
☐☐	11 October	Wolverhampton Wanderers	Football League
☐☐	18 October	Newcastle United	Football League
☐☐	1 November	Sheffield Wednesday	Football League
☐☐	15 November	West Bromwich Albion	Football League
☐☐	29 November	Everton – postponed	Football League
☐☐	17 December	Everton - abandoned	Football League
☐☐	20 December	West Ham United	Football League
☐☐	26 December	Crystal Palace	Football League
☐☐	7 January	Bradford City	FA Cup
☐☐	10 January	Derby County	Football League
☐☐	24 January	Crystal Palace	FA Cup
☐☐	31 January	Southampton	Football League
☐☐	14 February	Leeds United	Football League
☐☐	21 February	Stoke City	Football League
☐☐	6 March	Manchester United - postponed	Football League
☐☐	11 March	Everton	Football League
☐☐	21 March	Coventry City	Football League
☐☐	27 March	Nottingham Forest	Football League
☐☐	13 April	Manchester United	Football League
☐☐	2 May	Arsenal	Football League

☐ Handbook ☐ Season Ticket

Season Ticket

Handbook

13 August
Burnley

11 October
Wolverhampton Wanderers

29 November
Everton - postponed

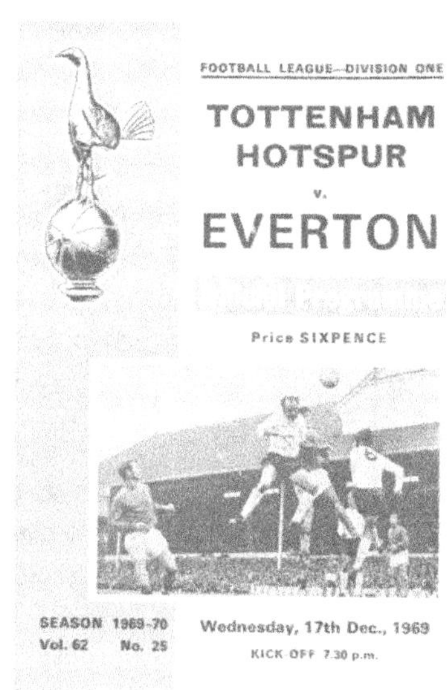

17 December
Everton - abandoned

26 December
Crystal Palace

7 January
Bradford City

14 February
Leeds United

6 March
Manchester United - postponed

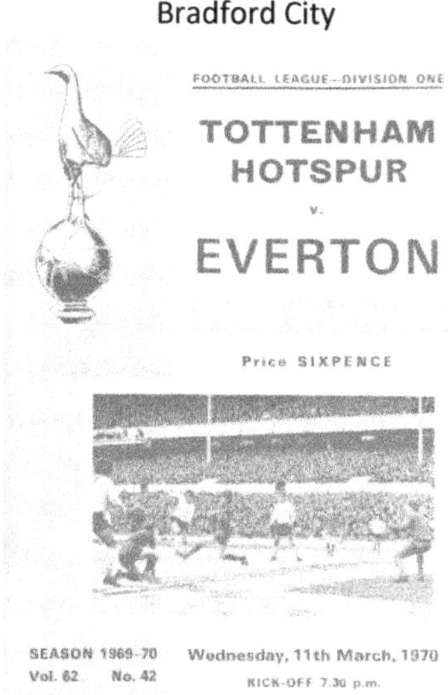

11 March
Everton

2 May
Arsenal

1969-70

AWAY

Date	Opponent	Competition
2 August	Heart of Midlothian	Friendly
4 August	Rangers	Friendly
9 August	Leeds United	Football League
19 August	Burnley	Football League
23 August	Crystal Palace	Football League
3 September	Wolverhampton Wanderers	Football League Cup
6 September	West Ham United	Football League
16 September	Arsenal	Football League
20 September	Derby County	Football League
4 October	Southampton	Football League
7 October	Liverpool	Football League
25 October	Stoke City	Football League
8 November	Nottingham Forest	Football League
22 November	Manchester United	Football League
6 December	Coventry City	Football League
13 December	Manchester City	Football League
27 December	Ipswich Town	Football League
3 January	Bradford City	FA Cup
17 January	Sunderland	Football League
28 January	Crystal Palace	FA Cup
7 February	Wolverhampton Wanderers	Football League
28 February	Newcastle United	Football League
14 March	Everton	Football League
28 March	West Bromwich Albion	Football League
30 March	Sheffield Wednesday	Football League
4 April	Chelsea	Football League
13 May	Valetta (Gzira)	Friendly
16 May	Sliema Wanderers (Gzira)	Friendly
17 May	MFA League XI (Gzira)	Friendly
	- Blue Review – Sliema Wanderers magazine	
	- Malta Spurs Supporters Club magazine	

2 August
Heart of Midlothian

4 August
Rangers

3 September
Wolverhampton Wanderers

20 September
Derby County

Nottingham Forest v Tottenham Hotspur

8 November
Nottingham Forest

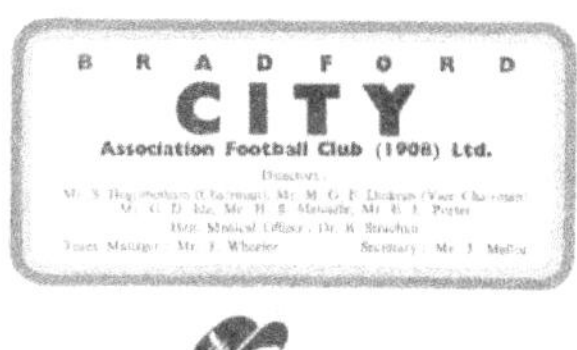

3 January
Bradford City

Football Association Cup
4th Round Replay

v.

TOTTENHAM H.

WEDNESDAY, 28th JANUARY 1970
Kick Off 7.30 p.m.

OFFICIAL PROGRAMME - 1/-

28 January
Crystal Palace

30 March
Sheffield Wednesday

Football Club
v
TOTTENHAM HOTSPUR
Saturday, 4th April, 3 p.m.
Football League Division 1 — Season 1969-70
OFFICIAL 1/- PROGRAMME

4 April
Chelsea

13 May
Valletta

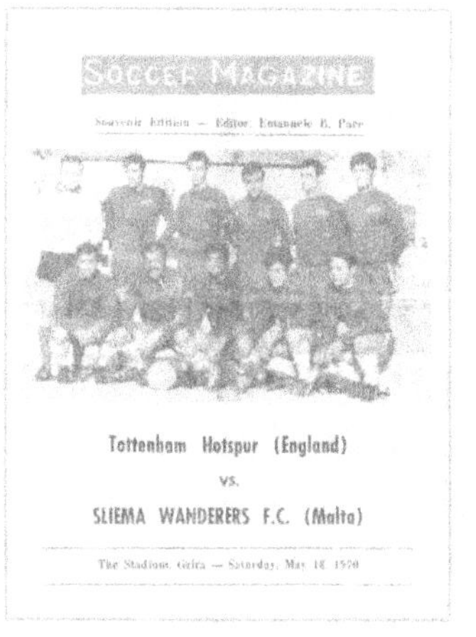

16 May
Sliema Wanderers

17 May
MFA League XI

1970-71

HOME

	Date	Opponent	Competition
☐☐	3 August	Rangers	Friendly
☐☐	15 August	West Ham United	Football League
☐☐	19 August	Leeds United	Football League
☐☐	29 August	Coventry City	Football League
☐☐	9 September	Swansea City	Football League Cup
☐☐	12 September	Blackpool	Football League
☐☐	16 September	Dunfermline Athletic	Texaco Cup
☐☐	26 September	Manchester City	Football League
☐☐	7 October	Sheffield United	Football League Cup
☐☐	10 October	Liverpool	Football League
☐☐	21 October	Motherwell	Texaco Cup
☐☐	24 October	Stoke City	Football League
☐☐	28 October	West Bromwich Albion	Football League Cup
☐☐	7 November	Burnley	Football League
☐☐	18 November	Coventry City	Football League Cup
☐☐	21 November	Newcastle United	Football League
☐☐	5 December	Manchester United	Football League
☐☐	19 December	Wolverhampton Wanderers	Football League
☐☐	23 December	Bristol City	Football League Cup
☐☐	2 January	Sheffield Wednesday	FA Cup
☐☐	16 January	Southampton	Football League
☐☐	30 January	Everton	Football League
☐☐	13 February	Nottingham Forest	FA Cup
☐☐	17 February	West Bromwich Albion	Football League
☐☐	10 March	Nottingham Forest	Football League
☐☐	13 March	Chelsea	Football League
☐☐	16 March	Liverpool	FA Cup
☐☐	7 April	Derby County	Football League
☐☐	10 April	Ipswich Town	Football League
☐☐	24 April	Crystal Palace	Football League
☐☐	28 April	Huddersfield Town	Football League
☐☐	3 May	Arsenal	Football League

☐ Handbook ☐ Season Ticket

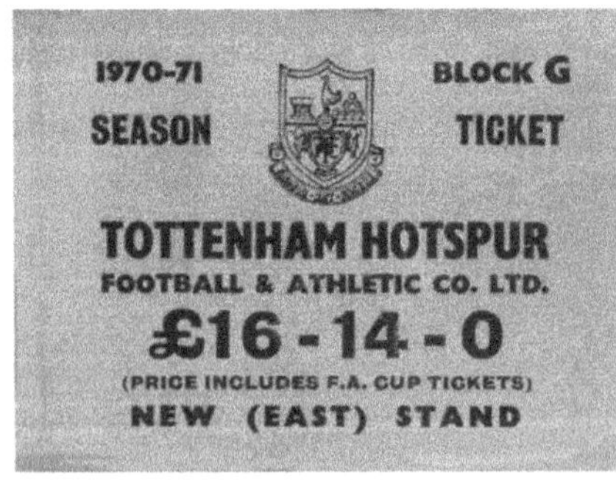

Season Ticket

Handbook

3 August
Rangers

9 September
Swansea City

16 September
Dunfermline Athletic

21 October
Motherwell

18 November
Coventry City

2 January
Sheffield Wednesday

13 February
Nottingham Forest

16 March
Liverpool

28 April
Huddersfield Town

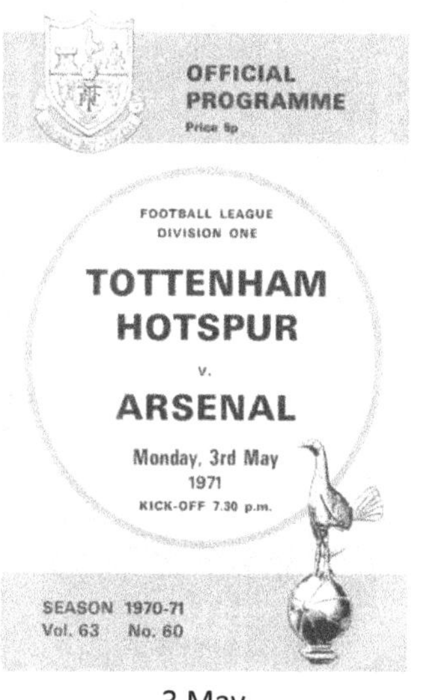

3 May
Arsenal

1970-71

AWAY

Date	Opponent	Competition
{ 7 August	1FC Cologne	Palma de Mallorca Tournament
{ 8 August	Atletico Madrid	Palma de Mallorca Tournament
22 August	Wolverhampton Wanderers	Football League
25 August	Southampton	Football League
1 September	Huddersfield Town	Football League
5 September	Arsenal	Football League
19 September	Crystal Palace	Football League
29 September	Dunfermline Athletic	Texaco Cup
3 October	Derby County	Football League
17 October	West Ham United	Football League
31 October	Nottingham Forest	Football League
3 November	Motherwell	Texaco Cup
14 November	Chelsea	Football League
28 November	Everton	Football League
12 December	West Bromwich Albion	Football League
16 December	Bristol City (dated 9 December)	Football League Cup
26 December	Ipswich Town - postponed	Football League
9 January	Leeds United	Football League
23 January	Carlisle United	FA Cup
6 February	Manchester United	Football League
20 February	Newcastle United	Football League
27 February	Aston Villa (Wembley)	Football League Cup
6 March	Liverpool	FA Cup
20 March	Burnley	Football League
23 March	Ipswich Town	Football League
3 April	Coventry City	Football League
12 April	Blackpool	Football League
17 April	Liverpool	Football League
1 May	Manchester City	Football League
5 May	Stoke City	Football League
29 May	All Japan XI (Kobe) – single match issue	Friendly
{ 29 May	All Japan XI (Kobe)	Friendly
{ 3 June	All Japan XI (Tokyo)	Friendly
{ 9 June	All Japan XI (Tokyo)	Friendly

7 & 8 August
Palma de Mallorca Tournament

1 September
Huddersfield Town

Texaco International League Competition
Dunfermline Athletic
versus
Tottenham Hotspur
Souvenir Programme - One Shilling

29 September
Dunfermline Athletic

3 October
Derby County

3 November
Motherwell

26 December
Ipswich Town - postponed

23 January
Carlisle United

6 March
Liverpool

12 April
Blackpool

1 May
Manchester City

29 May
All-Japan

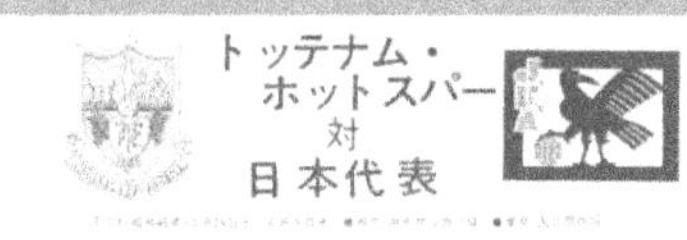

29 May, 3 & 9 June
All-Japan XI

1971-72

HOME

	Date	Opponent	Competition
☐☐	18 August	Newcastle United	Football League
☐☐	21 August	Huddersfield Town	Football League
☐☐	4 September	Liverpool	Football League
☐☐	18 September	Crystal Palace	Football League
☐☐	22 September	Torino	Anglo-Italian League Cup-Winners' Cup
☐☐	28 September	Keflavik	UEFA Cup
☐☐	2 October	Ipswich Town	Football League
☐☐	16 October	Wolverhampton Wanderers	Football League
☐☐	23 October	Nottingham Forest	Football League
☐☐	27 October	Preston North End	Football League Cup
☐☐	2 November	FC Nantes	UEFA Cup
☐☐	6 November	Everton	Division One
☐☐	17 November	Blackpool	Football League Cup
☐☐	20 November	West Bromwich Albion	Football League
☐☐	24 November	Arsenal	Football League
☐☐	4 December	Southampton	Football League
☐☐	8 December	Rapid Bucharest	UEFA Cup
☐☐	27 December	West Ham United	Football League
☐☐	5 January	Chelsea	Football League Cup
☐☐	8 January	Manchester City	Football League
☐☐	15 January	Carlisle United	FA Cup
☐☐	29 January	Leeds United	Football League
☐☐	5 February	Rotherham United	FA Cup
☐☐	19 February	Stoke City	Football League
☐☐	4 March	Manchester United	Football League
☐☐	11 March	Derby County	Football League
☐☐	21 March	Unizale Textile Arad	UEFA Cup
☐☐	25 March	Sheffield United	Football League
☐☐	31 March	Coventry City	Football League
☐☐	5 April	AC Milan	UEFA Cup
☐☐	15 April	Chelsea	Football League
☐☐	29 April	Leicester City	Football League
☐☐	17 May	Wolverhampton Wanderers	UEFA Cup

☐ Handbook ☐ Season Ticket

Season Ticket

Handbook

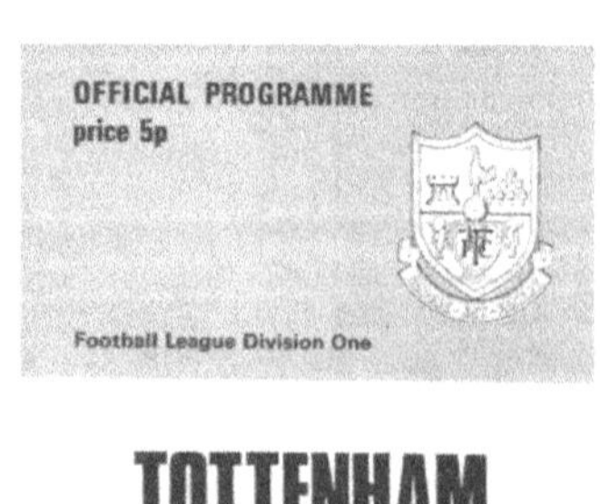

TOTTENHAM HOTSPUR

V

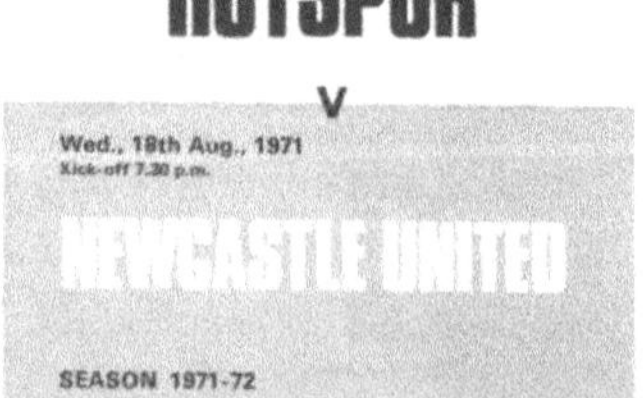

18 August
Newcastle United

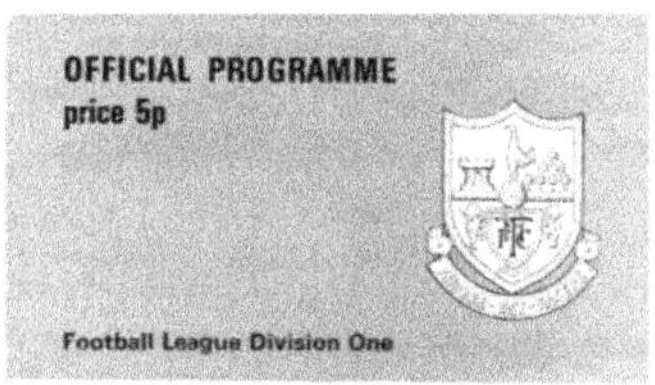

TOTTENHAM
HOTSPUR
v

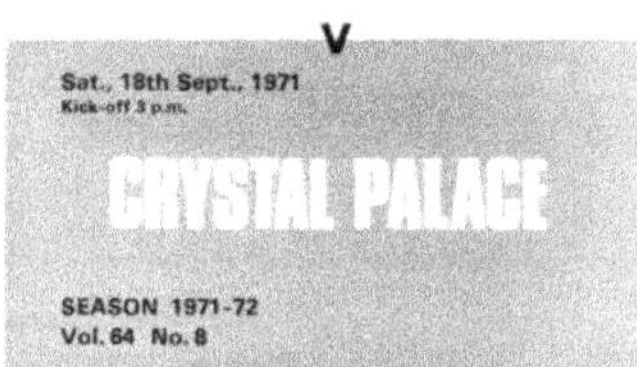

18 September
Crystal Palace

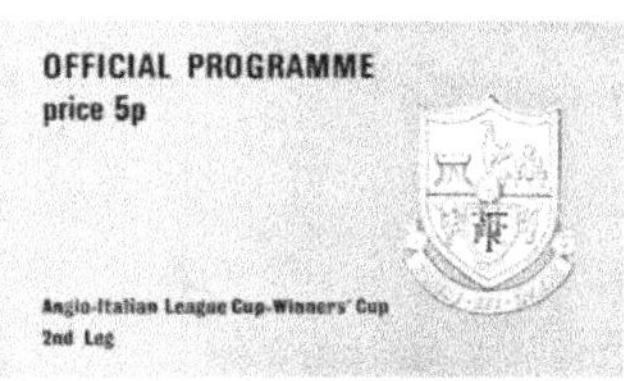

TOTTENHAM
HOTSPUR
v

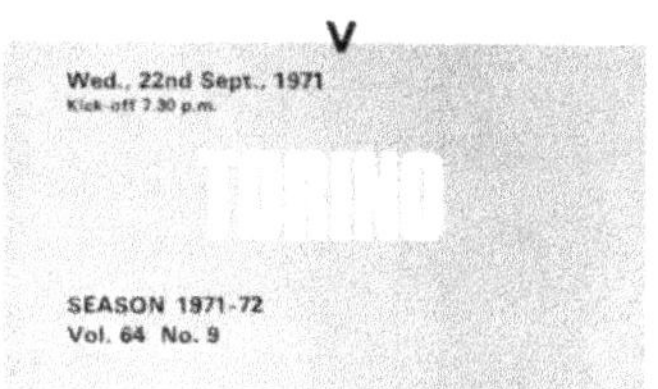

22 September
Torino

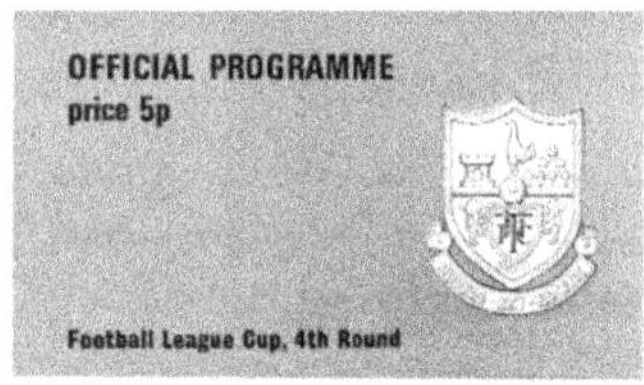

TOTTENHAM
HOTSPUR
v

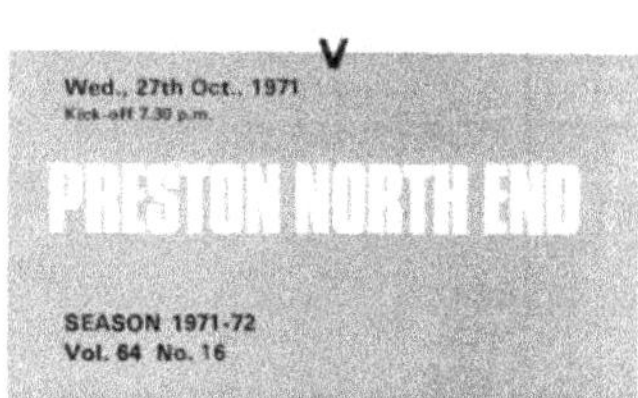

27 October
Preston North End

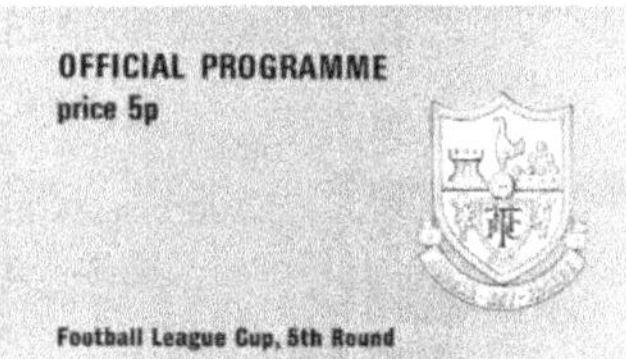

TOTTENHAM
HOTSPUR
v

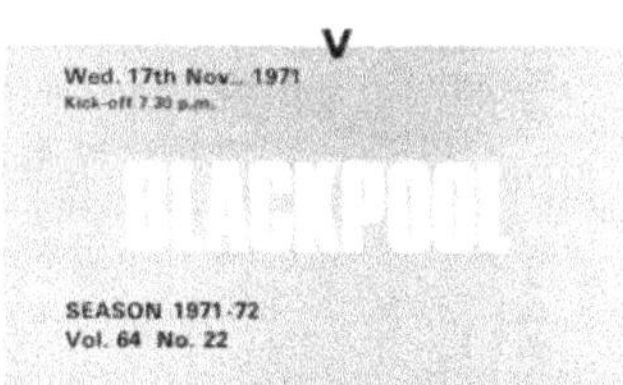

17 November
Blackpool

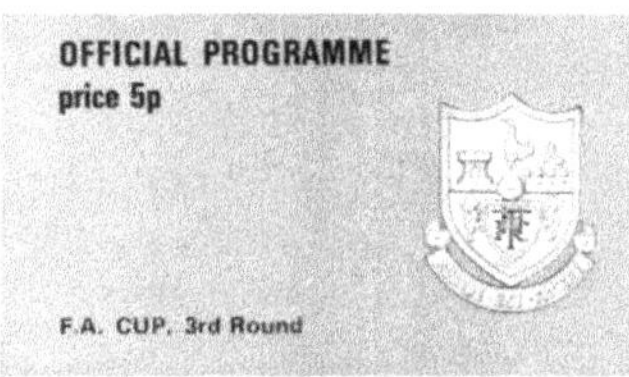

TOTTENHAM
HOTSPUR
v

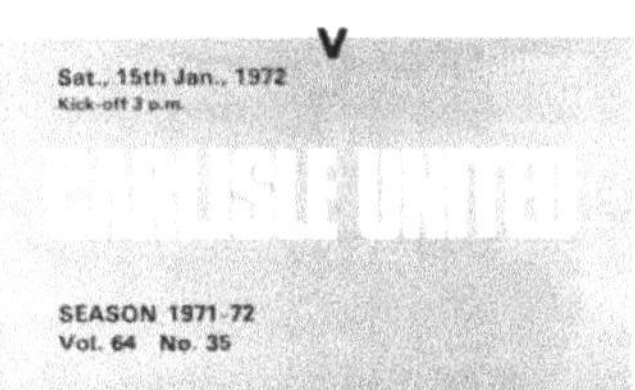

15 January
Carlisle United

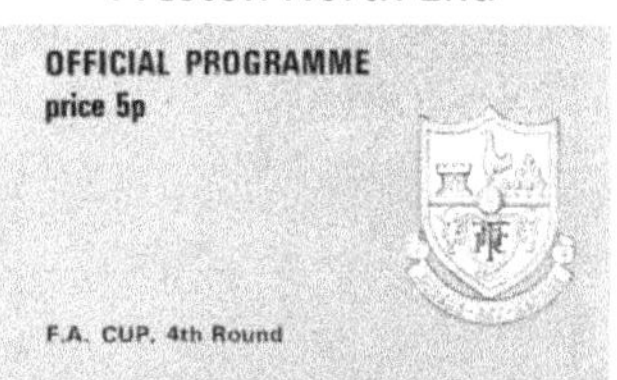

TOTTENHAM
HOTSPUR
v

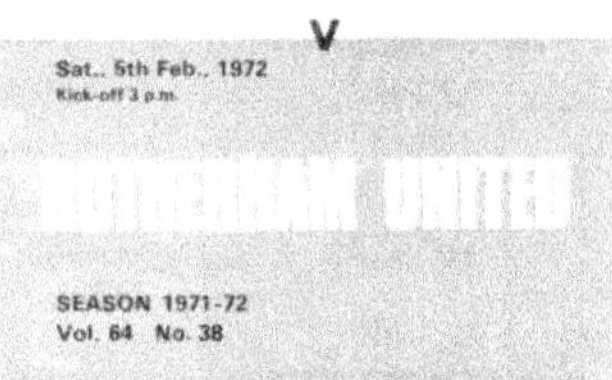

5 February
Rotherham United

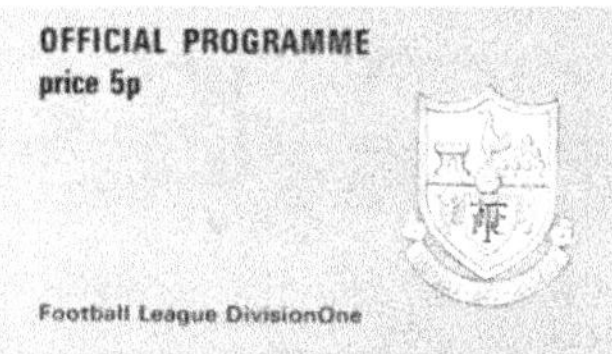

TOTTENHAM
HOTSPUR
v

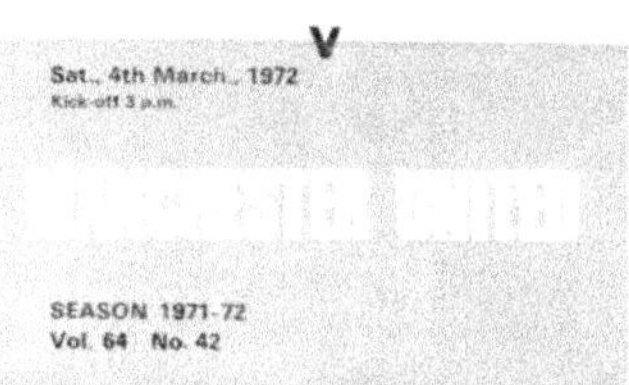

4 March
Manchester United

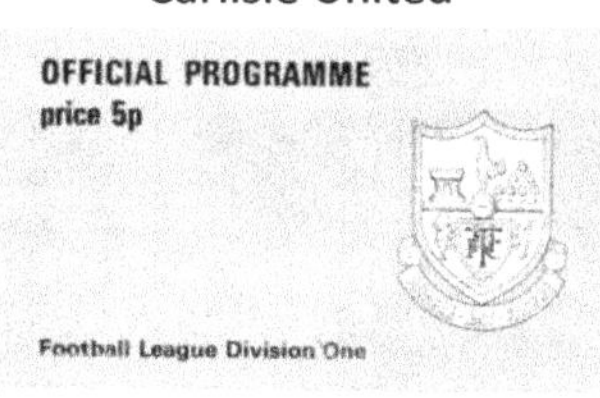

TOTTENHAM
HOTSPUR
v

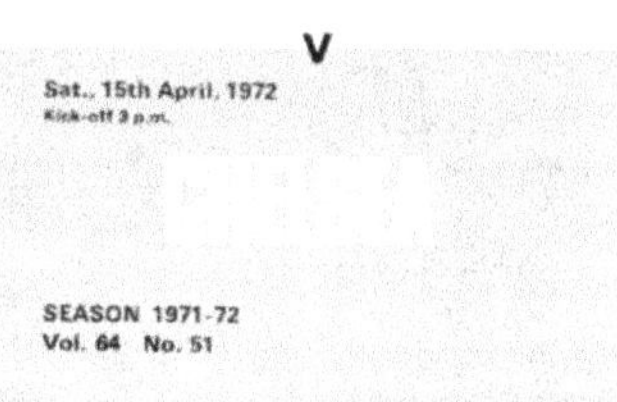

15 April
Chelsea

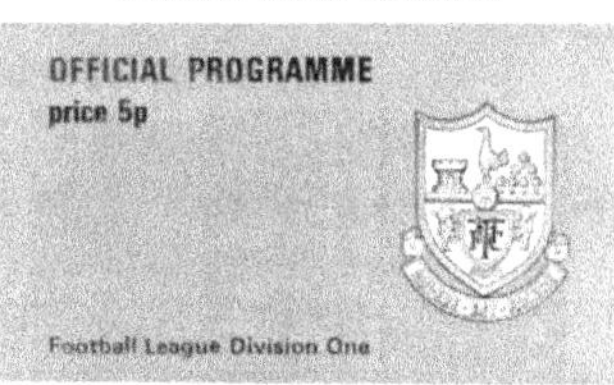

TOTTENHAM
HOTSPUR
v

29 April
Leicester City

1971-72

AWAY

Date	Opponent	Competition
7 August	Heart of Midlothian	Friendly
9 August	Rangers	Friendly
14 August	Wolverhampton Wanderers	Football League
25 August	Leeds United (Boothferry Park)	Football League
28 August	Manchester City	Football League
1 September	Torino	Anglo-Italian League Cup-Winner's Cup
8 September	West Bromwich Albion	Football League Cup
11 September	Sheffield United	Football League
14 September	Keflavik	UEFA Cup
25 September	Coventry City	Football League
6 October	Torquay United	Football League Cup
9 October	Derby County	Football League
	- VIP wraparound	
20 October	FC Nantes	UEFA Cup
30 October	Stoke City	Football League
8 November	Preston North End	Football League Cup
13 November	Manchester United	Football League
27 November	Chelsea	Football League
11 December	Leicester City	Football League
15 December	Rapid Bucharest	UEFA Cup
18 December	Liverpool	Football League
22 December	Chelsea	Football League Cup
1 January	Crystal Palace	Football League
18 January	Carlisle United	FA Cup
22 January	Newcastle United	Football League
12 February	Nottingham Forest	Football League
26 February	Everton	FA Cup
1 March	Everton	Football League
7 March	Unizale Textile Arad	UEFA Cup
18 March	Leeds United	FA Cup
28 March	Huddersfield Town	Football League
1 April	West Ham United	Football League
3 April	Ipswich Town	Football League
8 April	West Bromwich Albion	Football League
19 April	AC Milan	UEFA Cup
22 April	Southampton	Football League
3 May	Wolverhampton Wanderers	UEFA Cup
11 May	Arsenal	Football League
7 June	Maccabi Tel Aviv	Friendly

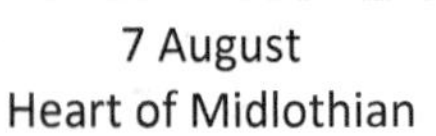

7 August
Heart of Midlothian

9 August
Rangers

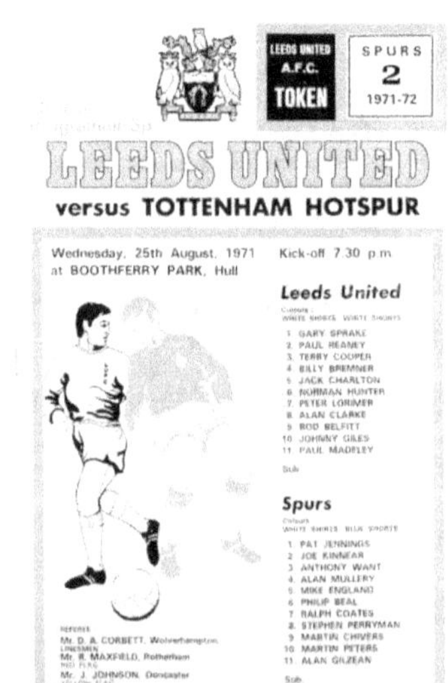

25 August
Leeds United

8 September
West Bromwich Albion

25 September
Coventry City

FOOTBALL LEAGUE CUP — 3rd Round

Wednesday, 6th October, 1971

Kick-off 7.30 p.m.

Torquay Utd. v Tottenham Hotspur

6 October
Torquay United

Derby County

Saturday, October 9, 1971
kick-off 3 p.m.
v TOTTENHAM HOTSPUR
League Division One

Complimentary Programme
(for internal use only)

9 October
Derby County - VIP wraparound issue

8 November
Preston North End

11 December
Leicester City

18 January
Carlisle United

1 March
Everton

FOOTBALL LEAGUE — DIVISION 1
TOTTENHAM HOTSPUR
TUESDAY, MARCH 28th, 1972 — Kick-off 7.30 p.m.

28 March
Huddersfield Town

1972-73

HOME

		Date	Opponent	Competition
		12 August	Coventry City	Football League
		23 August	Birmingham City	Football League
		26 August	Leeds United	Football League
		6 September	Huddersfield Town	Football League Cup
		9 September	Crystal Palace	Football League
		23 September	West Ham United	Football League
		27 September	Lyn Oslo	UEFA Cup
		7 October	Stoke City	Football League
		11 October	Middlesbrough	Football League Cup
		17 October	Feijenoord	Jimmy Greaves Testimonial
		21 October	Chelsea	Football League
		25 October	Olympiakos	UEFA Cup
		30 October	Middlesbrough	Football League Cup
		1 November	Millwall	Football League Cup
		11 November	West Bromwich Albion	Football League
		25 November	Liverpool	Football League
		29 November	Red Star Belgrade	UEFA Cup
		6 December	Liverpool	Football League Cup
		9 December	Arsenal	Football League
		23 December	Sheffield United	Football League
		30 December	Wolverhampton Wanderers	Football League Cup
		20 January	Ipswich Town	Football League
		7 February	Derby County	FA Cup
		10 February	Manchester City	Football League
		24 February	Everton	Football League
		7 March	Vitória Setúbal	UEFA Cup
		10 March	Norwich City	Football League
		24 March	Manchester United	Football League
		7 April	Southampton	Football League
		18 April	Derby County	Football League
		21 April	Leicester City	Football League
		25 April	Liverpool	UEFA Cup
		28 April	Newcastle United	Football League
		30 April	Wolverhampton Wanderers	Football League

☐ Handbook ☐ Season Ticket

Season Ticket

Handbook

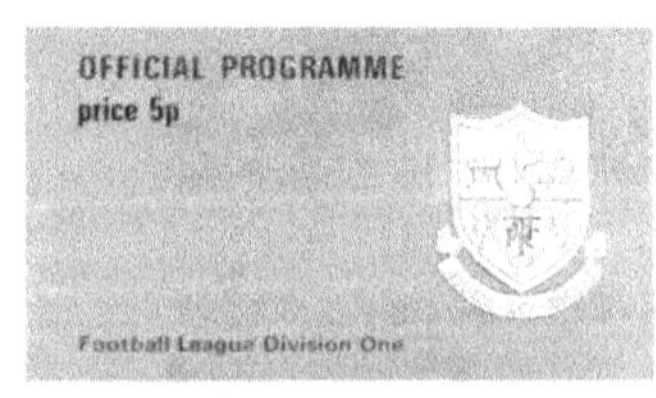

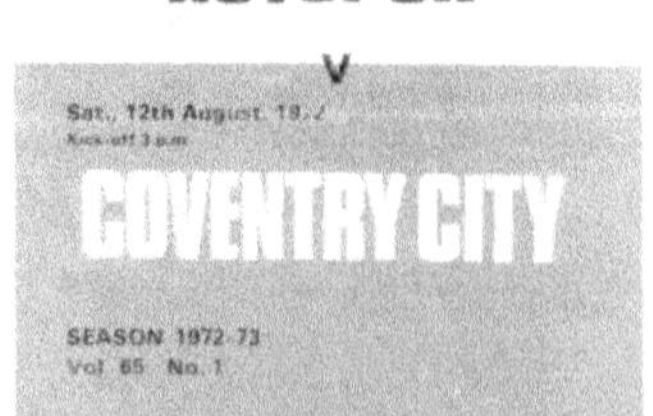

12 August
Coventry City

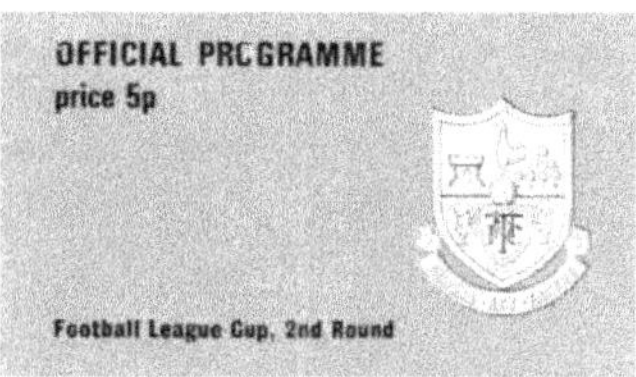

TOTTENHAM
HOTSPUR
v

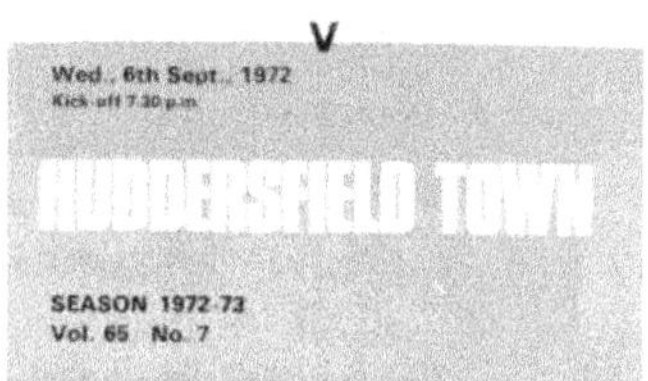

6 September
Huddersfield Town

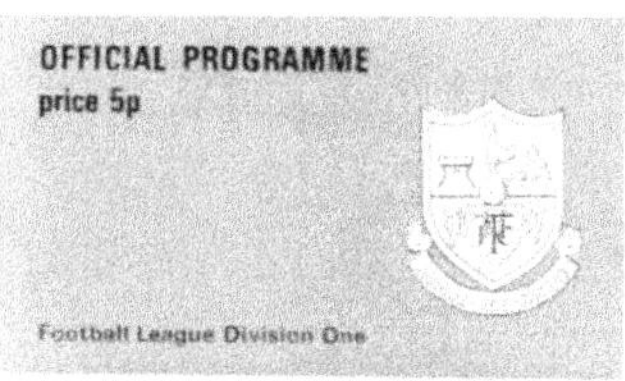

TOTTENHAM
HOTSPUR
v

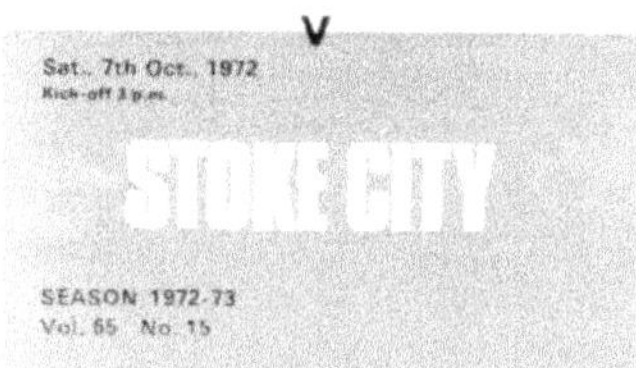

7 October
Stoke City

17 October
Feijenoord

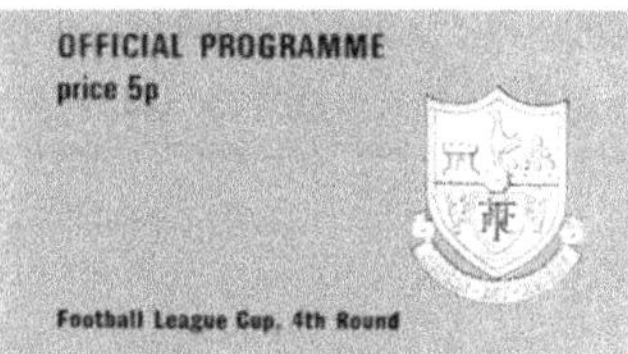

TOTTENHAM
HOTSPUR
v

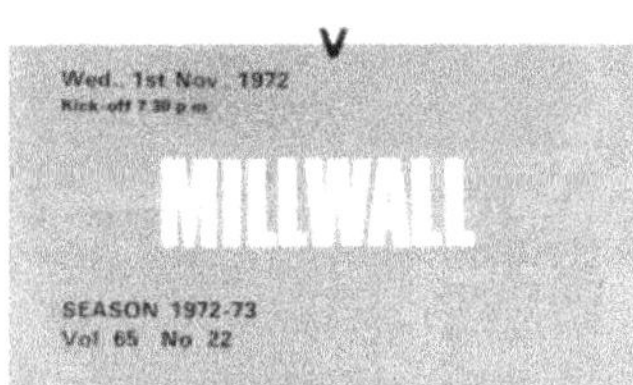

1 November
Millwall

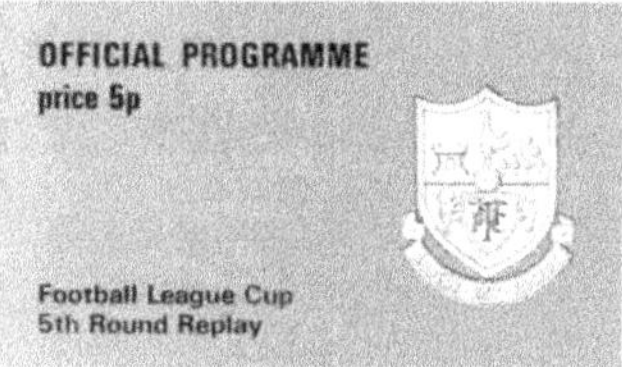

TOTTENHAM
HOTSPUR
v

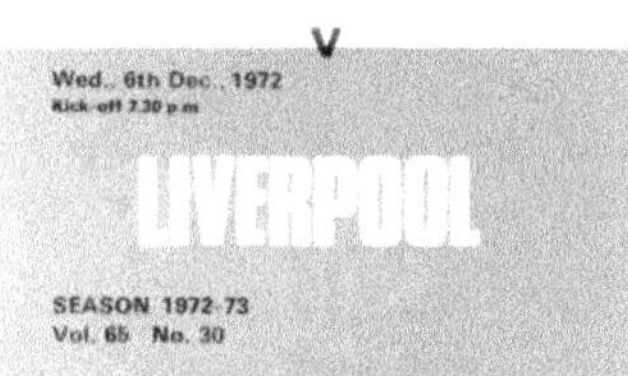

6 December
Liverpool

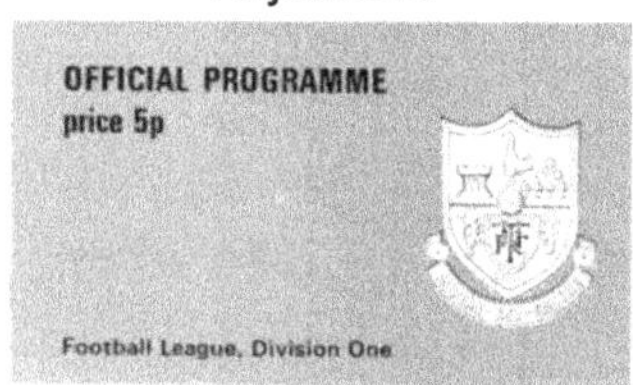

TOTTENHAM
HOTSPUR
v

10 February
Manchester City

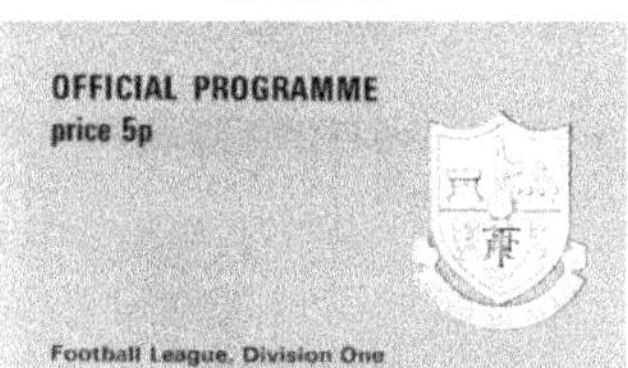

TOTTENHAM
HOTSPUR
v

24 March
Manchester United

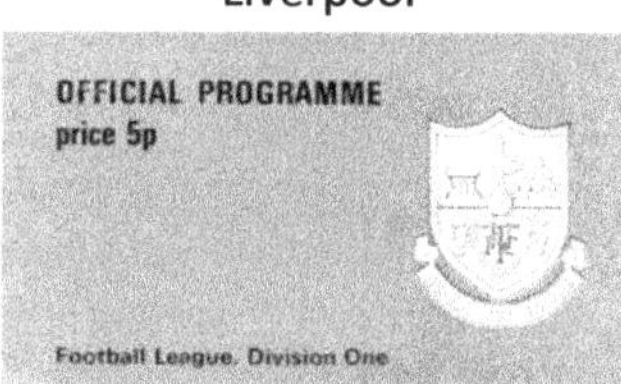

TOTTENHAM
HOTSPUR
v

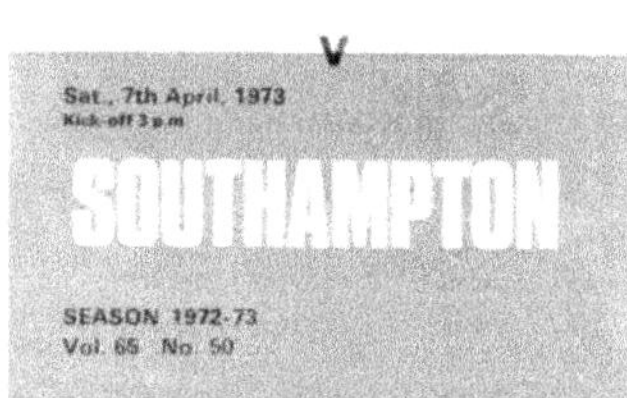

7 April
Southampton

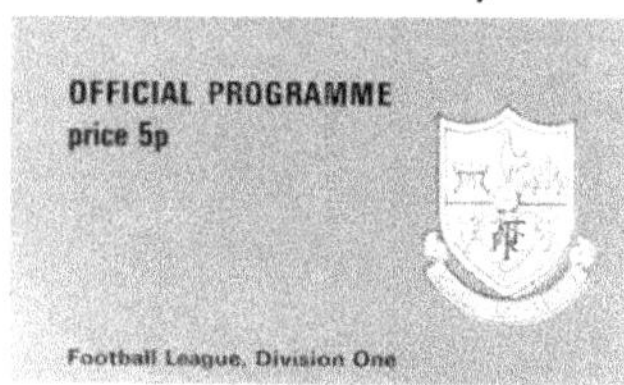

TOTTENHAM
HOTSPUR
v

30 April
Wolverhampton Wanderers

1972-73

AWAY

	Date	Opponent	Competition
☐☐	29 July	Bournemouth	Friendly
☐☐	2 August	Aston Villa	Friendly
☐☐	7 August	Celtic	Friendly
☐☐	16 August	West Bromwich Albion	Football League
☐☐	19 August	Wolverhampton Wanderers	Football League
☐☐	30 August	Newcastle United (dated 26 August)	Football League
☐☐	2 September	Ipswich Town	Football League
☐☐	13 September	Lyn Oslo	UEFA Cup
☐☐	16 September	Manchester City	Football League
☐☐	30 September	Derby County	Football League
☐☐	3 October	Middlesbrough	Football League Cup
☐☐	14 October	Norwich City	Football League
☐☐	28 October	Manchester United	Football League
☐☐	4 November	Birmingham City	Football League
☐☐	8 November	Olympiakos	UEFA Cup
☐☐	18 November	Leicester City	Football League
☐☐	2 December	Southampton	Football League
☐☐	4 December	Liverpool	Football League Cup
☐☐	13 December	Red Star Belgrade - magazine	UEFA Cup
☐☐	16 December	Everton	Football League
☐☐	20 December	Wolverhampton Wanderers	Football League Cup
☐☐	26 December	West Ham United	Football League
☐☐	6 January	Leeds United	Football League
☐☐	13 January	Margate	FA Cup
☐☐	27 January	Crystal Palace	Football League
☐☐	3 February	Derby County	FA Cup
☐☐	17 February	Coventry City	Football League
☐☐	3 March	Norwich City (Wembley)	Football League Cup
☐☐	14 March	Stoke City	Football League
☐☐	21 March	Vitória Setúbal	UEFA Cup
☐☐	31 March	Liverpool	Football League
☐☐	3 April	Chelsea	Football League
☐☐	10 April	Liverpool	UEFA Cup
☐☐	14 April	Arsenal	Football League
☐☐	2 May	Sheffield United	Football League

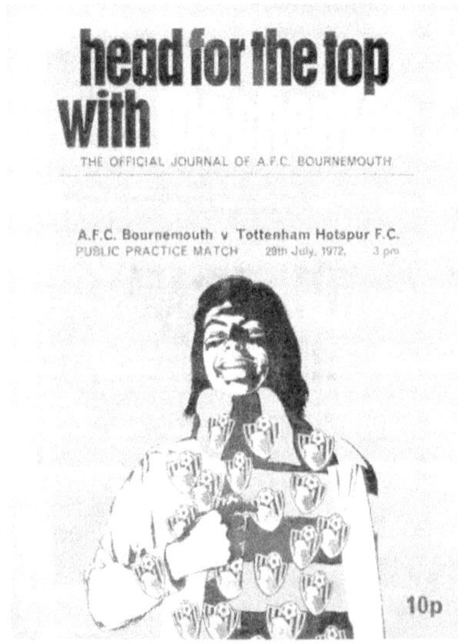

29 July
Bournemouth

2 August
Aston Villa

7 August
Celtic

30 August
Newcastle United

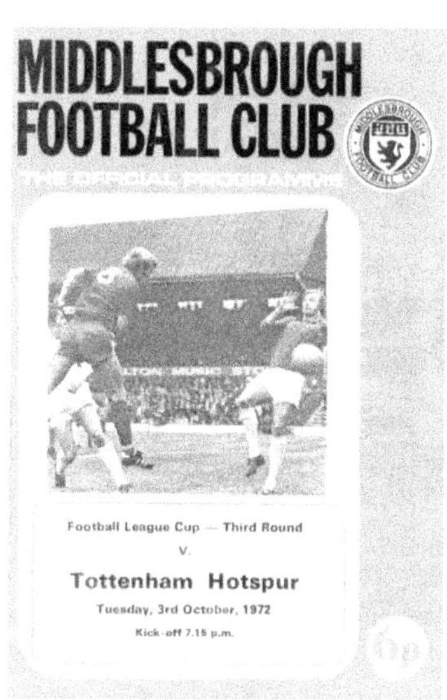

3 October
Middlesbrough

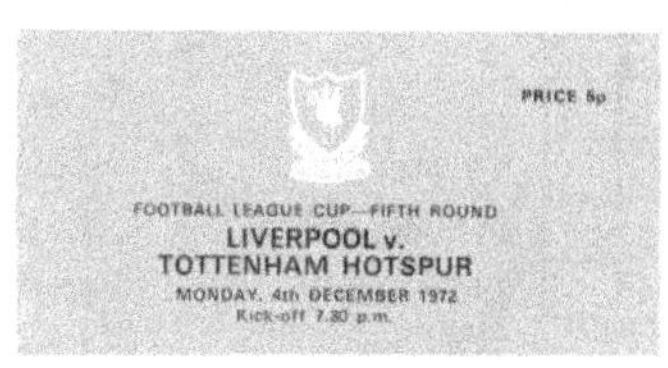

4 December
Liverpool

26 December
West Ham United

13 January
Margate

27 January
Crystal Palace

3 April
Chelsea

14 April
Arsenal

2 May
Sheffield United

1973-74

HOME

Date	Opponent	Competition
1 September	Leeds United	Football League
5 September	Burnley	Football League
15 September	Sheffield United	Football League
29 September	Derby County	Football League
3 October	Grasshoppers	UEFA Cup
13 October	Arsenal	Football League
27 October	Newcastle United	Football League
7 November	Aberdeen	UEFA Cup
10 November	Manchester United	Football League
24 November	Wolverhampton Wanderers	Football League
3 December	Bayern Munich	Phil Beal Testimonial
8 December	Stoke City	Football League
12 December	Dinamo Tbilisi	UEFA Cup
15 December	Manchester City	Football League
26 December	Queens Park Rangers	Football League
29 December	West Ham United	Football League
19 January	Coventry City	Football League
6 February	Birmingham City	Football League
9 February	Liverpool - postponed	Football League
23 February	Ipswich Town	Football League
16 March	Norwich City	Football League
20 March	1FC Cologne	UEFA Cup
30 March	Everton	Football League
3 April	Chelsea	Football League
13 April	Southampton	Football League
24 April	1FC Lokomotive Leipzig	UEFA Cup
27 April	Leicester City	Football League
8 May	Liverpool	Football League
21 May	Feijenoord	UEFA Cup

Handbook

Season Ticket

Season Ticket

Handbook

1 September
Leeds United

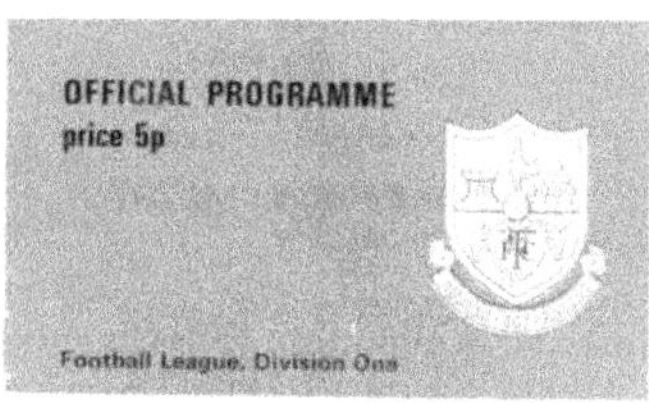

TOTTENHAM
HOTSPUR
v

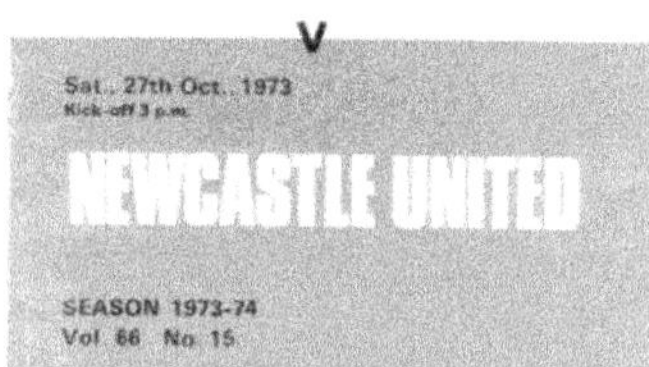

27 October
Newcastle United

3 December
Bayern Munich

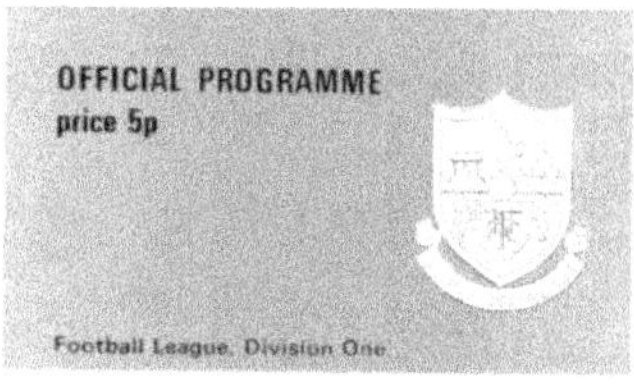

TOTTENHAM
HOTSPUR
v

15 December
Manchester City

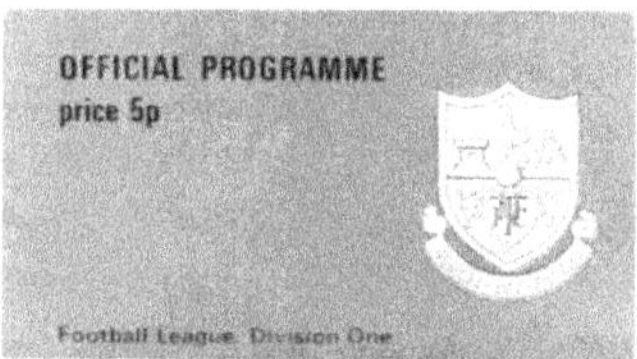

TOTTENHAM
HOTSPUR
v

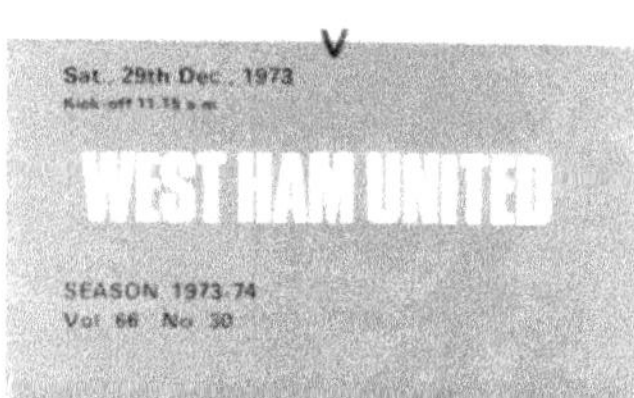

29 December
West Ham United

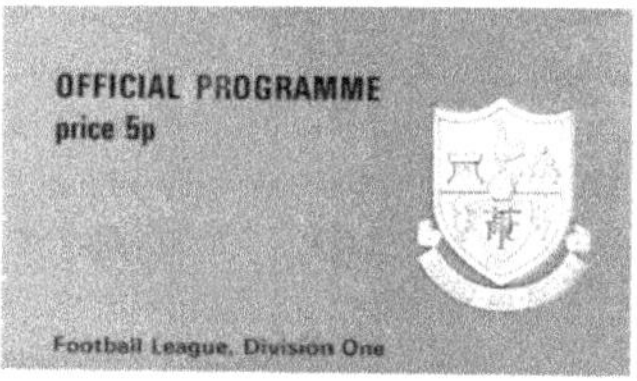

TOTTENHAM
HOTSPUR
v

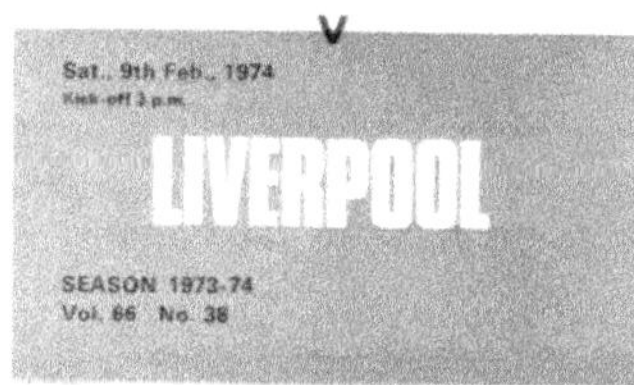

9 February
Liverpool - postponed

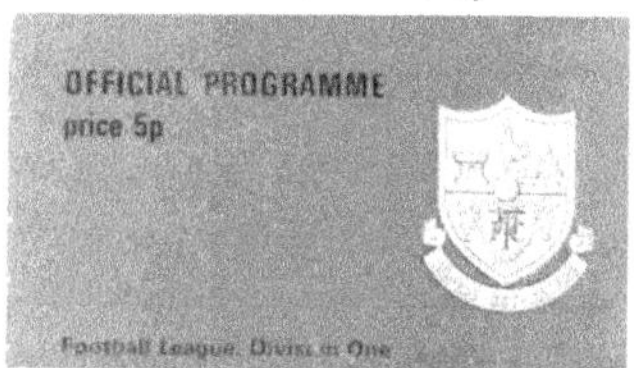

TOTTENHAM
HOTSPUR
v

16 March
Norwich City

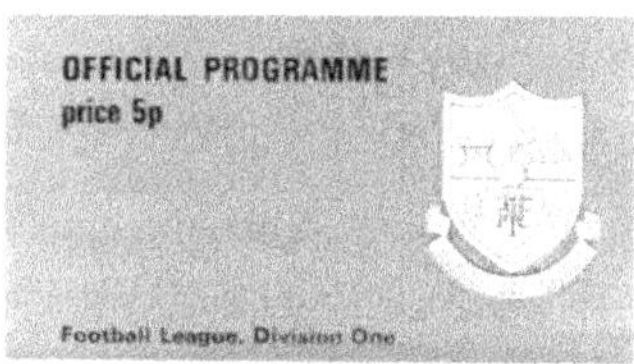

TOTTENHAM
HOTSPUR
v

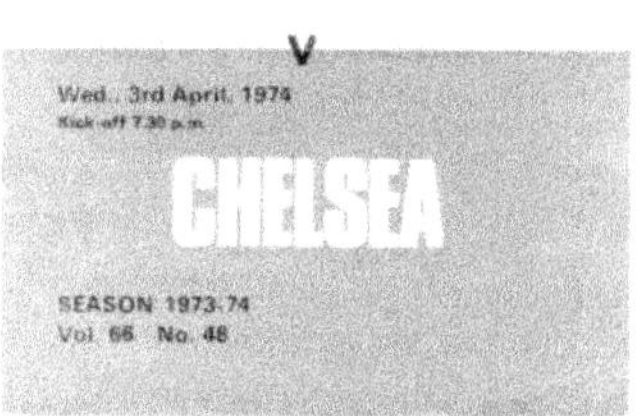

3 April
Chelsea

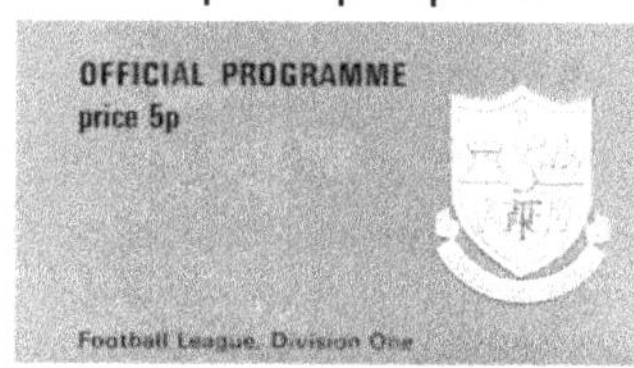

TOTTENHAM
HOTSPUR
v

13 April
Southampton

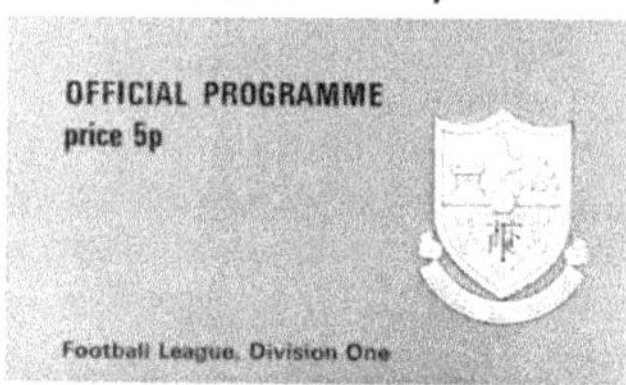

TOTTENHAM
HOTSPUR
v

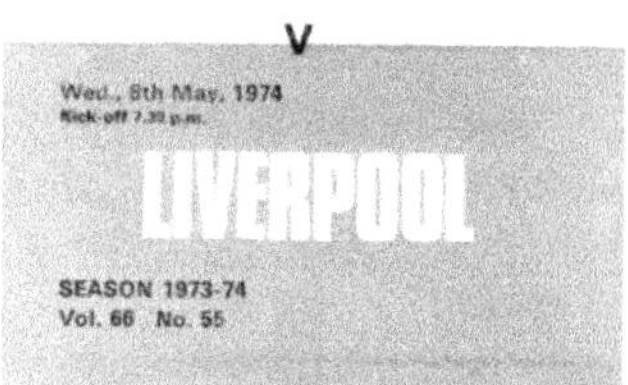

8 May
Liverpool

1973-74

AWAY

Date	Opponent	Competition
8 August	Ajax	Sjaak Swart Testimonial
11 August	Cardiff City	Friendly
18 August	Sunderland	Friendly
25 August	Coventry City	Football League
28 August	Birmingham City	Football League
8 September	West Ham United	Football League
11 September	Burnley	Football League
19 September	Grasshoppers	UEFA Cup
22 September	Liverpool	Football League
6 October	Ipswich Town	Football League
8 October	Queens Park Rangers	Football League Cup
20 October	Norwich City	Football League
24 October	Aberdeen	UEFA Cup
3 November	Everton	Football League
17 November	Southampton	Football League
28 November	Dinamo Tbilisi	UEFA Cup
1 December	Leicester City	Football League
22 December	Derby County	Football League
1 January	Leeds United	Football League
5 January	Leicester City	FA Cup
12 January	Sheffield United	Football League
2 February	Manchester City	Football League
16 February	Arsenal	Football League
2 March	Queens Park Rangers	Football League
6 March	1FC Cologne	UEFA Cup
23 March	Manchester United	Football League
6 April	Wolverhampton Wanderers	Football League
10 April	1FC Lokomotive Leipzig	UEFA Cup
15 April	Chelsea	Football League
20 April	Stoke City	Football League
11 May	Newcastle United	Football League
29 May	Feijenoord	UEFA Cup
	- De Sportgids	
	- Sport Blad Feyenoord	
{ 8 June	Mauritius Select XI (Curepipe)	Friendly
{ 13 June	Mauritius Select XI (Curepipe)	Friendly
{ 16 June	Mauritius Select XI (Curepipe)	Friendly

8 August
Ajax

11 August
Cardiff City

18 August
Sunderland

22 September
Liverpool

6 October
Ipswich Town

20 October
Norwich City

12 January
Sheffield United

2 February
Manchester City

23 March
Manchester United

6 April
Wolverhampton Wanderers

11 May
Newcastle United

8 – 16 June
Mauritius Select XI

1974-75

HOME

		Date	Opponent	Competition
☐	☐	17 August	Ipswich Town	Football League
☐	☐	28 August	Manchester City	Football League
☐	☐	31 August	Derby County	Football League
☐	☐	11 September	Middlesbrough	Football League Cup
☐	☐	14 September	West Ham United	Football League
☐	☐	28 September	Middlesbrough	Football League
☐	☐	5 October	Burnley	Football League
☐	☐	16 October	Carlisle United	Football League
☐	☐	19 October	Arsenal	Football League
☐	☐	9 November	Everton	Football League
☐	☐	23 November	Birmingham City	Football League
☐	☐	27 November	Red Star Belgrade	Alan Gilzean Testimonial
☐	☐	7 December	Newcastle United	Football League
☐	☐	21 December	Queens Park Rangers	Football League
☐	☐	28 December	Coventry City	Football League
☐	☐	8 January	Nottingham Forest	FA Cup
☐	☐	18 January	Sheffield United	Football League
☐	☐	8 February	Stoke City	Football League
☐	☐	22 February	Leicester City	Football League
☐	☐	22 March	Liverpool	Football League
☐	☐	28 March	Wolverhampton Wanderers	Football League
☐	☐	5 April	Luton Town	Football League
☐	☐	19 April	Chelsea	Football League
☐	☐	28 April	Leeds United	Football League

☐ Handbook ☐ Season Ticket

Season Ticket

Handbook

17 August
Ipswich Town

31 August
Derby County

5 October
Burnley

23 November
Birmingham City

27 November
Red Star Belgrade

21 December
Queens Park Rangers

18 January
Sheffield United

22 March
Liverpool

5 April
Luton Town

28 April
Leeds United

1974-75

AWAY

Date	Opponent	Competition
3 August	Heart of Midlothian	Friendly
7 August	Portsmouth	Friendly
10 August	Fulham	Friendly
21 August	Manchester City	Football League
24 August	Carlisle United	Football League
7 September	Liverpool	Football League
21 September	Wolverhampton Wanderers	Football League
12 October	Chelsea	Football League
26 October	Luton Town	Football League
2 November	Stoke City	Football League
16 November	Leicester City	Football League
18 November	Oxford United - cancelled	Rodney Smithson Testimonial
30 November	Sheffield United	Football League
4 December	Leeds United	Football League
14 December	Ipswich Town	Football League
26 December	West Ham United	Football League
4 January	Nottingham Forest	FA Cup
11 January	Newcastle United	Football League
24 January	Watford	Friendly
27 January	Enfield	Starlight Room Inauguration
1 February	Everton	Football League
15 February	Coventry City	Football League
18 February	Birmingham City	Football League
26 February	Red Star Belgrade	Friendly
1 March	Derby County	Football League
15 March	Middlesbrough	Football League
29 March	Queens Park Rangers	Football League
12 April	Burnley	Football League
26 April	Arsenal	Football League

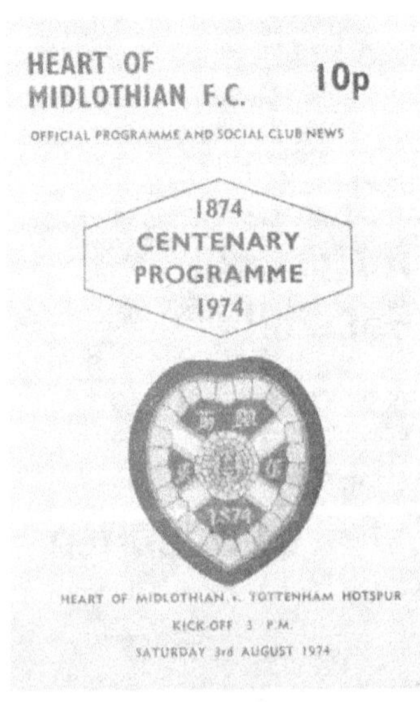

3 August
Heart of Midlothian

7 August
Portsmouth

Pre-Season Friendly

FULHAM
v
TOTTENHAM HOTSPUR

Saturday 10th August 1974
Kick off 3.00 pm

Official Programme Price 5p

10 August
Fulham

24 August
Carlisle United

18 November
Oxford United - cancelled

26 October
Luton Town

30 November
Sheffield United

14 December
Ipswich Town

24 January
Watford

27 January
Enfield

15 March
Middlesbrough

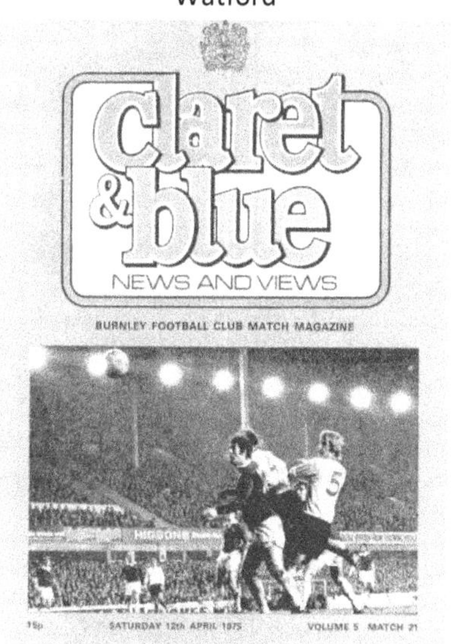

12 April
Burnley

1975-76

HOME

Date	Opponent	Competition
16 August	Middlesbrough	Football League
20 August	Ipswich Town	Football League
30 August	Norwich City	Football League
13 September	Derby County	Football League
27 September	Arsenal	Football League
18 October	Manchester City	Football League
22 October	Arsenal	Cyril Knowles Testimonial
1 November	Wolverhampton Wanderers	Football League
12 November	West Ham United	Football League Cup
15 November	Stoke City	Football League
29 November	Burnley	Football League
3 December	Doncaster Rovers	Football League Cup
10 December	Everton	Football League
13 December	Liverpool	Football League
26 December	Birmingham City	Football League
3 January	Stoke City	FA Cup
14 January	Newcastle United	Football League Cup
17 January	Manchester United	Football League
7 February	West Ham United	Football League
14 February	Queens Park Rangers	Football League
28 February	Leicester City	Football League
13 March	Aston Villa	Football League
27 March	Sheffield United	Football League
10 April	Leeds United	Football League
19 April	Coventry City	Football League
24 April	Newcastle United	Football League

☐ Handbook ☐ Season Ticket

Season Ticket

Handbook

16 August
Middlesbrough

DERBY COUNTY

Football League, Division One
Saturday, 13th September, 1975
Kick-off 3 p.m.
OFFICIAL PROGRAMME PRICE 10p

13 September
Derby County

v MANCHESTER CITY

Football League, Division One
Saturday, 18th October, 1975
Kick-off 3 p.m.
SEASON 1975-76
VOL. 68. NO. 11

18 October
Manchester City

22 October
Arsenal

DONCASTER ROVERS

Football League Cup, 5th Round,
Wednesday, 3rd December, 1975
Kick-off 7.30 p.m.
OFFICIAL PROGRAMME PRICE 10p

3 December
Doncaster Rovers

BIRMINGHAM CITY

Football League, Division One
Friday, 26th December, 1975
Kick-off 11.15 a.m.
OFFICIAL PROGRAMME PRICE 10p

26 December
Birmingham City

STOKE CITY

F.A. Cup, 3rd Round
Saturday, 3rd January, 1976
Kick-off 3 p.m.
OFFICIAL PROGRAMME PRICE 10p

3 January
Stoke City

QUEEN'S PARK RANGERS

Football League, Division One
Saturday, 14th February, 1976
Kick-off 3 p.m.
OFFICIAL PROGRAMME PRICE 10p

14 February
Queens Park Rangers

SHEFFIELD UNITED

Football League, Division One
Saturday, 27th March, 1976
Kick-off 3 p.m.
OFFICIAL PROGRAMME PRICE 10p

27 March
Sheffield United

NEWCASTLE UNITED

Football League, Division One
Saturday, 24th April, 1976
Kick-off 3 p.m.
OFFICIAL PROGRAMME PRICE 10p

24 April
Newcastle United

1975-76

AWAY

		Date	Opponent	Competition
		23 July	Rot-Weiss Essen	Friendly
		25 July	Karlsruher SC	Friendly
		29 July	Hanover 96	Friendly
		3 August	NAC Breda	Friendly
		8 August	Bristol Rovers	Friendly
		23 August	Liverpool	Football League
		25 August	West Ham United	Football League
		6 September	Manchester United	Football League
		9 September	Watford	Football League Cup
		20 September	Leeds United	Football League
		29 September	Stade Rennais	Friendly
		4 October	Newcastle United	Football League
		8 October	Crewe Alexandra	Football League Cup
		11 October	Aston Villa	Football League
		25 October	Leicester City	Football League
		27 October	Millwall	Barry Kitchener Testimonial
		8 November	Queens Park Rangers	Football League
		22 November	Manchester City	Football League
		24 November	West Ham United	Football League Cup
		6 December	Sheffield United	Football League
		20 December	Middlesbrough	Football League
		27 December	Coventry City	Football League
		10 January	Derby County	Football League
		21 January	Newcastle United	Football League Cup
		24 January	Stoke City (dated 7 January)	FA Cup
		31 January	Ipswich Town	Football League
		21 February	Stoke City	Football League
		24 February	Everton	Football League
		6 March	Norwich City	Football League
		16 March	Wolverhampton Wanderers	Football League
		20 March	Burnley	Football League
		23 March	Brighton & Hove Albion	Joe Kinnear Testimonial
		3 April	Arsenal	Football League
		5 April	Brann – cancelled	Friendly
		7 April	Norway XI - cancelled	Friendly
		17 April	Birmingham City	Football League
		21 April	North Herts XI (Stevenage)	Ray Dingwall Testimonial
		27 April	Toronto Metros-Croatia	Friendly
		1 May	Fijian Select XI (Lautoka)	Friendly
		3 May	Auckland FA XI (Auckland)	Friendly
		5 May	Wellington FA XI (Wellington)	Friendly
		9 May	Victoria (Melbourne)	Friendly
		12 May	Northern New South Wales (Newcastle)	Friendly
		16 May	Australian National XI (Sydney)	Friendly
		19 May	South Australia (Adelaide)	Friendly
		23 May	Western Australia (Perth)	Friendly

8 August
Bristol Rovers

23 March
Brighton & Hove Albion

5 April
Brann - cancelled

21 April
North Herts XI

3 May
Auckland FA XI

5 May
Wellington FA XI

16 May
Australian National XI

19 May
South Australia

23 May
Western Australia

1976-77

HOME

	Date	Opponent	Competition
☐☐	16 August	Royal Antwerp	Friendly
☐☐	25 August	Newcastle United	Football League
☐☐	28 August	Middlesbrough	Football League
☐☐	11 September	Leeds United	Football League
☐☐	22 September	Wrexham	Football League Cup
☐☐	25 September	Norwich City	Football League
☐☐	20 October	Birmingham City	Football League
☐☐	23 October	Coventry City	Football League
☐☐	30 October	Everton	Football League
☐☐	13 November	Bristol City	Football League
☐☐	23 November	Arsenal	Pat Jennings Test
☐☐	27 November	Stoke City	Football League
☐☐	11 December	Manchester City	Football League
☐☐	27 December	Arsenal	Football League
☐☐	1 January	West Ham United	Football League
☐☐	22 January	Ipswich Town	Football League
☐☐	12 February	Manchester United	Football League
☐☐	9 March	Liverpool	Football League
☐☐	12 March	West Bromwich Albion	Football League
☐☐	23 March	Derby County	Football League
☐☐	9 April	Queens Park Rangers	Football League
☐☐	16 April	Sunderland	Football League
☐☐	30 April	Aston Villa	Football League
☐☐	14 May	Leicester City	Football League

☐ Handbook ☐ Season Ticket

Season Ticket

Handbook

16 August
Royal Antwerp

28 August
Middlesbrough

22 September
Wrexham

30 October
Everton

23 November
Arsenal

27 December
Arsenal

12 February
Manchester United

9 March
Liverpool

9 April
Queens Park Rangers

14 May
Leicester City

1976-77

AWAY

Date	Opponent	Competition
24 July	VfL Osnabrück	Friendly
28 July	Eintracht Frankfurt	Friendly
31 July	1FC Cologne	Friendly
4 August	Baunatal	Friendly
6 August	Bad Honnef	Friendly
10 August	Swindon Town	Friendly
21 August	Ipswich Town	Football League
31 August	Middlesbrough	Football League Cup
4 September	Manchester United	Football League
18 September	Liverpool	Football League
2 October	West Bromwich Albion	Football League
9 October	Arsenal	Peter Simpson Testimonial
12 October	Napredak Kruševac	Friendly
16 October	Derby County	Football League
6 November	West Ham United	Football League
20 November	Sunderland	Football League
4 December	Aston Villa – postponed	Football League
18 December	Leicester City	Football League
3 January	Everton - postponed	Football League
8 January	Cardiff City	FA Cup
11 January	Queens Park Rangers (dated 29 December)	Football League
5 February	Middlesbrough	Football League
19 February	Leeds United	Football League
26 February	Newcastle United	Football League
5 March	Norwich City	Football League
19 March	Birmingham City	Football League
26 March	Everton	Football League
2 April	Coventry City	Football League
11 April	Arsenal	Football League
12 April	Bristol City	Football League
20 April	Aston Villa	Football League
23 April	Stoke City	Football League
7 May	Manchester City	Football League
17 May	Stord	Friendly
19 May	Sogndal	Friendly

28 July
Eintracht Frankfurt

4 August
Baunatal

Honnefer Fußballverein
1919 e.V.
Stadionpost

Welcome Spurs!

6 August
Bad Honnef

SWINDON TOWN FOOTBALL CLUB, THE COUNTY GROUND, SWINDON.
PRE-SEASON FRIENDLY MATCH

-0-0-0-0-0-0-0-0-0-0-0-0-0-0-0-0-

SWINDON TOWN V TOTTENHAM H/SPUR

Tuesday, 10th August, 1976

Kick-off:- 7.30 p.m.

-0-0-0-0-0-0-0-0-0-0-0-0-0-0-0-0-0-0-0-0-0-0-0-0-0-0-0-0-0-0-0-0-0-0-0-0-

OFFICIAL PROGRAMME PRICE TWO PENCE

-0-0-0-0-0-0-0-0-0-0-0-0-0-0-0-0-0-0-0-0-0-0-0-0-0-0-0-0-0-0-0-0-0-0-0-0-

SWINDON TOWN		TOTTENHAM H/SPUR
1. ALLEN J.		1. JENNINGS P.
2. McLAUGHLIN J.		2. NAYLOR T.
3. TAYLOR T.		3. McALLISTER D.
4. STROUD R.		4. PRATT J.
5. AIZLEWOOD S.	Referee	5. YOUNG
6. PROPHETT C.	Mr. T. Spencer.	6. OSGOOD K.
7. [illegible]		7. COATES R.
8. DIXON W.	Linesmen	8. PERRYMAN S.
9. GODDARD H.	Mr. P. Ackrill.	9. JONES C.
10. O'BRIEN G.	Mr. B. Uzzle.	10. ARMSTRONG
11. ANDERSON T.		11. NEIGHBOUR J.

Subs. GREEN A.
ROGERS D.
LYNCH S.

-0-0-0-0-0-0-0-0-0-0-0-0-0-0-0-0-0-

MATCH BALL DONATED BY
THE SWINDON & DISTRICT GROUP OF THE INSTITUTE OF ADVANCED MOTORISTS.

-0-0-0-0-0-0-0-0-0-0-0-0-0-0-

NEXT MATCH AT THE COUNTY GROUND
LEAGUE CUP I

SWINDON TOWN V NORTHAMPTON TOWN
SATURDAY, AUGUST 14th, 1976

Kick-off at 3.00 p.m.

10 August
Swindon Town

4 September
Manchester United

18 September
Liverpool

9 October
Arsenal

4 December
Aston Villa - postponed

3 January
Everton - postponed

8 January
Cardiff City

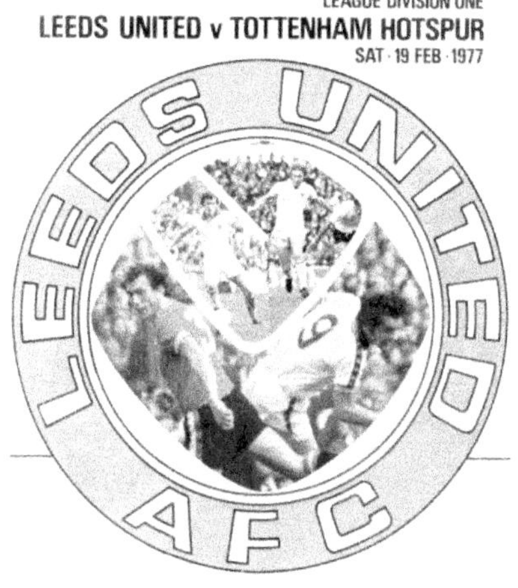

19 February
Leeds United

7 May
Manchester City

1977-78

HOME

Date	Opponent	Competition
20 August	Sheffield United	Football League
27 August	Notts County	Football League
31 August	Wimbledon	Football League Cup
10 September	Fulham	Football League
24 September	Luton Town	Football League
8 October	Oldham Athletic	Football League
22 October	Bristol Rovers	Football League
26 October	Coventry City	Football League Cup
5 November	Burnley	Football League
19 November	Brighton & Hove Albion	Football League
3 December	Southampton	Football League
17 December	Crystal Palace	Football League
27 December	Mansfield Town	Football League
31 December	Blackburn Rovers	Football League
7 January	Bolton Wanderers	FA Cup
21 January	Cardiff City	Football League
11 February	Blackpool	Football League
25 February	Orient	Football League
11 March	Charlton Athletic	Football League
22 March	Stoke City	Football League
27 March	Millwall	Football League
8 April	Bolton Wanderers	Football League
22 April	Sunderland	Football League
26 April	Hull City	Football League
12 May	Arsenal	John Pratt Testimonial

☐ Handbook

☐ Season Ticket

Season Ticket

Handbook

20 August
Sheffield United

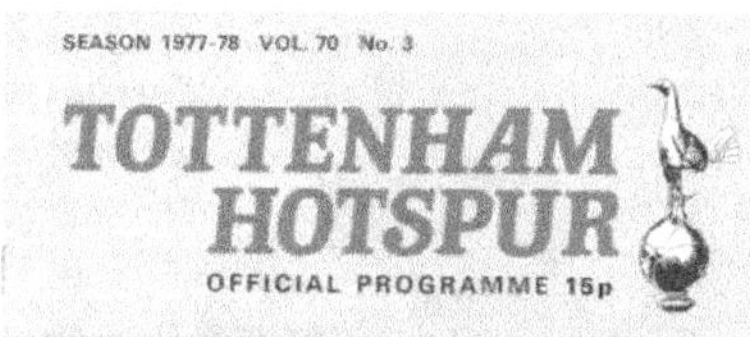

WIMBLEDON

Football League Cup, 2nd Round
Wednesday, 31st August, 1977 Kick-off 7.30 p.m.

31 August
Wimbledon

Football League, Division Two
Saturday, 22nd October, 1977 Kick-off 3.00 p.m.

BRISTOL ROVERS

22 October
Bristol Rovers

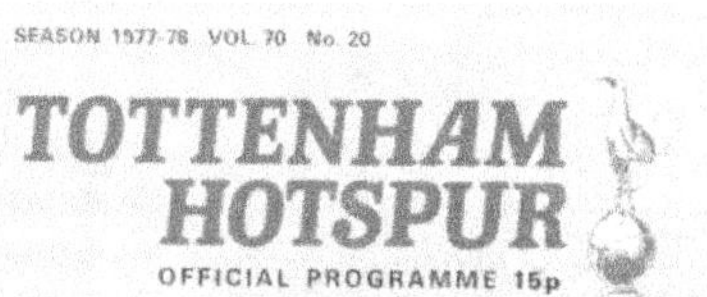

Football League, Division Two
Saturday, 19th November, 1977 Kick-off 3.00 p.m.

BRIGHTON AND HOVE ALBION

19 November
Brighton & Hove Albion

Football League, Division Two
Tuesday, 27th December, 1977 Kick-off 3.00 p.m.

MANSFIELD TOWN

27 December
Mansfield Town

Football League, Division Two
Saturday, 21st January, 1978 Kick-off 3.00 p.m.

CARDIFF CITY

21 January
Cardiff City

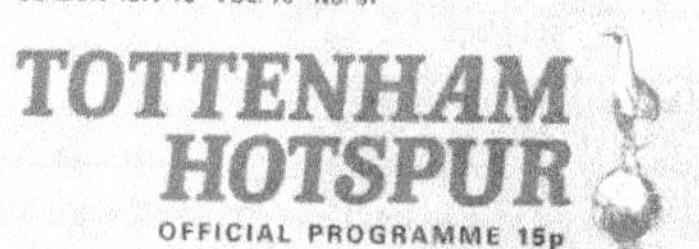

Football League, Division Two
Saturday, 25th February, 1978 Kick-off 3.00 p.m.

ORIENT

25 February
Orient

Football League Division Two
Monday, 27th March, 1978 Kick-off 3.00 p.m.

MILLWALL

27 March
Millwall

Football League Division Two
Wednesday, 26th April, 1978 Kick-off 7.30 p.m.

HULL CITY

26 April
Hull City

12 May
Arsenal

1977-78

AWAY

	Date	Opponent	Competition
☐	{ 7 August	Royal Union (Umeå)	Nolia Cup
☐	{ 10 August	Leicester City (Umeå)	Nolia Cup
☐	12 August	Norsjö IF	Friendly
☐	24 August	Blackburn Rovers	Football League
☐	3 September	Cardiff City	Football League
☐	17 September	Blackpool	Football League
☐	1 October	Orient	Football League
☐	4 October	Hull City	Football League
☐	15 October	Charlton Athletic	Football League
☐	29 October	Stoke City	Football League
☐	12 November	Crystal Palace	Football League
☐	22 November	Arsenal	Pat Rice Testimonial
☐	26 November	Bolton Wanderers	Football League
☐	10 December	Sunderland	Football League
☐	26 December	Millwall	Football League
☐	2 January	Sheffield United	Football League
☐	10 January	Bolton Wanderers	FA Cup
☐	14 January	Notts County	Football League
☐	4 February	Fulham	Football League
☐	22 February	Luton Town	Football League
☐	4 March	Oldham Athletic	Football League
☐	18 March	Bristol Rovers	Football League
☐	25 March	Mansfield Town	Football League
☐	1 April	Burnley	Football League
☐	15 April	Brighton & Hove Albion	Football League
☐	29 April	Southampton	Football League
☐	3 May	Truro City	Opening of Ground
☐	5 May	Orient	Angell & Blower Testimonial
☐	8 May	Aleppo	Friendly
☐	10 May	Syrian Police (Damascus)	Friendly
☐	15 May	Ham Kam	Friendly
☐	17 May	Kvik Halden	Friendly
☐	18 May	Karlstad	Friendly

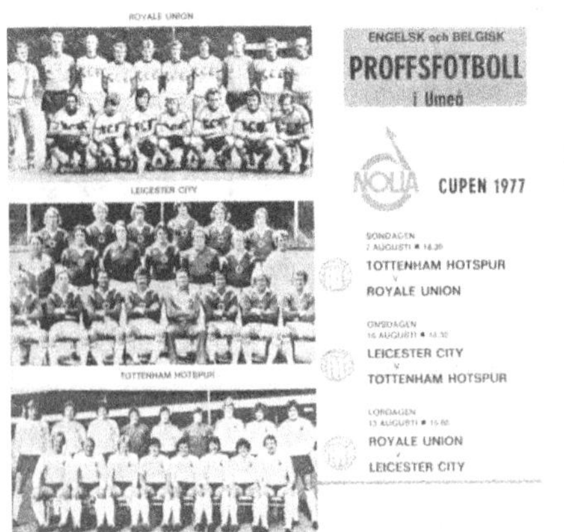

7 & 10 August
Nolia Cup

12 August
Norsjö IF

24 August
Blackburn Rovers

4 October
Hull City

22 November
Arsenal

10 January
Bolton Wanderers

25 March
Mansfield Town

SOUVENIR PROGRAMME
Grand Opening of New Ground

TRURO CITY AFC
v
TOTTENHAM
HOTSPUR

at
TREYEW ROAD, TRURO
on
WEDNESDAY 3rd MAY 1978
K.O. 6.45 p.m.

PROGRAMME 20p

3 May
Truro City

5 May
Orient

PROGRAM

HAM KAM
MØTER
TOTTENHAM
HOTSPUR

mandag 15/5 kl. 18.00

15 May
Ham Kam

VENNSKAPSKAMP I FOTBALL
Tottenham Hotspur - London
F. K. Kvik - Halden

Halden Stadion • 17. mai kl. 17.30

17 May
Kvik Halden

INTERNATIONELL MATCH
PA TINGVALLA 18 MAJ 1978

TOTTENHAM
●
KARLSTAD BK

ETT NWT ARRANGEMANG

GRAND HOTELL I KARLSTAD · V:A TORGGATAN 8
Tel. 054-11 52 40
Moderna rum till humana priser · frukost inkl
Festvåning · konferensrum · uppackningsrum
Egen parkering

18 May
Karlstad

1978-79

HOME

	Date	Opponent	Competition
☐☐	20 August	Official Players' Open Day (Cheshunt)	
☐☐	23 August	Aston Villa	Football League
☐☐	26 August	Chelsea	Football League
☐☐	6 September	Swansea City	Football League Cup
☐☐	9 September	Bristol City	Football League
☐☐	30 September	Coventry City	Football League
☐☐	14 October	Birmingham City	Football League
☐☐	28 October	Bolton Wanderers	Football League
☐☐	11 November	Nottingham Forest	Football League
☐☐	22 November	Liverpool	Football League
☐☐	25 November	Wolverhampton Wanderers	Football League
☐☐	9 December	Ipswich Town	Football League
☐☐	23 December	Arsenal	Football League
☐☐	1 January	Southampton - postponed	Football League
☐☐	10 January	Altrincham (dated 6 January)	FA Cup
☐☐	20 January	Leeds United	Football League
☐☐	3 February	Manchester City	Football League
☐☐	12 February	Wrexham	FA Cup
☐☐	3 March	Derby County	Football League
☐☐	10 March	Manchester United	FA Cup
☐☐	17 March	Norwich City	Football League
☐☐	28 March	Southampton	Football League
☐☐	7 April	Middlesbrough	Football League
☐☐	14 April	Queens Park Rangers	Football League
☐☐	21 April	Manchester United	Football League
☐☐	30 April	West Ham United	Steve Perryman Testimonial
☐☐	5 May	Everton	Football League
☐☐	14 May	West Bromwich Albion	Football League

☐ Handbook ☐ Season Ticket

Season Ticket

Handbook

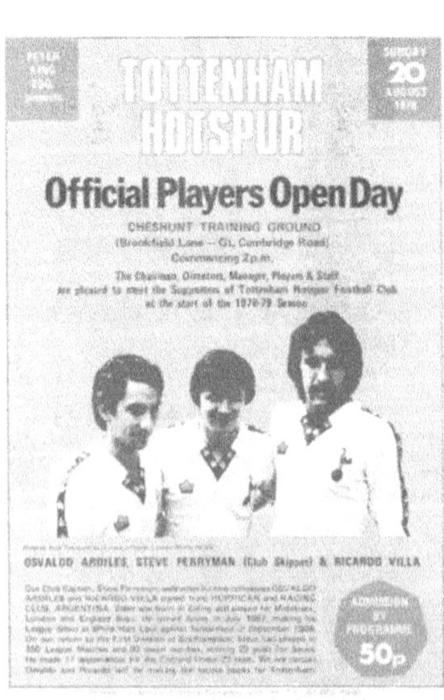

20 August
Official Players Open Day

23 August
Aston Villa

30 September
Coventry City

22 November
Liverpool

23 December
Arsenal

1 January
Southampton - postponed

10 March
Manchester United

7 April
Middlesbrough

30 April
West Ham United

14 May
West Bromwich Albion

1978-79

AWAY

5 August	Aberdeen	Friendly
8 August	Royal Antwerp	Friendly
10 August	VVV Venlo	Friendly
12 August	Bohemians	Friendly
19 August	Nottingham Forest	Football League
29 August	Swansea City	Football League Cup
2 September	Liverpool	Football League
16 September	Leeds United	Football League
19 September	Aldershot	John Anderson Testimonial
23 September	Manchester City	Football League
26 September	IFK Göteborg	Friendly
7 October	West Bromwich Albion	Football League
9 October	Saudi Arabian XI (Jeddah)	Friendly
16 October	Wolverhampton Wanderers	John McAlle Testimonial
21 October	Derby County	Football League
4 November	Norwich City	Football League
18 November	Chelsea	Football League
4 December	West Ham United	Billy Bonds Testimonial
16 December	Manchester United	Football League
18 December	Al Nasr	Friendly
26 December	Queens Park Rangers	Football League
30 December	Everton	Football League
13 January	Bristol City	Football League
16 January	Altrincham (Maine Road)	FA Cup
10 February	Coventry City	Football League
21 February	Wrexham (dated 15 February)	FA Cup
24 February	Birmingham City	Football League
28 February	Oldham Athletic	FA Cup
14 March	Manchester United	FA Cup
24 March	Aston Villa	Football League
31 March	Middlesbrough	Football League
3 April	Wolverhampton Wanderers	Football League
10 April	Arsenal	Football League
16 April	Southampton	Football League
24 April	Queens Park Rangers	Ian Gillard Testimonial
	- brochure	
28 April	Ipswich Town	Football League
8 May	Bolton Wanderers	Football League
11 May	Gillingham	Graham Knight Testimonial
16 May	Kuwait Army XI	Friendly
23 May	Malaysian Select XI (Kuala Lumpur)	Friendly
{ 27 May	Indonesia (Yokohama)	Japan Cup
{ 29 May	Japan "A" (Tokyo)	Japan Cup
{ 31 May	Fiorentina (Nishigaoka)	Japan Cup
{ 2 June	San Lorenzo (Tokyo)	Japan Cup
{ 4 June	Dundee United (Tokyo)	Japan Cup
6 June	Bermuda Select XI (Hamilton)	Friendly

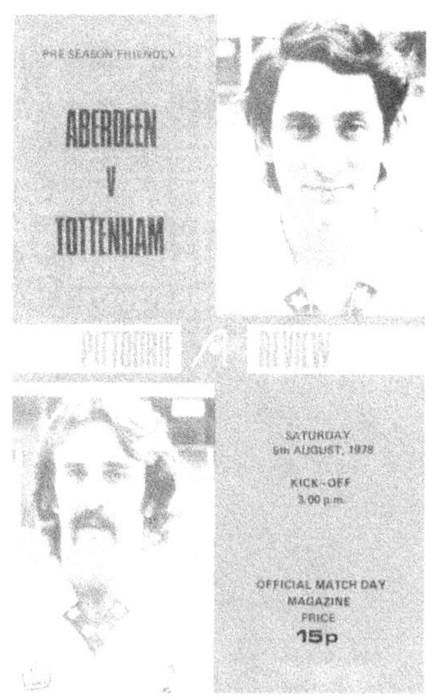

5 August
Aberdeen

8 August
Royal Antwerp

12 August
Bohemians

19 September
Aldershot

26 September
IFK Göteborg

18 December
Al Nasr

24 April
Queens Park Rangers

24 April
Queens Park Rangers - brochure

27 May – 4 June
Japan Cup

1979-80

HOME

	Date	Opponent	Competition
☐☐	18 August	Middlesbrough	Football League
☐☐	29 August	Manchester United	Football League Cup
☐☐	1 September	Manchester City	Football League
☐☐	2 September	Open Day (Cheshunt)	
☐☐	8 September	Brighton & Hove Albion	Football League
☐☐	22 September	West Bromwich Albion	Football League
☐☐	10 October	Norwich City	Football League
☐☐	13 October	Derby County	Football League
☐☐	27 October	Nottingham Forest	Football League
☐☐	10 November	Bolton Wanderers	Football League
☐☐	1 December	Manchester United	Football League
☐☐	15 December	Aston Villa	Football League
☐☐	29 December	Stoke City	Football League
☐☐	1 January	Wolverhampton Wanderers - postponed	Football League
☐☐	5 January	Manchester United	FA Cup
☐☐	30 January	Swindon Town	FA Cup
☐☐	2 February	Southampton	Football League
☐☐	16 February	Birmingham City	FA Cup
☐☐	27 February	Coventry City	Football League
☐☐	1 March	Leeds United	Football League
☐☐	8 March	Liverpool	FA Cup
☐☐	15 March	Crystal Palace	Football League
☐☐	29 March	Liverpool	Football League
☐☐	2 April	Ipswich Town	Football League
☐☐	7 April	Arsenal	Football League
☐☐	19 April	Everton	Football League
☐☐	23 April	Wolverhampton Wanderers	Football League
☐☐	29 April	Crystal Palace	Terry Naylor Testimonial
☐☐	3 May	Bristol City	Football League

☐ Handbook ☐ Season Ticket

Season Ticket

Handbook

18 August
Middlesbrough

2 September
Open Day

22 September
West Bromwich Albion

10 November
Bolton Wanderers

29 December
Stoke City

1 January
Wolverhampton Wanderers - post

8 March
Liverpool

7 April
Arsenal

29 April
Crystal Palace

3 May
Bristol City

1979-80

AWAY

Date	Opponent	Competition
2 August	Gillingham	Friendly
4 August	Oxford United	Friendly
7 August	Dundee United	Friendly
8 August	Aberdeen	Friendly
11 August	Orient	Friendly
22 August	Norwich City	Football League
25 August	Stoke City	Football League
5 September	Manchester United	Football League Cup
15 September	Southampton	Football League
29 September	Coventry City	Football League
6 October	Crystal Palace	Football League
20 October	Leeds United	Football League
3 November	Middlesbrough	Football League
6 November	Widad	Friendly
17 November	Liverpool	Football League
24 November	Everton	Football League
8 December	Bristol City	Football League
21 December	Ipswich Town	Football League
26 December	Arsenal	Football League
9 January	Manchester United	FA Cup
12 January	Manchester City	Football League
19 January	Brighton & Hove Albion	Football League
26 January	Swindon Town	FA Cup
9 February	West Bromwich Albion	Football League
23 February	Derby County	Football League
11 March	Nottingham Forest	Football League
22 March	Bolton Wanderers	Football League
5 April	Wolverhampton Wanderers	Football League
12 April	Manchester United	Football League
15 April	Crystal Palace	Martin Hinshelwood Testimonial
26 April	Aston Villa	Football League
5 May	Bournemouth	Keith Miller Testimonial
7 May	Hertford Town	Opening of Lights
11 May	Rapid/FC Austria XI (Vienna)	Friendly
13 May	Gais/Sturm Select XI (Graz)	Friendly

2 August
Gillingham

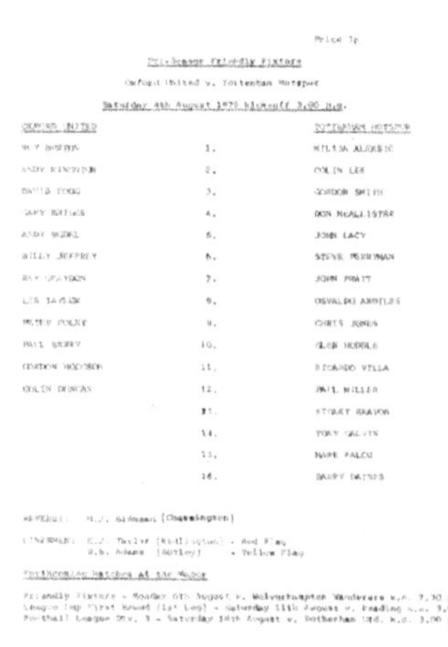
Pre-Season Friendly Fixture

Oxford United v. Tottenham Hotspur

Saturday 4th August 1979 Kick-off 3.00 p.m.

Oxford United		Tottenham Hotspur
[illegible]	1.	Milija Aleksic
[illegible]	2.	Colin Lee
[illegible]	3.	Gordon Smith
[illegible]	4.	Don McAllister
[illegible]	5.	John Lacy
Billy Jeffrey	6.	Steve Perryman
[illegible]	7.	John Pratt
Les Taylor	8.	Osvaldo Ardiles
Peter Foley	9.	Chris Jones
[illegible]	10.	Glen Hoddle
Gordon Hodgson	11.	Ricardo Villa
Colin Duncan	12.	Paul Miller
	13.	Stuart Beavon
	14.	Tony Galvin
	15.	Mark Falco
	16.	Barry Daines

[illegible]

4 August
Oxford United

8 August
Aberdeen

11 August
Orient

5 September
Manchester United

17 November
Liverpool

8 December
Bristol City

9 January
Manchester United

26 January
Swindon Town

15 April
Crystal Palace

5 May
Bournemouth

7 May
Hertford Town

1980-81

HOME

	Date	Opponent	Competition
☐☐	16 August	Nottingham Forest	Football League
☐☐	23 August	Brighton & Hove Albion	Football League
☐☐	31 August	Family Fun Day (Cheshunt)	
☐☐	3 September	Orient	Football League Cup
☐☐	6 September	Manchester United	Football League
☐☐	20 September	Sunderland	Football League
☐☐	24 September	Crystal Palace	Football League Cup
☐☐	11 October	Middlesbrough	Football League
☐☐	25 October	Coventry City	Football League
☐☐	4 November	Arsenal	Football League Cup
☐☐	8 November	Wolverhampton Wanderers	Football League
☐☐	12 November	Crystal Palace	Football League
☐☐	29 November	West Bromwich Albion	Football League
☐☐	13 December	Manchester City	Football League
☐☐	17 December	Ipswich Town	Football League
☐☐	26 December	Southampton	Football League
☐☐	7 January	Queens Park Rangers	FA Cup
☐☐	10 January	Birmingham City	Football League
☐☐	17 January	Arsenal	Football League
☐☐	24 January	Hull City	FA Cup
☐☐	7 February	Leeds United	Football League
☐☐	14 February	Coventry City	FA Cup
☐☐	21 February	Leicester City	Football League
☐☐	7 March	Exeter City	FA Cup
☐☐	11 March	Stoke City	Football League
☐☐	21 March	Aston Villa	Football League
☐☐	4 April	Everton	Football League
☐☐	18 April	Norwich City	Football League
☐☐	25 April	Liverpool	Football League
☐☐	11 May	West Ham United	Barry Daines Testimonial

☐ Handbook ☐ Season Ticket

Season Ticket

Handbook

16 August
Nottingham Forest

31 August
Family Fun Day

24 September
Crystal Palace

8 November
Wolverhampton Wanderers

29 November
West Bromwich Albion

26 December
Southampton

17 January
Arsenal

14 February
Coventry City

18 April
Norwich City

11 May
West Ham United

1980-81

AWAY

	Date	Opponent	Competition
☐☐	28 July	Southend United	Friendly
☐☐	30 July	Portsmouth	Friendly
☐☐	2 August	PSV (Beilen)	Friendly
☐☐	4 August	Rangers	Friendly
☐☐	5 August	Dundee United	Friendly
☐☐	8 August	Swansea City	Friendly
☐☐	19 August	Crystal Palace	Football League
☐☐	27 August	Orient	Football League Cup
☐☐	30 August	Arsenal	Football League
☐☐	13 September	Leeds United	Football League
☐☐	27 September	Leicester City	Football League
☐☐	30 September	Crystal Palace	Football League Cup
☐☐	4 October	Stoke City	Football League
☐☐	18 October	Aston Villa	Football League
☐☐	22 October	Manchester City	Football League
☐☐	1 November	Everton	Football League
☐☐	15 November	Nottingham Forest	Football League
☐☐	17 November	Weymouth	Friendly
☐☐	22 November	Birmingham City	Football League
☐☐	2 December	West Ham United	Football League Cup
☐☐	6 December	Liverpool	Football League
☐☐	20 December	Middlesbrough	Football League
☐☐	27 December	Norwich City	Football League
☐☐	3 January	Queens Park Rangers	FA Cup
☐☐	31 January	Brighton & Hove Albion	Football League
☐☐	2 February	Rothmans Combination XI (Jersey)	Friendly
☐☐	17 February	Manchester United	Football League
☐☐	28 February	Sunderland	Football League
☐☐	14 March	Ipswich Town	Football League
☐☐	28 March	Coventry City	Football League
☐☐	11 April	Wolverhampton Wanderers (Hillsborough)	FA Cup
☐☐	15 April	Wolverhampton Wanderers (Highbury)	FA Cup
☐☐	20 April	Southampton	Football League
☐☐	30 April	Wolverhampton Wanderers	Football League
☐☐	2 May	West Bromwich Albion	Football League
☐☐	9 May	Manchester City (Wembley)	FA Cup
☐☐	14 May	Manchester City (Wembley)	FA Cup
☐☐	24 May	Bahrain Select XI (Isa Town)	Friendly
☐☐	26 May	Kuwait Army XI	Friendly
☐☐	28 May	Bahrain Select XI (Isa Town)	Friendly
☐☐	10 June	Trabzonspor	Friendly
☐☐	13 June	Fenerbahçe	Friendly

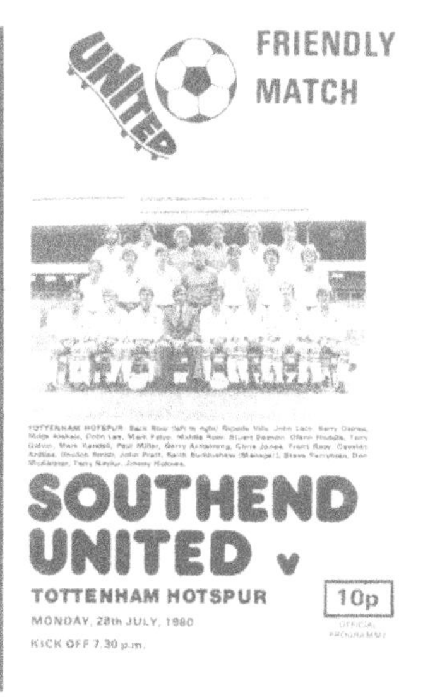

28 July
Southend United

30 July
Portsmouth

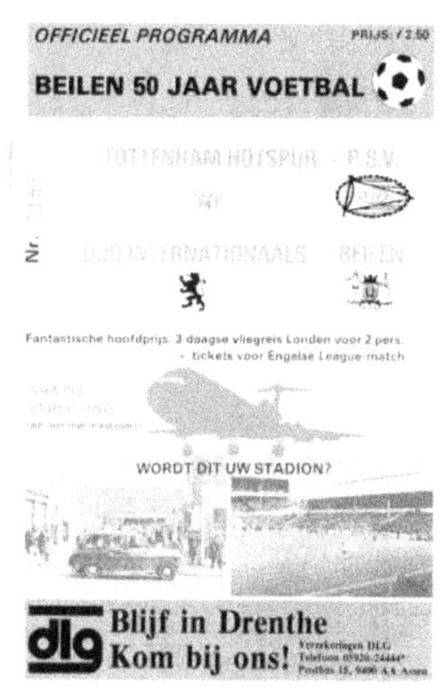

2 August
PSV

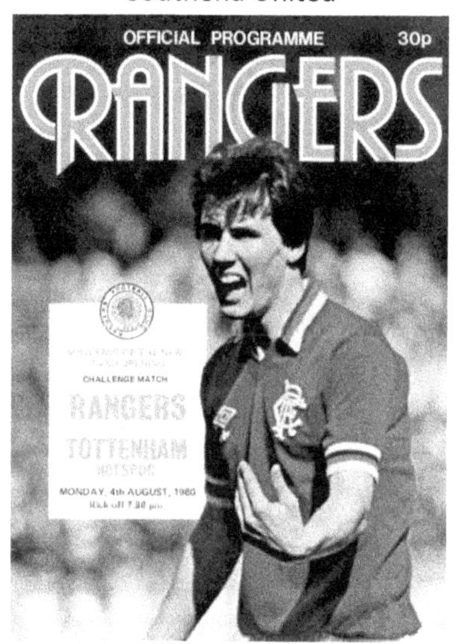

4 August
Rangers

5 August
Dundee United

8 August
Swansea City

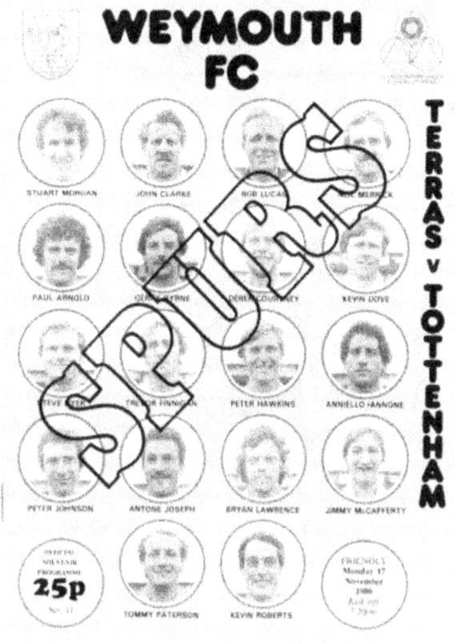

17 November
Weymouth

2 February
Rothmans Combination XI

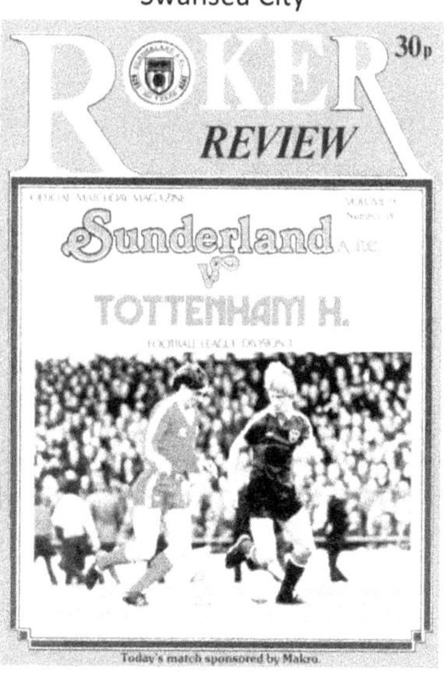

28 February
Sunderland

1981-82

HOME

Date	Opponent	Competition
23 August	Players' Family Open Day (Cheshunt)	
2 September	West Ham United	Football League
5 September	Aston Villa	Football League
19 September	Everton	Football League
29 September	Ajax	European Cup-Winners' Cup
3 October	Nottingham Forest	Football League
7 October	Manchester United	Football League Cup
10 October	Stoke City	Football League
24 October	Brighton & Hove Albion	Football League
4 November	Dundalk	European Cup-Winners' Cup
7 November	West Bromwich Albion	Football League
11 November	Wrexham	Football League Cup
21 November	Manchester United	Football League
2 December	Fulham	Football League Cup
5 December	Coventry City	Football League
28 December	Arsenal - postponed	Football League
2 January	Arsenal	FA Cup
18 January	Nottingham Forest	Football League Cup
23 January	Leeds United	FA Cup
27 January	Middlesbrough	Football League
6 February	Wolverhampton Wanderers	Football League
10 February	West Bromwich Albion	Football League Cup
13 February	Aston Villa	FA Cup
20 February	Manchester City	Football League
3 March	Eintracht Frankfurt	European Cup-Winners' Cup
20 March	Southampton	Football League
29 March	Arsenal	Football League
7 April	Barcelona	European Cup-Winners' Cup
10 April	Ipswich Town	Football League
14 April	Sunderland	Football League
24 April	Notts County	Football League
28 April	Birmingham City	Football League
3 May	Liverpool	Football League
5 May	Swansea City	Football League
8 May	Leeds United	Football League

☐ Handbook ☐ Season Ticket

Season Ticket

Handbook

23 August
Players Family Open Day

5 September
Aston Villa

24 October
Brighton & Hove Albion

21 November
Manchester United

28 December
Arsenal - postponed

23 January
Leeds United

6 February
Wolverhampton Wanderers

10 April
Ipswich Town

5 May
Swansea City

8 May
Leeds United

1981-82

AWAY

	Date	Opponent	Competition
☐☐	8 August	Glentoran	Friendly
☐☐	10 August	Limerick	Friendly
☐☐	12 August	Norwich City	Friendly
☐☐	16 August	Aberdeen	Willie Miller Testimonial
☐☐	22 August	Aston Villa (Wembley)	FA Charity Shield
☐☐	29 August	Middlesbrough	Football League
☐☐	12 September	Wolverhampton Wanderers	Football League
☐☐	16 September	Ajax	European Cup-Winners' Cup
☐☐	22 September	Swansea City	Football League
☐☐	26 September	Manchester City	Football League
☐☐	12 October	Luton Town	Paul Price Testimonial
☐☐	17 October	Sunderland	Football League
☐☐	21 October	Dundalk	European Cup-Winners' Cup
☐☐	28 October	Manchester United	Football League Cup
☐☐	31 October	Southampton	Football League
☐☐	14 November	Israel Select XI (Jaffa)	Friendly
☐☐	28 November	Notts County	Football League
☐☐	12 December	Leeds United	Football League
☐☐	22 December	Plymouth Argyle	Friendly
☐☐	29 December	Sporting Clube de Portugal	Friendly
☐☐	9 January	West Ham United - postponed	Football League
☐☐	30 January	Everton	Football League
☐☐	3 February	West Bromwich Albion	Football League Cup
☐☐	17 February	Aston Villa	Football League
☐☐	22 February	Rothmans Combination XI (Jersey)	Friendly
☐☐	27 February	Stoke City	Football League
☐☐	6 March	Chelsea	FA Cup
☐☐	9 March	Brighton & Hove Albion	Football League
☐☐	13 March	Liverpool (Wembley)	Football League Cup
☐☐	17 March	Eintracht Frankfurt	European Cup-Winners' Cup
☐☐	23 March	Birmingham City	Football League
☐☐	27 March	West Bromwich Albion	Football League
☐☐	3 April	Leicester City (Villa Park)	FA Cup
☐☐	12 April	Arsenal	Football League
☐☐	17 April	Manchester United	Football League
☐☐	21 April	Barcelona	European Cup-Winners' Cup
☐☐	1 May	Coventry City	Football League
☐☐	10 May	West Ham United	Football League
☐☐	12 May	Nottingham Forest	Football League
☐☐	15 May	Liverpool	Football League
☐☐	17 May	Ipswich Town	Football League
☐☐	22 May	Queens Park Rangers (Wembley)	FA Cup
☐☐	27 May	Queens Park Rangers (Wembley)	FA Cup

8 August
Glentoran

10 August
Limerick United

12 August
Norwich City

16 August
Aberdeen

12 October
Luton Town

22 December
Plymouth Argyle

9 January
West Ham United - postponed

22 February
Rothmans Combination XI

9 March
Brighton & Hove Albion

1982-83

HOME

	Date	Opponent	Competition
☐☐	28 August	Luton Town	Football League
☐☐	8 September	Southampton	Football League
☐☐	11 September	Manchester City	Football League
☐☐	25 September	Nottingham Forest	Football League
☐☐	28 September	Coleraine	European Cup-Winners' Cup
☐☐	6 October	Brighton & Hove Albion	Milk Cup
☐☐	9 October	Coventry City	Football League
☐☐	20 October	Bayern Munich	European Cup-Winners' Cup
☐☐	23 October	Notts County	Football League
☐☐	6 November	Watford	Football League
☐☐	20 November	West Ham United	Football League
☐☐	1 December	Luton Town	Milk Cup
☐☐	4 December	West Bromwich Albion	Football League
☐☐	18 December	Birmingham City	Football League
☐☐	28 December	Brighton & Hove Albion	Football League
☐☐	3 January	Everton	Football League
☐☐	8 January	Southampton	FA Cup
☐☐	19 January	Burnley	Milk Cup
☐☐	22 January	Sunderland	Football League
☐☐	29 January	West Bromwich Albion	FA Cup
☐☐	12 February	Swansea City	Football League
☐☐	26 February	Norwich City	Football League
☐☐	23 March	Aston Villa	Football League
☐☐	4 April	Arsenal	Football League
☐☐	16 April	Ipswich Town	Football League
☐☐	30 April	Liverpool	Football League
☐☐	11 May	Manchester United	Football League
☐☐	14 May	Stoke City	Football League

☐ Handbook ☐ Season Ticket

Season Ticket

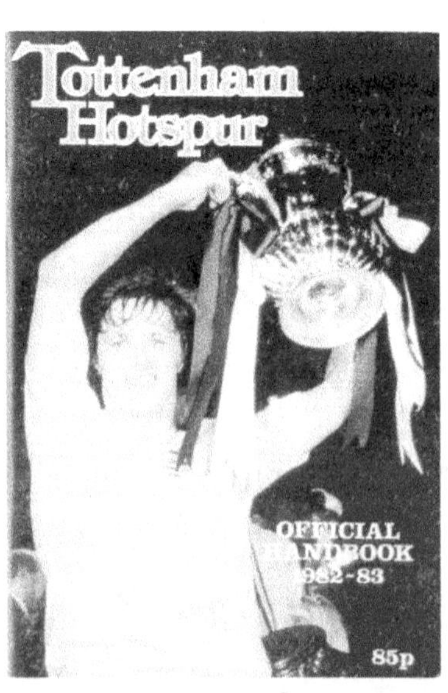

Handbook

28August
Luton Town

25 September
Nottingham Forest

23 October
Notts County

20 November
West Ham United

18 December
Birmingham City

8 January
Southampton

29 January
West Bromwich Albion

26 February
Norwich City

16 April
Ipswich Town

14 May
Stoke City

1982-83

AWAY

Date	Opponent	Competition
3 August	Scunthorpe United	Friendly
6 August	Lausanne-Sports	Friendly
8 August	Rangers	Friendly
13 August	Ajax	Amsterdam 707 Tournament
15 August	1FC Cologne (Amsterdam)	Amsterdam 707 Tournament
21 August	Liverpool (Wembley)	FA Charity Shield
31 August	Ipswich Town	Football League
4 September	Everton	Football League
15 September	Coleraine	European Cup-Winners' Cup
18 September	Sunderland	Football League
20 September	Barnet	Steve Brinkman Benefit
2 October	Swansea City	Football League
16 October	Norwich City	Football League
26 October	Brighton & Hove Albion	Milk Cup
30 October	Aston Villa	Football League
3 November	Bayern Munich	European Cup-Winners' Cup
9 November	Gillingham	Milk Cup
13 November	Manchester United	Football League
27 November	Liverpool	Football League
11 December	Stoke City	Football League
20 December	Borussia Monchengladbach (Tel Aviv)	Friendly
22 December	Israel Select XI (Tel Aviv)	Friendly
27 December	Arsenal	Football League
1 January	West Ham United	Football League
15 January	Luton Town	Football League
5 February	Manchester City	Football League
19 February	Everton	FA Cup
5 March	Notts County	Football League
12 March	Coventry City	Football League
19 March	Watford	Football League
26 March	Northerners' Athletic	Friendly
2 April	Brighton & Hove Albion	Football League
9 April	Nottingham Forest	Football League
19 April	Bristol Rovers	Centenary
23 April	West Bromwich Albion	Football League
3 May	Southampton	Football League
7 May	Birmingham City	Football League
17 May	Trinidad & Tobago (Port of Spain)	Friendly
20 May	ASL Trinidad	Friendly
23 May	Charlton Athletic	Colin Powell Testimonial
30 May	Aalesunds	Friendly
{ 4 June	Manchester United (Lobamba)	Royal Swazi Hotel Tournament
{ 11 June	Manchester United (Lobamba)	Royal Swazi Hotel Tournament

SCUNTHORPE UNITED

versus

TOTTENHAM HOTSPUR

(FA Cup Holders)

TUESDAY, 3rd AUGUST, 1982

OFFICIAL SOUVENIR PROGRAMME 25p

Kick off 7.30 p.m. Ground opens 6 p.m.

3 August
Scunthorpe United

LAUSANNE-SPORTS

LAUSANNE - SPORTS x TOTTENHAM HOTSPUR

Lausanne-Sports :	Tottenham Hotspur FC :
1. BURGENER Guy	1. CLEMENCE Ray
2. RAMSEY Ura	2. HUGHTON Chris
17. RYF Claude	3. MILLER Paul
4. BIZZINI Lucio	4. MABBUTT Gary
5. CHAPUISAT P.Albert	5. LACY John
14. PARIETTI Marcel (capt.)	6. BROOKE Gary
18. SCHEIWILER Fredy	7. ROBERTS Graham
15. PELLEGRINI Walter	8. ARCHIBALD Steve
9. KOK Robert	9. FALCO Mark
10. DI RAVELLO Robert	10. HODDLE Glenn (capt.)
11. DIERRENS Georges	11. CROOKS Garth
----	----
3. BATARDON Jean	12. GIBSON Terry
6. CASTELLA Gérard	14. CROOKE Ian
7. CRESCENZI Stéphane	15. O'REILLY Gary
8. DARIO John	GK. PARKS Tony
16. PFISTER Joko	
GK. MILANI Jean-Claude	

Arbitre : M. MACHERET - Juges de touche : MM. PICCAND / ABRISCHER

Ce match est organisé en collaboration avec le COQ SPORTIF

6 August
Lausanne-Sports

8 August
Rangers

13 & 15 August
Amsterdam 707 Tournament

20 September
Barnet

SOUVENIR PROGRAMME
Price: 25p

NORTHERNERS' ATHLETIC CLUB

vs.

TOTTENHAM HOTSPUR F.C.

AT CYCLING GROUNDS

SATURDAY
26th MARCH 1983

K.O. 4 p.m.

(LUCKY PROGRAMME WINNER WILL RECEIVE THE MATCH BALL, AUTOGRAPHED BY THE SPURS' PLAYERS)

LUCKY PROGRAMME Nº 1321

26 March
Northerners' Athletic

OFFICIAL OPENING

OF

1983/1984 FOOTBALL SEASON

TRINIDAD & TOBAGO CARIB FOOTBALL LEAGUE

AND

TRINIDAD & TOBAGO FOOTBALL ASSOCIATION

17TH MAY 1983

TOTTENHAM HOTSPUR -vs- T&T NATIONAL XI

AT THE

NATIONAL STADIUM

17 May
Trinidad & Tobago

KICK-OFF TIME: 8.00 p.m.

GAME: D.W.I.A. ASL SPORTS CLUB
-vs-
TOTTENHAM HOTSPUR

VENUE: QUEEN'S PARK OVAL

OFFICIALS: REFEREE: T. SIRIEDINGH

LINESMEN: J. DYER

G. DAY

4TH MAN: M. JOHN

DATE: MAY 20TH, 1983

20 May
ASL Trinidad

TOTTENHAM HOTSPUR

Soccer Safari

MANCHESTER UNITED

Classic

Commemorating the visit by Manchester United and Tottenham Hotspur to

SWAZILAND

JUNE 1983 · SPONSORED BY

Royal Swazi Hotel & Spa

SOUVENIR PROGRAMME R2,50

4 & 11 June
Royal Swazi Hotel Tournament

1983-84

HOME

Date	Opponent	Competition
21 August	West Ham United	Bill Nicholson Testimonial
	- white teamsheet	
	- yellow teamsheet	
29 August	Coventry City	Canon League
3 September	West Ham United	Canon League
17 September	Everton	Canon League
28 September	Drogheda United	UEFA Cup
2 October	Nottingham Forest	Canon League
	- teamsheet	
5 October	Lincoln City	Milk Cup
19 October	Feyenoord	UEFA Cup
29 October	Notts County	Canon League
9 November	Arsenal	Milk Cup
12 November	Liverpool	Canon League
26 November	Queens Park Rangers	Canon League
7 December	Bayern Munich	UEFA Cup
10 December	Southampton	Canon League
26 December	Arsenal	Canon League
2 January	Watford	Canon League
11 January	Fulham	FA Cup
14 January	Ipswich Town	Canon League
28 January	Norwich City	FA Cup
8 February	Sunderland	Canon League
11 February	Leicester City	Canon League
25 February	Birmingham City	Canon League
3 March	Stoke City	Canon League
7 March	FK Austria Vienna	UEFA Cup
17 March	West Bromwich Albion	Canon League
31 March	Wolverhampton Wanderers	Canon League
14 April	Luton Town	Canon League
18 April	Aston Villa	Canon League
25 April	Hajduk Split	UEFA Cup
5 May	Norwich City	Canon League
12 May	Manchester United	Canon League
23 May	Anderlecht	UEFA Cup
29 May	England XI	Keith Burkinshaw Testimonial

☐ Handbook

☐ Season Ticket

Season Ticket

Handbook

21 August
West Ham United

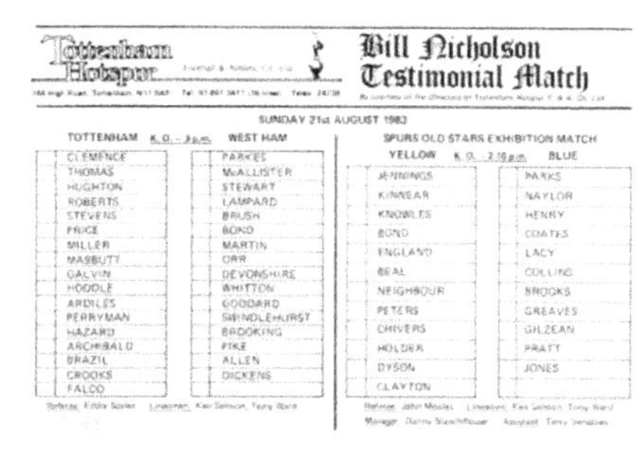

Tottenham Hotspur Football & Athletic Co. Ltd

Bill Nicholson Testimonial Match

SUNDAY 21st AUGUST 1983

TOTTENHAM K.O. – 3 p.m.	WEST HAM
CLEMENCE	PARKES
THOMAS	McALLISTER
HUGHTON	STEWART
ROBERTS	LAMPARD
STEVENS	BRUSH
PRICE	BOND
MILLER	MARTIN
MABBUTT	ORR
GALVIN	DEVONSHIRE
HODDLE	WHITTON
ARDILES	GODDARD
PERRYMAN	SWINDLEHURST
HAZARD	BROOKING
ARCHIBALD	PIKE
BRAZIL	ALLEN
CROOKS	DICKENS
FALCO	

SPURS OLD STARS EXHIBITION MATCH

YELLOW K.O. 2.10 p.m.	BLUE
JENNINGS	PARKS
KINNEAR	NAYLOR
KNOWLES	HENRY
BOND	COATES
ENGLAND	LACY
BEAL	COLLINS
NEIGHBOUR	BROOKS
PETERS	GREAVES
CHIVERS	GILZEAN
HOLDER	PRATT
DYSON	JONES
CLAYTON	

Abridged Particulars

Tottenham Hotspur plc

Offer for Sale by Sheppards and Chase of 3,800,000 new ordinary shares of 25p each at 100p per share payable in full on application

Tottenham Hotspur Football & Athletic Co. Ltd

748 High Road, Tottenham, N17 0AP. Tel: 01-801 3411 (16 lines) Telex: 24739

CANON LEAGUE – DIVISION 1

TOTTENHAM HOTSPUR v NOTTINGHAM FOREST

KICK-OFF – 2.35 p.m.

TOTTENHAM HOTSPUR	NOTTINGHAM FOREST
1 RAY CLEMENCE	1 HANS VAN BREUKELAN
2 CHRIS HUGHTON	2 VIV ANDERSON
3 TONY GALVIN	3 KENNY SWAIN
4 GRAHAM ROBERTS	4 COLIN TODD
5 GARY STEVENS	5 PAUL HART
6 STEVE PERRYMAN	6 IAN BOWYER
7 GARY MABBUTT	7 STEVEN WIGLEY
8 STEVE ARCHIBALD	8 IAN WALLACE
9 MARK FALCO	9 GARRY BIRTLES
10 GLENN HODDLE	10 STEVEN HODGE
11 ALAN BRAZIL	11 COLIN WALSH
Sub to be announced	Sub to be announced

Referee: A. ROBINSON (Portsmouth)

Linesmen: A.J. BUNCE (Oxford) and I.S. HEMLEY (Bedford)

Welcome home to White Hart Lane

21 August
West Ham United - teamsheet

2 October
Nottingham Forest

2 October
Nottingham Forest - teamsheet

5 October
Lincoln City

12 November
Liverpool

2 January
Watford

11 February
Leicester City

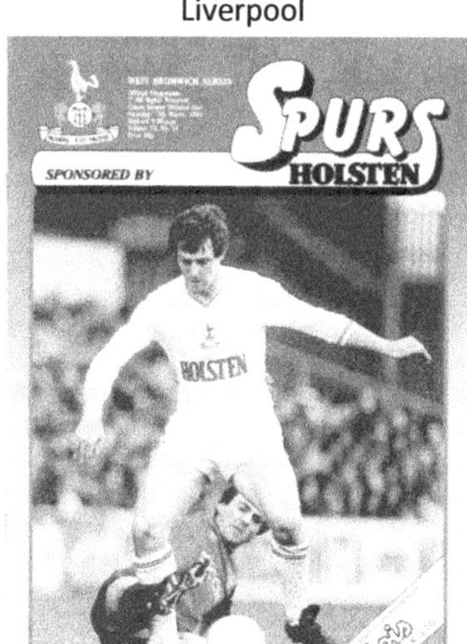

17 March
West Bromwich Albion

29 May
England XI

1983-84

AWAY

Date	Opponent	Competition
2 August	Hertford Town	Friendly
4 August	Enfield	Friendly
6 August	Brentford	Friendly
6 August	Aylesbury United	Friendly
9 August	Portsmouth	Friendly
12 August	Brighton & Hove Albion (dated 1982)	Friendly
16 August	Celtic	Friendly
17 August	Dundee United	Hamish McAlpine Testimonial
27 August	Ipswich Town	Canon League
7 September	West Bromwich Albion	Canon League
10 September	Leicester City	Canon League
14 September	Drogheda United	UEFA Cup
24 September	Watford	Canon League
8 October	Vale Recreation	Friendly
15 October	Wolverhampton Wanderers	Canon League
22 October	Birmingham City	Canon League
26 October	Lincoln City	Milk Cup
2 November	Feyenoord	UEFA Cup
5 November	Stoke City	Canon League
19 November	Luton Town	Canon League
23 November	Bayern Munich	UEFA Cup
	- Die Blaue issue	
3 December	Norwich City	Canon League
16 December	Manchester United	Canon League
27 December	Aston Villa	Canon League
31 December	West Ham United	Canon League
7 January	Fulham	FA Cup
21 January	Everton	Canon League
1 February	Norwich City	FA Cup
4 February	Nottingham Forest	Canon League
21 February	Notts County	Canon League
10 March	Liverpool	Canon League
21 March	FK Austria Vienna	UEFA Cup
24 March	Coventry City	Canon League
26 March	Wimbledon	Dave Bassett Testimonial
7 April	Sunderland	Canon League
11 April	Hajduk Split - magazine	UEFA Cup
21 April	Arsenal	Canon League
28 April	Queens Park Rangers	Canon League
7 May	Southampton	Canon League
9 May	Anderlecht	UEFA Cup
18 May	West Ham United	Pat Holland Testimonial
{ 2 June	Liverpool (Lobamba)	Royal Swazi Sun Challenge
{ 9 June	Liverpool (Lobamba)	Royal Swazi Sun Challenge

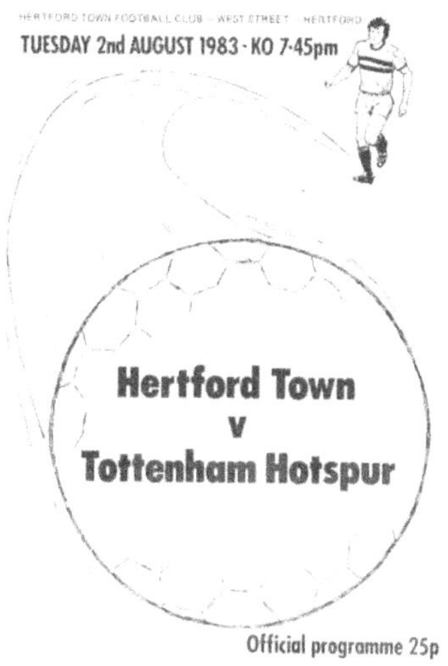

2 August
Hertford Town

4 August
Enfield

6 August
Brentford

9 August
Portsmouth

12 August
Brighton & Hove Albion

OFFICIAL PROGRAMME 40p CELTIC PARK

v

TUESDAY 16th AUGUST 1983
KICK-OFF 7.30 p.m.

16 August
Celtic

17 August
Dundee United

VALE RECREATION F.C.
presents
Vale Recreation
(Guernsey Champions)

Tottenham Hotspur
(Football League Division One)
CORBET FIELD · SATURDAY 8th OCTOBER 1983
Kick-off 6.30 p.m.
Souvenir Programme 20p

8 October
Vale Recreation

2 & 9 June
Royal Swazi Sun Challenge

1984-85

HOME

	Date	Opponent	Competition
☐☐	20 August	Fulham	Peter Southey Memorial
☐☐	27 August	Leicester City	Canon League
☐☐	1 September	Norwich City	Canon League
☐☐	15 September	Queens Park Rangers	Canon League
☐☐	29 September	Luton Town	Canon League
☐☐	3 October	SC Braga	UEFA Cup
☐☐	9 October	Halifax Town	Milk Cup
☐☐	12 October	Liverpool	Canon League
☐☐	27 October	Stoke City	Canon League
☐☐	31 October	Liverpool	Milk Cup
☐☐	3 November	West Bromwich Albion	Canon League
☐☐	7 November	Club Brugge	UEFA Cup
☐☐	24 November	Chelsea	Canon League
☐☐	28 November	Bohemians Prague	UEFA Cup
☐☐	5 December	Sunderland	Milk Cup
☐☐	8 December	Newcastle United	Canon League
☐☐	26 December	West Ham United	Canon League
☐☐	29 December	Sunderland	Canon League
☐☐	5 January	Charlton Athletic	FA Cup
☐☐	9 February	Sheffield Wednesday - postponed	Canon League
☐☐	6 March	Real Madrid	UEFA Cup
☐☐	12 March	Manchester United	Canon League
☐☐	23 March	Southampton	Canon League
☐☐	30 March	Aston Villa	Canon League
☐☐	3 April	Everton	Canon League
☐☐	17 April	Arsenal	Canon League
☐☐	20 April	Ipswich Town	Canon League
☐☐	4 May	Coventry City	Canon League
☐☐	11 May	Watford	Canon League
☐☐	14 May	Sheffield Wednesday	Canon League
☐☐	17 May	Nottingham Forest	Canon League

☐ Handbook ☐ Season Ticket

Season Ticket

Handbook

20 August
Fulham

15 September
Queens Park Rangers

9 October
Halifax Town

8 December
Newcastle United

26 December
West Ham United

9 February
Sheffield Wednesday - postponed

30 March
Aston Villa

17 April
Arsenal

14 May
Sheffield Wednesday

17 May
Nottingham Forest

1984-85

AWAY

Date	Opponent	Competition
27 July	Stjørdals-Blink	Friendly
29 July	Östersunds	Friendly
30 July	Viking	Friendly
4 August	Enfield	Friendly
6 August	Nice	Friendly
11 August	Brentford	Friendly
16 August	Manchester City	Friendly
18 August	Sheffield United	Friendly
25 August	Everton	Canon League
4 September	Sunderland	Canon League
8 September	Sheffield Wednesday	Canon League
12 September	Real Madrid	Gregorio Benito Testimonial
19 September	SC Braga	UEFA Cup
22 September	Aston Villa	Canon League
26 September	Halifax Town	Milk Cup
6 October	Southampton	Canon League
14 October	Malta FA XI	Friendly
20 October	Manchester United	Canon League
24 October	Club Brugge	UEFA Cup
10 November	Nottingham Forest	Canon League
13 November	Sutton United	Larry Pritchard Testimonial
17 November	Ipswich Town	Canon League
21 November	Sunderland	Milk Cup
1 December	Coventry City	Canon League
12 December	Bohemians Prague	UEFA Cup
15 December	Watford	Canon League
22 December	Norwich City	Canon League
1 January	Arsenal	Canon League
12 January	Queens Park Rangers	Canon League
23 January	Charlton Athletic	FA Cup
27 January	Liverpool	FA Cup
2 February	Luton Town	Canon League
23 February	West Bromwich Albion	Canon League
2 March	Stoke City	Canon League
8 March	Kuwait National XI (Amman)	Friendly
16 March	Liverpool	Canon League
20 March	Real Madrid	UEFA Cup
6 April	West Ham United	Canon League
8 April	Guernsey FA XI	Friendly
13 April	Leicester City	Canon League
27 April	Chelsea	Canon League
29 April	Bristol Rovers	Bristol Brain Cancer Research Fund
6 May	Newcastle United	Canon League
8 May	Arsenal	Pat Jennings Farewell
23 May	Seiko - magazine	Friendly
{ 29 May	Australia Soccer Federation (Melbourne)	$200,000 International Tournament
{ 1 June	Udinese (Sydney)	$200,000 International Tournament
{ 5 June	Vasco da Gama (Adelaide)	$200,000 International Tournament
{ 9 June	Udinese (Melbourne)	$200,000 International Tournament

29 July
Östersunds

4 August
Enfield

11 August
Brentford

16 August
Manchester City

18 August
Sheffield United

15 October
Malta FA XI

8 April
Guernsey

29 April
Bristol Rovers

29 May – 9 June
$200,000 International Tournament

1985-86

HOME

	Date	Opponent	Competition
☐☐	4 August	Arsenal	Glenn Hoddle Testimonial
☐☐		- teamsheet	
☐☐	17 August	Watford	Canon League
☐☐	26 August	Everton	Canon League
☐☐	4 September	Chelsea	Canon League
☐☐	7 September	Newcastle United	Canon League
☐☐	21 September	Sheffield Wednesday	Canon League
☐☐	2 October	Southampton	Screensport Super
☐☐	26 October	Leicester City	Canon League
☐☐	30 October	Orient	Milk Cup
☐☐	6 November	Wimbledon	Milk Cup
☐☐	9 November	Luton Town	Canon League
☐☐	20 November	Portsmouth	Milk Cup
☐☐	23 November	Queens Park Rangers	Canon League
☐☐	7 December	Oxford United	Canon League
☐☐	21 December	Ipswich Town	Canon League
☐☐	26 December	West Ham United	Canon League
☐☐	8 January	Oxford United	FA Cup
☐☐	11 January	Nottingham Forest	Canon League
☐☐	14 January	Liverpool	Screensport Super
☐☐	18 January	Manchester City	Canon League
☐☐	29 January	Notts County	FA Cup
☐☐	5 February	Everton	Screensport Super
☐☐	8 February	Coventry City	Canon League
☐☐	16 February	Everton - postponed	FA Cup
☐☐	2 March	Liverpool	Canon League
☐☐		- teamsheet	
☐☐	4 March	Everton	FA Cup
☐☐	8 March	West Bromwich Albion	Canon League
☐☐	29 March	Arsenal	Canon League
☐☐	16 April	Birmingham City	Canon League
☐☐	19 April	Manchester United	Canon League
☐☐	1 May	Internazionale	Ossie Ardiles Benefit
☐☐	3 May	Aston Villa	Canon League
☐☐	5 May	Southampton	Canon League

☐ Handbook ☐ Season Ticket

Season Ticket

Handbook

4 August
Arsenal

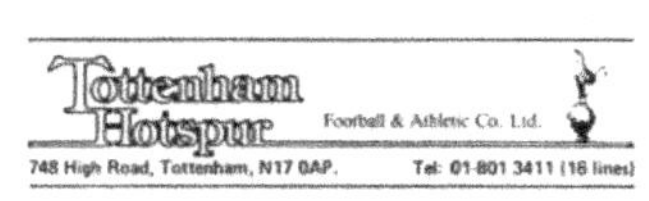

748 High Road, Tottenham, N17 0AP. Tel: 01-801 3411 (16 lines)

GLENN HODDLE TESTIMONIAL

TOTTENHAM HOTSPUR v ARSENAL

SUNDAY, 4th AUGUST 1985
KICK-OFF 3 p.m.

1. RAY CLEMENCE	1. JOHN LUKIC
2. PAUL ALLEN	2. VIV ANDERSON
3. CHRIS HUGHTON	3. KENNY SANSOM
4. GRAHAM ROBERTS	4. STEVE WILLIAMS
5. PAUL MILLER	5. DAVID O'LEARY
6. STEVE PERRYMAN	6. TOMMY CATON
7. OSVALDO ARDILES	7. STEWART ROBSON
8. MARK FALCO	8. CHARLIE NICHOLAS
9. CHRIS WADDLE	9. PAUL MARINER
10. GLENN HODDLE	10. TONY WOODCOCK
11. TONY GALVIN	11. GRAHAM RIX
12. DANNY THOMAS	12. IAN ALLINSON
14. JOHN CHIEDOZIE	14. TONY ADAMS
15. DAVE LEWORTHY	15. PAUL DAVIS

Referee: A. W. WARD (London)

Linesmen: P. DACE (Herts.) P. VOSPER (Middx.)

4 August
Arsenal - teamsheet

7 September
Newcastle United

2 October
Southampton

6 November
Wimbledon

21 December
Ipswich Town

16 February
Everton - postponed

29 March
Arsenal

1 May
Internazionale

5 May
Southampton

1985-86

AWAY

	Date	Opponent	Competition
☐☐	18 July	Wycombe Wanderers (Bisham Abbey)	Friendly
☐☐	24 July	Chesterfield	Friendly
☐☐	27 July	Bournemouth	Friendly
☐☐	31 July	Plymouth Argyle	Friendly
☐☐	3 August	Exeter City	Friendly
☐☐	10 August	Norwich City	Friendly
☐☐	21 August	Oxford United	Canon League
☐☐	24 August	Ipswich Town	Canon League
☐☐	31 August	Manchester City	Canon League
☐☐	10 September	Fareham Town	Friendly
☐☐	14 September	Nottingham Forest	Canon League
☐☐	23 September	Orient	Milk Cup
☐☐	28 September	Liverpool	Canon League
☐☐	5 October	West Bromwich Albion	Canon League
☐☐	14 October	Maidstone United	Brian Thompson Testimonial
☐☐	20 October	Coventry City	Canon League
☐☐	2 November	Southampton	Canon League
☐☐	16 November	Manchester United	Canon League
☐☐	27 November	Portsmouth	Milk Cup
☐☐	30 November	Aston Villa	Canon League
☐☐	3 December	Liverpool	Screensport Super Cup
☐☐	10 December	Portsmouth	Milk Cup
☐☐	14 December	Watford	Canon League
☐☐	17 December	Southampton	Screensport Super Cup
☐☐	28 December	Chelsea	Canon League
☐☐	1 January	Arsenal	Canon League
☐☐	4 January	Oxford United	FA Cup
☐☐	25 January	Notts County	FA Cup
☐☐	1 February	Everton	Canon League
☐☐	10 February	Jersey Select XI	Friendly
☐☐	22 February	Sheffield Wednesday	Canon League
☐☐	15 March	Birmingham City	Canon League
☐☐	19 March	Everton	Screensport Super Cup
☐☐	22 March	Newcastle United	Canon League
☐☐	31 March	West Ham United	Canon League
☐☐	5 April	Leicester City	Canon League
☐☐	6 April	Rangers	Friendly
☐☐	12 April	Luton Town	Canon League
☐☐	22 April	Chelmsford City	Colin Johnson Testimonial
☐☐	26 April	Queens Park Rangers	Canon League
☐☐	9 May	Brentford	Danis Salman Testimonial
☐☐	12 May	West Ham United	Gerhardt Ampofo Testimonial

10p

CHESTERFIELD v TOTTENHAM HOTSPUR

Wednesday 24th July 1985 Kick-off 7.30pm

Welcome back to Saltergate after what seems a remarkably short summer break following the Club's great triumph last season. As a thank you to our loyal supporters, the Board has arranged this evening's friendly fixture against one of the top club sides in the world, Tottenham Hotspur, seven times F.A. Cup winners, twice League Champions and five times European finalists.

It's been a busy 10 weeks since the end of 1984-85 for many people here at Chesterfield F.C. Manager John Duncan, an ex-Spurs player, has been very active in the transfer market bringing in, from Newport County, Tony Reid, Dave Caldwell (Mansfield), Charlie Williamson (Owls) and Swindon's Paul Batty, whilst Big Bob Newton, John Matthews and John Seasman have moved on to pastures new.

Off the field, we've a new Commercial Manager and part-time player, goalkeeper Jim Brown, and Dave Asher has come to the Club to run 'Top Score', the League's own Pool which could reap enormous benefits for all participating clubs. In the wake of the tragedies at Bradford and Brussels, changes have been made to certain sections of the ground, most notably the closing of the small enclosure in front of the stand to allow for fire and safety exits to be constructed.

Another major change is the formation of the Midland Intermediate League, which gives our younger players the opportunity of playing against the likes of Aston Villa, WBA, Nottingham Forest and Leicester City. These games will be played on Saturdays, so if you can't get to a first team away fixture, pop along to Saltergate and support the reserves.

If you want to keep up to date with all the Saltergate News and Views, make sure you get your copy of 'The Spire', Chesterfield F.C.'s matchday programme, available at each home game starting with the opening league match of the season against Bury on August 17th. It's too good to miss!

24 July
Chesterfield

27 July
Bournemouth

10p 10p

PLYMOUTH ARGYLE F.C.
WELCOME
TOTTENHAM HOTSPUR F.C.
TO
HOME PARK

A Football Friendly

Kick Off 7.30 p.m

10p 10p

31 July
Plymouth Argyle

EXETER
CITY FC
SOUVENIR
PROGRAMME

EXETER CITY v TOTTENHAM

Pre Season Friendly

SATURDAY 3rd AUGUST 1985
Kick-off 3.00 p.m.

PROGRAMME 20p

3 August
Exeter City

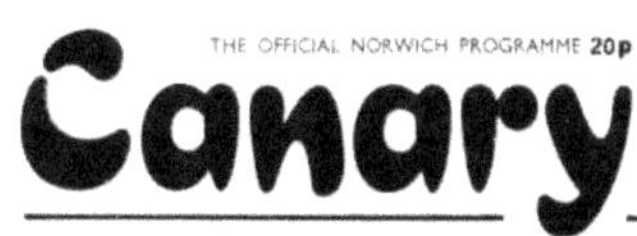

Pre Season Friendly – Saturday 10 August 1985
Kick-off 3.00 p.m.

NORWICH CITY

v

TOTTENHAM HOTSPUR

Preceded by
NORWICH CITY YOUTH
v
SV PH ALMELO (Holland)
Kick-off 1.00 p.m.

OFFICIAL CLUB SPONSORS

10 August
Norwich City

10 September
Fareham Town

BRIAN THOMPSON TESTIMONIAL MATCH

MAIDSTONE UNITED v
TOTTENHAM HOTSPUR

SOUVENIR PROGRAMME 50p

14 October
Maidstone United

6 April
Rangers

22 April
Chelmsford City

1986-87

HOME

Date	Opponent	Competition
2 August	Rangers	Paul Miller Testimonial
25 August	Newcastle United	Today League
30 August	Manchester City	Today League
13 September	Chelsea	Today League
27 September	Everton	Today League
4 October	Luton Town	Today League
8 October	Barnsley	Littlewoods Challenge Cup
18 October	Sheffield Wednesday	Today League
29 October	Birmingham City	Littlewoods Challenge Cup
1 November	Wimbledon	Today League
4 November	SV Hamburg	Friendly
15 November	Coventry City	Today League
29 November	Nottingham Forest	Today League
13 December	Watford	Today League
26 December	West Ham United	Today League
4 January	Arsenal	Today League
	- teamsheet	
10 January	Scunthorpe United	FA Cup
24 January	Aston Villa	Today League
31 January	Crystal Palace	FA Cup
2 February	West Ham United	Littlewoods Challenge Cup
14 February	Southampton	Today League
21 February	Newcastle United	FA Cup
25 February	Leicester City	Today League
1 March	Arsenal	Littlewoods Challenge Cup
	- teamsheet	
4 March	Arsenal	Littlewoods Challenge Cup
7 March	Queens Park Rangers	Today League
22 March	Liverpool	Today League
	- teamsheet	
4 April	Norwich City	Today League
20 April	West Ham United	Today League
25 April	Oxford United	Today League
4 May	Manchester United	Today League

☐ Handbook

☐ Season Ticket

Season Ticket

Handbook

2 August
Rangers

25 August
Newcastle United

8 October
Barnsley

4 November
Hamburg

4 January
Arsenal

Arsenal

Get on the ball . . .
. . . make that call
SPURS LINE
0898-100-500
News • Views • Information

4 January
Arsenal - teamsheet

10 January
Scunthorpe United

25 February
Leicester City

4 April
Norwich City

4 May
Manchester United

1986-87

AWAY

		Date	Opponent	Competition
		4 August	Aldershot	Friendly
		8 August	Brighton & Hove Albion	Gerry Ryan Testimonial
		12 August	Gillingham	Mark Weatherly Testimonial
		19 August	PSV Eindhoven (Barcelona)	XXI Trofeu Joan Gamper
		20 August	AC Milan (Barcelona)	XXI Trofeu Joan Gamper
		23 August	Aston Villa	Today League
		2 September	Southampton	Today League
		6 September	Arsenal	Today League
		20 September	Leicester City	Today League
		23 September	Barnsley	Littlewoods Challenge Cup
		11 October	Liverpool	Today League
		25 October	Queens Park Rangers	Today League
		8 November	Norwich City	Today League
		22 November	Oxford United	Today League
		26 November	Cambridge United	Littlewoods Challenge Cup
		7 December	Manchester United	Today League
		16 December	Bermuda National XI (Hamilton)	Friendly
		20 December	Chelsea	Today League
		27 December	Coventry City	Today League
		1 January	Charlton Athletic	Today League
		17 January	Newcastle United - postponed	Today League
		20 January	Linfield	Roy Coyle Testimonial
		27 January	West Ham United	Littlewoods Challenge Cup
		8 February	Arsenal	Littlewoods Challenge Cup
		15 March	Wimbledon	FA Cup
		25 March	Newcastle United	Today League
		28 March	Luton Town	Today League
		7 April	Sheffield Wednesday	Today League
		11 April	Watford (Villa Park)	FA Cup
		15 April	Manchester City	Today League
		20 April	West Ham United	Today League
		22 April	Wimbledon	Today League
		2 May	Nottingham Forest	Today League
		9 May	Watford	Today League
		11 May	Everton	Today League
		16 May	Coventry City (Wembley)	FA Cup
		28 May	Millonarios	Miami Classic

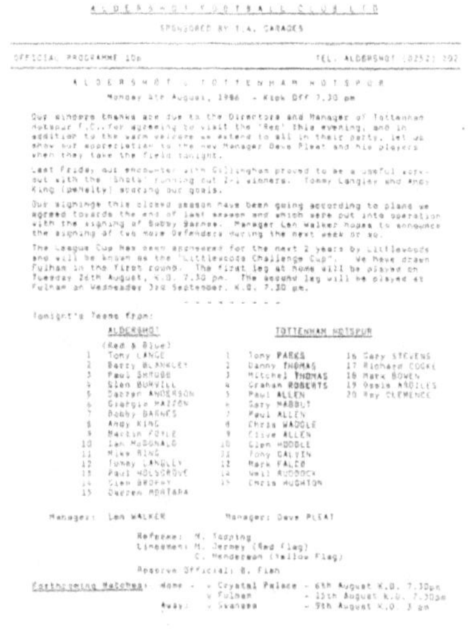

ALDERSHOT FOOTBALL CLUB LTD

SPONSORED BY T.A. GARAGES

OFFICIAL PROGRAMME 10p — TEL. ALDERSHOT (0252) 202

ALDERSHOT v TOTTENHAM HOTSPUR

Monday 4th August, 1986 - Kick Off 7.30 pm

Our sincere thanks are due to the Directors and Manager of Tottenham Hotspur F.C. for agreeing to visit the 'Rec' this evening, and in addition to the warm welcome we extend to all in their party, let us show our appreciation to the new Manager Dave Pleat and his players when they take the field tonight.

Last Friday our encounter with Gillingham proved to be a useful work-out with the 'Shots' running out 2-1 winners. Tommy Langley and Andy King (penalty) scoring our goals.

Our signings this closed season have been going according to plans we agreed towards the end of last season and which were put into operation with the signing of Bobby Barnes. Manager Len Walker hopes to announce the signing of two more Defenders during the next week or so.

The League Cup has been sponsored for the next 2 years by Littlewoods and will be known as the "Littlewoods Challenge Cup". We have drawn Fulham in the first round. The first leg at home will be played on Tuesday 26th August, K.O. 7.30 pm. The second leg will be played at Fulham on Wednesday 3rd September, K.O. 7.30 pm.

Tonight's Teams from:

ALDERSHOT (Red & Blue)	TOTTENHAM HOTSPUR	
1 Tony LANGE	1 Tony PARKS	16 Gary STEVENS
2 Barry BLANKLEY	2 Danny THOMAS	17 Richard COOKE
3 Paul SHRUBB	3 Mitchel THOMAS	18 Mark BOWEN
4 Glen BURVILL	4 Graham ROBERTS	19 Ossie ARDILES
5 Darren ANDERSON	5 Paul ALLEN	20 Ray CLEMENCE
6 Giorgio MAZZON	6 Gary MABBUTT	
7 Bobby BARNES	7 Paul ALLEN	
8 Andy KING	8 Chris WADDLE	
9 Martin FOYLE	9 Clive ALLEN	
10 Ian McDONALD	10 Glen HODDLE	
11 Mike RING	11 Tony GALVIN	
12 Tommy LANGLEY	12 Mark FALCO	
13 Paul HOLSGROVE	14 Neil RUDDOCK	
14 Glen BROPHY	15 Chris HUGHTON	
15 Darren MORTARA		

Manager: Len WALKER — Manager: Dave PLEAT

Referee: M. Tedding
Linesmen: M. Jermey (Red Flag)
C. Henderson (Yellow Flag)

Reserve Official: B. Fish

Forthcoming Matches: Home - v Crystal Palace - 6th August K.O. 7.30pm
v Fulham - 13th August K.O. 7.30pm
Away: v Swansea - 9th August K.O. 3 pm

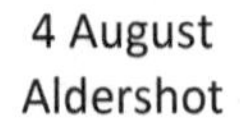

4 August
Aldershot

8 August
Brighton & Hove Albion

12 August
Gillingham

23 August
Aston Villa

23 September
Barnsley

25 October
Queens Park Rangers

26 November
Cambridge United

16 December
Bermuda

17 January
Newcastle United - postponed

ROY COYLE TESTIMONIAL

Linfield
(Irish League Champions 1981-86)
VERSUS
Tottenham Hotspur
AT WINDSOR PARK, BELFAST
ON TUESDAY, JANUARY 20, 1987
KICK-OFF — 7.30 P.M.
Official Souvenir Programme: 50p

20 January
Linfield

28 March
Luton Town

11 May
Everton

1987-88

HOME

Date	Opponent	Competition
10 August	Arsenal	Chris Hughton Testimonial
19 August	Newcastle United	Barclays League
22 August	Chelsea	Barclays League
1 September	Oxford United	Barclays League
12 September	Southampton	Barclays League
3 October	Sheffield Wednesday	Barclays League
7 October	Torquay United	Littlewoods Challenge Cup
18 October	Arsenal	Barclays League
	- teamsheet	
20 October	West Ham United	Tony Galvin Testimonial
31 October	Wimbledon	Barclays League
14 November	Queens Park Rangers	Barclays League
28 November	Liverpool	Barclays League
13 December	Charlton Athletic	Barclays League
	- teamsheet	
28 December	West Ham United	Barclays League
1 January	Watford	Barclays League
16 January	Coventry City	Barclays League
15 February	AS Monaco	Friendly
23 February	Manchester United	Barclays League
1 March	Derby County	Barclays League
9 March	Everton	Barclays League
12 March	Norwich City	Barclays League
26 March	Nottingham Forest	Barclays League
28 March	Manchester United	Danny Thomas Benefit
2 April	Portsmouth	Barclays League
4 May	Luton Town	Barclays League

☐ Handbook ☐ Season Ticket

Season Ticket

Handbook

10 August
Arsenal

19 August
Newcastle United

18 October
Arsenal

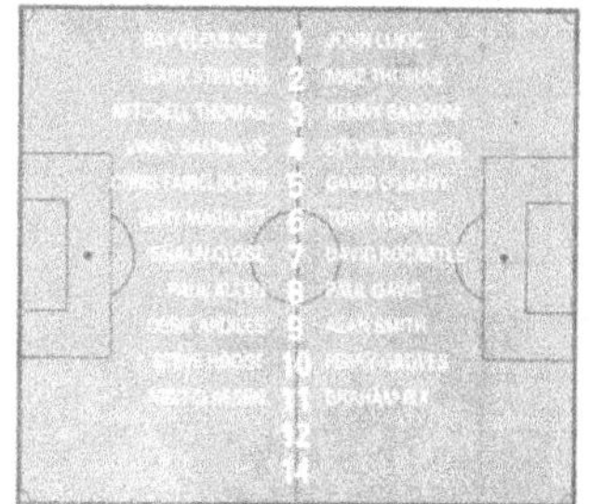

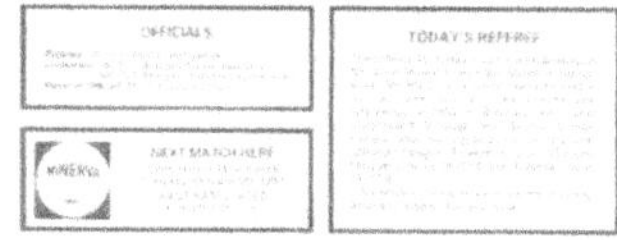

18 October
Arsenal - teamsheet

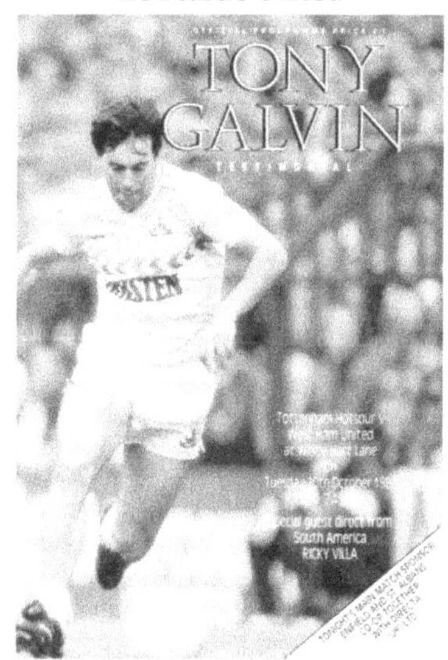

20 October
West Ham United

31 October
Wimbledon

15 February
AS Monaco

12 March
Norwich City

28 March
Manchester United

4 May
Luton Town

1987-88

AWAY

Date	Opponent	Competition
23 July	Exeter City	Friendly
25 July	Bournemouth	Friendly
30 July	Örebro SK	Friendly
1 August	Lansi Uudenmaan District (Karjaa)	Friendly
3 August	IFK/VSK Västerås Select XI	Friendly
5 August	Marsta IK	Friendly
6 August	Team "Norrettan" (Gävle)	Friendly
15 August	Coventry City	Barclays League
29 August	Watford	Barclays League
5 September	Everton	Barclays League
19 September	West Ham United	Barclays League
23 September	Torquay United	Littlewoods Challenge Cup
26 September	Manchester United	Barclays League
10 October	Norwich City	Barclays League
24 October	Nottingham Forest	Barclays League
28 October	Aston Villa	Littlewoods Challenge Cup
4 November	Portsmouth	Barclays League
10 November	St Alban's City	Friendly
21 November	Luton Town	Barclays League
5 December	Brentford	Friendly
20 December	Derby County	Barclays League
26 December	Southampton	Barclays League
2 January	Chelsea	Barclays League
9 January	Oldham Athletic	FA Cup
23 January	Newcastle United	Barclays League
30 January	Port Vale	FA Cup
13 February	Oxford United	Barclays League
19 February	West Bromwich Albion	Mick Brown Benefit
27 February	Sheffield Wednesday	Barclays League
6 March	Arsenal	Barclays League
19 March	Wimbledon	Barclays League
4 April	Queens Park Rangers	Barclays League
15 April	Hull City	Jeff Radcliffe Testimonial
23 April	Liverpool	Barclays League
26 April	Crystal Palace	Jim Cannon Testimonial
2 May	Charlton Athletic	Barclays League
6 May	Barnet	Kevin Millett Testimonial
10 May	Euskadi (Bilbao)	Friendly

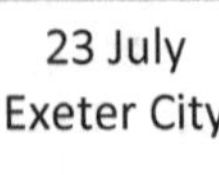

23 July
Exeter City

25 July
Bournemouth

30 July
Örebro SK

1 August
Lansi Uudenmaan District

3 August
IFK/VSK Västerås Select XI

5 August
Marsta IK

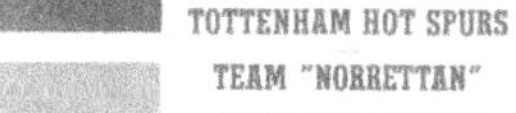

6 August
Team "Norrettan"

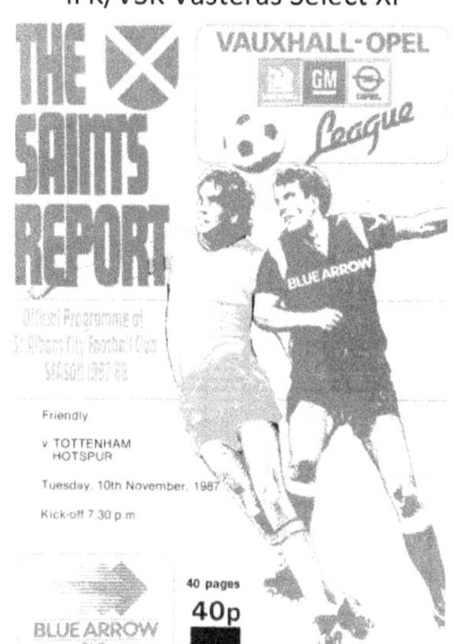

10 November
St Albans City

5 December
Brentford

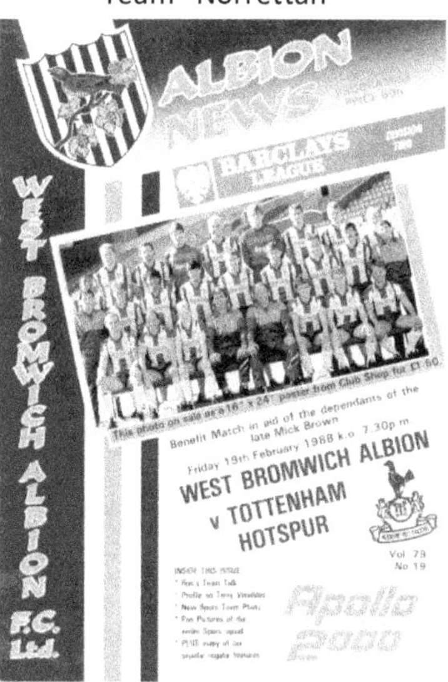

19 February
West Bromwich Albion

15 April
Hull City

6 May
Barnet

1988-89

HOME

☐☐	27 August	Coventry City - postponed	Barclays League
☐☐	10 September	Arsenal	Barclays League
☐☐	24 September	Middlesbrough	Barclays League
☐☐	1 October	Manchester United	Barclays League
☐☐	11 October	Notts County	Littlewoods Challenge Cup
☐☐	25 October	Southampton	Barclays League
☐☐	1 November	Blackburn Rovers	Littlewoods Challenge Cup
☐☐	5 November	Derby County	Barclays League
☐☐	12 November	Wimbledon	Barclays League
☐☐	23 November	Coventry City	Barclays League
☐☐	26 November	Queens Park Rangers	Barclays League
☐☐	10 December	Millwall	Barclays League
☐☐	26 December	Luton Town	Barclays League
☐☐	31 December	Newcastle United	Barclays League
☐☐	15 January	Nottingham Forest	Barclays League
☐☐		- teamsheet	
☐☐	17 January	AC Monaco	Friendly
☐☐	11 February	Charlton Athletic	Barclays League
☐☐	21 February	Norwich City	Barclays League
☐☐	1 March	Aston Villa	Barclays League
☐☐	4 March	Bordeaux	Friendly
☐☐	26 March	Liverpool	Barclays League
☐☐	1 April	West Ham United	Barclays League
☐☐	12 April	Sheffield Wednesday	Barclays League
☐☐	22 April	Everton	Barclays League

☐ Handbook ☐ Season Ticket

Season Ticket

Handbook

27 August
Coventry City - postponed

5 November
Derby County

26 November
Queens Park Rangers

26 December
Luton Town

15 January
Nottingham Forest

Tottenham Hotspur

BOBBY MIMMS	1	STEVE SUTTON
GUY BUTTERS	2	BRIAN LAWS
MITCHELL THOMAS	3	STUART PEARCE
TERRY FENWICK	4	DES WALKER
CHRIS FAIRCLOUGH	5	TERRY WILSON
GARY MABBUTT	6	STEVE HODGE
PAUL WALSH	7	FRANZ CARR
GUDNI BERGSSON	8	NEIL WEBB
CHRIS WADDLE	9	TOMMY GAYNOR
PAUL STEWART	10	LEE CHAPMAN
PAUL ALLEN	11	GARY PARKER
CHRIS HUGHTON	12	NIGEL CLOUGH
JOHN MONCUR	14	PHILIP STARBUCK

Nottingham Forest

OFFICIALS

NEXT MATCH HERE

A S MONACO

TODAY'S REFEREE

Tottenham Hotspur

15 January
Nottingham Forest - teamsheet

17 January
AS Monaco

4 March
Bordeaux

26 March
Liverpool

22 April
Everton

1988-89

AWAY

Date	Opponent	Match
26 July	Vederslav/Danningelanda IF	Friendly
28 July	Trelleborgs FF	Friendly
31 July	GAIS	Friendly
2 August	Jönköpings Södra IF	Friendly
7 August	Dundee United	David Narey Testimonial
10 August	Reading	Martin Hicks Testimonial
{ 13 August	Arsenal (Wembley)	Makita International Tournament
{ 14 August	AC Milan (Wembley)	Makita International Tournament
16 August	Chelsea	Colin Pates Testimonial
21 August	West Ham United - teamsheet	Alvin Martin Testimonial
3 September	Newcastle United	Barclays League
6 September	Swansea City	Michael Hughes Benefit
17 September	Liverpool	Barclays League
27 September	Notts County	Littlewoods Challenge Cup
8 October	Charlton Athletic	Barclays League
18 October	Home Farm	Friendly
22 October	Norwich City	Barclays League
29 October	Aston Villa	Barclays League
9 November	Blackburn Rovers	Littlewoods Challenge Cup
20 November	Sheffield Wednesday	Barclays League
29 November	Southampton	Littlewoods Challenge Cup
3 December	Everton	Barclays League
17 December	West Ham United	Barclays League
2 January	Arsenal	Barclays League
7 January	Bradford City	FA Cup
21 January	Middlesbrough	Barclays League
28 January	Portsmouth - cancelled	Friendly
5 February	Manchester United	Barclays League
25 February	Southampton	Barclays League
11 March	Derby County	Barclays League
18 March	Coventry City	Barclays League
22 March	Nottingham Forest	Barclays League
28 March	Luton Town	Barclays League
4 April	Charlton Athletic	Steve Gritt Testimonial
15 April	Wimbledon	Barclays League
29 April	Millwall	Barclays League
13 May	Queens Park Rangers	Barclays League

26 July
Vederslav/Danningelanda IF

28 July
Trelleborgs FF

Matchsponsor: it-bolagen
som omfattar: Industri- och terminalanläggningar
IT Construktion · Göteborgs Nya Golv · Projektbyggen

31 July
GAIS

2 August
Jönköpings Södra IF

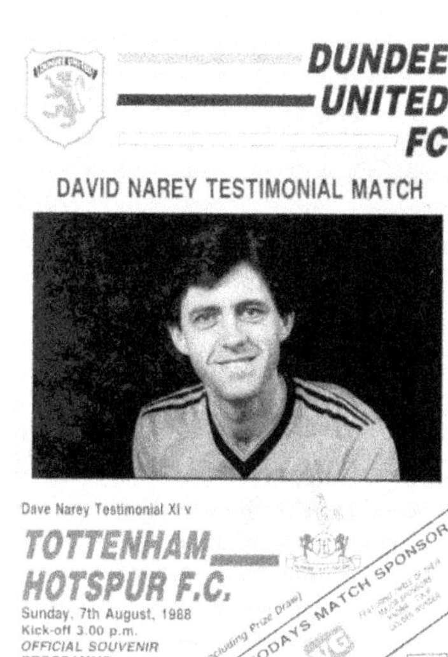

7 August
Dundee United

10 August
Reading

13 & 14 August
Makita International Tournament

21 August
West Ham United

WEST HAM UNITED FOOTBALL CO. LTD.
Boleyn Ground, Green Street, Upton Park, London, E.13

ALVIN MARTIN TESTIMONIAL

WEST HAM UNITED

VERSUS

TOTTENHAM HOTSPUR

Sunday 21 August 1988 Kick-off 3 p.m.

West Ham United	Tottenham Hotspur
TOM McALISTER	1 BOBBY MIMMS
PHIL PARKES	2 MITCHELL THOMAS
ALLEN McKNIGHT	3 CHRIS HUGHTON
RAY STEWART	4 TERRY FENWICK
STEVE POTTS	5 CHRIS FAIRCLOUGH
JULIAN DICKS	6 GARY MABBUTT
GEORGE PARRIS	7 PAUL WALSH
TOMMY McQUEEN	8 PAUL GASCOIGNE
TONY GALE	9 CHRIS WADDLE
ALVIN MARTIN	10 PAUL MORAN
PAUL HILTON	11 PAUL ALLEN
GARY STRODDER	12 PAUL STEWART
LIAM BRADY	13 BRIAN STATHAM
KEVIN KEEN	14 DAVID HOWELLS
ALAN DEVONSHIRE	15 MARK STIMSON
MARK WARD	16 PHILIP GRAY
ALAN DICKENS	
LEROY ROSENIOR	
DAVID KELLY	
STUART SLATER	
EAMONN DOLAN	
STEWART ROBSON	

Referee: D. VICKERS (Goodmayes, Essex)
Linesman (Red Trim): J. MOULES (Dartford, Kent)
Linesman (Yellow Trim): B. O'LEARY (Dagenham, Essex)

AVCO TRUST
OFFICIAL SPONSORS TO THE CLUB

ADMISSION PRICES
NO TRANSFERS
All prices include V.A.T.

21 August
West Ham United - teamsheet

6 September
Swansea City

18 October
Home Farm

28 January
Portsmouth - cancelled

1989-90

HOME

	Date	Opponent	Competition
☐☐	19 August	Luton Town	Barclays League
☐☐	16 September	Chelsea	Barclays League
☐☐	20 September	Southend United	Littlewoods Challenge Cup
☐☐	30 September	Queens Park Rangers	Barclays League
☐☐	18 October	Arsenal	Barclays League
☐☐	21 October	Sheffield Wednesday	Barclays League
☐☐	11 November	Wimbledon	Barclays League
☐☐	25 November	Derby County	Barclays League
☐☐	29 November	Tranmere Rovers	Littlewoods Challenge Cup
☐☐	9 December	Everton	Barclays League
☐☐	26 December	Millwall	Barclays League
☐☐	30 December	Nottingham Forest	Barclays League
☐☐	6 January	Southampton	FA Cup
☐☐	13 January	Manchester City	Barclays League
☐☐	24 January	Nottingham Forest	Littlewoods Challenge Cup
☐☐	4 February	Norwich City	Barclays League
☐☐	21 February	Aston Villa	Barclays League
☐☐	3 March	Crystal Palace	Barclays League
☐☐	10 March	Charlton Athletic	Barclays League
☐☐	21 March	Liverpool	Barclays League
☐☐	14 April	Coventry City	Barclays League
☐☐	21 April	Manchester United	Barclays League
☐☐	1 May	Northern Ireland XI	Danny Blanchflower Benefit
☐☐	5 May	Southampton	Barclays League

☐ Handbook

☐ Season Ticket

Season Ticket

Handbook

19 August
Luton Town

20 September
Southend United

18 October
Arsenal

29 November
Tranmere Rovers

26 December
Millwall

4 February
Norwich City

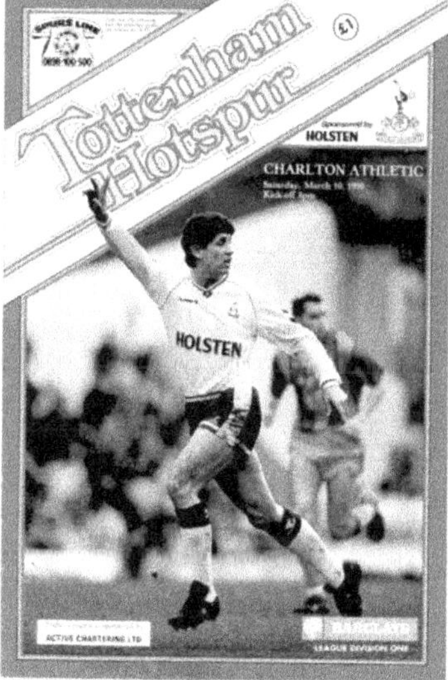

10 March
Charlton Athletic

14 April
Coventry City

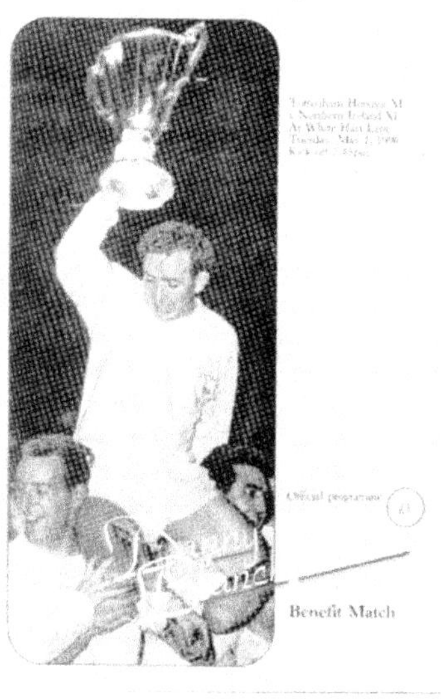

1 May
Northern Ireland XI

5 May
Southampton

1989-90

AWAY

Date	Opponent	Competition
23 July	Bohemians	Friendly
25 July	Cork City	Friendly
6 August	Rangers	Friendly
8 August	Viking	Friendly
10 August	Brann	Friendly
11 August	Dinamo Bucharest (Madrid)	Trofeo Villa De Madrid
13 August	Atletico Madrid	Trofeo Villa De Madrid
22 August	Everton	Barclays League
26 August	Manchester City	Barclays League
9 September	Aston Villa	Barclays League
23 September	Norwich City	Barclays League
4 October	Southend United	Littlewoods Challenge Cup
14 October	Charlton Athletic	Barclays League
25 October	Manchester United	Littlewoods Challenge Cup
29 October	Liverpool	Barclays League
31 October	Caen (Cherbourg)	La Presse De La Manche Centenary
4 November	Southampton	Barclays League
6 November	Leicester City	Paul Ramsey Testimonial
	- teamsheet	
18 November	Crystal Palace	Barclays League
22 November	Tranmere Rovers	Littlewoods Challenge Cup
2 December	Luton Town	Barclays League
16 December	Manchester United	Barclays League
1 January	Coventry City	Barclays League
17 January	Nottingham Forest	Littlewoods Challenge Cup
20 January	Arsenal	Barclays League
26 January	Plymouth Argyle	Geoff Crudgington Testimonial
10 February	Chelsea	Barclays League
24 February	Derby County	Barclays League
17 March	Queens Park Rangers	Barclays League
31 March	Sheffield Wednesday	Barclays League
3 April	Brighton 1983	Graham Moseley Testimonial
7 April	Nottingham Forest	Barclays League
16 April	Millwall	Barclays League
23 April	Vålerenga	Friendly
28 April	Wimbledon	Barclays League

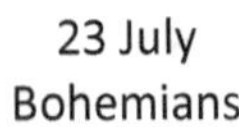

23 July
Bohemians

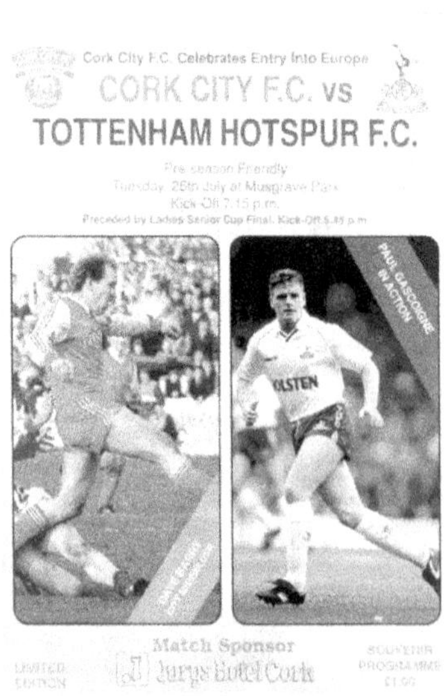

25 July
Cork City

6 August
Rangers

8 August
Viking

10 August
Brann

4 October
Southend United

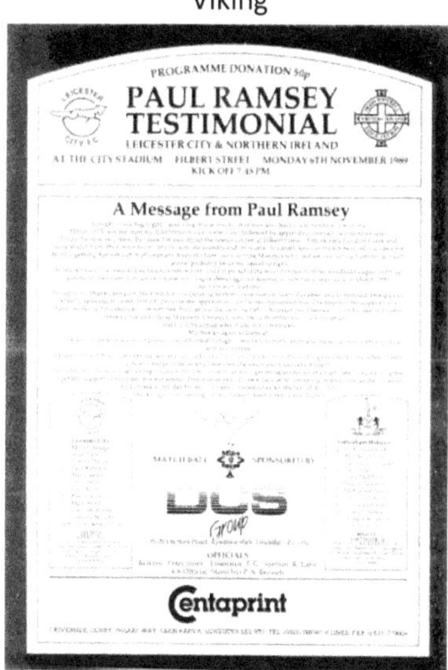

6 November
Leicester City

6 November
Leicester City - teamsheet

22 November
Tranmere Rovers

26 January
Plymouth Argyle

3 April
Brighton & Hove Albion 1983

23 April
Vålerenga

1990-91

HOME

	Date	Opponent	Competition
☐☐	17 August	West Ham United	Ray Clemence Benefit
☐☐	25 August	Manchester City	Barclays League
☐☐	8 September	Derby County	Barclays League
☐☐	22 September	Crystal Palace	Barclays League
☐☐	26 September	Hartlepool United	Rumbelows League Cup
☐☐	29 September	Aston Villa	Barclays League
☐☐	20 October	Sheffield United	Barclays League
☐☐	30 October	Bradford City	Rumbelows League Cup
☐☐	4 November	Liverpool	Barclays League
☐☐		*- The Match*	
☐☐	10 November	Wimbledon	Barclays League
☐☐	24 November	Norwich City	Barclays League
☐☐	8 December	Sunderland	Barclays League
☐☐	22 December	Luton Town	Barclays League
☐☐	1 January	Manchester United	Barclays League
☐☐	12 January	Arsenal	Barclays League
☐☐	23 January	Chelsea	Rumbelows League Cup
☐☐	26 January	Oxford United	FA Cup
☐☐	2 February	Leeds United	Barclays League
☐☐	2 March	Chelsea	Barclays League
☐☐	10 March	Notts County	FA Cup
☐☐	23 March	Queens Park Rangers	Barclays League
☐☐	30 March	Coventry City	Barclays League
☐☐	6 April	Southampton	Barclays League
☐☐	24 April	Everton	Barclays League
☐☐	4 May	Nottingham Forest	Barclays League

☐ Handbook ☐ Season Ticket

Season Ticket

Handbook

17 August
West Ham United

22 September
Crystal Palace

20 October
Sheffield United

4 November
Liverpool - *The Match* issue

22 December
Luton Town

12 January
Arsenal

26 January
Oxford United

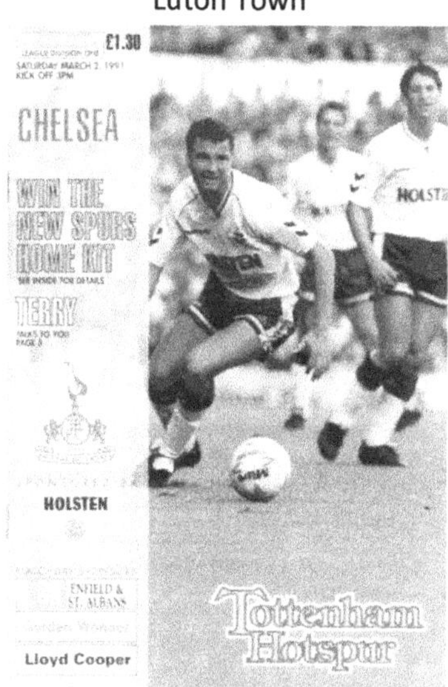

2 March
Chelsea

30 March
Coventry City

4 May
Nottingham Forest

1990-91

AWAY

Date	Opponent	Competition
1 August	Shelbourne	Friendly
3 August	Derry City	Friendly
7 August	Brann	Friendly
9 August	Viking	Friendly
11 August	Sogndal	Friendly
13 August	Heart of Midlothian	Friendly
20 August	Southend United	Friendly
28 August	Sunderland	Barclays League
1 September	Arsenal	Barclays League
15 September	Leeds United	Barclays League
6 October	Queens Park Rangers	Barclays League
9 October	Hartlepool United	Rumbelows League Cup
13 October	Arsenal	Graham Rix Testimonial
27 October	Nottingham Forest	Barclays League
12 November	West Ham United	Billy Bonds Testimonial
18 November	Everton - Gabriel edition	Barclays League
	- Kendall edition	
	- *The Match* (Gabriel edition)	
27 November	Sheffield United	Rumbelows League Cup
1 December	Chelsea	Barclays League
15 December	Manchester City	Barclays League
26 December	Coventry City	Barclays League
29 December	Southampton	Barclays League
5 January	Blackpool	FA Cup
16 January	Chelsea	Rumbelows League Cup
20 January	Derby County	Barclays League
	- *The Match*	
16 February	Portsmouth	FA Cup
23 February	Wimbledon	Barclays League
16 March	Aston Villa	Barclays League
1 April	Luton Town	Barclays League
10 April	Norwich City	Barclays League
14 April	Arsenal (Wembley)	FA Cup
17 April	Crystal Palace	Barclays League
20 April	Sheffield United	Barclays League
11 May	Liverpool	Barclays League
18 May	Nottingham Forest (Wembley)	FA Cup
20 May	Manchester United	Barclays League
{ 2 June	Vasco da Gama (Kobe)	Kirin Cup
{ 5 June	Thailand (Nagoya)	Kirin Cup
{ 9 June	Japan (Tokyo)	Kirin Cup

1 August
Shelbourne

3 August
Derry City

7 August
Brann

9 August
Viking

11 August
Sogndal

13 August
Heart of Midlothian

20 August
Southend United

20 January
Derby County - *The Match* issue

2 – 9 June
Kirin Cup

1991-92

HOME

		Date	Opponent	Competition
☐	☐	24 August	Chelsea	Barclays League
☐	☐	4 September	Sparkasse Stockerau	European Cup-Winners' Cup
☐	☐	14 September	Queens Park Rangers	Barclays League
☐	☐	28 September	Manchester United	Barclays League
☐	☐	2 October	Hajduk Split	European Cup-Winners' Cup
☐	☐	9 October	Swansea City	Rumbelows League Cup
☐	☐	19 October	Manchester City	Barclays League
☐	☐	23 October	Porto	European Cup-Winners' Cup
☐	☐	10 November	Spurs '81-82	Cyril Knowles Mem
☐	☐	16 November	Luton Town	Barclays League
☐	☐	23 November	Sheffield United	Barclays League
☐	☐	7 December	Notts County	Barclays League
☐	☐	18 December	Liverpool	Barclays League
☐	☐	26 December	Nottingham Forest	Barclays League
☐	☐	28 December	Norwich City	Barclays League
☐	☐	8 January	Norwich City	Rumbelows League Cup
☐	☐	14 January	Aston Villa	FA Cup
☐	☐	18 January	Southampton	Barclays League
☐	☐	25 January	Oldham Athletic	Barclays League
☐	☐	16 February	Crystal Palace	Barclays League
☐	☐	22 February	Arsenal	Barclays League
☐	☐	1 March	Nottingham Forest	Rumbelows League Cup
☐	☐	7 March	Leeds United	Barclays League
☐	☐	14 March	Sheffield Wednesday	Barclays League
☐	☐	18 March	Feyenoord	European Cup-Winners' Cup
☐	☐	28 March	Coventry City	Barclays League
☐	☐	1 April	West Ham United	Barclays League
☐	☐	4 April	Aston Villa	Barclays League
☐	☐	18 April	Wimbledon	Barclays League
☐	☐	25 April	Everton	Barclays League

☐ Handbook ☐ Season Ticket

Season Ticket

12809
CUP TIE VOUCHER BOOK
Tottenham Hotspur Football Club
SEASON 1991/92

This voucher book will admit the holder to all Cup Ties played at White Hart Lane NOT covered by season tickets during Season 1991/92.

Block, Row and Seat details are listed on the computer ticket attached to the back of the cover of this voucher book.

THIS BOOK CANNOT BE REPLACED IF LOST

Cup Tie Voucher Book

Handbook

24 August
Chelsea

28 September
Manchester United

10 November
Spurs '81-82

7 December
Notts County

28 December
Norwich City

8 January
Norwich City

25 January
Oldham Athletic

22 February
Chelsea

28 March
Coventry City

25 April
Everton

1991-92

AWAY

Date	Opponent	Competition
23 July	Sligo Rovers	Glencar Spring Water Challenge
25 July	Drogheda United	Friendly
27 July	Shelbourne	Friendly
30 July	Brann	Friendly
1 August	Bryne	Friendly
4 August	Celtic	Friendly
10 August	Arsenal (Wembley)	Tennents FA Charity Shield
{11 August	Messina (Catanzaro)	Nicola Ceravolo Memorial Tournament
{13 August	Catanzaro	Nicola Ceravolo Memorial Tournament
17 August	Southampton	Barclays League
21 August	Sparkasse Stockerau (Vienna)	European Cup-Winners' Cup
28 August	Nottingham Forest	Barclays League
31 August	Norwich City	Barclays League
7 September	Aston Villa	Barclays League
17 September	Hajduk Split (Linz)	European Cup-Winners' Cup
21 September	Wimbledon	Barclays League
25 September	Swansea City	Rumbelows League Cup
5 October	Everton	Barclays League
26 October	West Ham United	Barclays League
29 October	Grimsby Town	Rumbelows League Cup
2 November	Sheffield Wednesday	Barclays League
7 November	Porto - magazine	European Cup-Winners' Cup
1 December	Arsenal	Barclays League
	- *The Match*	
4 December	Coventry City	Rumbelows League Cup
14 December	Leeds United	Barclays League
22 December	Crystal Palace	Barclays League
1 January	Coventry City	Barclays League
5 January	Aston Villa	FA Cup
11 January	Chelsea	Barclays League
1 February	Manchester City	Barclays League
9 February	Nottingham Forest	Rumbelows League Cup
4 March	Feyenoord	European Cup-Winners' Cup
11 March	Luton Town	Barclays League
21 March	Liverpool	Barclays League
7 April	Notts County	Barclays League
11 April	Queens Park Rangers	Barclays League
14 April	Sheffield United	Barclays League
20 April	Oldham Athletic	Barclays League
2 May	Manchester United	Barclays League
5 May	Cardiff City	Harry Parsons Testimonial
8 May	Garreth Roberts' Hull City XI	Garreth Roberts Testimonial

23 July
Sligo Rovers

25 July
Drogheda United

27 July
Shelbourne

1 August
Bryne

4 August
Celtic

11 & 13 August
Nicola Ceravolo Memorial Tournament

29 October
Grimsby Town

5 May
Cardiff City

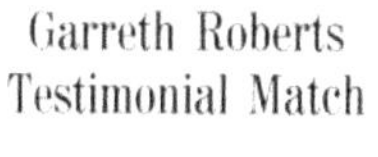

8 May
Garreth Roberts' Hull City XI

1992-93

HOME

	Date	Opponent	Competition
☐☐	19 August	Coventry City	FA Premier League
☐☐	22 August	Crystal Palace	FA Premier League
☐☐	2 September	Sheffield United	FA Premier League
☐☐	5 September	Everton	FA Premier League
☐☐	19 September	Manchester United	FA Premier League
☐☐	21 September	Brentford	Coca Cola Cup
☐☐	17 October	Middlesbrough	FA Premier League
☐☐	20 October	Lazio	Capital Cup
☐☐	31 October	Liverpool	FA Premier League
☐☐	21 November	Aston Villa	FA Premier League
☐☐	5 December	Chelsea	FA Premier League
☐☐	12 December	Arsenal	FA Premier League
☐☐	28 December	Nottingham Forest	FA Premier League
☐☐	16 January	Sheffield Wednesday	FA Premier League
☐☐	27 January	Ipswich Town	FA Premier League
☐☐	7 February	Southampton	FA Premier League
☐☐	14 February	Wimbledon	FA Cup
☐☐	20 February	Leeds United	FA Premier League
☐☐	27 February	Queens Park Rangers	FA Premier League
☐☐	24 March	Manchester City	FA Premier League
☐☐	9 April	Norwich City	FA Premier League
☐☐	17 April	Oldham Athletic	FA Premier League
☐☐	27 April	Real Madrid	Fiorucci Cup
	27 April	Internazionale	Fiorucci Cup
☐☐	1 May	Wimbledon	FA Premier League
☐☐	5 May	Blackburn Rovers	FA Premier League

☐ Handbook ☐ Season Ticket

Season Ticket

Handbook

19 August
Coventry City

19 September
Manchester United

20 October
Lazio

21 November
Aston Villa

12 December
Arsenal

16 January
Sheffield Wednesday

20 February
Leeds United

24 March
Manchester City

27 April
Fiorucci Cup

5 May
Blackburn Rovers

1992-93

AWAY

	Date	Opponent	Competition
	25 July	Heart of Midlothian	Friendly
	29 July	Brighton & Hove Albion	Friendly
	1 August	Glenavon	Friendly
	3 August	West Bromwich Albion	Friendly
	5 August	Sunderland	City Celebration
	8 August	Watford	Friendly
	10 August	Portsmouth	Friendly
	15 August	Southampton	FA Premier League
	25 August	Leeds United	FA Premier League
	30 August	Ipswich Town	FA Premier League
	14 September	Coventry City	FA Premier League
	23 September	Lazio	Capital Cup
	27 September	Sheffield Wednesday	FA Premier League
	3 October	Queens Park Rangers	FA Premier League
	7 October	Brentford	Coca Cola Cup
	25 October	Wimbledon	FA Premier League
	28 October	Manchester City	Coca Cola Cup
	7 November	Blackburn Rovers	FA Premier League
	10 November	Swansea City	Harold Woolacott Testimonial
	28 November	Manchester City	FA Premier League
	2 December	Nottingham Forest	Coca Cola Cup
	19 December	Oldham Athletic	FA Premier League
	26 December	Norwich City	FA Premier League
	2 January	Marlow (White Hart Lane)	FA Cup
	9 January	Manchester United	FA Premier League
	24 January	Norwich City	FA Cup
	30 January	Crystal Palace	FA Premier League
	10 February	Everton	FA Premier League
	2 March	Sheffield United	FA Premier League
	7 March	Manchester City	FA Cup
	10 March	Aston Villa	FA Premier League
	20 March	Chelsea	FA Premier League
	28 March	Crystal Palace	Malcolm Allison Testimonial
	4 April	Arsenal (Wembley)	FA Cup
	12 April	Nottingham Forest	FA Premier League
	20 April	Middlesbrough	FA Premier League
	23 April	Real Zaragoza	Friendly
	8 May	Liverpool	FA Premier League
	11 May	Arsenal	FA Premier League
	14 May	Enfield	Eddie Baily Testimonial

25 July
Heart of Midlothian

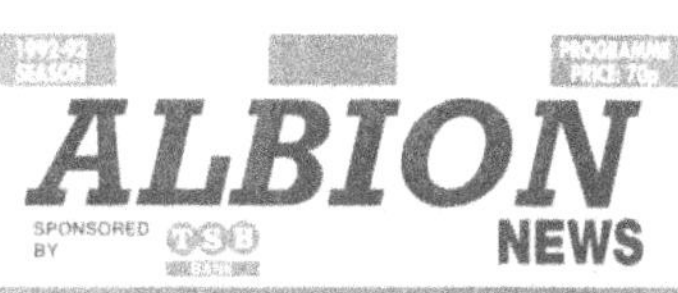

29 July
Brighton & Hove Albion

1 August
Glenavon

3 August
West Bromwich Albion

5 August
Sunderland

8 August
Watford

10 August
Portsmouth

2 January
Marlow

14 May
Enfield

1993-94

HOME

Date	Opponent	Competition
31 July	Lazio	Makita International Tournament
1 August	Chelsea	Makita International Tournament
16 August	Arsenal	FA Carling Premiership
21 August	Manchester City	FA Carling Premiership
1 September	Chelsea	FA Carling Premiership
18 September	Oldham Athletic	FA Carling Premiership
3 October	Everton	FA Carling Premiership
6 October	Burnley	Coca Cola Cup
23 October	Swindon Town	FA Carling Premiership
20 November	Leeds United	FA Carling Premiership
24 November	Wimbledon	FA Carling Premiership
1 December	Blackburn Rovers	Coca Cola Cup
4 December	Newcastle United	FA Carling Premiership
18 December	Liverpool	FA Carling Premiership
27 December	Norwich City	FA Carling Premiership
1 January	Coventry City	FA Carling Premiership
12 January	Aston Villa	Coca Cola Cup
15 January	Manchester United	FA Carling Premiership
19 January	Peterborough United	FA Cup
5 February	Sheffield Wednesday	FA Carling Premiership
12 February	Blackburn Rovers	FA Carling Premiership
2 March	Aston Villa	FA Carling Premiership
5 March	Sheffield United	FA Carling Premiership
19 March	Ipswich Town	FA Carling Premiership
4 April	West Ham United	FA Carling Premiership
23 April	Southampton	FA Carling Premiership
7 May	Queens Park Rangers	FA Carling Premiership

☐ Handbook ☐ Season Ticket

Season Ticket

Handbook

31 July & 1 August
Makita International Tournament

18 September
Oldham Athletic

23 October
Swindon Town

24 November
Wimbledon

27 December
Norwich City

15 January
Manchester United

5 February
Sheffield Wednesday

5 March
Sheffield United

23 April
Southampton

7 May
Queens Park Rangers

1993-94

AWAY

16 July	Brian Lenihan Shelbourne XI	Friendly
18 July	Drogheda United	Friendly
23 July	Team Nord-Trøndelag (Steinkjer)	Friendly
25 July	Lyn Oslo	Tom Sundby Testimonial
27 July	Team Porsgrunn	Friendly
6 August	Brentford	Keith Millen Testimonial
9 August	Peterborough United	Friendly
14 August	Newcastle United	FA Carling Premiership
25 August	Liverpool	FA Carling Premiership
28 August	Aston Villa	FA Carling Premiership
11 September	Sheffield United	FA Carling Premiership
22 September	Burnley	Coca Cola Cup
26 September	Ipswich Town	FA Carling Premiership
11 October	Brann	Friendly
16 October	Manchester United	FA Carling Premiership
19 October	Hartlepool United	Cyril Knowles Memorial
27 October	Derby County	Coca Cola Cup
30 October	Blackburn Rovers	FA Carling Premiership
6 November	Southampton	FA Carling Premiership
27 November	Queens Park Rangers	FA Carling Premiership
6 December	Arsenal	FA Carling Premiership
11 December	Manchester City	FA Carling Premiership
28 December	West Ham United	FA Carling Premiership
3 January	Sheffield Wednesday	FA Carling Premiership
8 January	Peterborough United	FA Cup
22 January	Swindon Town	FA Carling Premiership
29 January	Ipswich Town	FA Cup
15 February	Atletico Madrid (Jerez)	Friendly
27 February	Chelsea	FA Carling Premiership
16 March	Oldham Athletic - postponed	FA Carling Premiership
26 March	Everton	FA Carling Premiership
2 April	Norwich City	FA Carling Premiership
9 April	Coventry City	FA Carling Premiership
17 April	Leeds United	FA Carling Premiership
30 April	Wimbledon	FA Carling Premiership
5 May	Oldham Athletic (dated 20 April)	FA Carling Premiership

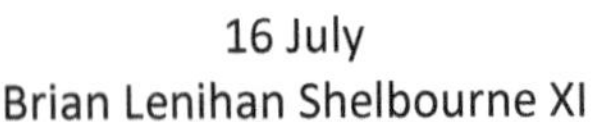
16 July
Brian Lenihan Shelbourne XI

18 July
Drogheda United

23 July
Team Nord-Trøndelag

25 July
Lyn Oslo

27 July
Team Porsgrunn

6 August
Brentford

9 August
Peterborough United

22 September
Burnley

19 October
Hartlepool United

8 January
Peterborough United

16 March
Oldham Athletic - postponed

5 May
Oldham Athletic

1994-95

HOME

Date	Opponent	Competition
24 August	Everton	FA Carling Premiership
27 August	Manchester United	FA Carling Premiership
12 September	Southampton	FA Carling Premiership
24 September	Nottingham Forest	FA Carling Premiership
4 October	Watford	Coca Cola Cup
8 October	Queens Park Rangers	FA Carling Premiership
29 October	West Ham United	FA Carling Premiership
19 November	Aston Villa	FA Carling Premiership
23 November	Chelsea	FA Carling Premiership
3 December	Newcastle United	FA Carling Premiership
10 December	Sheffield Wednesday	FA Carling Premiership
27 December	Crystal Palace	FA Carling Premiership
2 January	Arsenal	FA Carling Premiership
7 January	Altrincham	FA Cup
21 January	Manchester City - postponed	FA Carling Premiership
5 February	Blackburn Rovers	FA Carling Premiership
18 February	Southampton	FA Cup
25 February	Wimbledon	FA Carling Premiership
8 March	Ipswich Town	FA Carling Premiership
18 March	Leicester City	FA Carling Premiership
22 March	Liverpool	FA Carling Premiership
11 April	Manchester City	FA Carling Premiership
17 April	Norwich City	FA Carling Premiership
9 May	Coventry City	FA Carling Premiership
14 May	Leeds United	FA Carling Premiership

☐ Handbook ☐ Season Ticket

Season Ticket

Handbook

24 August
Everton

24 September
Nottingham Forest

29 October
West Ham United

3 December
Newcastle United

27 December
Crystal Palace

21 January
Manchester City - postponed

18 February
Southampton

22 March
Liverpool

17 April
Norwich City

14 May
Leeds United

1994-95

AWAY

Date	Opponent	Competition
22 July	Bournemouth	Richard Cooke Testimonial
26 July	Cambridge United	Friendly
29 July	Bristol City	Friendly
2 August	Brighton and Hove Albion	Friendly
6 August	Watford	Friendly
9 August	Shelbourne	Friendly
20 August	Sheffield Wednesday	FA Carling Premiership
30 August	Ipswich Town	FA Carling Premiership
17 September	Leicester City	FA Carling Premiership
21 September	Watford	Coca Cola Cup
1 October	Wimbledon	FA Carling Premiership
15 October	Leeds United	FA Carling Premiership
22 October	Manchester City	FA Carling Premiership
26 October	Notts County	Coca Cola Cup
5 November	Blackburn Rovers	FA Carling Premiership
11 November	Reading	Friendly
26 November	Liverpool	FA Carling Premiership
17 December	Everton	FA Carling Premiership
26 December	Norwich City	FA Carling Premiership
31 December	Coventry City	FA Carling Premiership
14 January	West Ham United	FA Carling Premiership
25 January	Aston Villa	FA Carling Premiership
29 January	Sunderland	FA Cup
11 February	Chelsea	FA Carling Premiership
22 February	Newcastle United - postponed	FA Carling Premiership
1 March	Southampton	FA Cup
4 March	Nottingham Forest	FA Carling Premiership
11 March	Liverpool	FA Cup
15 March	Manchester United	FA Carling Premiership
2 April	Southampton	FA Carling Premiership
9 April	Everton (Elland Road)	FA Cup
14 April	Crystal Palace	FA Carling Premiership
29 April	Arsenal	FA Carling Premiership
3 May	Newcastle United	FA Carling Premiership
6 May	Queens Park Rangers	FA Carling Premiership
21 May	Eastern/Kitchee Select (Hong Kong)	Euro-Asia Challenge
24 May	Guangzhou	Friendly
26 May	Singapore Lions	Pioneer Challenge

22 July
Bournemouth

26 July
Cambridge United

29 July
Bristol City

2 August
Brighton & Hove Albion

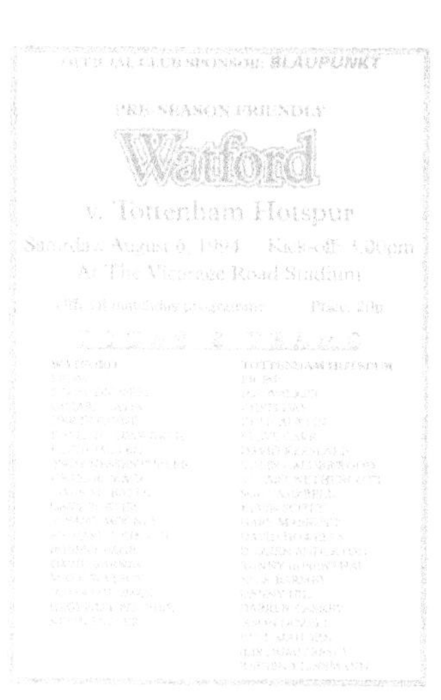

6 August
Watford

9 August
Shelbourne

20 August
Sheffield Wednesday

26 October
Notts County

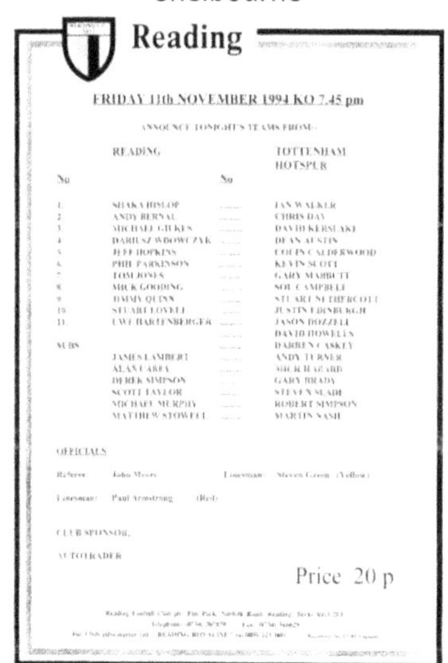
Reading

FRIDAY 11th NOVEMBER 1994 KO 7.45 pm

ANNOUNCE TONIGHT'S TEAMS FROM:-

No	READING	No	TOTTENHAM HOTSPUR
1	SHAKA HISLOP		IAN WALKER
2	ANDY BERNAL		CHRIS DAY
3	MICHAEL GILKES		DAVID KERSLAKE
4	DARIUSZ WDOWCZYK		DEAN AUSTIN
5	JEFF HOPKINS		COLIN CALDERWOOD
6	PHIL PARKINSON		KEVIN SCOTT
7	TOM JONES		GARY MABBUTT
8	MICK GOODING		SOL CAMPBELL
9	JIMMY QUINN		STUART NETHERCOTT
10	STUART LOVELL		JUSTIN EDINBURGH
11	UWE HARTENBERGER		JASON DOZZELL
			DAVID HOWELLS
SUBS			DARREN CASKEY
	JAMES LAMBERT		ANDY TURNER
	ALAN CAREY		NICK HAZARD
	DEREK SIMPSON		GARY BRADY
	SCOTT TAYLOR		STEVEN SLADE
	MICHAEL MURPHY		ROBERT SIMPSON
	MATTHEW STOWELL		MARTIN NASH

OFFICIALS

Referee: John Moore Linesman: Steven Green (Yellow)

Linesman: Paul Armstrong (Red)

CLUB SPONSOR:

AUTOTRADER

Price 20 p

11 November
Reading

22 February
Newcastle United - postponed

6 May
Queens Park Rangers

21 May
Eastern/Kitchee Select

1995-96

HOME

		Date	Opponent	Competition
☐	☐	12 August	Newcastle United	Gary Mabbutt Testimonial
☐	☐	23 August	Aston Villa	FA Carling Premiership
☐	☐	26 August	Liverpool	FA Carling Premiership
☐	☐	9 September	Leeds United	FA Carling Premiership
☐	☐	20 September	Chester City	Coca Cola Cup
☐	☐	30 September	Wimbledon	FA Carling Premiership
☐	☐	14 October	Nottingham Forest	FA Carling Premiership
☐	☐	29 October	Newcastle United	FA Carling Premiership
☐	☐	18 November	Arsenal	FA Carling Premiership
☐	☐	2 December	Everton	FA Carling Premiership
☐	☐	9 December	Queens Park Rangers	FA Carling Premiership
☐	☐	23 December	Bolton Wanderers	FA Carling Premiership
☐	☐	1 January	Manchester United	FA Carling Premiership
☐	☐	13 January	Manchester City	FA Carling Premiership
☐	☐	17 January	Hereford United	FA Cup
☐	☐	27 January	Wolverhampton Wanderers	FA Cup
☐	☐	12 February	West Ham United	FA Carling Premiership
☐	☐	24 February	Sheffield Wednesday	FA Carling Premiership
☐	☐	2 March	Southampton	FA Carling Premiership
☐	☐	9 March	Nottingham Forest	FA Cup
☐	☐	16 March	Blackburn Rovers	FA Carling Premiership
☐	☐	30 March	Coventry City	FA Carling Premiership
☐	☐	8 April	Middlesbrough	FA Carling Premiership
☐	☐	27 April	Chelsea	FA Carling Premiership

☐ Handbook ☐ Season Ticket

Season Ticket

Handbook

12 August
Newcastle United

26 August
Liverpool

20 September
Chester City

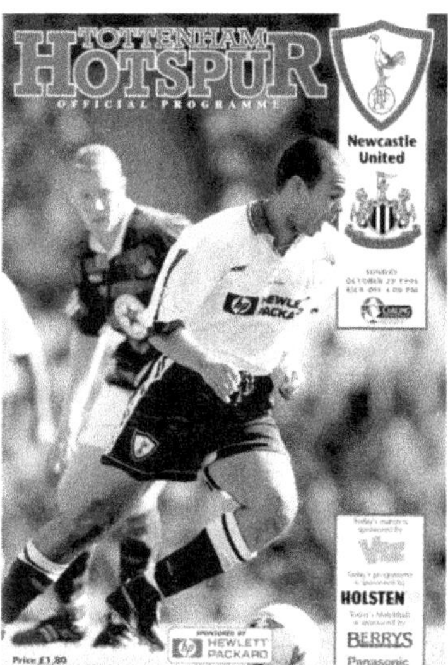

29 October
Newcastle United

9 December
Queens Park Rangers

17 January
Hereford United

24 February
Sheffield Wednesday

9 March
Nottingham Forest

30 March
Coventry City

27 April
Chelsea

1995-96

AWAY

		Date	Opponent	Competition
		22 July	Silkeborg (Bjerringbro)	Friendly
		23 July	Halmstad (Vinberg)	Friendly
		24 July	IFK Göteborg (Varberg)	Friendly
		26 July	Hässleholm	Friendly
		29 July	Sampdoria (Ibrox Park)	Ibrox International Tournament
		30 July	Steaua Bucharest (Ibrox Park)	Ibrox International Tournament
		2 August	Derby County	Friendly
		5 August	Watford	Friendly
		19 August	Manchester City	FA Carling Premiership
		30 August	West Ham United	FA Carling Premiership
		16 September	Sheffield Wednesday	FA Carling Premiership
		25 September	Queens Park Rangers	FA Carling Premiership
		4 October	Chester City	Coca Cola Cup
		22 October	Everton	FA Carling Premiership
		25 October	Coventry City	Coca Cola Cup
		4 November	Coventry City	FA Carling Premiership
		21 November	Middlesbrough	FA Carling Premiership
		25 November	Chelsea	FA Carling Premiership
		16 December	Wimbledon	FA Carling Premiership
		26 December	Southampton	FA Carling Premiership
		30 December	Blackburn Rovers	FA Carling Premiership
		6 January	Hereford United	FA Cup
		21 January	Aston Villa	FA Carling Premiership
		3 February	Liverpool	FA Carling Premiership
		7 February	Wolverhampton Wanderers	FA Cup
		19 February	Nottingham Forest - abandoned	FA Cup
		28 February	Nottingham Forest	FA Cup
		20 March	Bolton Wanderers	FA Carling Premiership
		24 March	Manchester United	FA Carling Premiership
		6 April	Nottingham Forest	FA Carling Premiership
		15 April	Arsenal	FA Carling Premiership
		2 May	Leeds United	FA Carling Premiership
		5 May	Newcastle United	FA Carling Premiership

22 July
Silkeborg

23 July
Halmstad

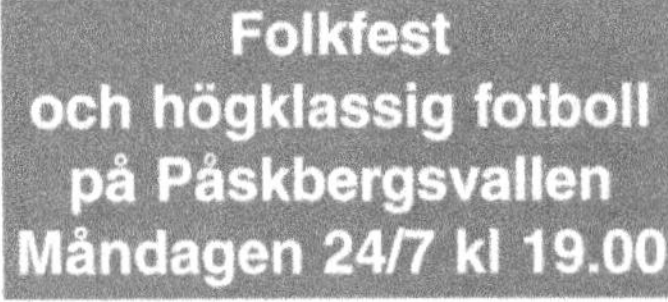

24 July
IFK Göteborg

1905  1995

Jubileumsmatch

IFK HÄSSLEHOLM

vs

TOTTENHAM HOTSPURS FC

Onsdagen den 26 Juli 1995

kl. 19.30

Österås IP

26 July
Hässleholm

29 July
Sampdoria

30 July
Steaua Bucharest

2 August
Derby County

5 August
Watford

4 October
Chester City

6 January
Hereford United

19 February
Nottingham Forest - abandoned

28 February
Nottingham Forest

1996-97

HOME

	Date	Opponent	Competition
☐☐	21 August	Derby County	FA Carling Premiership
☐☐	24 August	Everton	FA Carling Premiership
☐☐	7 September	Newcastle United	FA Carling Premiership
☐☐	22 September	Leicester City	FA Carling Premiership
☐☐	25 September	Preston North End	Coca Cola Cup
☐☐	12 October	Aston Villa	FA Carling Premiership
☐☐	23 October	Sunderland	Coca Cola Cup
☐☐	2 November	West Ham United	FA Carling Premiership
☐☐	16 November	Sunderland	FA Carling Premiership
☐☐	2 December	Liverpool	FA Carling Premiership
☐☐	21 December	Sheffield Wednesday	FA Carling Premiership
☐☐	26 December	Southampton	FA Carling Premiership
☐☐	12 January	Manchester United	FA Carling Premiership
☐☐	29 January	Blackburn Rovers	FA Carling Premiership
☐☐	1 February	Chelsea	FA Carling Premiership
☐☐	15 February	Arsenal	FA Carling Premiership
☐☐	1 March	Nottingham Forest	FA Carling Premiership
☐☐	15 March	Leeds United	FA Carling Premiership
☐☐	5 April	Wimbledon	FA Carling Premiership
☐☐	24 April	Middlesbrough	FA Carling Premiership
☐☐	11 May	Coventry City	FA Carling Premiership

☐ Handbook ☐ Season Ticket

Season Ticket

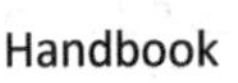

Handbook

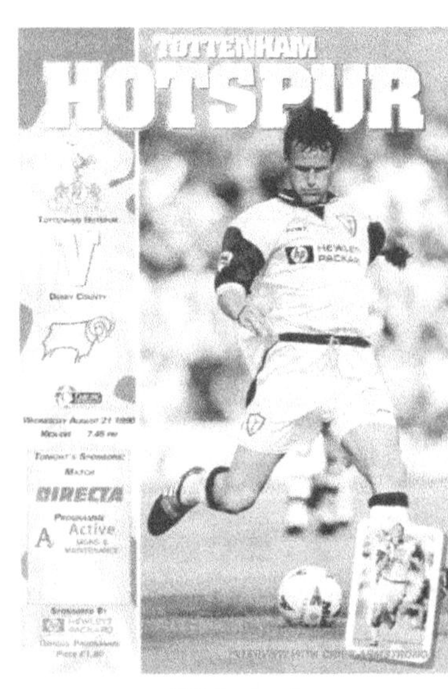

21 August
Derby County

22 September
Leicester City

23 October
Sunderland

16 November
Sunderland

21 December
Sheffield Wednesday

29 January
Blackburn Rovers

15 February
Arsenal

15 March
Leeds United

24 April
Middlesbrough

11 May
Coventry City

1996-97

AWAY

		Date	Opponent	Competition
		23 July	Ham-Kam (Hamar Stadion)	Friendly
		25 July	Odd Grenland (dated 27 July)	Friendly
		26 July	Raufoss	Friendly
		31 July	Brentford	Friendly
		3 August	Reading	Friendly
		7 August	Southend United	CTA International Trophy
		10 August	Charlton Athletic	Colin Walsh Testimonial
		17 August	Blackburn Rovers	FA Carling Premiership
		4 September	Wimbledon	FA Carling Premiership
		14 September	Southampton	FA Carling Premiership
		17 September	Preston North End	Coca Cola Cup
		29 September	Manchester United	FA Carling Premiership
		19 October	Middlesbrough	FA Carling Premiership
		26 October	Chelsea	FA Carling Premiership
		24 November	Arsenal	FA Carling Premiership
		27 November	Bolton Wanderers	Coca Cola Cup
		7 December	Coventry City	FA Carling Premiership
		14 December	Leeds United	FA Carling Premiership
		28 December	Newcastle United	FA Carling Premiership
		1 January	Leicester City - postponed	FA Carling Premiership
		5 January	Manchester United	FA Cup
		19 January	Nottingham Forest	FA Carling Premiership
		24 February	West Ham United	FA Carling Premiership
		4 March	Sunderland	FA Carling Premiership
		19 March	Leicester City	FA Carling Premiership
		22 March	Derby County	FA Carling Premiership
		9 April	Sheffield Wednesday	FA Carling Premiership
		12 April	Everton	FA Carling Premiership
		19 April	Aston Villa	FA Carling Premiership
		3 May	Liverpool	FA Carling Premiership

LAGOPPSTILLING

Briskeby Gressbane 23.07.96

Ham Kam Tottenham Hotspur

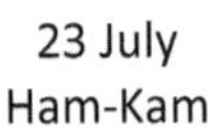

23 July
Ham-Kam

25 July
Odd Grenland

RAUFOSS TOTTENHAM

DOMMER:

26 July
Raufoss

31 July
Brentford

3 August
Reading

7 August
Southend United

10 August
Charlton Athletic

17 August
Blackburn Rovers

1 January
Leicester City - postponed

5 January
Manchester United

12 April
Everton

3 May
Liverpool

1997-98

HOME

	Date	Opponent	Competition
☐☐	2 August	Fiorentina	David Howells Testimonial
☐☐	10 August	Manchester United	FA Carling Premiership
☐☐	23 August	Derby County	FA Carling Premiership
☐☐	27 August	Aston Villa	FA Carling Premiership
☐☐	17 September	Carlisle United	Coca Cola Cup
☐☐	20 September	Blackburn Rovers	FA Carling Premiership
☐☐	27 September	Wimbledon	FA Carling Premiership
☐☐	15 October	Derby County	Coca Cola Cup
☐☐	19 October	Sheffield Wednesday	FA Carling Premiership
☐☐	1 November	Leeds United	FA Carling Premiership
☐☐	24 November	Crystal Palace	FA Carling Premiership
☐☐	6 December	Chelsea	FA Carling Premiership
☐☐	20 December	Barnsley	FA Carling Premiership
☐☐	28 December	Arsenal	FA Carling Premiership
☐☐	5 January	Fulham	FA Cup
☐☐	17 January	West Ham United	FA Carling Premiership
☐☐	24 January	Barnsley	FA Cup
☐☐	14 February	Leicester City	FA Carling Premiership
☐☐	1 March	Bolton Wanderers	FA Carling Premiership
☐☐	14 March	Liverpool	FA Carling Premiership
☐☐	4 April	Everton	FA Carling Premiership
☐☐	13 April	Coventry City	FA Carling Premiership
☐☐	25 April	Newcastle United	FA Carling Premiership
☐☐	10 May	Southampton	FA Carling Premiership

☐ Handbook ☐ Season Ticket

Season Ticket

Handbook

2 August
Fiorentina

27 August
Aston Villa

15 October
Derby County

24 November
Crystal Palace

20 December
Barnsley

17 January
West Ham United

14 February
Leicester City

14 March
Liverpool

4 April
Everton

10 May
Southampton

1997-98

AWAY

		Date	Opponent	Competition
		15 July	Ski	Friendly
		17 July	Faaberg	Friendly
		18 July	Fredrikstad	Friendly
		21 July	Rosenborg	Friendly
		23 July	Leyton Orient	Friendly
		26 July	Swindon Town	Friendly
		29 July	Oxford United	Oxfordshire "Bill Halsey" Memorial Trophy
		13 August	West Ham United	FA Carling Premiership
		30 August	Arsenal	FA Carling Premiership
		13 September	Leicester City	FA Carling Premiership
		23 September	Bolton Wanderers	FA Carling Premiership
		30 September	Carlisle United	Coca Cola Cup
		4 October	Newcastle United	FA Carling Premiership
		25 October	Southampton	FA Carling Premiership
		8 November	Liverpool	FA Carling Premiership
		29 November	Everton	FA Carling Premiership
		13 December	Coventry City	FA Carling Premiership
		26 December	Aston Villa	FA Carling Premiership
		10 January	Manchester United	FA Carling Premiership
		31 January	Derby County	FA Carling Premiership
		4 February	Barnsley	FA Cup
		7 February	Blackburn Rovers	FA Carling Premiership
		21 February	Sheffield Wednesday	FA Carling Premiership
		4 March	Leeds United	FA Carling Premiership
		28 March	Crystal Palace	FA Carling Premiership
		11 April	Chelsea	FA Carling Premiership
		18 April	Barnsley	FA Carling Premiership
		2 May	Wimbledon	FA Carling Premiership

15 July
Ski

17 July
Faaberg

18 July
Fredrikstad

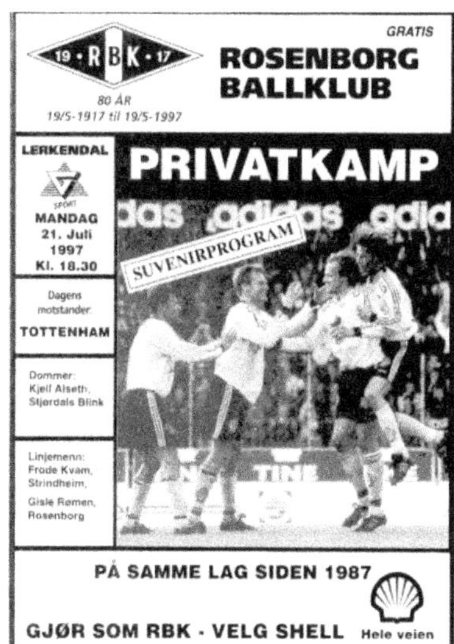

21 July
Rosenborg

23 July
Leyton Orient

26 July
Swindon Town

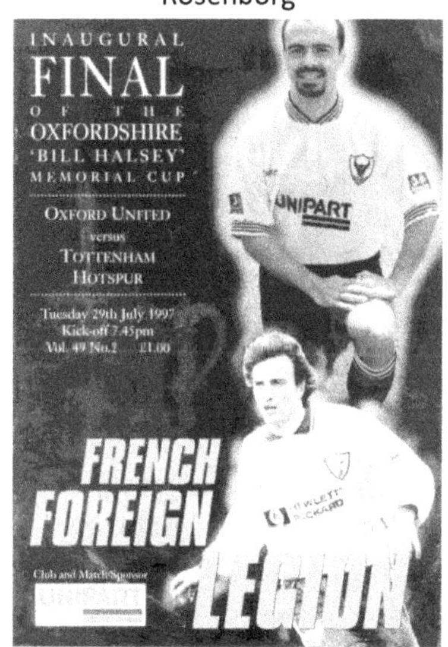

29 July
Oxford United

13 August
West Ham United

30 September
Carlisle United

25 October
Southampton

13 December
Coventry City

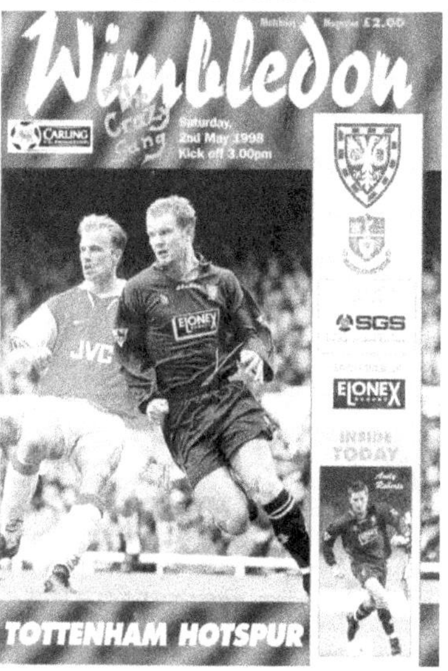

2 May
Wimbledon

1998-99

HOME

	Date	Opponent	Competition
☐☐	22 August	Sheffield Wednesday	FA Carling Premiership
☐☐	9 September	Blackburn Rovers	FA Carling Premiership
☐☐	13 September	Middlesbrough	FA Carling Premiership
☐☐	23 September	Brentford	Worthington Cup
☐☐	26 September	Leeds United	FA Carling Premiership
☐☐	24 October	Newcastle United	FA Carling Premiership
☐☐	2 November	Charlton Athletic	FA Carling Premiership
☐☐	21 November	Nottingham Forest	FA Carling Premiership
☐☐	2 December	Manchester United	Worthington Cup
☐☐	5 December	Liverpool	FA Carling Premiership
☐☐	12 December	Manchester United	Premiership
☐☐	28 December	Everton	FA Carling Premiership
☐☐	2 January	Watford	FA Cup
☐☐	16 January	Wimbledon	FA Carling Premiership
☐☐	27 January	Wimbledon	Worthington Cup
☐☐	2 February	Wimbledon	FA Cup
☐☐	6 February	Coventry City	FA Carling Premiership
☐☐	24 February	Leeds United	FA Cup
☐☐	27 February	Derby County	FA Carling Premiership
☐☐	2 March	Southampton	FA Carling Premiership
☐☐	13 March	Aston Villa	FA Carling Premiership
☐☐	3 April	Leicester City	FA Carling Premiership
☐☐	24 April	West Ham United	FA Carling Premiership
☐☐	5 May	Arsenal	FA Carling Premiership
☐☐	10 May	Chelsea	FA Carling Premiership

☐ Handbook

☐ Season Ticket

Season Ticket

Handbook

22 August
Sheffield Wednesday

23 September
Brentford

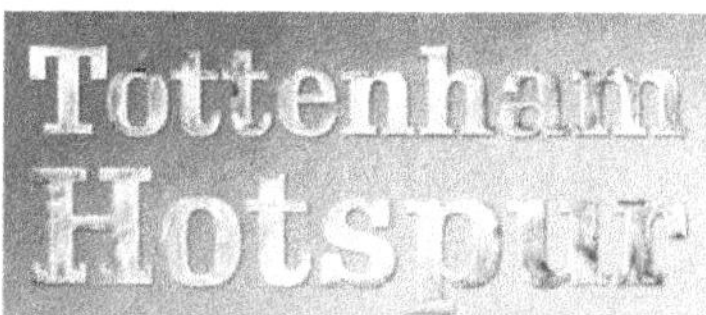

2 November
Charlton Athletic

2 December
Manchester United

28 December
Everton

16 January
Wimbledon

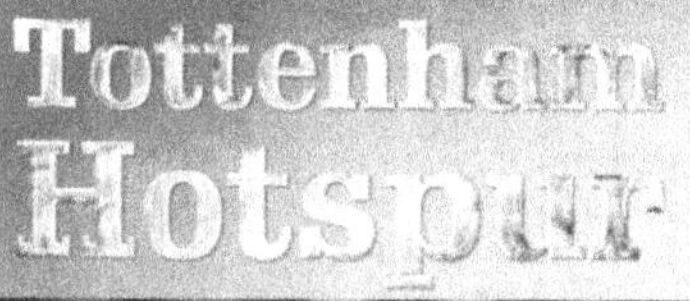

27 February
Derby County

13 March
Aston Villa

24 April
West Ham United

10 May
Chelsea

1998-99

AWAY

	Date	Opponent	Competition
☐ ☐	10 July	Grasshopper Club	Friendly
☐ ☐	15 July	Peterborough United	Friendly
☐ ☐	19 July	Brøndby	Friendly
☐ ☐	22 July	Birmingham City	Friendly
☐ ☐	25 July	Celtic	Friendly
☐ ☐	29 July	Norwich City	Friendly
☐ ☐	1 August	Queens Park Rangers	Friendly
☐ ☐	5 August	De Tubanters	Friendly
☐ ☐	8 August	Feyenoord	Friendly
☐ ☐	11 August	St Albans City	Friendly
☐ ☐	15 August	Wimbledon	FA Carling Premiership
☐ ☐	29 August	Everton	FA Carling Premiership
☐ ☐	15 September	Brentford	Worthington Cup
☐ ☐	19 September	Southampton	FA Carling Premiership
☐ ☐	3 October	Derby County	FA Carling Premiership
☐ ☐	19 October	Leicester City	FA Carling Premiership
☐ ☐	27 October	Northampton Town	Worthington Cup
☐ ☐	7 November	Aston Villa	FA Carling Premiership
☐ ☐	10 November	Liverpool	Worthington Cup
☐ ☐	14 November	Arsenal	FA Carling Premiership
☐ ☐	28 November	West Ham United	FA Carling Premiership
☐ ☐	19 December	Chelsea	FA Carling Premiership
☐ ☐	26 December	Coventry City	FA Carling Premiership
☐ ☐	9 January	Sheffield Wednesday	FA Carling Premiership
☐ ☐	23 January	Wimbledon	FA Cup
☐ ☐	30 January	Blackburn Rovers	FA Carling Premiership
☐ ☐	13 February	Leeds United	FA Cup
☐ ☐	16 February	Wimbledon	Worthington Cup
☐ ☐	20 February	Middlesbrough	FA Carling Premiership
☐ ☐	10 March	Leeds United	FA Carling Premiership
☐ ☐	16 March	Barnsley	FA Cup
☐ ☐	21 March	Leicester City (Wembley)	Worthington Cup
☐ ☐	5 April	Newcastle United	FA Carling Premiership
☐ ☐	11 April	Newcastle United (Old Trafford)	FA Cup
☐ ☐	17 April	Nottingham Forest	FA Carling Premiership
☐ ☐	20 April	Charlton Athletic	FA Carling Premiership
☐ ☐	1 May	Liverpool	FA Carling Premiership
☐ ☐	16 May	Manchester United	FA Carling Premiership

Datum: Freitag 10. Juli 1998 Anspielzeit: 19.00 Uhr
Spieltag: Vorbereitungsspiel

Grasshopper-Club – Tottenham Hotspurs

Schiedsrichter: Dieter Schoch Linienrichter: Käppeli Ruedi, Buragina Franco

Aufstellung Grasshopper Club Zürich		Aufstellung Tottenham Hotspurs	
18	Walker Philipp	1	Walker Ian
2	Haas Bernt	2	Carr Stephen
3	Christ Sven	3	Tramezzani Paolo
5	Tararache Mihai	4	Berti Nicola
6	Mazzarelli Giuseppe	5	Vega Ramon
9	Tikva Avraham	6	Scales John
10	Kavelashvili Michail	7	Fox Ruel
14	Vogel Johann	8	Clemence Stephen
16	Smiljanic Boris	9	Allen Rory
18	Magnin Joel	11	Sinton Andy
20	Magro Feliciano	14	Ginola David
13	Savic Nenad	10	Armstrong Chris
15	Cabanas Ricardo	12	Edinburgh Justin
17	Zanni Reto	13	Brown Simon
21	Berner Bruno	15	Dominguez Jose
24	Pena	16	Saib Moussa
25	Al-Enazi Mohamed	17	[illegible]
1	Zuberbühler Pascal		

Bemerkungen: Verletzt: Comisetti, Esposito, Gren, Nemsadze, Türkyilmaz

Bemerkungen: Verletzt:

10 July
Grasshopper Club

15 July
Peterborough United

19 July
Brøndby

22 July
Birmingham City

25 July
Celtic

29 July
Norwich City

1 August
Queens Park Rangers

5 August
De Tubanters

8 August
Feyenoord

11 August
St Albans City

15 September
Brentford

27 October
Northampton Town

1999-2000

HOME

	Date	Opponent	Competition
☐☐	9 August	Newcastle United	FA Carling Premiership
☐☐	14 August	Everton	FA Carling Premiership
☐☐	28 August	Leeds United	FA Carling Premiership
☐☐	16 September	Zimbru Chişinău	UEFA Cup
☐☐	19 September	Coventry City	FA Carling Premiership
☐☐	3 October	Leicester City	FA Carling Premiership
☐☐	13 October	Crewe Alexandra	Worthington Cup
☐☐	23 October	Manchester United	FA Carling Premiership
☐☐	28 October	1FC Kaiserslautern	UEFA Cup
☐☐	7 November	Arsenal	FA Carling Premiership
☐☐	6 December	West Ham United	FA Carling Premiership
☐☐	12 December	Newcastle United	FA Cup
☐☐	26 December	Watford	Premiership
☐☐	3 January	Liverpool	FA Carling Premiership
☐☐	22 January	Sheffield Wednesday	FA Carling Premiership
☐☐	5 February	Chelsea	FA Carling Premiership
☐☐	4 March	Bradford City	FA Carling Premiership
☐☐	11 March	Southampton	FA Carling Premiership
☐☐	3 April	Middlesbrough	FA Carling Premiership
☐☐	15 April	Aston Villa	FA Carling Premiership
☐☐	22 April	Wimbledon	FA Carling Premiership
☐☐	29 April	Derby County	FA Carling Premiership
☐☐	14 May	Sunderland	FA Carling Premiership

☐ Handbook ☐ Season Ticket

Season Ticket

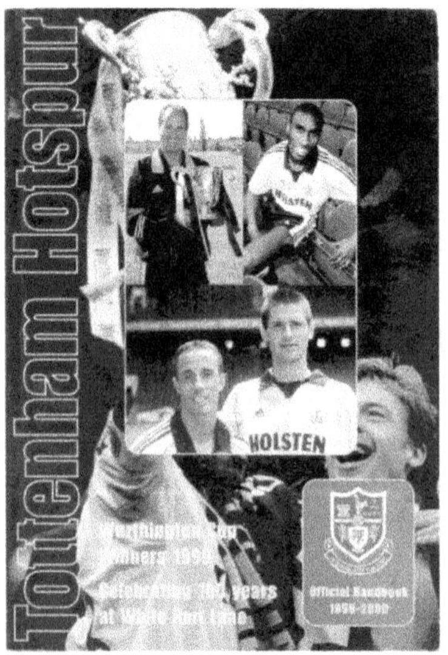

Handbook

9 August
Newcastle United

19 September
Coventry City

13 October
Crewe Alexandra

7 November
Arsenal

12 December
Newcastle United

22 January
Sheffield Wednesday

5 February
Chelsea

11 March
Southampton

15 April
Aston Villa

14 May
Sunderland

1999-2000

AWAY

		Date	Opponent	Competition
		15 July	Elfsborg (Varberg)	Friendly
		17 July	Lysekil	Friendly
		20 July	GAIS - light green issue	Friendly
			- dark green issue	
			- white issue	
		24 July	Heart of Midlothian	Friendly
		28 July	Queens Park Rangers	Friendly
		31 July	Wolverhampton Wanderers	Friendly
		7 August	West Ham United	FA Carling Premiership
		21 August	Sheffield Wednesday	FA Carling Premiership
		3 September	Bishop's Stortford	Opening of Ground
		12 September	Bradford City	FA Carling Premiership
		26 September	Wimbledon	FA Carling Premiership
		30 September	Zimbru Chişinău	UEFA Cup
		16 October	Derby County	FA Carling Premiership
		31 October	Sunderland	FA Carling Premiership
		4 November	1FC Kaiserslautern	UEFA Cup
		20 November	Southampton	FA Carling Premiership
		28 November	Newcastle United	FA Carling Premiership
		1 December	Fulham	Worthington Cup
		18 December	Middlesbrough	FA Carling Premiership
		22 December	Newcastle United	FA Cup
		29 December	Aston Villa	FA Carling Premiership
		12 January	Chelsea	FA Carling Premiership
		15 January	Everton	FA Carling Premiership
		12 February	Leeds United	FA Carling Premiership
		26 February	Coventry City	FA Carling Premiership
		19 March	Arsenal	FA Carling Premiership
		25 March	Watford	FA Carling Premiership
		9 April	Liverpool	FA Carling Premiership
		19 April	Leicester City	FA Carling Premiership
		6 May	Manchester United	FA Carling Premiership
		9 May	Portsmouth	Justin Edinburgh Testimonial

15 July
Elfsborg

17 July
Lysekils

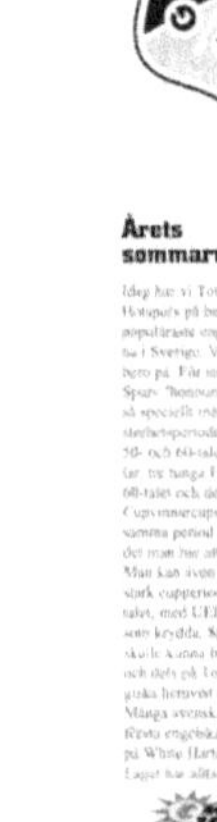

20 July
GAIS

24 July
Heart of Midlothian

28 July
Queens Park Rangers

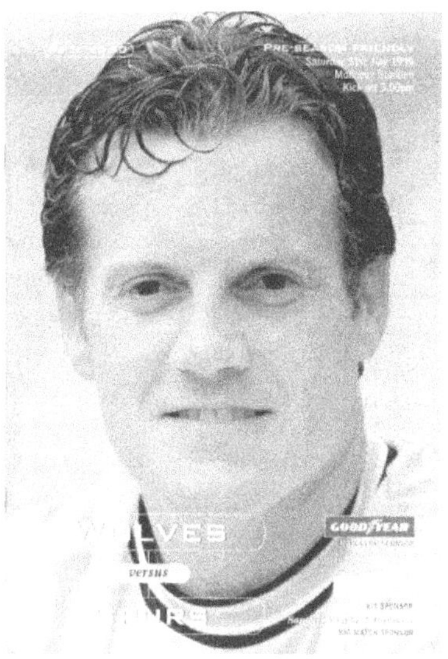

31 July
Wolverhampton Wanderers

3 September
Bishop's Stortford

16 October
Derby County

31 October
Sunderland

1 December
Fulham

15 January
Everton

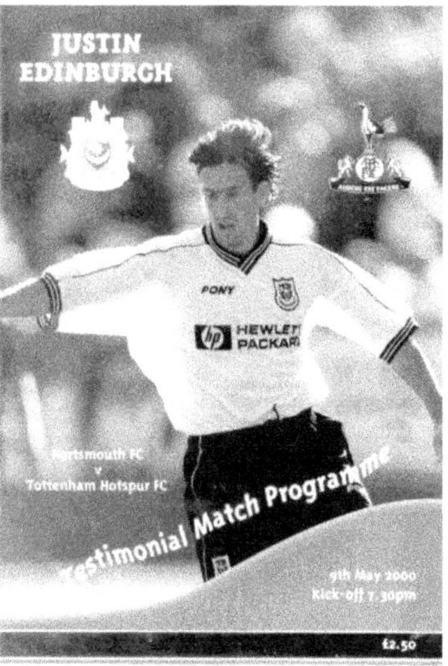

9 May
Portsmouth

2000-01

HOME

		Date	Opponent	Competition
☐	☐	19 August	Ipswich Town	FA Carling Premiership
☐	☐	5 September	Everton	FA Carling Premiership
☐	☐	11 September	West Ham United	FA Carling Premiership
☐	☐	23 September	Manchester City	FA Carling Premiership
☐	☐	26 September	Brentford	Worthington Cup
☐	☐	21 October	Derby County	FA Carling Premiership
☐	☐	31 October	Birmingham City	Worthington Cup
☐	☐	4 November	Sunderland	FA Carling Premiership
☐	☐	19 November	Liverpool	FA Carling Premiership
☐	☐	25 November	Leicester City	FA Carling Premiership
☐	☐	18 December	Arsenal	FA Carling Premiership
☐	☐	23 December	Middlesbrough	FA Carling Premiership
☐	☐	2 January	Newcastle United	FA Carling Premiership
☐	☐	20 January	Southampton	FA Carling Premiership
☐	☐	3 February	Charlton Athletic	FA Carling Premiership
☐	☐	17 February	Stockport County	FA Cup
☐	☐	24 February	Leeds United	FA Carling Premiership
☐	☐	17 March	Coventry City	FA Carling Premiership
☐	☐	10 April	Bradford City	FA Carling Premiership
☐	☐	17 April	Chelsea	FA Carling Premiership
☐	☐	28 April	Aston Villa	FA Carling Premiership
☐	☐	19 May	Manchester United	FA Carling Premiership

☐ Handbook ☐ Season Ticket

Season Ticket

Handbook

19 August
Ipswich Town

11 September
West Ham United

21 October
Derby County

4 November
Sunderland

18 December
Arsenal

20 January
Southampton

17 February
Stockport County

17 March
Coventry City

10 April
Bradford City

19 May
Manchester United

2000-01

AWAY

		Date	Opponent	Competition
		19 July	AIK Skelleftea (Byske)	Friendly
		22 July	Tervarit - large colour	Friendly
			- small black/white	
			- newspaper	
		24 July	Bodens	Friendly
		29 July	Birmingham City	Friendly
		2 August	Fulham	Simon Morgan Testimonial
		5 August	Queens Park Rangers	Danny Maddix Testimonial
		8 August	Peterborough United	Friendly
		12 August	Vitesse Arnhem	Friendly
		22 August	Middlesbrough	FA Carling Premiership
		26 August	Newcastle United	FA Carling Premiership
		16 September	Charlton Athletic	FA Carling Premiership
		19 September	Brentford	Worthington Cup
		30 September	Leeds United	FA Carling Premiership
		14 October	Coventry City	FA Carling Premiership
		28 October	Chelsea	FA Carling Premiership
		11 November	Aston Villa	FA Carling Premiership
		2 December	Manchester United	FA Carling Premiership
		9 December	Bradford City	FA Carling Premiership
		27 December	Southampton	FA Carling Premiership
		30 December	Ipswich Town	FA Carling Premiership
		6 January	Leyton Orient	FA Cup
		13 January	Everton	FA Carling Premiership
		31 January	West Ham United	FA Carling Premiership
		7 February	Charlton Athletic	FA Cup
		10 February	Manchester City	FA Carling Premiership
		3 March	Derby County	FA Carling Premiership
		11 March	West Ham United	FA Cup
		31 March	Arsenal	FA Carling Premiership
		8 April	Arsenal (Old Trafford)	FA Cup
		14 April	Sunderland	FA Carling Premiership
		22 April	Liverpool	FA Carling Premiership
		5 May	Leicester City	FA Carling Premiership

19 July
AIK Skelleftea

22 July
Tervarit

22 July
Tervarit - newspaper issue

24 July
Bodens

29 July
Birmingham City

2 August
Fulham

5 August
Queens Park Rangers

8 August
Peterborough United

12 August
Vitesse Arnhem

9 December
Bradford City

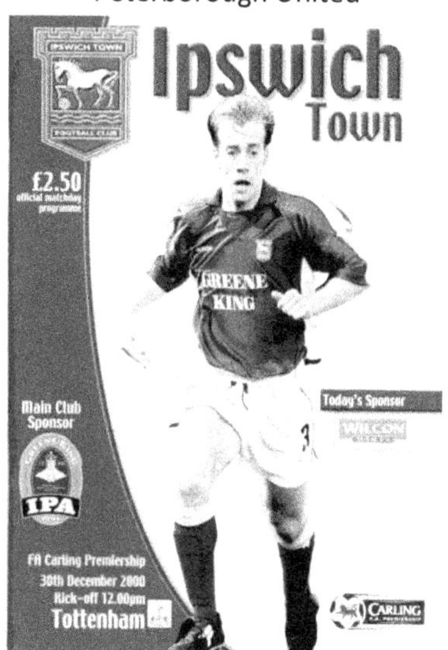

30 December
Ipswich Town

3 March
Derby County

2001-02

HOME

		Date	Opponent	Competition
☐	☐	8 August	Fiorentina	Bill Nicholson Testimonial
☐	☐	18 August	Aston Villa	FA Barclaycard Premiership
☐	☐	9 September	Southampton	FA Barclaycard Premiership
☐	☐	13 September	Torquay United	Worthington Cup
☐	☐	16 September	Chelsea	FA Barclaycard Premiership
☐	☐	29 September	Manchester United	FA Barclaycard Premiership
☐	☐	15 October	Derby County	FA Barclaycard Premiership
☐	☐	27 October	Middlesbrough	FA Barclaycard Premiership
☐	☐	17 November	Arsenal	FA Barclaycard Premiership
☐	☐	3 December	Bolton Wanderers	FA Barclaycard Premiership
☐	☐	11 December	Bolton Wanderers	Worthington Cup
☐	☐	15 December	Fulham	FA Barclaycard Premiership
☐	☐	22 December	Ipswich Town	FA Barclaycard Premiership
☐	☐	1 January	Blackburn Rovers	FA Barclaycard Premiership
☐	☐	19 January	Everton	FA Barclaycard Premiership
☐	☐	23 January	Chelsea	Worthington Cup
☐	☐	26 January	Bolton Wanderers -postponed	FA Cup
☐	☐	30 January	Newcastle United	FA Barclaycard Premiership
☐	☐	5 February	Bolton Wanderers	FA Cup
☐	☐	9 February	Leicester City	FA Barclaycard Premiership
☐	☐	17 February	Tranmere Rovers	FA Cup
☐	☐	2 March	Sunderland	FA Barclaycard Premiership
☐	☐	10 March	Chelsea	FA Cup
☐	☐	18 March	Charlton Athletic	FA Barclaycard Premiership
☐	☐	1 April	Leeds United	FA Barclaycard Premiership
☐	☐	13 April	West Ham United	FA Barclaycard Premiership
☐	☐	27 April	Liverpool	FA Barclaycard Premiership

☐ Handbook ☐ Season Ticket

Season Ticket

Handbook

8 August
Fiorentina

18 August
Aston Villa

29 September
Manchester United

27 October
Middlesbrough

17 November
Arsenal

11 December
Bolton Wanderers

26 January
Bolton Wanderers - postponed

9 February
Leicester City

10 March
Chelsea

27 April
Liverpool

2001-02

AWAY

		Date	Opponent	Competition
		13 July	Stevenage Borough	Friendly
		17 July	Swindon Town	Friendly
		19 July	Leyton Orient	Steve Castle Testimonial
		21 July	Wycombe Wanderers	Friendly
		25 July	Portsmouth	Friendly
		1 August	Reading	Friendly
		4 August	Millwall	Keith Stevens Benefit
		7 August	Luton Town	Friendly
		12 August	AEK Athens - Greek issue with Spurs badge	Friendly
			- Greek issue without Spurs badge	Friendly
			- English issue	Friendly
		20 August	Everton	FA Barclaycard Premiership
		25 August	Blackburn Rovers	FA Barclaycard Premiership
		19 September	Sunderland	FA Barclaycard Premiership
		22 September	Liverpool	FA Barclaycard Premiership
		9 October	Tranmere Rovers	Worthington Cup
		21 October	Newcastle United	FA Barclaycard Premiership
		4 November	Leeds United	FA Barclaycard Premiership
		24 November	West Ham United	FA Barclaycard Premiership
		29 November	Fulham	Worthington Cup
		8 December	Charlton Athletic	FA Barclaycard Premiership
		26 December	Southampton	FA Barclaycard Premiership
		29 December	Aston Villa	FA Barclaycard Premiership
		9 January	Chelsea	Worthington Cup
		12 January	Ipswich Town	FA Barclaycard Premiership
		16 January	Coventry City	FA Cup
		2 February	Derby County	FA Barclaycard Premiership
		24 February	Blackburn Rovers (Millennium Stadium)	Worthington Cup
		6 March	Manchester United	FA Barclaycard Premiership
		12 March	Chelsea	FA Barclaycard Premiership
		24 March	Fulham	FA Barclaycard Premiership
		30 March	Middlesbrough	FA Barclaycard Premiership
		6 April	Arsenal	FA Barclaycard Premiership
		20 April	Bolton Wanderers	FA Barclaycard Premiership
		12 May	Leicester City	FA Barclaycard Premiership

13 July
Stevenage Borough

17 July
Swindon Town

19 July
Leyton Orient

21 July
Wycombe Wanderers

25 July
Portsmouth

1 August
Reading

4 August
Millwall

7 August
Luton Town

12 August
AEK - Greek edition (both badges)

12 August
AEK - English edition (both badges)

12 August
AEK - Greek edition (AEK badge only)

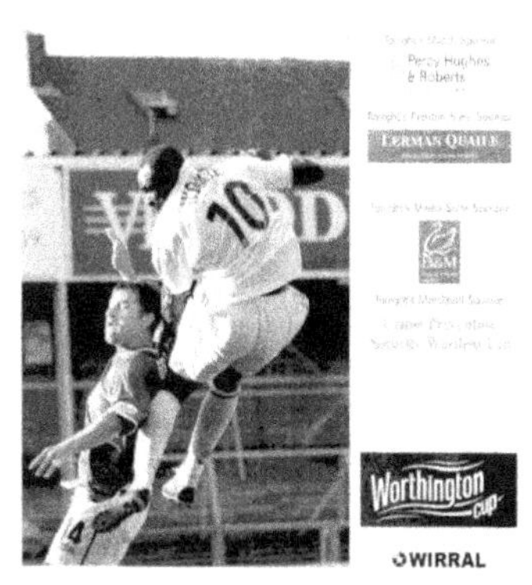

9 October
Tranmere Rovers

2002-03

HOME

	Date	Opponent	Competition
☐☐	7 August	Celtic	Friendly
☐☐	11 August	Lazio	Friendly
☐☐	24 August	Aston Villa	FA Barclaycard Premiership
☐☐	31 August	Southampton	FA Barclaycard Premiership
☐☐	15 September	West Ham United	FA Barclaycard Premiership
☐☐	28 September	Middlesbrough	FA Barclaycard Premiership
☐☐	1 October	Cardiff City	Worthington Cup
☐☐	17 October	DC United	Tottenham Tribute Trust
☐☐	20 October	Bolton Wanderers	FA Barclaycard Premiership
☐☐	3 November	Chelsea	FA Barclaycard Premiership
☐☐	24 November	Leeds United	FA Barclaycard Premiership
☐☐	8 December	West Bromwich Albion	FA Barclaycard Premiership
☐☐	15 December	Arsenal	FA Barclaycard Premiership
☐☐	26 December	Charlton Athletic	FA Barclaycard Premiership
☐☐	12 January	Everton	FA Barclaycard Premiership
☐☐	29 January	Newcastle United	FA Barclaycard Premiership
☐☐	8 February	Sunderland	FA Barclaycard Premiership
☐☐	24 February	Fulham	FA Barclaycard Premiership
☐☐	16 March	Liverpool	FA Barclaycard Premiership
☐☐	5 April	Birmingham City	FA Barclaycard Premiership
☐☐	18 April	Manchester City	FA Barclaycard Premiership
☐☐	27 April	Manchester United	FA Barclaycard Premiership
☐☐	11 May	Blackburn Rovers	FA Barclaycard Premiership

☐ Handbook ☐ Season Ticket

Season Ticket

Handbook

7 August
Celtic

11 August
Lazio

15 September
West Ham United

17 October
DC United

3 November
Chelsea

26 December
Charlton Athletic

12 January
Everton

24 February
Fulham

16 March
Liverpool

11 May
Blackburn Rovers

2002-03

AWAY

		Date	Opponent	Competition
		21 July	Stevenage Borough	Friendly
		23 July	Colchester United	Richard Wilkins Testimonial
		25 July	Bournemouth	Friendly
		27 July	Gillingham	Friendly
		28 July	Queens Park Rangers	Friendly
		31 July	Crystal Palace	Simon Rodger Testimonial
		3 August	Watford	Nigel Gibbs Testimonial
		4 August	Feyenoord	Friendly
		17 August	Everton	FA Barclaycard Premiership
		27 August	Charlton Athletic	FA Barclaycard Premiership
		11 September	Fulham	FA Barclaycard Premiership
		21 September	Manchester United	FA Barclaycard Premiership
		6 October	Blackburn Rovers	FA Barclaycard Premiership
		26 October	Liverpool	FA Barclaycard Premiership
		6 November	Burnley	Worthington Cup
		10 November	Sunderland	FA Barclaycard Premiership
		16 November	Arsenal	FA Barclaycard Premiership
		30 November	Birmingham City	FA Barclaycard Premiership
		23 December	Manchester City	FA Barclaycard Premiership
		29 December	Newcastle United	FA Barclaycard Premiership
		1 January	Southampton	FA Barclaycard Premiership
		4 January	Southampton	FA Cup
		18 January	Aston Villa	FA Barclaycard Premiership
		1 February	Chelsea	FA Barclaycard Premiership
		1 March	West Ham United	FA Barclaycard Premiership
		4 March	Bohemians	Friendly
		24 March	Bolton Wanderers	FA Barclaycard Premiership
		12 April	Leeds United	FA Barclaycard Premiership
		21 April	West Bromwich Albion	FA Barclaycard Premiership
		3 May	Middlesbrough	FA Barclaycard Premiership
		14 May	DC United	Friendly

21 July
Stevenage Borough

23 July
Colchester United

25 July
Bournemouth

27 July
Gillingham

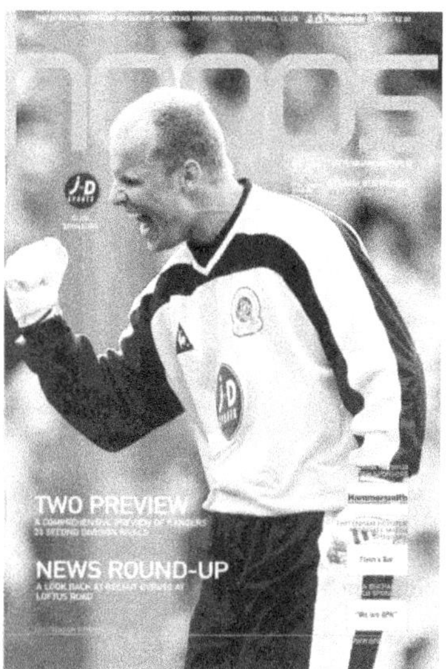

28 July
Queens Park Rangers

31 July
Crystal Palace

3 August
Watford

4 August
Feyenoord

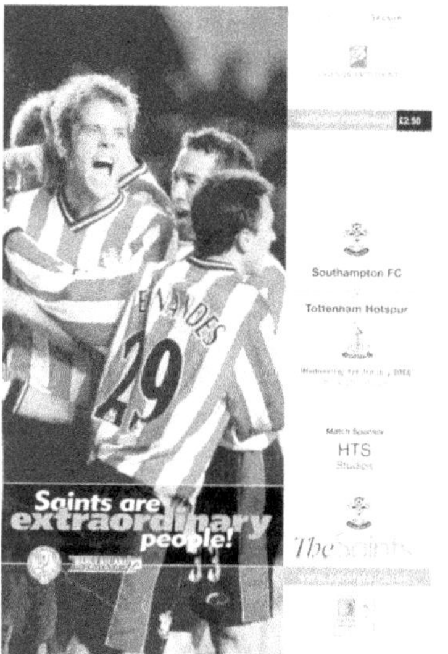

1 January
Southampton

4 January
Southampton

4 March
Bohemians

D.C. UNITED

TOTTENHAM HOTSPUR

14 May
DC United

2003-04

HOME

		Date	Opponent	Competition
☐	☐	3 August	PSV Eindhoven	Friendly
☐	☐	10 August	Sporting Clube de Portugal	Friendly
☐	☐	23 August	Leeds United	FA Barclaycard Premiership
☐	☐	30 August	Fulham	FA Barclaycard Premiership
☐	☐	20 September	Southampton	FA Barclaycard Premiership
☐	☐	4 October	Everton	FA Barclaycard Premiership
☐	☐	26 October	Middlesbrough	FA Barclaycard Premiership
☐	☐	29 October	West Ham United	Carling Cup
☐	☐	1 November	Bolton Wanderers	FA Barclaycard Premiership
☐	☐	23 November	Aston Villa	FA Barclaycard Premiership
☐	☐	3 December	Manchester City	Carling Cup
☐	☐	6 December	Wolverhampton Wanderers	FA Barclaycard Premiership
☐	☐	17 December	Middlesbrough	Carling Cup
☐	☐	21 December	Manchester United	FA Barclaycard Premiership
☐	☐	28 December	Charlton Athletic	FA Barclaycard Premiership
☐	☐	3 January	Crystal Palace	FA Cup
☐	☐	7 January	Birmingham City	FA Barclaycard Premiership
☐	☐	17 January	Liverpool	FA Barclaycard Premiership
☐	☐	4 February	Manchester City	FA Cup
☐	☐	7 February	Portsmouth	FA Barclaycard Premiership
☐	☐	22 February	Leicester City	FA Barclaycard Premiership
☐	☐	14 March	Newcastle United	FA Barclaycard Premiership
☐	☐	3 April	Chelsea	FA Barclaycard Premiership
☐	☐	12 April	Manchester City	FA Barclaycard Premiership
☐	☐	25 April	Arsenal	FA Barclaycard Premiership
☐	☐	8 May	Blackburn Rovers	FA Barclaycard Premiership

☐ Yearbook ☐ Season Ticket

Season Ticket

Yearbook

3 August
PSV Eindhoven

10 August
Sporting Clube de Portugal

20 September
Southampton

29 October
West Ham United

23 November
Aston Villa

28 December
Charlton Athletic

17 January
Liverpool

22 February
Leicester City

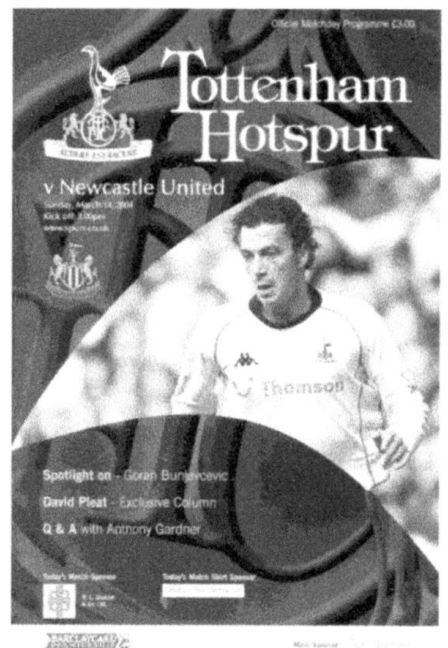

14 March
Newcastle United

8 May
Blackburn Rovers

2003-04

AWAY

Date	Opponent	Competition
16 July	Stevenage Borough	Friendly
19 July	Wycombe Wanderers	Dave Jones Testimonial
20 July	Oxford United	Friendly
22 July	Norwich City	Friendly
26 July	Orlando Pirates (Durban)	SA 2010 Bid
29 July	Kaizer Chiefs (Cape Town)	SA 2010 Bid
16 August	Birmingham City	FA Barclaycard Premiership
27 August	Liverpool	FA Barclaycard Premiership
13 September	Chelsea	FA Barclaycard Premiership
24 September	Coventry City	Carling Cup
28 September	Manchester City	FA Barclaycard Premiership
19 October	Leicester City	FA Barclaycard Premiership
8 November	Arsenal	FA Barclaycard Premiership
29 November	Blackburn Rovers	FA Barclaycard Premiership
13 December	Newcastle United	FA Barclaycard Premiership
26 December	Portsmouth	FA Barclaycard Premiership
10 January	Leeds United	FA Barclaycard Premiership
25 January	Manchester City	FA Cup
31 January	Fulham	FA Barclaycard Premiership
11 February	Charlton Athletic	FA Barclaycard Premiership
9 March	Middlesbrough	FA Barclaycard Premiership
20 March	Manchester United	FA Barclaycard Premiership
27 March	Southampton	FA Barclaycard Premiership
9 April	Everton	FA Barclaycard Premiership
17 April	Bolton Wanderers	FA Barclaycard Premiership
2 May	Aston Villa	FA Barclaycard Premiership
15 May	Wolverhampton Wanderers	FA Barclaycard Premiership

16 July
Stevenage Borough

19 July
Wycombe Wanderers

20 July
Oxford United

22 July
Norwich City

26 July
Orlando Pirates

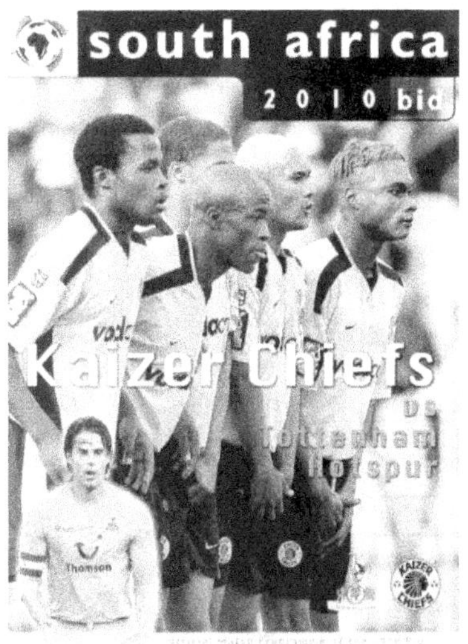

29 July
Kaizer Chiefs

16 August
Birmingham City

19 October
Leicester City

26 December
Portsmouth

11 February
Charlton Athletic

2 May
Aston Villa

15 May
Wolverhampton Wanderers

2004-05

HOMES

	Date	Opponent	Competition
☐☐	7 August	Cagliari	Friendly
☐☐	14 August	Liverpool	FA Barclays Premiership
☐☐	28 August	Birmingham City	FA Barclays Premiership
☐☐	12 September	Norwich City	FA Barclays Premiership
☐☐	25 September	Manchester United	FA Barclays Premiership
☐☐	23 October	Bolton Wanderers	FA Barclays Premiership
☐☐	6 November	Charlton Athletic	FA Barclays Premiership
☐☐	13 November	Arsenal	FA Barclays Premiership
☐☐	28 November	Middlesbrough	FA Barclays Premiership
☐☐	1 December	Liverpool	Carling Cup
☐☐	18 December	Southampton	FA Barclays Premiership
☐☐	28 December	Crystal Palace	FA Barclays Premiership
☐☐	1 January	Everton	FA Barclays Premiership
☐☐	8 January	Brighton and Hove Albion	FA Cup
☐☐	15 January	Chelsea	FA Barclays Premiership
☐☐	5 February	Portsmouth	FA Barclays Premiership
☐☐	12 February	West Bromwich Albion	FA Cup
☐☐	20 February	Nottingham Forest	FA Cup
☐☐	26 February	Fulham	FA Barclays Premiership
☐☐	19 March	Manchester City	FA Barclays Premiership
☐☐	10 April	Newcastle United	FA Barclays Premiership
☐☐	20 April	West Bromwich Albion	FA Barclays Premiership
☐☐	1 May	Aston Villa	FA Barclays Premiership
☐☐	15 May	Blackburn Rovers	FA Barclays Premiership

☐ Yearbook ☐ Season Ticket

Season Ticket

Yearbook

7 August
Cagliari

12 September
Norwich City

23 October
Bolton Wanderers

6 November
Charlton Athletic

1 December
Liverpool

28 December
Crystal Palace

15 January
Chelsea

20 February
Nottingham Forest

19 March
Manchester City

15 May
Blackburn Rovers

2004-05

AWAY

	Date	Opponent	Competition
☐☐	13 July	Falkenbergs	Friendly
☐☐	15 July	FC Copenhagen (Gothenberg)	Friendly
☐☐	17 July	Trollhättan	Friendly
☐☐	20 July	Stevenage Borough	Friendly
☐☐	24 July	Hull City	Friendly
☐☐	25 July	Sheffield United	Friendly
☐☐	28 July	Rangers	Walter Tull Trophy
☐☐	31 July	Nottingham Forest	Friendly
☐☐	3 August	Feyenoord (Seville)	Kappa Cup
☐☐	5 August	Partizan Belgrade (Seville)	Kappa Cup
☐☐	10 August	Celtic	Friendly
☐☐	21 August	Newcastle United	FA Barclays Premiership
☐☐	25 August	West Bromwich Albion	FA Barclays Premiership
☐☐	19 September	Chelsea	FA Barclays Premiership
☐☐	22 September	Oldham Athletic	Carling Cup
☐☐	2 October	Everton	FA Barclays Premiership
☐☐	18 October	Portsmouth	FA Barclays Premiership
☐☐	27 October	Bolton Wanderers	Carling Cup
☐☐	30 October	Fulham	FA Barclays Premiership
☐☐	9 November	Burnley	Carling Cup
☐☐	22 November	Aston Villa	FA Barclays Premiership
☐☐	04 December	Blackburn Rovers	FA Barclays Premiership
☐☐	11 December	Manchester City	FA Barclays Premiership
☐☐	26 December	Norwich City	FA Barclays Premiership
☐☐	4 January	Manchester United	FA Barclays Premiership
☐☐	22 January	Crystal Palace	FA Barclays Premiership
☐☐	29 January	West Bromwich Albion	FA Cup
☐☐	1 February	Bolton Wanderers	FA Barclays Premiership
☐☐	2 March	Nottingham Forest	FA Cup
☐☐	5 March	Southampton	FA Barclays Premiership
☐☐	13 March	Newcastle United	FA Cup
☐☐	16 March	Charlton Athletic	FA Barclays Premiership
☐☐	2 April	Birmingham City	FA Barclays Premiership
☐☐	16 April	Liverpool	FA Barclays Premiership
☐☐	25 April	Arsenal	FA Barclays Premiership
☐☐	7 May	Middlesbrough	FA Barclays Premiership
☐☐	20 May	Club M (Mauritius) - Spurs badge	Friendly
☐☐		- MFA badge	

13 July
Falkenbergs

15 July
Copenhagen

17 July
Trollhättan

20 July
Stevenage Borough

24 July
Hull City

25 July
Sheffield United

28 July
Rangers

31 July
Nottingham Forest

10 August
Celtic

16 March
Charlton Athletic

20 May
Club M (MFA badge)

20 May
Club M (TH badge)

2005-06

HOME

	Date	Opponent	Competition
☐☐	6 August	Porto	Friendly
☐☐	20 August	Middlesbrough	FA Barclays Premiership
☐☐	27 August	Chelsea	FA Barclays Premiership
☐☐	10 September	Liverpool	FA Barclays Premiership
☐☐	26 September	Fulham	FA Barclays Premiership
☐☐	15 October	Everton	FA Barclays Premiership
☐☐	29 October	Arsenal	FA Barclays Premiership
☐☐	20 November	West Ham United	FA Barclays Premiership
☐☐	3 December	Sunderland	FA Barclays Premiership
☐☐	12 December	Portsmouth	FA Barclays Premiership
☐☐	26 December	Birmingham City	FA Barclays Premiership
☐☐	31 December	Newcastle United	FA Barclays Premiership
☐☐	21 January	Aston Villa	FA Barclays Premiership
☐☐	5 February	Charlton Athletic	FA Barclays Premiership
☐☐	19 February	Wigan Athletic	FA Barclays Premiership
☐☐	5 March	Blackburn Rovers	FA Barclays Premiership
☐☐	27 March	West Bromwich Albion	FA Barclays Premiership
☐☐	8 April	Manchester City	FA Barclays Premiership
☐☐	17 April	Manchester United	FA Barclays Premiership
☐☐	30 April	Bolton Wanderers	FA Barclays Premiership

☐ Handbook

☐ Season Ticket

6 August
Porto

26 September
Fulham

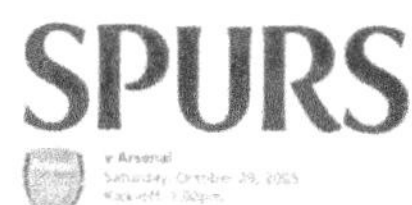

29 October
Arsenal

20 November
West Ham United

26 December
Birmingham City

21 January
Aston Villa

19 February
Wigan Athletic

27 March
West Bromwich Albion

8 April
Manchester City

30 April
Bolton Wanderers

2005-06

AWAY

Date	Opponent	Competition
9 July	Stevenage Borough	Friendly
{16 July	Boca Juniors (Suwon)	Peace Cup
{18 July	Sundowns (Suwon)	Peace Cup
{21 July	Real Sociedad (Ulsan)	Peace Cup
{24 July	Olympique Lyonnais (Seoul)	Peace Cup
30 July	Reading	Friendly
13 August	Portsmouth	FA Barclays Premiership
24 August	Blackburn Rovers	FA Barclays Premiership
17 September	Aston Villa	FA Barclays Premiership
20 September	Grimsby Town	Carling Cup
1 October	Charlton Athletic	FA Barclays Premiership
22 October	Manchester United	FA Barclays Premiership
7 November	Bolton Wanderers	FA Barclays Premiership
26 November	Wigan Athletic	FA Barclays Premiership
18 December	Middlesbrough	FA Barclays Premiership
28 December	West Bromwich Albion	FA Barclays Premiership
4 January	Manchester City	FA Barclays Premiership
8 January	Leicester City	FA Cup
14 January	Liverpool	FA Barclays Premiership
31 January	Fulham	FA Barclays Premiership
12 February	Sunderland	FA Barclays Premiership
11 March	Chelsea	FA Barclays Premiership
18 March	Birmingham City	FA Barclays Premiership
1 April	Newcastle United	FA Barclays Premiership
15 April	Everton	FA Barclays Premiership
22 April	Arsenal	FA Barclays Premiership
7 May	West Ham United	FA Barclays Premiership

9 July
Stevenage Borough

16 - 24 July
Peace Cup

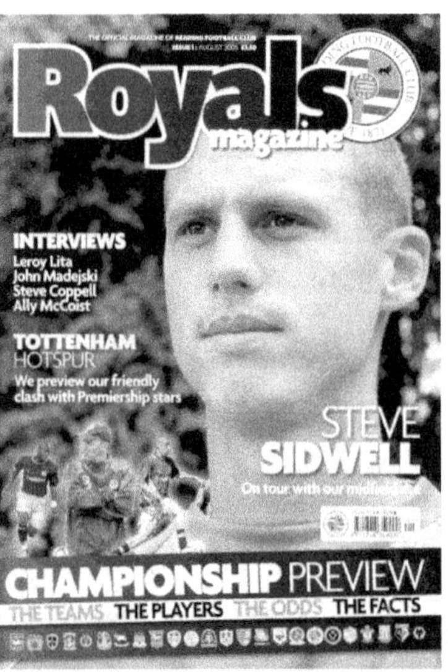

30 July
Reading

17 September
Aston Villa

20 September
Grimsby Town

1 October
Charlton Athletic

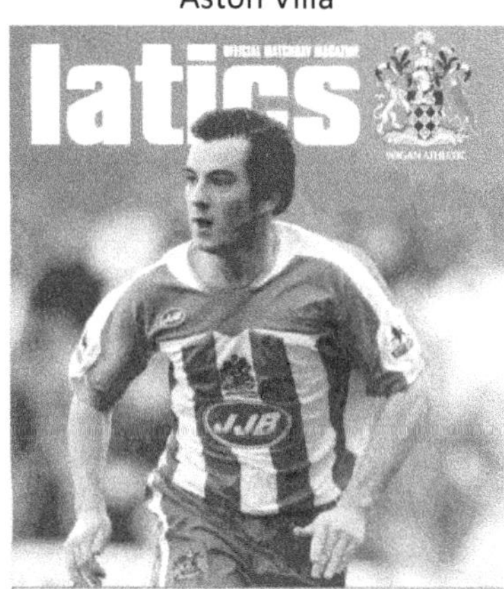

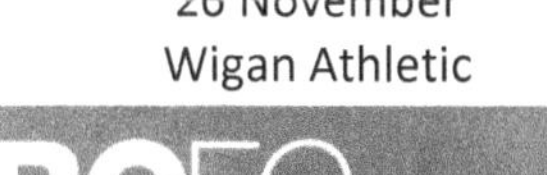

26 November
Wigan Athletic

4 January
Manchester City

14 January
Liverpool

18 March
Birmingham City

1 April
Newcastle United

15 April
Everton

2006-07

HOME

	Date	Opponent	Competition
☐☐	30 July	Internazionale	Friendly
☐☐	12 August	Real Sociedad	Friendly
☐☐	22 August	Sheffield United	FA Barclays Premiership
☐☐	26 August	Everton	FA Barclays Premiership
☐☐	17 September	Fulham	FA Barclays Premiership
☐☐	28 September	Slavia Prague	UEFA Cup
☐☐	1 October	Portsmouth	FA Barclays Premiership
☐☐	22 October	West Ham United	FA Barclays Premiership
☐☐	2 November	Club Brugge	UEFA Cup
☐☐	5 November	Chelsea	FA Barclays Premiership
☐☐	8 November	Port Vale	Carling Cup
☐☐	26 November	Wigan Athletic	FA Barclays Premiership
☐☐	5 December	Middlesbrough	FA Barclays Premiership
☐☐	9 December	Charlton Athletic	FA Barclays Premiership
☐☐	14 December	Dinamo Bucharest	UEFA Cup
☐☐	20 December	Southend United	Carling Cup
☐☐	26 December	Aston Villa	FA Barclays Premiership
☐☐	30 December	Liverpool	FA Barclays Premiership
☐☐	14 January	Newcastle United	FA Barclays Premiership
☐☐	17 January	Cardiff City	FA Cup
☐☐	24 January	Arsenal	Carling Cup
☐☐	27 January	Southend United	FA Cup
☐☐	4 February	Manchester United	FA Barclays Premiership
☐☐	25 February	Bolton Wanderers	FA Barclays Premiership
☐☐	14 March	SC Braga	UEFA Cup
☐☐	17 March	Watford	FA Barclays Premiership
☐☐	19 March	Chelsea	FA Cup
☐☐	1 April	Reading	FA Barclays Premiership
☐☐	12 April	Sevilla	UEFA Cup
☐☐	21 April	Arsenal	FA Barclays Premiership
☐☐	10 May	Blackburn Rovers	FA Barclays Premiership
☐☐	13 May	Manchester City	FA Barclays Premiership

☐ Handbook

☐ Season Ticket

Season Ticket

Handbook

30 July
Internazionale

12 August
Real Sociedad

17 September
Fulham

22 October
West ham United

8 November
Port Vale

26 December
Aston Villa

17 January
Cardiff City

25 February
Bolton Wanderers

21 April
Arsenal

13 May
Manchester City

2006-07

AWAY

Date	Opponent	Competition
13 July	Girondins de Bordeaux (Albertville)	Friendly
14 July	OGC Nice (Evian)	Friendly
18 July	Celta Vigo (Annecy)	Friendly
22 July	Birmingham City	Friendly
25 July	Stevenage Borough	Friendly
5 August	Borussia Dortmund	Friendly
19 August	Bolton Wanderers	FA Barclays Premiership
9 September	Manchester United	FA Barclays Premiership
14 September	Slavia Prague	UEFA Cup
23 September	Liverpool	FA Barclays Premiership
14 October	Aston Villa	FA Barclays Premiership
19 October	Besiktas	UEFA Cup
25 October	Milton Keynes Dons	Carling Cup
28 October	Watford	FA Barclays Premiership
12 November	Reading	FA Barclays Premiership
19 November	Blackburn Rovers	FA Barclays Premiership
23 November	Bayer 04 Leverkusen	UEFA Cup
2 December	Arsenal	FA Barclays Premiership
17 December	Manchester City	FA Barclays Premiership
23 December	Newcastle United	FA Barclays Premiership
1 January	Portsmouth	FA Barclays Premiership
7 January	Cardiff City	FA Cup
20 January	Fulham	FA Barclays Premiership
31 January	Arsenal	Carling Cup
10 February	Sheffield United	FA Barclays Premiership
18 February	Fulham	FA Cup
21 February	Everton	FA Barclays Premiership
4 March	West Ham United	FA Barclays Premiership
8 March	SC Braga	UEFA Cup
11 March	Chelsea	FA Cup
5 April	Sevilla	UEFA Cup
7 April	Chelsea	FA Barclays Premiership
15 April	Wigan Athletic	FA Barclays Premiership
28 April	Middlesbrough	FA Barclays Premiership
7 May	Charlton Athletic	FA Barclays Premiership

22 July
Birmingham City

25 July
Stevenage Borough

19 August
Bolton Wanderers

14 October
Aston Villa

25 October
Milton Keynes Dons

12 November
Reading

17 December
Manchester City

7 January
Cardiff City

20 January
Fulham

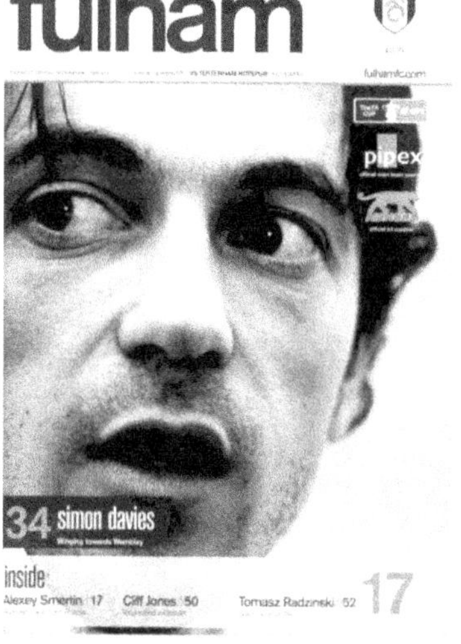

18 February
Fulham

21 February
Everton

7 May
Charlton Athletic

2007-08

HOME

Date	Opponent	Competition
4 August	Torino	Friendly
14 August	Everton	Barclays Premier League
18 August	Derby County	Barclays Premier League
15 September	Arsenal	Barclays Premier League
20 September	Anorthosis Famagusta	UEFA Cup
26 September	Middlesbrough	Carling Cup
1 October	Aston Villa	Barclays Premier League
25 October	Getafe	UEFA Cup
28 October	Blackburn Rovers	Barclays Premier League
31 October	Blackpool	Carling Cup
11 November	Wigan Athletic	Barclays Premier League
29 November	Aalborg BK	UEFA Cup
2 December	Birmingham City	Barclays Premier League
9 December	Manchester City	Barclays Premier League
26 December	Fulham	Barclays Premier League
29 December	Reading	Barclays Premier League
5 January	Reading	FA Cup
19 January	Sunderland	Barclays Premier League
22 January	Arsenal	Carling Cup
2 February	Manchester United	Barclays Premier League
21 February	Slavia Prague	UEFA Cup
6 March	PSV Eindhoven	UEFA Cup
9 March	West Ham United	Barclays Premier League
19 March	Chelsea	Barclays Premier League
22 March	Portsmouth	Barclays Premier League
30 March	Newcastle United	Barclays Premier League
12 April	Middlesbrough	Barclays Premier League
26 April	Bolton Wanderers	Barclays Premier League
11 May	Liverpool	Barclays Premier League

☐ Handbook ☐ Season Ticket

Season Ticket Handbook

4 August
Torino

18 August
Derby County

15 September
Arsenal

1 October
Aston Villa

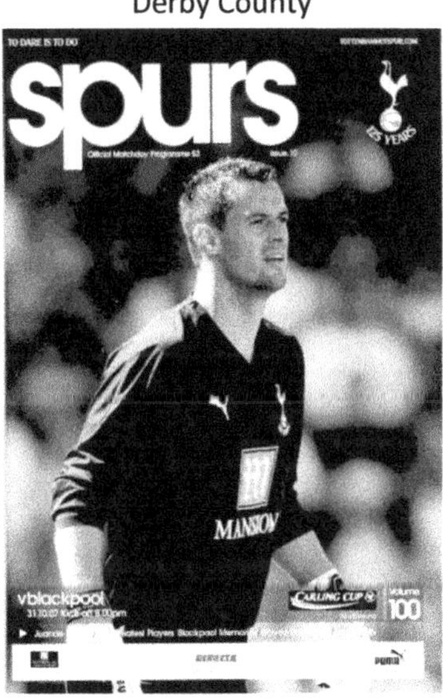

31 October
Blackpool

11 November
Wigan Athletic

26 December
Fulham

2 February
Manchester United

19 March
Chelsea

11 May
Liverpool

2007-08

AWAY

	Date	Opponent	Competition
☐☐	7 July	Stevenage Borough	Friendly
☐☐	12 July	St Patrick's Athletic (dated 12 June)	Friendly
☐☐	{ 21 July	Kaizer Chiefs (Durban)	Vodacom Challenge
☐☐	{ 24 July	Orlando Pirates (Cape town)	Vodacom Challenge
☐☐	{ 28 July	Orlando Pirates (Pretoria)	Vodacom Challenge
☐☐	1 August	Leyton Orient	Friendly
☐☐	11 August	Sunderland	Barclays Premier League
☐☐	26 August	Manchester United	Barclays Premier League
☐☐	1 September	Fulham	Barclays Premier League
☐☐	23 September	Bolton Wanderers	Barclays Premier League
☐☐	4 October	Anorthosis Famagusta	UEFA Cup
☐☐	7 October	Liverpool	Barclays Premier League
☐☐	22 October	Newcastle United	Barclays Premier League
☐☐	3 November	Middlesbrough	Barclays Premier League
☐☐	8 November	Hapoel Tel Aviv	UEFA Cup
☐☐	25 November	West Ham United	Barclays Premier League
☐☐	6 December	Anderlecht	UEFA Cup
☐☐	15 December	Portsmouth	Barclays Premier League
☐☐	18 December	Manchester City	Carling Cup
☐☐	22 December	Arsenal	Barclays Premier League
☐☐	1 January	Aston Villa	Barclays Premier League
☐☐	9 January	Arsenal	Carling Cup
☐☐	12 January	Chelsea	Barclays Premier League
☐☐	15 January	Reading	FA Cup
☐☐	27 January	Manchester United	FA Cup
☐☐	30 January	Everton	Barclays Premier League
☐☐	9 February	Derby County	Barclays Premier League
☐☐	14 February	Slavia Prague	UEFA Cup
☐☐	24 February	Chelsea (Wembley)	Carling Cup
☐☐	1 March	Birmingham City	Barclays Premier League
☐☐	12 March	PSV Eindhoven	UEFA Cup
☐☐	16 March	Manchester City	Barclays Premier League
☐☐	5 April	Blackburn Rovers	Barclays Premier League
☐☐	19 April	Wigan Athletic	Barclays Premier League
☐☐	3 May	Reading	Barclays Premier League

7 July
Stevenage Borough

12 July
St Patrick's Athletic

21 – 28 July
Vodacom Challenge

1 August
Leyton Orient

23 September
Bolton Wanderers

3 November
Middlesbrough

1 January
Aston Villa

15 January
Reading

9 February
Derby County

16 March
Manchester City

5 April
Blackburn Rovers

3 May
Reading

2008-09

HOME

		Date	Opponent	Competition
☐	☐	10 August	Roma	Friendly
☐	☐	23 August	Sunderland	Barclays Premier League
☐	☐	15 September	Aston Villa	Barclays Premier League
☐	☐	18 September	Wisła Kraków	UEFA Cup
☐	☐	21 September	Wigan Athletic	Barclays Premier League
☐	☐	5 October	Hull City	Barclays Premier League
☐	☐	26 October	Bolton Wanderers	Barclays Premier League
☐	☐	1 November	Liverpool	Barclays Premier League
☐	☐	6 November	Dinamo Zagreb	UEFA Cup
☐	☐	12 November	Liverpool	Carling Cup
☐	☐	23 November	Blackburn Rovers	Barclays Premier League
☐	☐	30 November	Everton	Barclays Premier League
☐	☐	13 December	Manchester United	Barclays Premier League
☐	☐	18 December	Spartak Moscow	UEFA Cup
☐	☐	26 December	Fulham	Barclays Premier League
☐	☐	2 January	Wigan Athletic	FA Cup
☐	☐	6 January	Burnley	Carling Cup
☐	☐	18 January	Portsmouth	Barclays Premier League
☐	☐	27 January	Stoke City	Barclays Premier League
☐	☐	8 February	Arsenal	Barclays Premier League
☐	☐	26 February	Shakhtar Donetsk	UEFA Cup
☐	☐	4 March	Middlesbrough	Barclays Premier League
☐	☐	22 March	Chelsea	Barclays Premier League
☐	☐	11 April	West Ham United	Barclays Premier League
☐	☐	19 April	Newcastle United	Barclays Premier League
☐	☐	2 May	West Bromwich Albion	Barclays Premier League
☐	☐	16 May	Manchester City	Barclays Premier League

☐ Handbook - Ramos printing
☐ - Redknapp printing

☐ Season Ticket

Handbook

Handbook
Ramos printing

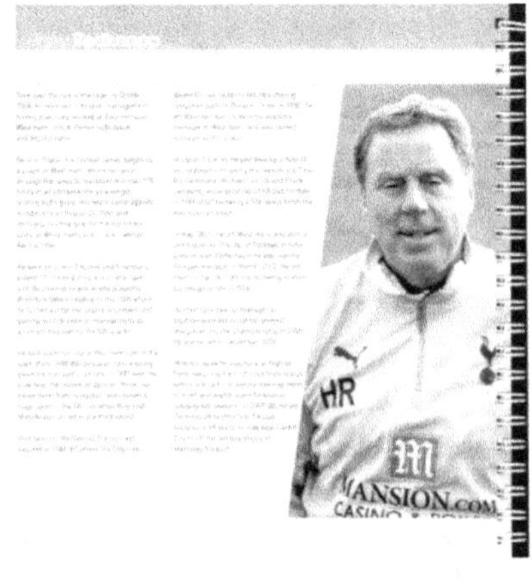

Handbook
Redknapp printing

Season Ticket

10 August
Roma

15 September
Aston Villa

30 November
Everton

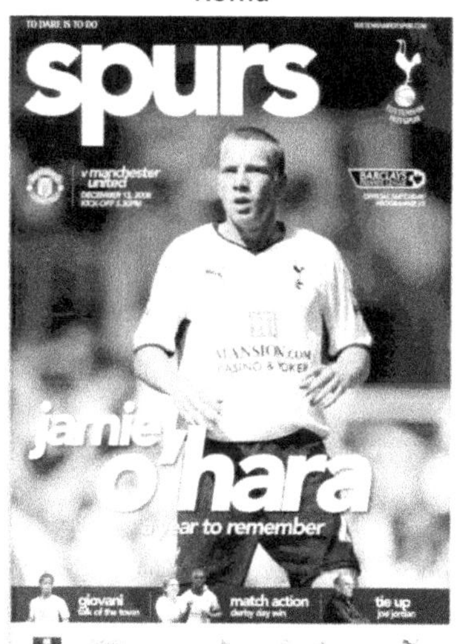

13 December
Manchester United

2 January
Wigan Athletic

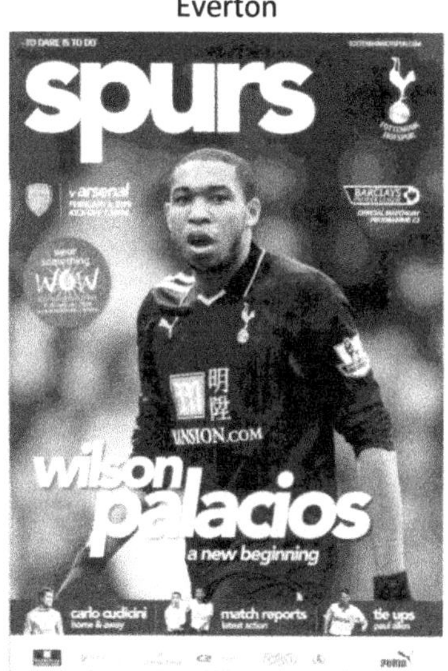

8 February
Arsenal

11 April
West Ham United

16 May
Manchester City

2008-09

AWAY

Date	Opponent		Competition
24 July	Hercules		Friendly
28 July	Norwich City		Friendly
30 July	Leyton Orient		Friendly
{ 1 August	Celtic (Rotterdam)		Feyenoord Jubileum Toernooi
{ 3 August	Borussia Dortmund (Rotterdam)		Feyenoord Jubileum Toernooi
		- Stadion Sport Nieuws	
16 August	Middlesbrough	- red Issue	Barclays Premier League
		- white Issue	Barclays Premier League
31 August	Chelsea		Barclays Premier League
24 September	Newcastle United		Carling Cup
28 September	Portsmouth		Barclays Premier League
2 October	Wisła Kraków		UEFA Cup
19 October	Stoke City		Barclays Premier League
23 October	Udinese - black		UEFA Cup
	- newspaper		
	- fold-out		
29 October	Arsenal		Barclays Premier League
9 November	Manchester City		Barclays Premier League
15 November	Fulham		Barclays Premier League
27 November	NEC Nijmegen		UEFA Cup
3 December	Watford		Carling Cup
8 December	West Ham United		Barclays Premier League
21 December	Newcastle United		Barclays Premier League
28 December	West Bromwich Albion		Barclays Premier League
11 January	Wigan Athletic		Barclays Premier League
21 January	Burnley		Carling Cup
24 January	Manchester United		FA Cup
30 January	Bolton Wanderers		Barclays Premier League
19 February	Shakhtar Donetsk		UEFA Cup
23 February	Hull City		Barclays Premier League
1 March	Manchester United (Wembley)		Carling Cup
7 March	Sunderland		Barclays Premier League
15 March	Aston Villa		Barclays Premier League
4 April	Blackburn Rovers		Barclays Premier League
25 April	Manchester United		Barclays Premier League
9 May	Everton		Barclays Premier League
24 May	Liverpool		Barclays Premier League
	Spartak Moscow – group stage programme		UEFA Cup

28 July
Norwich City

30 July
Leyton Orient

1 & 3 August
Feyenoord Jubileum Toernooi

1 & 3 August - Feyenoord Jubileum Toernooi - Stadion Sport Nieuws edition

16 August
Middlesbrough - white issue

16 August
Middlesbrough - red issue

29 October
Arsenal

8 December
West Ham United

28 December
West Bromwich Albion

23 February
Hull City

9 May
Everton

24 May
Liverpool

2009-10

HOME

		Date	Opponent	Competition
☐	☐	9 August	Olympiacos	Friendly
☐	☐	16 August	Liverpool	Barclays Premier League
☐	☐	29 August	Birmingham City	Barclays Premier League
☐	☐	12 September	Manchester United	Barclays Premier League
☐	☐	26 September	Burnley	Barclays Premier League
☐	☐	24 October	Stoke City	Barclays Premier League
☐	☐	27 October	Everton	Carling Cup
☐	☐	7 November	Sunderland	Barclays Premier League
☐	☐	22 November	Wigan Athletic	Barclays Premier League
☐	☐	12 December	Wolverhampton Wanderers	Barclays Premier League
☐	☐	16 December	Manchester City	Barclays Premier League
☐	☐	28 December	West Ham United	Barclays Premier League
☐	☐	2 January	Peterborough United	FA Cup
☐	☐	16 January	Hull City	Barclays Premier League
☐	☐	23 January	Leeds United	FA Cup
☐	☐	26 January	Fulham	Barclays Premier League
☐	☐	6 February	Aston Villa	Barclays Premier League
☐	☐	24 February	Bolton Wanderers	FA Cup
☐	☐	28 February	Everton	Barclays Premier League
☐	☐	13 March	Blackburn Rovers	Barclays Premier League
☐	☐	24 March	Fulham	FA Cup
☐	☐	27 March	Portsmouth	Barclays Premier League
☐	☐	14 April	Arsenal	Barclays Premier League
☐	☐	17 April	Chelsea	Barclays Premier League
☐	☐	1 May	Bolton Wanderers	Barclays Premier League

☐ Handbook ☐ Season Ticket

Season Ticket

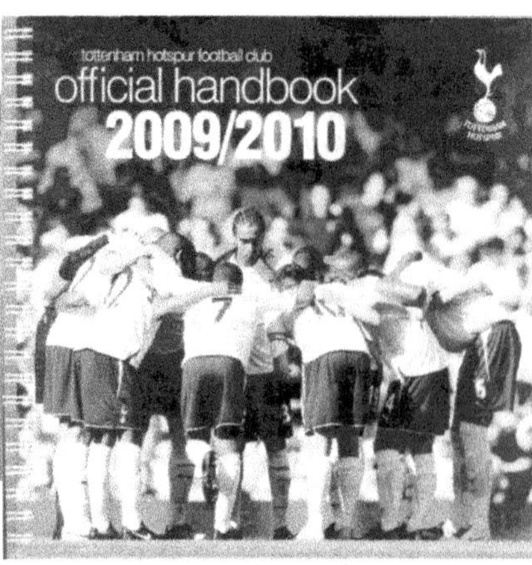

Handbook

9 August
Olympiacos

12 September
Manchester United

27 October
Everton

22 November
Wigan Athletic

28 December
West Ham United

2 January
Peterborough United

28 February
Everton

24 March
Fulham

14 April
Arsenal

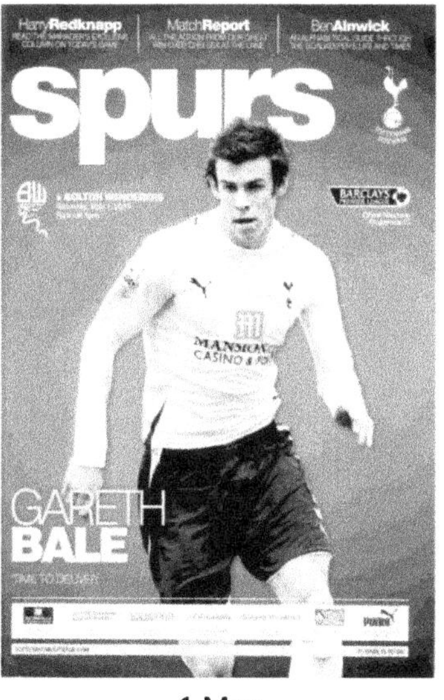

1 May
Bolton Wanderers

2009-10

AWAY

Date	Opponent	Competition
15 July	Exeter City	Friendly
17 July	Bournemouth	Friendly
21 July	Peterborough United	Friendly
{ 24 July	Barcelona (Wembley)	Wembley Cup
{ 26 July	Celtic (Wembley)	Wembley Cup
{ 29 July	West Ham United (Beijing)	Barclays Asia Trophy
{ 31 July	Hull City (Beijing)	Barclays Asia Trophy
2 August	South China (Hong Kong)	Panasonic Invitation Cup
19 August	Hull City	Barclays Premier League
23 August	West Ham United	Barclays Premier League
26 August	Doncaster Rovers	Carling Cup
20 September	Chelsea	Barclays Premier League
23 September	Preston North End	Carling Cup
3 October	Bolton Wanderers	Barclays Premier League
17 October	Portsmouth	Barclays Premier League
31 October	Arsenal	Barclays Premier League
28 November	Aston Villa	Barclays Premier League
1 December	Manchester United	Carling Cup
6 December	Everton	Barclays Premier League
19 December	Blackburn Rovers	Barclays Premier League
26 December	Fulham	Barclays Premier League
10 January	Liverpool - postponed	Barclays Premier League
20 January	Liverpool	Barclays Premier League
30 January	Birmingham City	Barclays Premier League
3 February	Leeds United	FA Cup
10 February	Wolverhampton Wanderers	Barclays Premier League
14 February	Bolton Wanderers	FA Cup
21 February	Wigan Athletic	Barclays Premier League
6 March	Fulham	FA Cup
20 March	Stoke City	Barclays Premier League
3 April	Sunderland	Barclays Premier League
11 April	Portsmouth (Wembley)	FA Cup
24 April	Manchester United	Barclays Premier League
5 May	Manchester City	Barclays Premier League
9 May	Burnley	Barclays Premier League
	- limited edition	

15 July
Exeter City

17 July
Bournemouth

21 July
Peterborough United

24 & 26 July
Wembley Cup

29 & 31 July
Barclays Asia Trophy

26 August
Doncaster Rovers

28 November
Aston Villa

10 January
Liverpool - postponed

30 January
Birmingham City

6 March
Fulham

9 May
Burnley

9 May
Burnley - limited edition

2010-11

HOME

Date	Opponent	Competition
29 July	Villarreal	Friendly
7 August	Fiorentina	Friendly
14 August	Manchester City	Barclays Premier League
25 August	BSC Young Boys	Champions League
28 August	Wigan Athletic	Barclays Premier League
18 September	Wolverhampton Wanderers	Barclays Premier League
21 September	Arsenal	Carling Cup
29 September	FC Twente	Champions League
2 October	Aston Villa	Barclays Premier League
23 October	Everton	Barclays Premier League
2 November	Internazionale	Champions League
9 November	Sunderland	Barclays Premier League
13 November	Blackburn Rovers	Barclays Premier League
24 November	Werder Bremen	Champions League
28 November	Liverpool	Barclays Premier League
12 December	Chelsea	Barclays Premier League
28 December	Newcastle United	Barclays Premier League
1 January	Fulham	Barclays Premier League
9 January	Charlton Athletic	FA Cup
16 January	Manchester United	Barclays Premier League
5 February	Bolton Wanderers	Barclays Premier League
9 March	AC Milan	Champions League
19 March	West Ham United	Barclays Premier League
9 April	Stoke City	Barclays Premier League
13 April	Real Madrid	Champions League
20 April	Arsenal	Barclays Premier League
23 April	West Bromwich Albion	Barclays Premier League
7 May	Blackpool	Barclays Premier League
22 May	Birmingham City	Barclays Premier League

☐ Handbook ☐ Season Ticket

Handbook

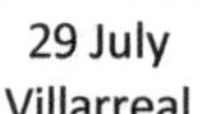

29 July
Villarreal

7 August
Fiorentina

21 September
Arsenal

23 October
Everton

13 November
Blackburn

28 December
Newcastle United

9 January
Charlton Athletic

5 February
Bolton Wanderers

9 April
Stoke City

23 April
West Bromwich Albion

7 May
Blackpool

2010-11

AWAY

Date	Opponent	Competition
10 July	Bournemouth	Friendly
17 July	San Jose Earthquakes	Friendly
{ 22 July	New York Red Bulls	Barclays New York Challenge
{ 25 July	Sporting Club de Portugal (New York)	Barclays New York Challenge
3 August	Benfica	Eusebio Cup
17 August	BSC Young Boys	Champions League
21 August	Stoke City	Barclays Premier League
11 September	West Bromwich Albion	Barclays Premier League
14 September	Werder Bremen	Champions League
25 September	West Ham United	Barclays Premier League
16 October	Fulham	Barclays Premier League
20 October	Internazionale - La Interista	Champions League
	- Il Calcio Mondiale	
30 October	Manchester United	Barclays Premier League
6 November	Bolton Wanderers	Barclays Premier League
20 November	Arsenal	Barclays Premier League
4 December	Birmingham City	Barclays Premier League
7 December	FC Twente	Champions League
19 December	Blackpool - postponed	Barclays Premier League
26 December	Aston Villa	Barclays Premier League
5 January	Everton	Barclays Premier League
22 January	Newcastle United	Barclays Premier League
30 January	Fulham	FA Cup
2 February	Blackburn Rovers	Barclays Premier League
12 February	Sunderland	Barclays Premier League
15 February	AC Milan - Il Milanista	Champions League
	- Metro Stadio	
22 February	Blackpool	Barclays Premier League
6 March	Wolverhampton Wanderers	Barclays Premier League
2 April	Wigan Athletic	Barclays Premier League
5 April	Real Madrid – Media Punta	Champions League
30 April	Chelsea	Barclays Premier League
10 May	Manchester City	Barclays Premier League
15 May	Liverpool	Barclays Premier League

10 July
Bournemouth

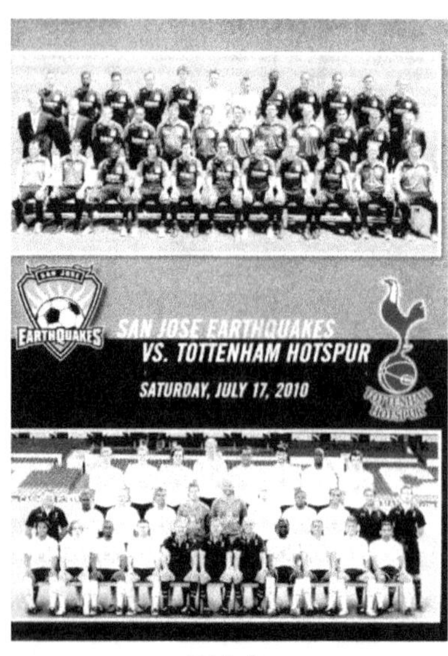

17 July
San Jose Earthquakes

22 & 25 July
Barclays New York Challenge

16 October
Fulham

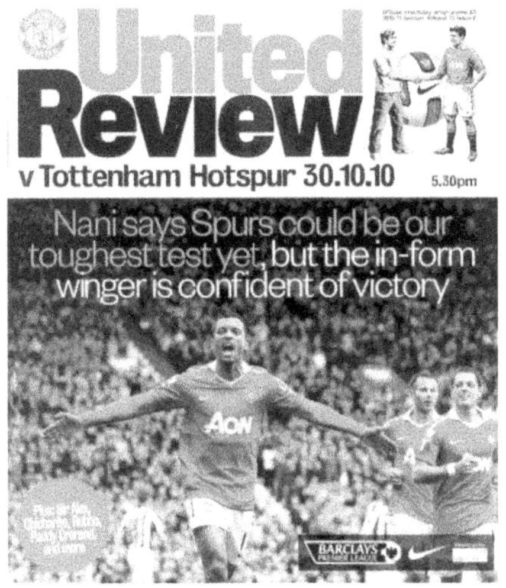

30 October
Tottenham Hotspur

4 December
Birmingham City

19 December
Blackpool - postponed

26 December
Aston Villa

2 February
Blackburn Rovers

6 March
Wolverhampton Wanderers

2 April
Wigan Athletic

15 May
Liverpool

2011-12

HOME

		Date	Opponent	Competition
		6 August	Athletic Bilbao	Friendly
		25 August	Heart of Midlothian	Europa League
		28 August	Manchester City	Barclays Premier League
		18 September	Liverpool	Barclays Premier League
		29 September	Shamrock Rovers	Europa League
		2 October	Arsenal	Barclays Premier League
		20 October	Rubin Kazan	Europa League
		30 October	Queens Park Rangers	Barclays Premier League
		21 November	Aston Villa	Barclays Premier League
		30 November	PAOK	Europa League
		3 December	Bolton Wanderers	Barclays Premier League
		18 December	Sunderland	Barclays Premier League
		22 December	Chelsea	Barclays Premier League
		3 January	West Bromwich Albion	Barclays Premier League
		7 January	Cheltenham Town	FA Cup
		11 January	Everton	Barclays Premier League
		14 January	Wolverhampton Wanderers	Barclays Premier League
		31 January	Wigan Athletic	Barclays Premier League
		11 February	Newcastle United	Barclays Premier League
		4 March	Manchester United	Barclays Premier League
		7 March	Stevenage	FA Cup
		17 March	Bolton Wanderers - abandoned	FA Cup
		21 March	Stoke City	Barclays Premier League
		27 March	Bolton Wanderers	FA Cup
		1 April	Swansea City	Barclays Premier League
		9 April	Norwich City	Barclays Premier League
		29 April	Blackburn Rovers	Barclays Premier League
		13 May	Fulham	Barclays Premier League

☐ Handbook ☐ Season Ticket

Handbook

6 August
Athletic Bilbao

28 August
Manchester City

18 September
Liverpool

30 October
Queens Park Rangers

21 November
Aston Villa

18 December
Sunderland

7 January
Cheltenham Town

11 February
Newcastle United

7 March
Stevenage

17 March
Bolton Wanderers - abandoned

13 May
Fulham

2011-12

AWAY

Date	Opponent	Competition
{ 16 July	Kaizer Chiefs (Polokwane)	Vodacom Challenge
{ 19 July	Orlando Pirates (Nelspruit)	Vodacom Challenge
{ 23 July	Orlando Pirates (Johannesburg)	Vodacom Challenge
30 July	Brighton & Hove Albion	Stadium Opening
18 August	Heart of Midlothian	Europa League
22 August	Manchester United	Barclays Premier League
10 September	Wolverhampton Wanderers	Barclays Premier League
15 September	PAOK	Europa League
21 September	Stoke City	Carling Cup
24 September	Wigan Athletic	Barclays Premier League
16 October	Newcastle United	Barclays Premier League
23 October	Blackburn Rovers	Barclays Premier League
3 November	Rubin Kazan	Europa League
6 November	Fulham	Barclays Premier League
26 November	West Bromwich Albion	Barclays Premier League
11 December	Stoke City	Barclays Premier League
15 December	Shamrock Rovers	Europa League
27 December	Norwich City	Barclays Premier League
31 December	Swansea City	Barclays Premier League
22 January	Manchester City	Barclays Premier League
27 January	Watford	FA Cup
6 February	Liverpool	Barclays Premier League
19 February	Stevenage	FA Cup
26 February	Arsenal	Barclays Premier League
10 March	Everton	Barclays Premier League
24 March	Chelsea	Barclays Premier League
7 April	Sunderland	Barclays Premier League
15 April	Chelsea (Wembley)	FA Cup
21 April	Queens Park Rangers	Barclays Premier League
2 May	Bolton Wanderers	Barclays Premier League
6 May	Aston Villa	Barclays Premier League

16 - 23 July
Vodacom Challenge

30 July
Brighton & Hove Albion

20 September
Stoke City

6 November
Fulham

26 November
West Bromwich Albion

31 December
Swansea City

27 January
Watford

19 February
Stevenage

10 March
Everton

7 April
Sunderland

21 April
Queens Park Rangers

6 May
Aston Villa

2012-13

HOME

		Date	Opponent	Competition
		25 August	West Bromwich Albion	Barclays Premier League
		1 September	Norwich City	Barclays Premier League
		20 September	Lazio	Europa League
		23 September	Queens Park Rangers	Barclays Premier League
		7 October	Aston Villa	Barclays Premier League
		20 October	Chelsea	Barclays Premier League
		3 November	Wigan Athletic	Barclays Premier League
		8 November	NK Maribor	Europa League
		25 November	West Ham United	Barclays Premier League
		28 November	Liverpool	Barclays Premier League
		6 December	Panathinaikos	Europa League
		16 December	Swansea City	Barclays Premier League
		22 December	Stoke City	Barclays Premier League
		1 January	Reading	Barclays Premier League
		5 January	Coventry City	FA Cup
		20 January	Manchester United	Barclays Premier League
		9 February	Newcastle United	Barclays Premier League
		14 February	Olympique Lyonnais	Europa League
		3 March	Arsenal	Barclays Premier League
		7 March	Internazionale	Europa League
		17 March	Fulham	Barclays Premier League
		4 April	FC Basel 1893	Europa League
		7 April	Everton	Barclays Premier League
		21 April	Manchester City	Barclays Premier League
		4 May	Southampton	Barclays Premier League
		19 May	Sunderland	Barclays Premier League

☐ Handbook

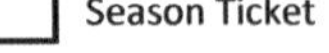
☐ Season Ticket

Handbook

25 August
West Bromwich Albion

23 September
Queens Park Rangers

20 October
Chelsea

25 November
West Ham United

28 November
Liverpool

22 December
Stoke City

20 January
Manchester United

9 February
Newcastle United

17 March
Fulham

21 April
Manchester City

19 May
Sunderland

2012-13

AWAY

		Date	Opponent	Competition
		18 July	Stevenage	Friendly
		24 July	LA Galaxy	Friendly
		28 July	Liverpool (Baltimore)	Friendly
		31 July	New York Red Bulls	Barclays New York Cup
		5 August	Watford	Lloyd Doyley Testimonial
		9 August	Valencia	Trofeo Estrella Damm
		18 August	Newcastle United	Barclays Premier League
		16 September	Reading	Barclays Premier League
		26 September	Carlisle United	Capital One Cup
		29 September	Manchester United	Barclays Premier League
		4 October	Panathinaikos	Europa League
		25 October	NK Maribor	Europa League
		28 October	Southampton	Barclays Premier League
		31 October	Norwich City	Capital One Cup
		11 November	Manchester City	Barclays Premier League
		17 November	Arsenal	Barclays Premier League
		22 November	Lazio - Cittaceleste	Europa League
		1 December	Fulham	Barclays Premier League
		9 December	Everton	Barclays Premier League
		26 December	Aston Villa	Barclays Premier League
		29 December	Sunderland	Barclays Premier League
		12 January	Queens Park Rangers	Barclays Premier League
		27 January	Leeds United	FA Cup
		30 January	Norwich City	Barclays Premier League
		3 February	West Bromwich Albion	Barclays Premier League
		21 February	Olympique Lyonnais – La Tribune	Europa League
		25 February	West Ham United	Barclays Premier League
		10 March	Liverpool	Barclays Premier League
		14 March	Internazionale	Europa League
		30 March	Swansea City	Barclays Premier League
		11 April	FC Basel 1893	Europa League
		27 April	Wigan Athletic	Barclays Premier League
		8 May	Chelsea	Barclays Premier League
		12 May	Stoke City	Barclays Premier League
		23 May	Jamaica Reggae Boys (Bahamas)	Friendly

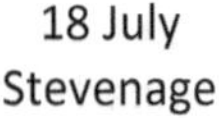
18 July
Stevenage

24 July
LA Galaxy

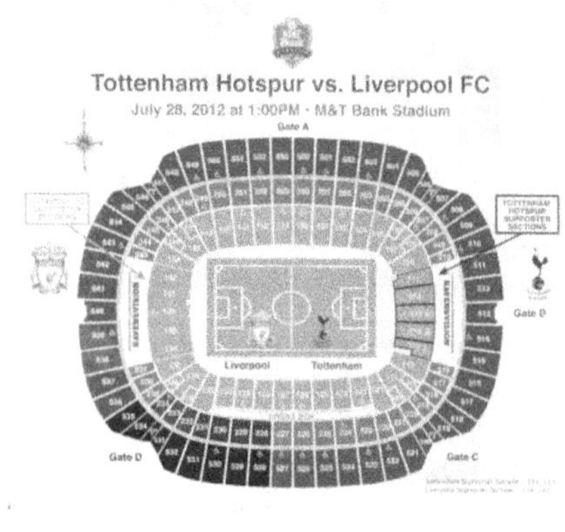

28 July
Liverpool

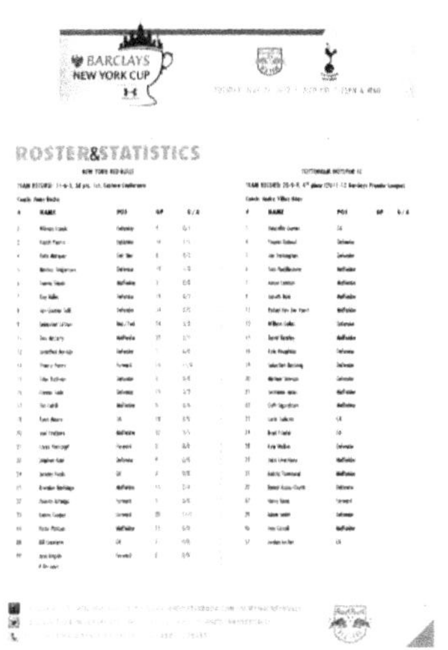

31 July
New York Red Bulls

5 August
Watford

26 September
Carlisle United

31 October
Norwich City

26 December
Aston Villa

30 January
Norwich City

25 February
West Ham United

12 May
Stoke City

23 May
Jamaica Reggae Boys

2013-14

HOME

Date	Opponent	Competition
10 August	Espanyol	Friendly
25 August	Swansea City	Barclays Premier League
29 August	Dinamo Tbilisi	Europa League
14 September	Norwich City	Barclays Premier League
19 September	Tromsø	Europa League
28 September	Chelsea	Barclays Premier League
6 October	West Ham United	Barclays Premier League
27 October	Hull City	Barclays Premier League
30 October	Hull City	Capital One Cup
7 November	FC Sheriff	Europa League
10 November	Newcastle United	Barclays Premier League
1 December	Manchester United	Barclays Premier League
12 December	Anzhi Makhachkala	Europa League
15 December	Liverpool	Barclays Premier League
18 December	West Ham United	Capital One Cup
26 December	West Bromwich Albion	Barclays Premier League
29 December	Stoke City	Barclays Premier League
11 January	Crystal Palace	Barclays Premier League
29 January	Manchester City	Barclays Premier League
9 February	Everton	Barclays Premier League
27 February	Dnipro	Europa League
2 March	Cardiff City	Barclays Premier League
13 March	Benfica	Europa League
16 March	Arsenal	Barclays Premier League
23 March	Southampton	Barclays Premier League
7 April	Sunderland	Barclays Premier League
19 April	Fulham	Barclays Premier League
11 May	Aston Villa	Barclays Premier League
12 May	Ledley Guest XI	Ledley King Testimonial

Handbook

Season Ticket

Handbook

10 August
Espanyol

14 September
Norwich City

6 October
West Ham United

30 October
Hull City

1 December
Manchester City

18 December
West Ham United

29 January
Manchester City

2 March
Cardiff City

23 March
Southampton

19 April
Fulham

12 May
Ledley Guest XI

2013-14

AWAY

Date	Opponent	Competition
16 July	Swindon Town	Friendly
19 July	Colchester United	Friendly
{ 24 July	Sunderland (Hong Kong)	Barclays Asia Trophy
{ 27 July	South China (Hong Kong)	Barclays Asia Trophy
3 August	AS Monaco	Friendly
18 August	Crystal Palace	Barclays Premier League
22 August	Dinamo Tbilisi	Europa League
1 September	Arsenal	Barclays Premier League
21 September	Cardiff City	Barclays Premier League
24 September	Aston Villa	Capital One Cup
3 October	Anzhi Makhachkala (Ramenskoye) – A3 prog	Europa League
	- A4 brochure	
20 October	Aston Villa	Barclays Premier League
24 October	FC Sheriff	Europa League
3 November	Everton	Barclays Premier League
24 November	Manchester City	Barclays Premier League
28 November	Tromsø	Europa League
4 December	Fulham	Barclays Premier League
7 December	Sunderland	Barclays Premier League
22 December	Southampton	Barclays Premier League
1 January	Manchester United	Barclays Premier League
4 January	Arsenal	FA Cup
19 January	Swansea City	Barclays Premier League
1 February	Hull City	Barclays Premier League
12 February	Newcastle United	Barclays Premier League
20 February	Dnipro - B3 size	Europa League
	- A4 size	
23 February	Norwich City	Barclays Premier League
8 March	Chelsea	Barclays Premier League
20 March	Benfica	Europa League
30 March	Liverpool	Barclays Premier League
12 April	West Bromwich Albion	Barclays Premier League
26 April	Stoke City	Barclays Premier League
3 May	West Ham United	Barclays Premier League

16 July
Swindon Town

19 July
Colchester United

24 & 27 July
Barclays Asia Trophy

3 August
AS Monaco

18 August
Crystal Palace

22 September
Cardiff City

24 September
Aston Villa

20 October
Aston Villa

4 January
Arsenal

1 February
Hull City

23 February
Norwich City

26 April
Stoke City

2014-15

HOME

		9 August	Schalke 04	Friendly
		24 August	Queens Park Rangers	Barclays Premier League
		28 August	AEL Limassol – Goal News	Europa League
		31 August	Liverpool	Barclays Premier League
		21 September	West Bromwich Albion	Barclays Premier League
		24 September	Nottingham Forest	Capital One Cup
		2 October	Besiktas	Europa League
		5 October	Southampton	Barclays Premier League
		23 October	Asteras Tripolis	Europa League
		26 October	Newcastle United	Barclays Premier League
		29 October	Brighton & Hove Albion	Capital One Cup
		9 November	Stoke City	Barclays Premier League
		27 November	Partizan Belgrade	Europa League
		30 November	Everton	Barclays Premier League
		6 December	Crystal Palace	Barclays Premier League
		17 December	Newcastle United	Capital One Cup
		20 December	Burnley	Barclays Premier League
		28 December	Manchester United	Barclays Premier League
		1 January	Chelsea	Barclays Premier League
		14 January	Burnley	FA Cup
		17 January	Sunderland	Barclays Premier League
		21 January	Sheffield United	Capital One Cup
		24 January	Leicester City	FA Cup
		7 February	Arsenal	Barclays Premier League
		19 February	Fiorentina	Europa League
		22 February	West Ham United	Barclays Premier League
		4 March	Swansea City	Barclays Premier League
		21 March	Leicester City	Barclays Premier League
		11 April	Aston Villa	Barclays Premier League
		3 May	Manchester City	Barclays Premier League
		16 May	Hull City	Barclays Premier League

☐ Handbook ☐ Season Ticket

Handbook

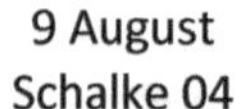

9 August
Schalke 04

31 August
Liverpool

24 September
Nottingham Forest

5 October
Southampton

26 October
Newcastle United

9 November
Stoke City

20 December
Burnley

17 January
Sunderland

4 March
Swansea City

21 March
Leicester City

16 May
Hull City

2014-15

AWAY

Date	Opponent	Competition
19 July	Seattle Sounders - Soccer Seattle issue	Friendly
	- Matchday issue	
23 July	Toronto - programme	Friendly
	- official player card	
26 July	Chicago Fire	Friendly
2 August	Celtic (Helsinki)	Friendly
16 August	West Ham United	Barclays Premier League
21 August	AEL Limassol – Goal News	Europa League
13 September	Sunderland	Barclays Premier League
18 September	Partizan Belgrade	Europa League
27 September	Arsenal	Barclays Premier League
18 October	Manchester City	Barclays Premier League
2 November	Aston Villa	Barclays Premier League
6 November	Asteras Tripolis	Europa League
23 November	Hull City	Barclays Premier League
3 December	Chelsea	Barclays Premier League
11 December	Besiktas	Europa League
14 December	Swansea City	Barclays Premier League
26 December	Leicester City	Barclays Premier League
5 January	Burnley	FA Cup
10 January	Crystal Palace	Barclays Premier League
28 January	Sheffield United	Capital One Cup
31 January	West Bromwich Albion	Barclays Premier League
10 February	Liverpool	Barclays Premier League
26 February	Fiorentina - il Brivido Sportivo	Europa League
	- tutto-viola	
1 March	Chelsea (Wembley)	Capital One Cup
7 March	Queens Park Rangers	Barclays Premier League
15 March	Manchester United	Barclays Premier League
5 April	Burnley	Barclays Premier League
19 April	Newcastle United	Barclays Premier League
25 April	Southampton	Barclays Premier League
9 May	Stoke City	Barclays Premier League
24 May	Everton	Barclays Premier League
27 May	Malaysia XI (Kuala Lumpur)	AIA Cup
30 May	Sydney FC	AIA Cup

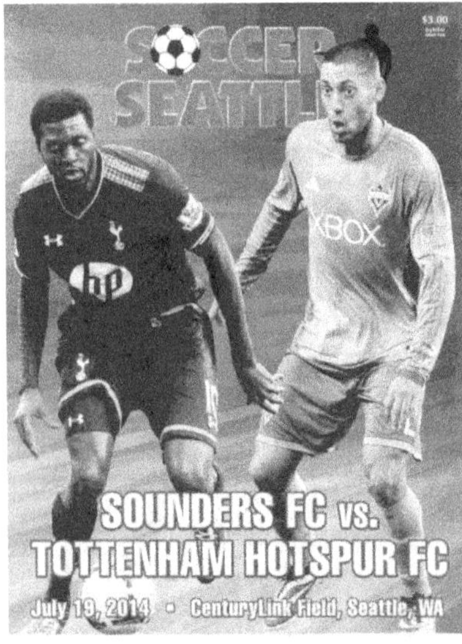

19 July
Seattle Sounders - Soccer Seattle issue

19 July
Seattle Sounders - Matchday issue

23 July
Toronto - programme

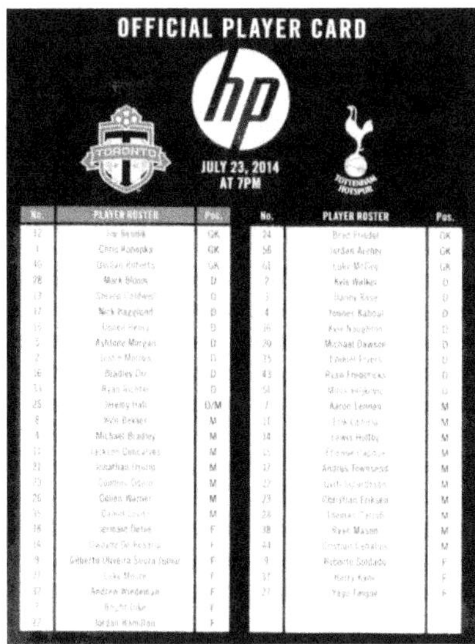

23 July
Toronto - official player card

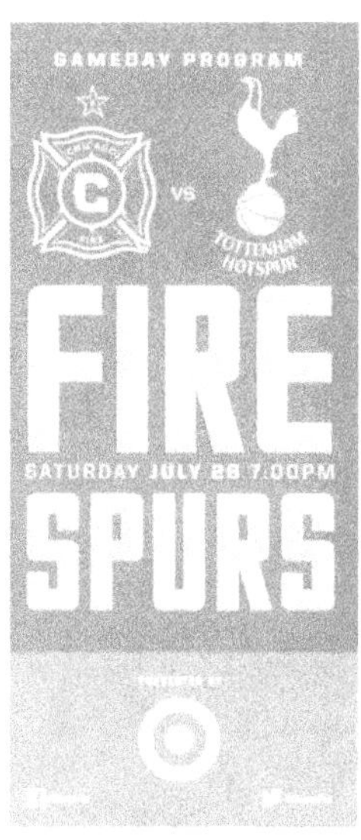

26 July
Chicago Fire

2 August
Celtic

2 November
Aston Villa

14 December
Swansea City

5 January
Burnley

19 April
Newcastle United

27 May
Malaysia XI

30 May
Sydney

2015-16

HOME

		Date	Opponent	Competition
☐	☐	15 August	Stoke City	Barclays Premier League
☐	☐	29 August	Everton	Barclays Premier League
☐	☐	17 September	Qarabag	Europa League
☐	☐	20 September	Crystal Palace	Barclays Premier League
☐	☐	23 September	Arsenal	Capital One Cup
☐	☐	26 September	Manchester City	Barclays Premier League
☐	☐	17 October	Liverpool	Barclays Premier League
☐	☐	2 November	Aston Villa	Barclays Premier League
☐	☐	5 November	Anderlecht	Europa League
☐	☐	22 November	West Ham United	Barclays Premier League
☐	☐	29 November	Chelsea	Barclays Premier League
☐	☐	10 December	AS Monaco	Europa League
☐	☐	13 December	Newcastle United	Barclays Premier League
☐	☐	26 December	Norwich City	Barclays Premier League
☐	☐	10 January	Leicester City	FA Cup
☐	☐	13 January	Leicester City	Barclays Premier League
☐	☐	16 January	Sunderland	Barclays Premier League
☐	☐	6 February	Watford	Barclays Premier League
☐	☐	21 February	Crystal Palace	FA Cup
☐	☐	25 February	Fiorentina	Europa League
☐	☐	28 February	Swansea City	Barclays Premier League
☐	☐	5 March	Arsenal	Barclays Premier League
☐	☐	17 March	Borussia Dortmund	Europa League
☐	☐	20 March	Bournemouth	Barclays Premier League
☐	☐	10 April	Manchester United	Barclays Premier League
☐	☐	25 April	West Bromwich Albion	Barclays Premier League
☐	☐	8 May	Southampton	Barclays Premier League

☐ Handbook ☐ Season Ticket

Handbook

15 August
Stoke City

20 September
Crystal Palace

17 October
Liverpool

22 November
West Ham United

26 December
Norwich City

10 January
Leicester City

6 February
Watford

21 February
Crystal Palace

5 March
Arsenal

25 April
West Bromwich Albion

8 May
Southampton

2015-16

AWAY

		Date	Opponent	Competition
		29 July	MLS All-Stars (Denver)	Friendly
		4 August	Real Madrid (Munich)	Audi Cup
		5 August	AC Milan (Munich)	Audi Cup
		8 August	Manchester United	Barclays Premier League
		22 August	Leicester City	Barclays Premier League
		13 September	Sunderland	Barclays Premier League
		1 October	AS Monaco	Europa League
		4 October	Swansea City	Barclays Premier League
		22 October	Anderlecht	Europa League
		25 October	Bournemouth	Barclays Premier League
		8 November	Arsenal	Barclays Premier League
		26 November	Qarabag	Europa League
		5 December	West Bromwich Albion	Barclays Premier League
		19 December	Southampton	Barclays Premier League
		28 December	Watford	Barclays Premier League
		3 January	Everton	Barclays Premier League
		20 January	Leicester City	FA Cup
		23 January	Crystal Palace	Barclays Premier League
		30 January	Colchester United	FA Cup
		2 February	Norwich City	Barclays Premier League
		14 February	Manchester City	Barclays Premier League
		18 February	Fiorentina – tutto-viola	Europa League
		2 March	West Ham United	Barclays Premier League
		10 March	Borussia Dortmund	Europa League
		13 March	Aston Villa	Barclays Premier League
		2 April	Liverpool	Barclays Premier League
		18 April	Stoke City	Barclays Premier League
		2 May	Chelsea	Barclays Premier League
		15 May	Newcastle United	Barclays Premier League

2015 MLS ALL-STAR GAME ROSTER

29 July
MLS All-Stars

4 August
Real Madrid

5 August
AC Milan

13 September
Sunderland

4 October
Swansea City

28 December
Watford

30 January
Colchester United

14 February
Manchester City

2 March
West Ham United

13 March
Aston Villa

18 April
Stoke City

15 May
Newcastle United

2016-17

HOME

		Date	Opponent	Competition
☐	☐	20 August	Crystal Palace	Premier League
☐	☐	27 August	Liverpool	Premier League
☐	☐	14 September	AS Monaco (Wembley)	Champions League
☐	☐	18 September	Sunderland	Premier League
☐	☐	21 September	Gillingham	EFL Cup
☐	☐		- Gillingham production	
☐	☐	2 October	Manchester City	Premier League
☐	☐	29 October	Leicester City	Premier League
☐	☐	2 November	Bayer 04 Leverkusen (Wembley)	Champions League
☐	☐	19 November	West Ham United	Premier League
☐	☐	3 December	Swansea City	Premier League
☐	☐	7 December	CSKA Moscow (Wembley)	Champions League
☐	☐	14 December	Hull City	Premier League
☐	☐	18 December	Burnley	Premier League
☐	☐	4 January	Chelsea	Premier League
☐	☐	8 January	Aston Villa	FA Cup
☐	☐	14 January	West Bromwich Albion	Premier League
☐	☐	28 January	Wycombe Wanderers	FA Cup
☐	☐	4 February	Middlesbrough	Premier League
☐	☐	23 February	KAA Gent (Wembley)	Europa League
☐	☐	26 February	Stoke City	Premier League
☐	☐	5 March	Everton	Premier League
☐	☐	12 March	Millwall	FA Cup
☐	☐	19 March	Southampton	Premier League
☐	☐	8 April	Watford	Premier League
☐	☐	15 April	Bournemouth	Premier League
☐	☐	30 April	Arsenal	Premier League
☐	☐	14 May	Manchester United	Premier League
☐	☐	14 May	The Finale (Farewell Ceremony)	

☐ Handbook ☐ Season Ticket

Handbook

20 August
Crystal Palace

21 September
Gillingham

21 September
Gillingham - Gillingham production

29 October
Leicester City

3 December
Swansea City

18 December
Burnley

28 January
Wycombe Wanderers

27 February
Stoke City

12 March
Millwall

15 April
Bournemouth

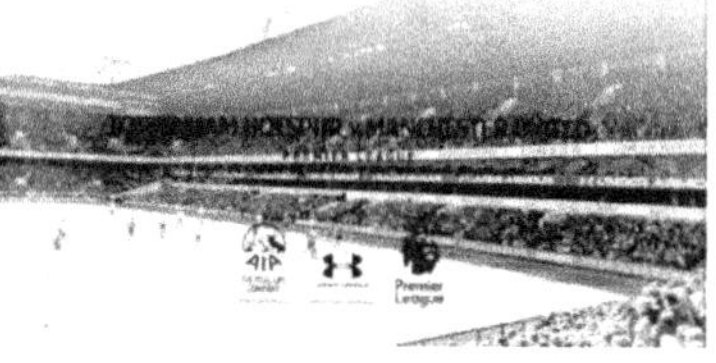

14 May
Manchester United

2016-17

AWAY

	Date	Opponent	Competition
☐	26 July	Juventus (Melbourne)	International Champions Cup
☐	29 July	Atletico Madrid (Melbourne)	International Champions Cup
☐ ☐	5 August	Internazionale (Oslo)	Pirelli Trophy
☐ ☐	13 August	Everton	Premier League
☐ ☐	10 September	Stoke City	Premier League
☐ ☐	24 September	Middlesbrough	Premier League
☐ ☐	27 September	CSKA Moscow	Champions League
☐ ☐	15 October	West Bromwich Albion	Premier League
☐ ☐	18 October	Bayer 04 Leverkusen	Champions League
☐ ☐	22 October	Bournemouth	Premier League
☐ ☐	25 October	Liverpool	EFL Cup
☐ ☐	6 November	Arsenal	Premier League
☐ ☐	22 November	AS Monaco	Champions League
☐ ☐	26 November	Chelsea	Premier League
☐ ☐	11 December	Manchester United	Premier League
☐ ☐	28 December	Southampton	Premier League
☐ ☐	1 January	Watford	Premier League
☐ ☐	21 January	Manchester City	Premier League
☐ ☐	31 January	Sunderland	Premier League
☐ ☐	11 February	Liverpool	Premier League
☐ ☐	16 February	KAA Gent	Europa League
☐ ☐	19 February	Fulham	FA Cup
☐ ☐	1 April	Burnley	Premier League
☐ ☐	5 April	Swansea City	Premier League
☐ ☐	22 April	Chelsea (Wembley)	FA Cup
☐ ☐	26 April	Crystal Palace	Premier League
☐ ☐	5 May	West Ham United	Premier League
☐ ☐	18 May	Leicester City	Premier League
☐ ☐	21 May	Hull City	Premier League
☐ ☐	26 May	Kitchee (Hong Kong)	Jockey Club Kitchee Centre Challenge Cup

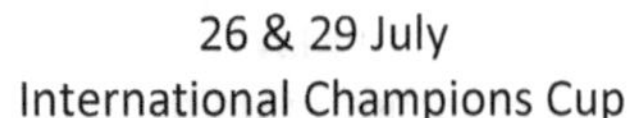

26 & 29 July
International Champions Cup

24 September
Middlesbrough

25 October
Liverpool

6 November
Arsenal

11 December
Manchester United

1 January
Watford

19 February
Fulham

1 April
Burnley

18 May
Leicester City

21 May
Hull City - cover 1

21 May
Hull City - cover 2

26 May
Kitchee

2017-18

HOME

Date	Opponent	Competition
5 August	Juventus (Wembley)	Friendly
20 August	Chelsea (Wembley)	Premier League
27 August	Burnley (Wembley)	Premier League
13 September	Borussia Dortmund (Wembley)	Champions League
16 September	Swansea City (Wembley)	Premier League
19 September	Barnsley (Wembley)	Carabao Cup
14 October	Bournemouth (Wembley)	Premier League
22 October	Liverpool (Wembley)	Premier League
25 October	West Ham United (Wembley)	Carabao Cup
1 November	Real Madrid (Wembley)	Champions League
5 November	Crystal Palace (Wembley)	Premier League
25 November	West Bromwich Albion (Wembley)	Premier League
6 December	APOEL (Wembley)	Champions League
9 December	Stoke City (Wembley)	Premier League
13 December	Brighton and Hove Albion (Wembley)	Premier League
26 December	Southampton (Wembley)	Premier League
4 January	West Ham United (Wembley)	Premier League
7 January	Wimbledon (Wembley)	FA Cup
13 January	Everton (Wembley)	Premier League
31 January	Manchester United (Wembley)	Premier League
7 February	Newport County (Wembley)	FA Cup
10 February	Arsenal (Wembley)	Premier League
28 February	Rochdale (Wembley)	FA Cup
3 March	Huddersfield Town (Wembley)	Premier League
7 March	Juventus (Wembley)	Champions League
14 April	Manchester City (Wembley)	Premier League
30 April	Watford (Wembley)	Premier League
9 May	Newcastle United (Wembley)	Premier League
13 May	Leicester City (Wembley)	Premier League

☐ Handbook ☐ Season Ticket

Handbook

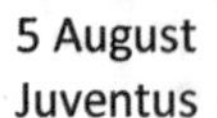
5 August
Juventus

27 August
Burnley

14 October
Bournemouth

22 October
Liverpool

5 November
Crystal Palace

13 December
Brighton & Hove Albion

7 January
Wimbledon

7 February
Newport County

10 February
Arsenal

30 April
Watford

13 May
Leicester City

2017-18

AWAY

		22 July	Paris Saint-Germain (Orlando)	International Champions Cup
		25 July	AS Roma (Harrison)	International Champions Cup
		29 July	Manchester City (Nashville)	International Champions Cup
		13 August	Newcastle United	Premier League
		9 September	Everton	Premier League
		23 September	West Ham United	Premier League
		26 September	APOEL	Champions League
		30 September	Huddersfield Town	Premier League
		17 October	Real Madrid	Champions League
		28 October	Manchester United	Premier League
		18 November	Arsenal	Premier League
		21 November	Borussia Dortmund	Champions League
		28 November	Leicester City	Premier League
		2 December	Watford	Premier League
		16 December	Manchester City	Premier League
		23 December	Burnley	Premier League
		2 January	Swansea City	Premier League
		21 January	Southampton	Premier League
		27 January	Newport County	FA Cup
		4 February	Liverpool	Premier League
		13 February	Juventus – Juve Toro	Champions League
		18 February	Rochdale	FA Cup
		25 February	Crystal Palace	Premier League
		11 March	Bournemouth	Premier League
		17 March	Swansea City	FA Cup
		1 April	Chelsea	Premier League
		7 April	Stoke City	Premier League
		17 April	Brighton & Hove Albion	Premier League
		21 April	Manchester United (Wembley)	FA Cup
		5 May	West Bromwich Albion	Premier League

22 July
Paris Saint Germain

25 July
AS Roma

29 July
Manchester City

13 August
Newcastle United

9 September
Everton

30 September
Huddersfield Town

23 December
Burnley

27 January
Newport County

18 February
Rochdale

11 March
Bournemouth

7 April
Stoke City

5 May
West Bromwich Albion

2018-19

HOME

	Date	Opponent	Competition
☐☐	18 August	Fulham (Wembley)	Premier League
☐☐	15 September	Liverpool (Wembley)	Premier League
☐☐	26 September	Watford (Milton Keynes)	Carabao Cup
☐☐	3 October	Barcelona (Wembley)	Champions League
☐☐	6 October	Cardiff City (Wembley)	Premier League
☐☐	29 October	Manchester City (Wembley)	Premier League
☐☐	6 November	PSV (Wembley)	Champions League
☐☐	24 November	Chelsea (Wembley)	Premier League
☐☐	28 November	Internazionale (Wembley)	Champions League
☐☐	5 December	Southampton (Wembley)	Premier League
☐☐	15 December	Burnley (Wembley)	Premier League
☐☐	26 December	Bournemouth (Wembley)	Premier League
☐☐	29 December	Wolverhampton Wanderers (Wembley)	Premier League
☐☐	8 January	Chelsea (Wembley)	Carabao Cup
☐☐	13 January	Manchester United (Wembley)	Premier League
☐☐	30 January	Watford (Wembley)	Premier League
☐☐	2 February	Newcastle United (Wembley)	Premier League
☐☐	10 February	Leicester City (Wembley)	Premier League
☐☐	13 February	Borussia Dortmund (Wembley)	Champions League
☐☐	2 March	Arsenal (Wembley)	Premier League
☐☐	3 April	Crystal Palace	Premier League
☐☐	9 April	Manchester City	Champions League
☐☐	13 April	Huddersfield Town	Premier League
☐☐	23 April	Brighton & Hove Albion	Premier League
☐☐	27 April	West Ham United	Premier League
☐☐	30 April	Ajax	Champions League
☐☐	12 May	Everton	Premier League

☐ Handbook ☐ Season Ticket

Handbook

18 August
Fulham

26 September
Watford

29 October
Manchester City

24 November
Chelsea

15 December
Burnley

29 December
Wolverhampton Wanderers

13 January
Manchester United

2 February
Newcastle United

2 March
Arsenal

3 April
Crystal Palace

12 May
Everton

2018-19

AWAY

Date	Opponent	Competition
25 July	AS Roma (San Diego)	International Champions Cup
28 July	Barcelona (Pasadena)	International Champions Cup
31 July	AC Milan (Minneapolis)	International Champions Cup
4 August	Girona	Trofeu Costa Brava
11 August	Newcastle United	Premier League
27 August	Manchester United	Premier League
2 September	Watford	Premier League
18 September	Internazionale	Champions League
22 September	Brighton & Hove Albion	Premier League
29 September	Huddersfield Town	Premier League
20 October	West Ham United	Premier League
24 October	PSV	Champions League
31 October	West Ham United	Carabao Cup
3 November	Wolverhampton Wanderers	Premier League
10 November	Crystal Palace	Premier League
2 December	Arsenal	Premier League
8 December	Leicester City	Premier League
11 December	Barcelona	Champions League
19 December	Arsenal	Carabao Cup
23 December	Everton	Premier League
1 January	Cardiff City	Premier League
4 January	Tranmere Rovers	FA Cup
20 January	Fulham	Premier League
24 January	Chelsea	Carabao Cup
27 January	Crystal Palace	FA Cup
23 February	Burnley	Premier League
27 February	Chelsea	Premier League
5 March	Borussia Dortmund	Champions League
9 March	Southampton	Premier League
31 March	Liverpool	Premier League
17 April	Manchester City	Champions League
20 April	Manchester City	Premier League
4 May	Bournemouth	Premier League
8 May	Ajax	Champions League
1 June	Liverpool (Madrid)	Champions League

11 August
Newcastle United

2 September
Watford

20 October
West Ham United

31 October
West ham United

3 November
Wolverhampton Wanderers

2 December
Arsenal

23 December
Everton

1 January
Cardiff City

4 January
Tranmere Rovers

23 February
Burnley

31 March
Liverpool

4 May
Bournemouth

2019-20

HOME

		Date	Opponent	Competition
☐	☐	4 August	Internazionale	International Champions Cup
☐	☐	10 August	Aston Villa	Premier League
☐	☐	25August	Newcastle United	Premier League
☐	☐	14 September	Crystal Palace	Premier League
☐	☐	28 September	Southampton	Premier League
☐	☐	1 October	Bayern Munich	Champions League
☐	☐	19 October	Watford	Premier League
☐	☐	22 October	Red Star Belgrade	Champions League
☐	☐	9 November	Sheffield United	Premier League
☐	☐	26 November	Olympiakos	Champions League
☐	☐	30 November	Bournemouth	Premier League
☐	☐	7 December	Burnley	Premier League
☐	☐	22 December	Chelsea	Premier League
☐	☐	26 December	Brighton & Hove Albion	Premier League
☐	☐	11 January	Liverpool	Premier League
☐	☐	14 January	Middlesbrough	FA Cup
☐	☐	22 January	Norwich City	Premier League
☐	☐	2 February	Manchester City	Premier League
☐	☐	5 February	Southampton	FA Cup
☐	☐	19 February	Red Bull Leipzig	Champions League
☐	☐	1 March	Wolverhampton Wanderers	Premier League
☐	☐	4 March	Norwich City	FA Cup
☐	☐	15 March	Manchester United - postponed	Premier League
☐	☐	19 June	Manchester United	Premier League
☐	☐	23 June	West Ham United	Premier League
☐	☐	6 July	Everton	Premier League
☐	☐	12 July	Arsenal	Premier League
☐	☐	19 July	Leicester City	Premier League

☐ Handbook ☐ Season Ticket

Handbook

4 August
Internazionale

10 August
Aston Villa

19 October
Watford

30 November
Bournemouth

26 December
Brighton & Hove Albion

11 January
Liverpool

2 February
Manchester City

5 February
Southampton

1 March
Wolverhampton Wanderers

15 March
Manchester United - postponed

19 July
Leicester City

2019-20

AWAY

		Date	Opponent	Competition
		21 July	Juventus (Singapore)	International Champions Cup
		25 July	Manchester United (Shanghai)	International Champions Cup
		30 July	Real Madrid (Munich)	Audi Cup
		31 July	Bayern Munich	Audi Cup
		17 August	Manchester City	Premier League
		1 September	Arsenal	Premier League
		18 September	Olympiakos	Champions League
		21 September	Leicester City	Premier League
		24 September	Colchester United	Carabao Cup
		5 October	Brighton & Hove Albion	Premier League
		27 October	Liverpool	Premier League
		3 November	Everton	Premier League
		6 November	Red Star Belgrade	Champions League
		23 November	West Ham United	Premier League
		4 December	Manchester United	Premier League
		11 December	Bayern Munich	Champions League
		15 December	Wolverhampton Wanderers	Premier League
		28 December	Norwich City	Premier League
		1 January	Southampton	Premier League
		5 January	Middlesbrough	FA Cup
		18 January	Watford	Premier League
		25 January	Southampton	FA Cup
		16 February	Aston Villa	Premier League
		22 February	Chelsea	Premier League
		7 March	Burnley	Premier League
		10 March	Red Bull Leipzig - German edition	Champions League
			- English edition	
		2 July	Sheffield United - four match issue	Premier League
			- single match issue	
		9 July	Bournemouth (teamsheet)	Premier League
		15 July	Newcastle United	Premier League
		26 July	Crystal Palace	Premier League

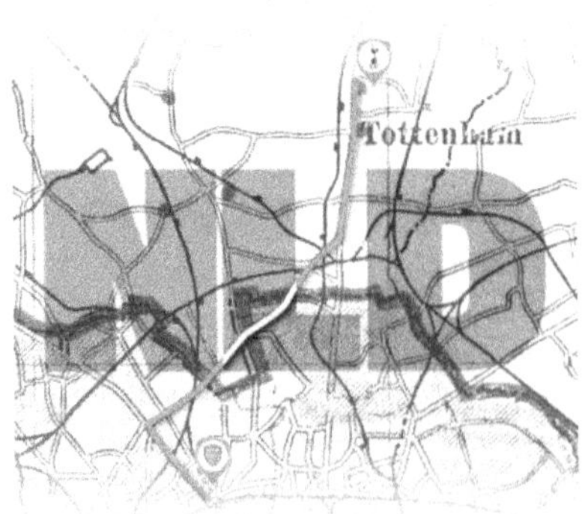

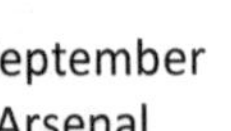

17 August
Manchester City

1 September
Arsenal

24 September
Colchester United

5 October
Brighton & Hove Albion

Martin Peters

28 December
Norwich City

5 January
Middlesbrough

25 January
Southampton

16 February
Aston Villa

7 March
Burnley

2 July
Sheffield United - four match issue

2 July
Sheffield United - single match issue

9 July
Bournemouth - teamsheet

CUP FINALS

6 May 1961
FA Cup
Leicester City

5 May 1962
FA Cup
Burnley

15 May 1963
European Cup-Winners' Cup
Atletico Madrid

15 May 1963
European Cup-Winners' Cup
Atletico Madrid – stadium issue

20 May 1967
FA Cup
Chelsea

27 February 1971
Football League Cup
Aston Villa

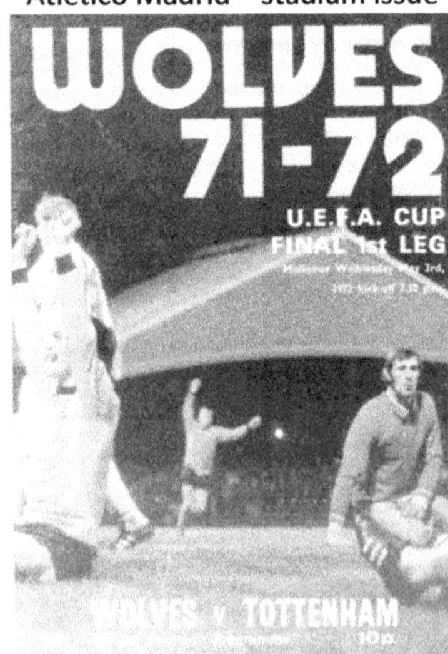

3 May 1972
UEFA Cup – 1st leg
Wolverhampton Wanderers

17 May 1972
UEFA Cup – 2nd leg
Wolverhampton Wanderers

3 March 1973
Football League Cup
Norwich City

CUP FINALS

21 May 1974
UEFA Cup – 1st leg
Feijenoord

29 May 1974
UEFA Cup – 2nd leg
Feijenoord

29 May 1974
UEFA Cup – 2nd leg
Feyenoord - De Sportgids

29 May 1974
UEFA Cup – 2nd leg
Feyenoord - Sport Blad Feyenoord

9 May 1981
FA Cup
Manchester City

14 May 1981
FA Cup Replay
Manchester City

13 March 1982
Football League Milk Cup
Liverpool

22 May 1982
FA Cup
Queens Park Rangers

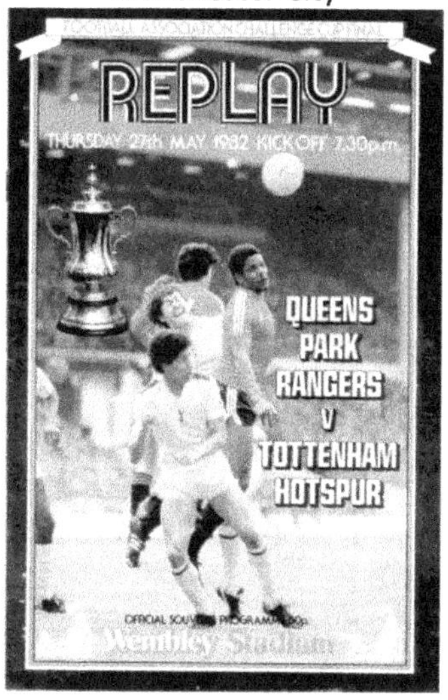

27 May 1982
FA Cup Replay
Queens Park Rangers

CUP FINALS

9 May 1984
UEFA Cup – 1st leg
Anderlecht

29 May 1984
UEFA Cup – 2nd leg
Anderlecht

16 May 1987
FA Cup
Coventry City

18 May 1991
FA Cup
Nottingham Forest

21 March 1999
Worthington Cup
Leicester City

24 February 2002
Worthington Cup
Blackburn Rovers

24 February 2008
Carling Cup
Chelsea

1 March 2009
Carling Cup
Manchester United

1 March 2015
Carling Cup
Chelsea

CUP FINALS

1 June 2019
Champions League
Liverpool

SEMI-FINALS

THE FOOTBALL ASSOCIATION
CHALLENGE CUP

SEMI-FINAL TIE

BLACKPOOL
v.
TOTTENHAM HOTSPUR
AT
Villa Park, Birmingham
SATURDAY, MARCH 13th, 1948
KICK-OFF 3 P.M.

OFFICIAL PROGRAMME SIXPENCE

13 March 1948
FA Cup
Blackpool

THE FOOTBALL ASSOCIATION
CHALLENGE CUP

SEMI-FINAL TIE

BLACKPOOL
v.
TOTTENHAM HOTSPUR
At VILLA PARK, BIRMINGHAM
SATURDAY, MARCH 21st, 1953

OFFICIAL PROGRAMME ISSUED BY ASTON VILLA F.C.
SIXPENCE

21 March 1953
FA Cup
Blackpool

OFFICIAL PROGRAMME

THE FOOTBALL ASSOCIATION
CHALLENGE CUP

SEMI-FINAL TIE

MANCHESTER CITY
v.
TOTTENHAM HOTSPUR
VILLA PARK, BIRMINGHAM
SATURDAY, MARCH 17th, 1956

PRICE - 6d.

17 March 1956
FA Cup
Manchester City

OFFICIAL PROGRAMME

THE FOOTBALL ASSOCIATION
CHALLENGE CUP

SEMI-FINAL TIE

TOTTENHAM HOTSPUR
BURNLEY
VILLA PARK, BIRMINGHAM
SATURDAY, MARCH 18th, 1961

PRICE - 6d.

18 March 1961
FA Cup
Burnley

31 March 1962
FA Cup
Manchester United

21 March 1962
European Cup – 1st leg
Benfica - O Benfica newspaper

EUROPEAN CUP
Semi-Final, Second Leg

TOTTENHAM
HOTSPUR
VERSUS
BENFICA
(PORTUGAL)

Thursday, 5th April, 1962
Kick-off 7.45 p.m.

OFFICIAL PROGRAMME
6d.

5 April 1962
European Cup – 2nd leg
Benfica

OFK BEOGRAD

POLUFINALE KUPA
POBEDNIKA KUPOVA EVROPE

TOTTENHAM

24 April 1963
European Cup-Winners' Cup – 1st leg
OFK Belgrade

1 May 1963
European Cup-Winners' Cup – 2nd leg
OFK Belgrade

SEMI-FINALS

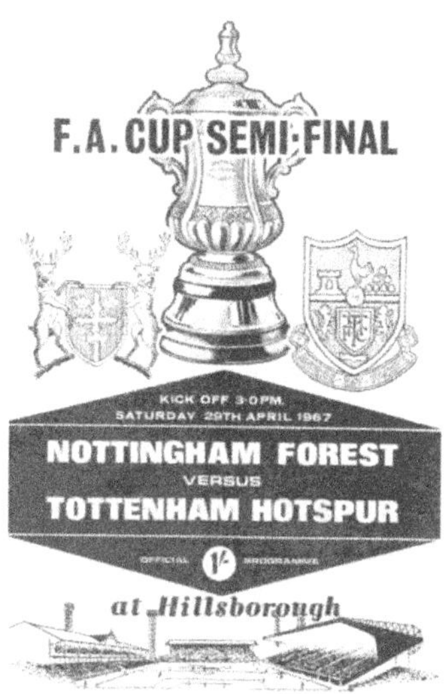

29 April 1967
FA Cup
Nottingham Forest

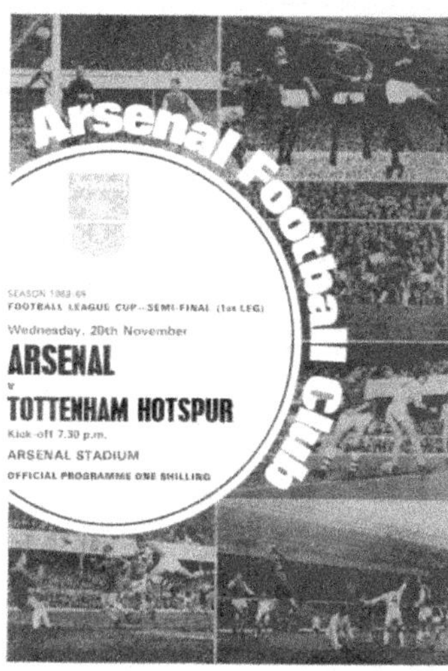

20 November 1968
Football League Cup – 1st leg
Arsenal

4 December 1968
Football League Cup – 2nd leg
Arsenal

16 December 1970
Football League Cup – 1st leg
Bristol City

23 December 1970
Football League Cup – 2nd leg
Bristol City

22 December 1971
Football League Cup – 1st leg
Chelsea

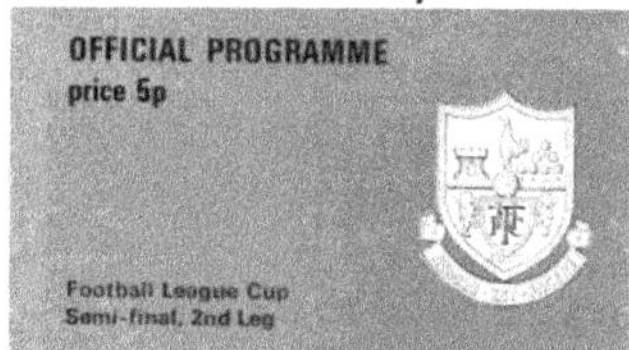

TOTTENHAM
HOTSPUR
v

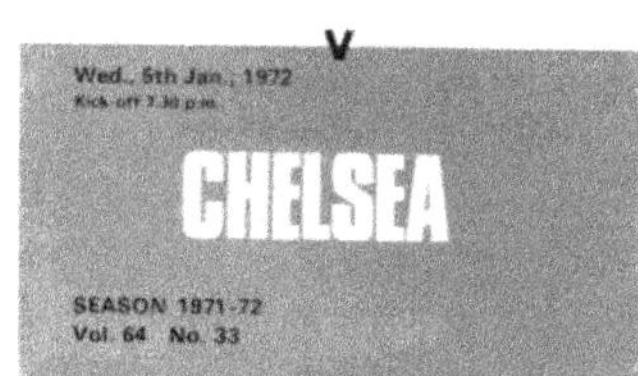

5 January 1972
Football League Cup – 2nd leg
Chelsea

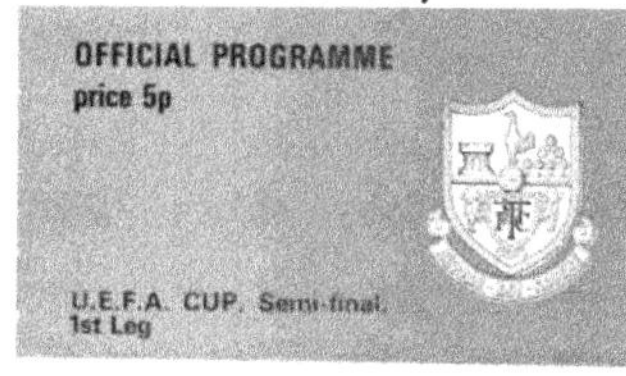

TOTTENHAM
HOTSPUR
v

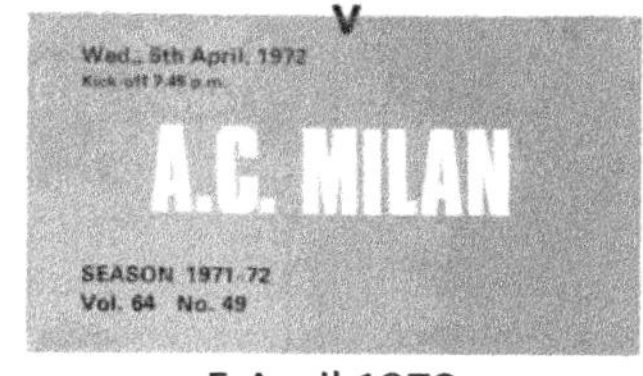

5 April 1972
UEFA Cup – 1st leg
AC Milan

20 December 1972
Football League Cup – 1st leg
Wolverhampton Wanderers

SEMI-FINALS

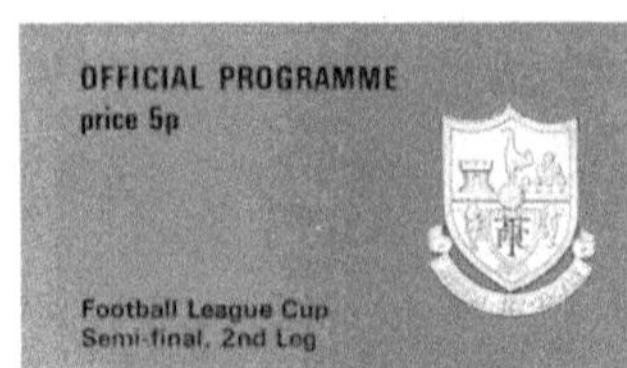

30 December 1972
Football League Cup – 2nd leg
Wolverhampton Wanderers

10 April 1973
UEFA Cup – 1st leg
Liverpool

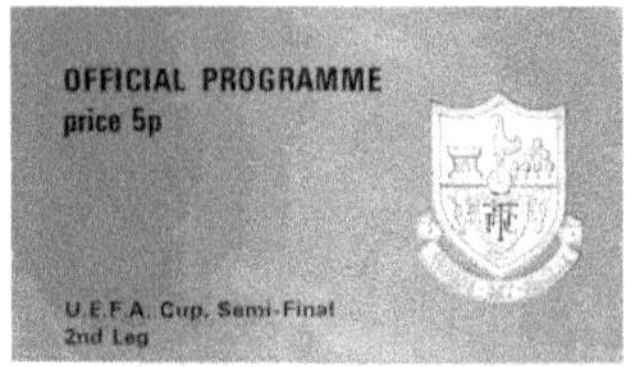

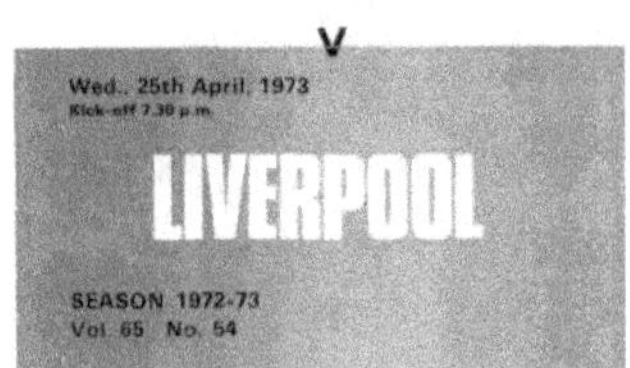

25 April 1973
UEFA Cup – 2nd leg
Liverpool

10 April 1974
UEFA Cup – 1st leg
1FC Lokomotive Leipzig

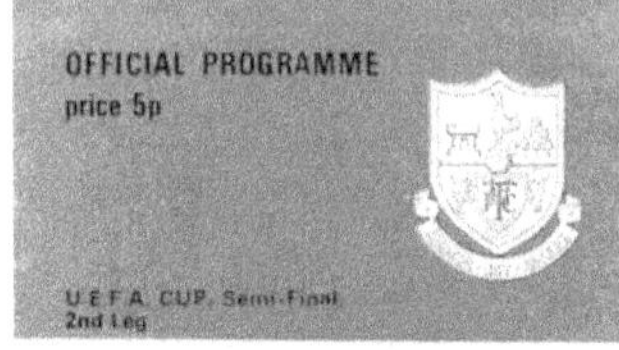

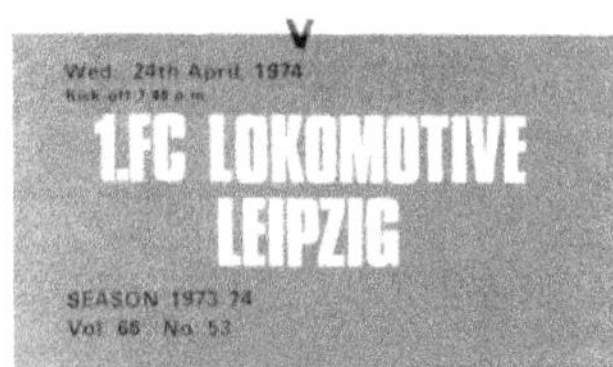

24 April 1974
UEFA Cup – 2nd leg
1FC Lokomotive Leipzig

14 January 1976
Football League Cup – 1st leg
Newcastle United

21 January 1976
Football League Cup – 2nd leg
Newcastle United

11 April 1981
FA Cup
Wolverhampton Wanderers

15 April 1981
FA Cup Replay
Wolverhampton Wanderers

SEMI-FINALS

3 February 1982
Football League Cup – 1st leg
West Bromwich Albion

10 February 1982
Football League Cup – 2nd leg
West Bromwich Albion

3 April 1982
FA Cup
Leicester City

7 April 1982
UEFA Cup – 1st leg
Barcelona

11 April 1984
UEFA Cup – 1st leg
Hajduk Split - magazine

25 April 1984
UEFA Cup – 2nd leg
Hajduk Split

5 February 1986
Screen Sport Super Cup – 1st leg
Everton

19 March 1986
Screen Sport Super Cup – 2nd leg
Everton

8 February 1987
Littlewoods Cup – 1st leg
Arsenal

SEMI-FINALS

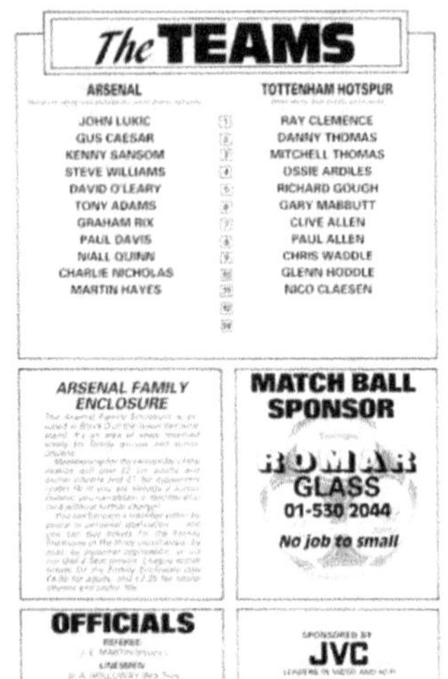

The TEAMS

ARSENAL		TOTTENHAM HOTSPUR
JOHN LUKIC	1	RAY CLEMENCE
GUS CAESAR	2	DANNY THOMAS
KENNY SANSOM	3	MITCHELL THOMAS
STEVE WILLIAMS	4	OSSIE ARDILES
DAVID O'LEARY	5	RICHARD GOUGH
TONY ADAMS	6	GARY MABBUTT
GRAHAM RIX	7	CLIVE ALLEN
PAUL DAVIS	8	PAUL ALLEN
NIALL QUINN	9	CHRIS WADDLE
CHARLIE NICHOLAS	10	GLENN HODDLE
MARTIN HAYES	11	NICO CLAESEN

ARSENAL FAMILY ENCLOSURE

MATCH BALL SPONSOR

ROMAR GLASS

01-530 2044

No job to small

OFFICIALS

SPONSORED BY JVC

8 February 1987
Littlewoods Cup – 1st leg
Arsenal - teamsheet

1 March 1987
Littlewoods Cup – 2nd leg
Arsenal

Tottenham Hotspur

RAY CLEMENCE
DANNY THOMAS
MITCHELL THOMAS
RICHARD GOUGH
OSSIE ARDILES
GARY MABBUTT
CHRIS WADDLE
PAUL ALLEN
GLENN HODDLE
CLIVE ALLEN
NICO CLAESEN
MARTIN HAYES
DAVID ROCASTLE
CHARLIE NICHOLAS
PAUL DAVIS
NIALL QUINN
TONY ADAMS
GRAHAM RIX
DAVID O'LEARY
KENNY SANSOM
VIV ANDERSON
JOHN LUKIC

Arsenal

OFFICIALS

Next match here
QUEENS PARK RANGERS

£1.99.

1 March 1987
Littlewoods Cup – 2nd leg
Arsenal - teamsheet

4 March 1987
Littlewoods Cup Replay
Arsenal

11 April 1987
FA Cup
Watford

14 April 1991
FA Cup
Arsenal

9 February 1992
Rumbelows Cup – 1st leg
Nottingham Forest

4 April 1993
FA Cup
Arsenal

9 April 1995
FA Cup
Everton

SEMI-FINALS

27 January 1999
Worthington Cup – 1st leg
Wimbledon

16 February 1999
Worthington Cup – 2nd leg
Wimbledon

11 April 1999
FA Cup
Newcastle United

8 April 2001
FA Cup
Arsenal

9 January 2002
Worthington Cup – 1st leg
Chelsea

23 January 2002
Worthington Cup – 2nd leg
Chelsea

24 January 2007
Carling Cup – 2nd leg
Arsenal

31 January 2007
Carling Cup – 2nd leg
Arsenal

9 January 2008
Carling Cup – 1st leg
Arsenal

SEMI-FINALS

22 January 2008
Carling Cup – 2nd leg
Arsenal

6 January 2009
Carling Cup – 1st leg
Burnley

21 January 2009
Carling Cup – 2nd leg
Burnley

11 April 2010
FA Cup
Portsmouth

15 April 2012
FA Cup
Chelsea

21 January 2015
Carling Cup – 1st leg
Sheffield United

28 January 2015
Carling Cup – 2nd leg
Sheffield United

22 April 2017
FA Cup
Chelsea

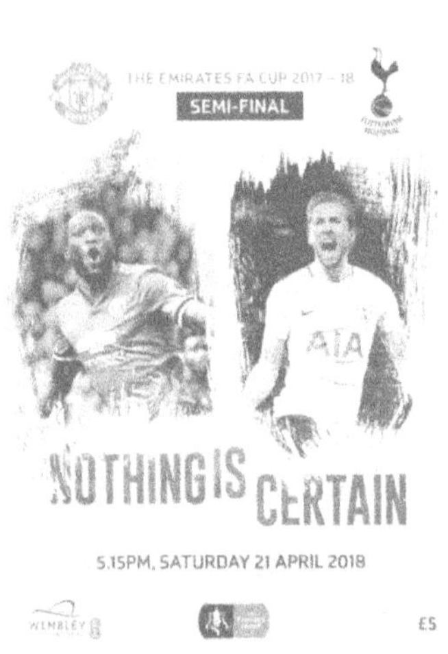

21 April 2018
FA Cup
Manchester United

SEMI-FINALS

8 January 2019
Carabao Cup – 1st leg
Chelsea

24 January 2019
Carabao Cup – 2nd leg
Chelsea

30 April 2019
Champions League – 1st leg
Ajax

8 May 2019
Champions League – 2nd leg
Ajax

CHARITY SHIELD

COPYRIGHT ALL RIGHTS RESERVED

TOTTENHAM HOTSPUR

FOOTBALL AND ATHLETIC COMPANY, LIMITED

Official Programme

AND RECORD OF THE CLUB

PRICE TWOPENCE

VOL. XLIV. No. 12. MONDAY, SEPTEMBER 24th, 1951

F.A. CHARITY SHIELD

DO YOU ? KNOW

THE ENFIELD CENTRAL BAND WILL PLAY AT EACH HOME GAME

24 September 1951
Newcastle United

PRICE THREEPENCE

TOTTENHAM HOTSPUR

FOOTBALL AND ATHLETIC COMPANY LIMITED

Official Programme

COPYRIGHT ALL RIGHTS RESERVED

SATURDAY, 12th AUGUST, 1961 Vol. 54 No. 1

Approach of

A NEW SEASON

12 August 1961
FA XI

11 August 1962
Ipswich Town

12 August 1967
Manchester United

22 August 1981
Aston Villa

21 August 1982
Liverpool

10 August 1991
Arsenal

EUROPEAN MATCHES

13 September 1961
European Cup
Gornik Zabrze - away

20 September 1961
European Cup
Gornik Zabrze - home

1 November 1961
European Cup
Feijenoord - away

15 November 1961
European Cup
Feijenoord - home

14 February 1962
European Cup
Dukla Prague - away

26 February 1962
European Cup
Dukla Prague - home

31 October 1962
European Cup-Winners' Cup – 1st leg
Rangers - home

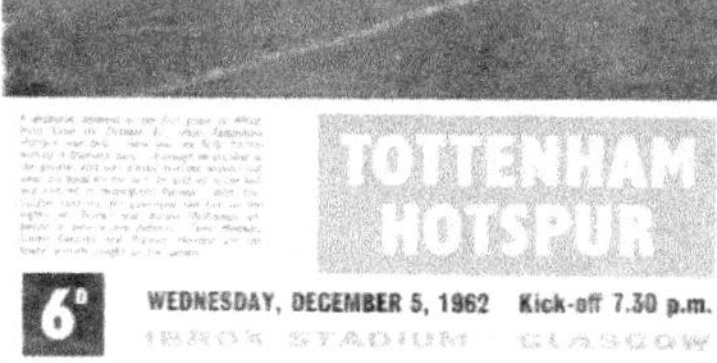

11 December 1962
European Cup-Winners' Cup – 2nd leg
Rangers - away

SLOVAN BRATISLAVA CHZJD

5 March 1963
European Cup-Winners' Cup – 1st leg
Slovan Bratislava - away

EUROPEAN MATCHES

14 March 1963
European Cup-Winners' Cup – 2nd leg
Slovan Bratislava - home

27 November 1963
European Cup-Winners' Cup – 1st leg
Manchester United - home - postponed

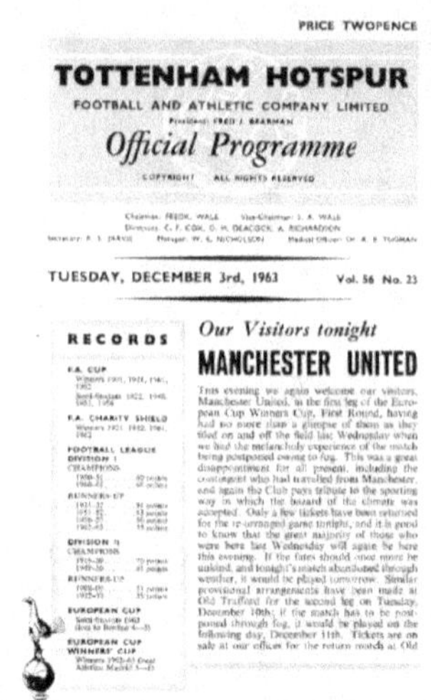

3 December 1963
European Cup-Winners' Cup – 1st leg
Manchester United - home

10 December 1963
European Cup-Winners' Cup – 2nd leg
Manchester United - away

20 September 1967
European Cup-Winners' Cup – 1st leg
Hajduk Split - away

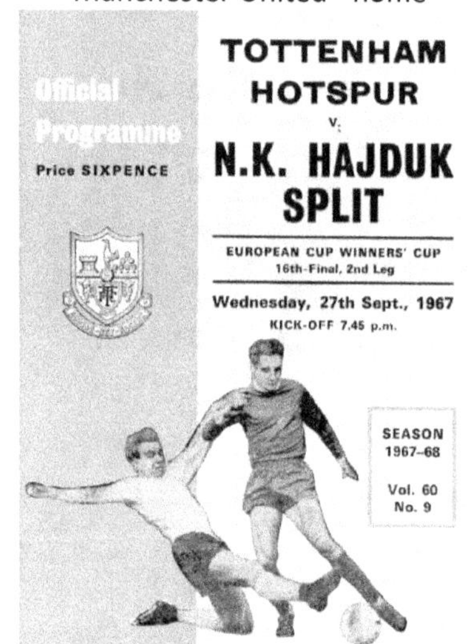

27 September 1967
European Cup-Winners' Cup – 2nd leg
Hajduk Split - home

29 November 1967
European Cup-Winners' Cup – 1st leg
Olympique Lyonnais - away

13 December 1967
European Cup-Winners' Cup – 2nd leg
Olympique Lyonnais - home

14 September 1971
UEFA Cup – 1st leg
Keflavik - away

EUROPEAN MATCHES

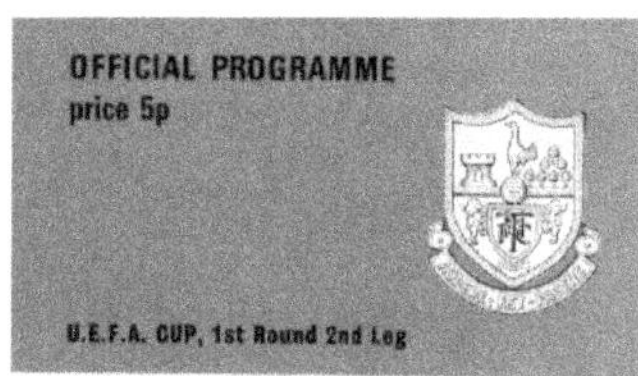

TOTTENHAM HOTSPUR

v

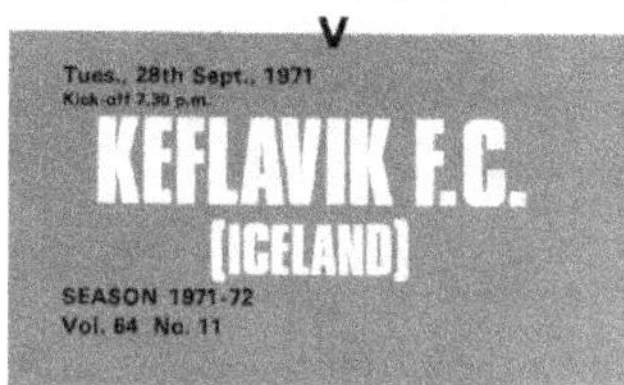

28 September 1971
UEFA Cup – 2nd leg
Keflavik - home

20 October 1971
UEFA Cup – 1st leg
Nantes - away

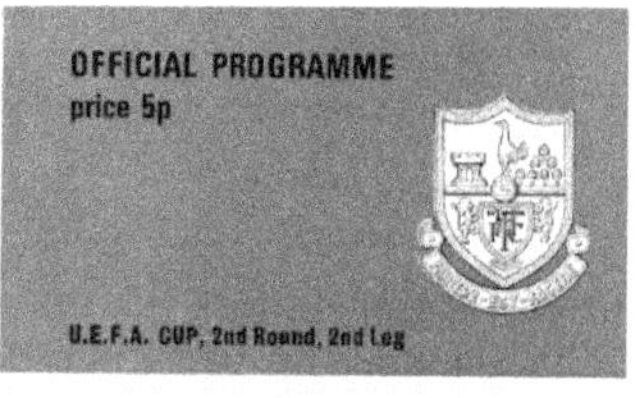

TOTTENHAM HOTSPUR

v

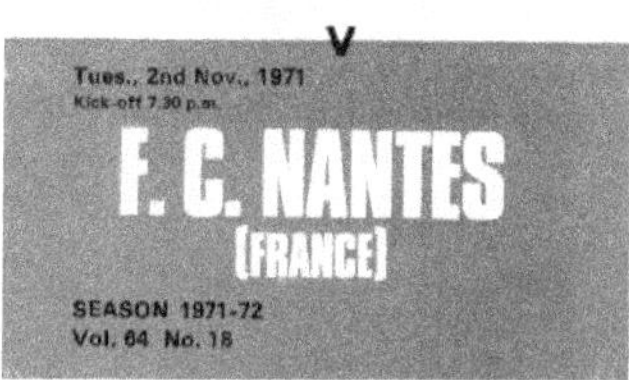

2 November 1971
UEFA Cup – 2nd leg
Nantes - home

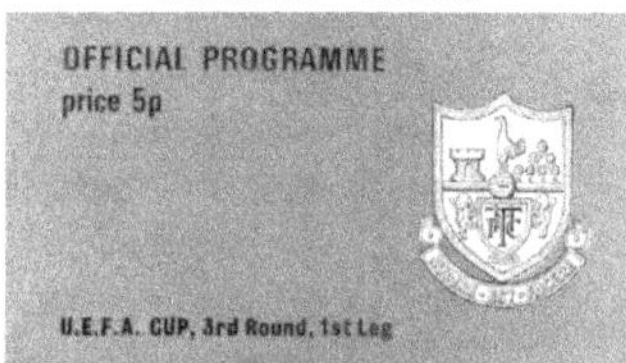

TOTTENHAM HOTSPUR

v

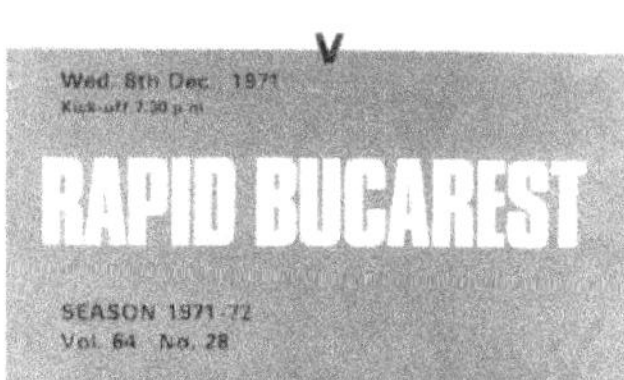

8 December 1971
UEFA Cup – 1st leg
Rapid Bucharest - home

CLUBUL SPORTIV Rapid BUCURESTI — FONDAT IN 1923

UN CORDIAL "BUN-VENIT!" OASPETILOR NOSTRI - DELEGATIA DE SPORTIVI SI CONDUCATORI REPREZENTAND CLUBUL ENGLEZ TOTTENHAM LONDRA CONDUSA DE DOMNUL C.F. COX,

IN NUMELE CLUBULUI SPORTIV RAPID, ADRESAM OASPETILOR NOSTRI - BRIGAZII DE ARBITRI ITALIENI, AVAND-O LA CENTRU PE AURELIO ANGONESE, PRECUM SI OBSERVATORUL UEFA PETR VLADIMIR, CELE MAI CALDE URARI.

AZI, INCEPAND DE LA ORA 13,30 PE STADIONUL "23 AUGUST" ARE LOC MECIUL REVANSA DIN "CUPA UEFA". MULT SUCCES ECHIPEI RAPID BUCURESTI!

ECHIPELE:

RAPID BUCURESTI	TOTTENHAM LONDRA
1. NECULA RADUCANU	1. JENNINGS
2. ION POP	2. EVANS
3. ALEXANDRU BOC	3. KNOWLES
4. NICOLAE LUPESCU	4. ENGLAND
5. GHEORGHE CODREA	5. COATES
6. CONSTANTIN DINU	6. BEAL
7. ION DUMITRU	7. PERRYMAN
8. MARIAN PETREANU	8. MULLERY
9. EMIL DANIEL	9. PETERS
10. ALEXANDRU NEAGU	10. GILZEAN
11. TEOFIL CODREANU	11. CHIVERS
12. CONSTANTIN NASTURESCU	12. NAYLOR
13. IORDAN ANGHELESCU	13. PEARCE

ANTRENORI:

BAZIL MARIAN	BILL NICHOLSON
A. SAMUREANU	

ARBITRII: ANGONESE
STAGNOLI, TRINCHERI (ITALIA)

PRESEDINTE CLUB RAPID,
PETRE CAPRA

15 December 1971
UEFA Cup – 2nd leg
Rapid Bucharest - away

7 March 1972
UEFA Cup – 1st leg
Unizale Textile Arad - away

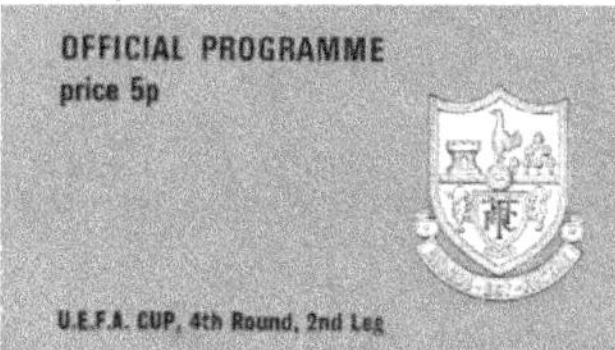

TOTTENHAM HOTSPUR

v

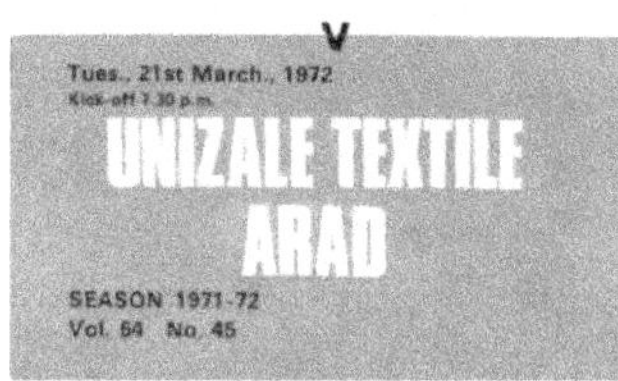

21 March 1972
UEFA Cup – 2nd leg
Unizale Textile Arad - home

13 September 1972
UEFA Cup – 1st leg
Lyn Oslo - away

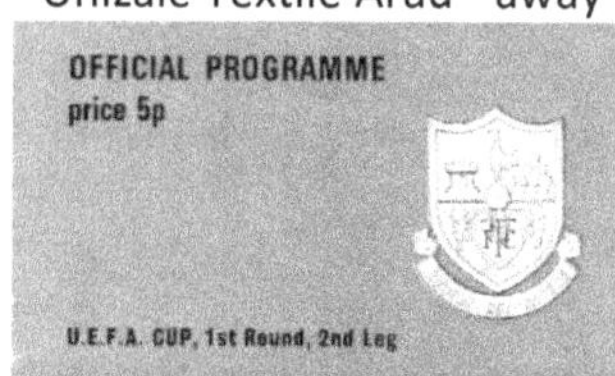

TOTTENHAM HOTSPUR

v

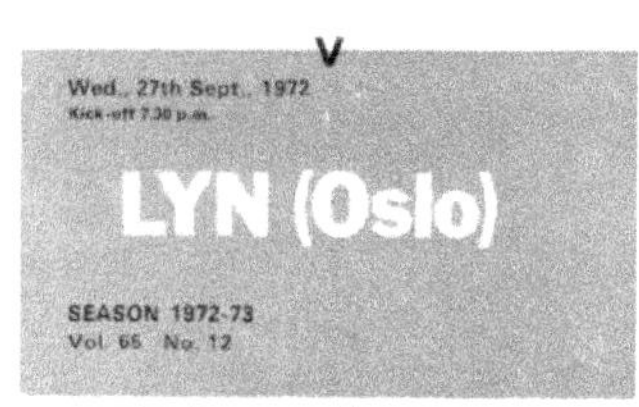

27 September 1972
UEFA Cup – 2nd leg
Lyn Oslo - home

EUROPEAN MATCHES

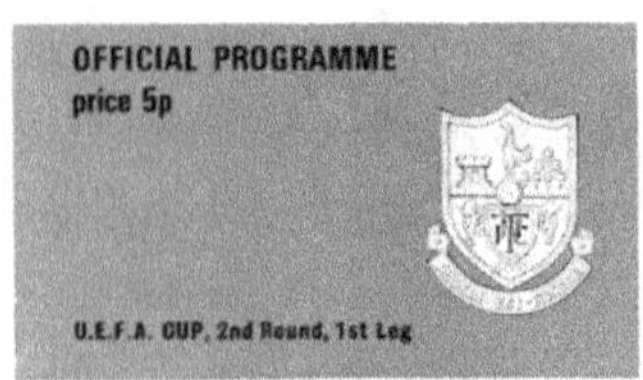

TOTTENHAM
HOTSPUR
v

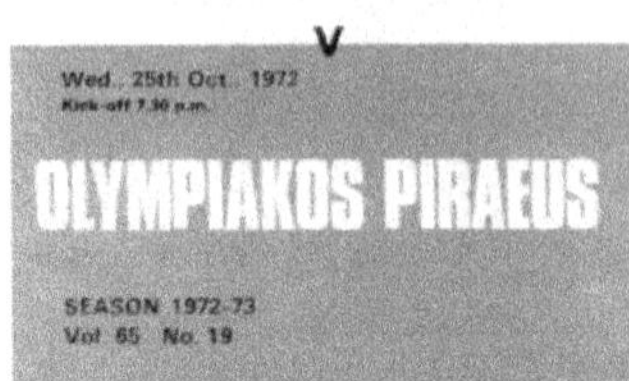

25 October 1972
UEFA Cup – 1st leg
Olympiakos - home

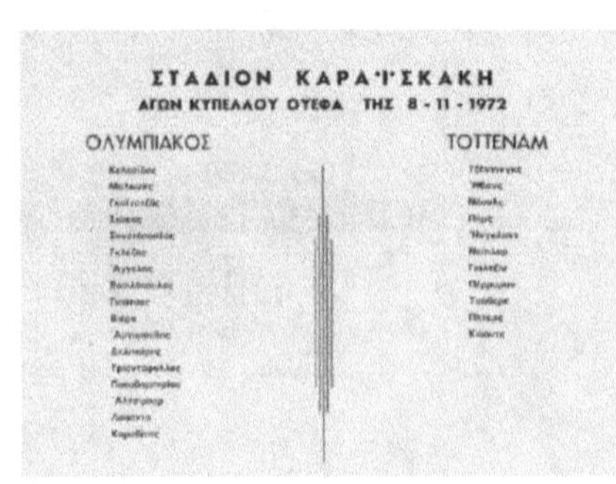

8 November 1972
UEFA Cup – 2nd leg
Olympiakos - away

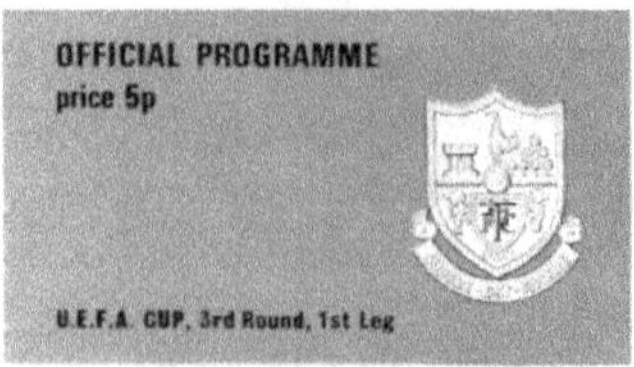

TOTTENHAM
HOTSPUR
v

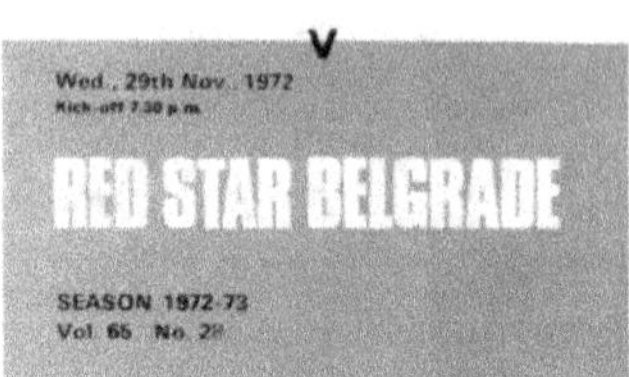

29 November 1972
UEFA Cup – 1st leg
Red Star Belgrade - home

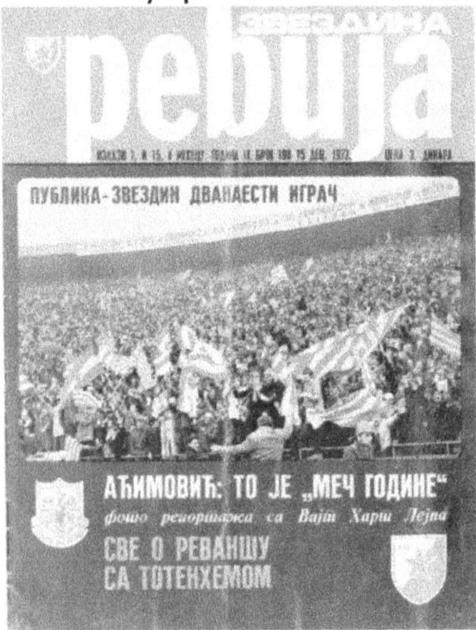

13 December 1972
UEFA Cup – 2nd leg
Red Star Belgrade - away - magazine

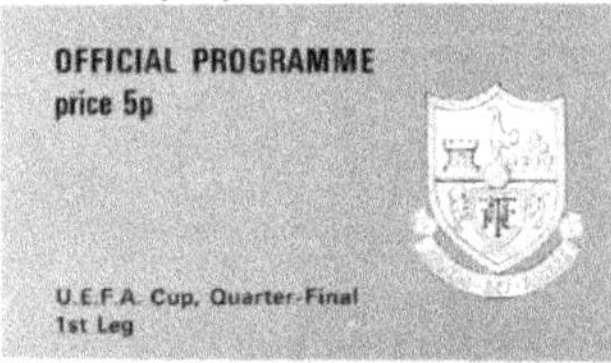

TOTTENHAM
HOTSPUR
v

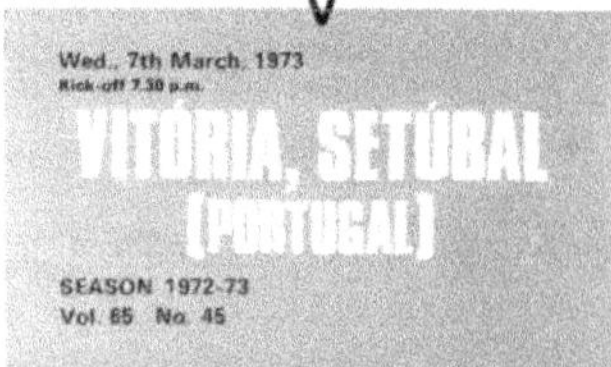

7 March 1973
UEFA Cup – 1st leg
Vitória Setúbal - home

19 September 1973
UEFA Cup – 1st leg
Grasshoppers - away

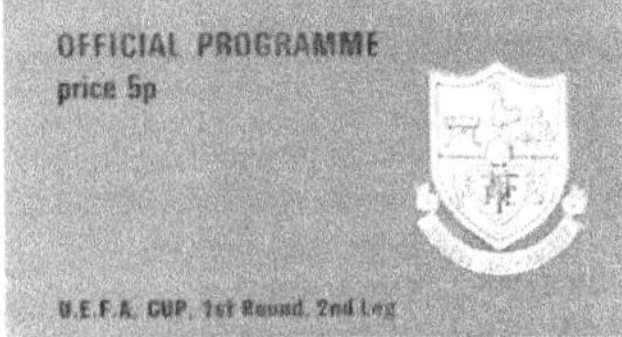

TOTTENHAM
HOTSPUR
v

3 October 1973
UEFA Cup – 2nd leg
Grasshoppers - home

24 October 1973
UEFA Cup – 1st leg
Aberdeen - away

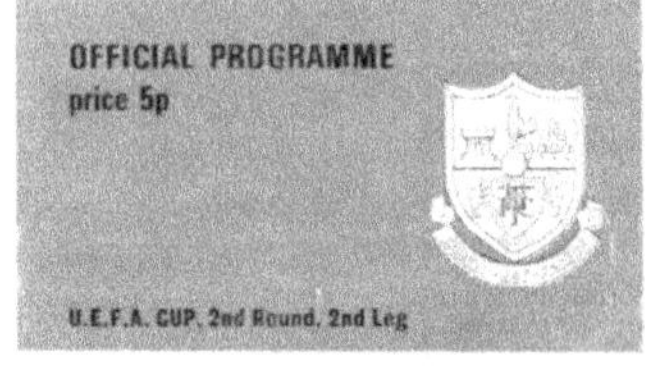

TOTTENHAM
HOTSPUR
v

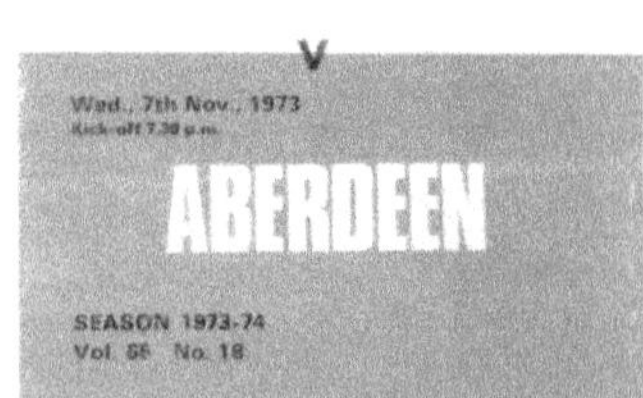

7 November 1973
UEFA Cup – 2nd leg
Aberdeen - home

EUROPEAN MATCHES

28 November 1973
UEFA Cup – 1st leg
Dinamo Tbilisi - away

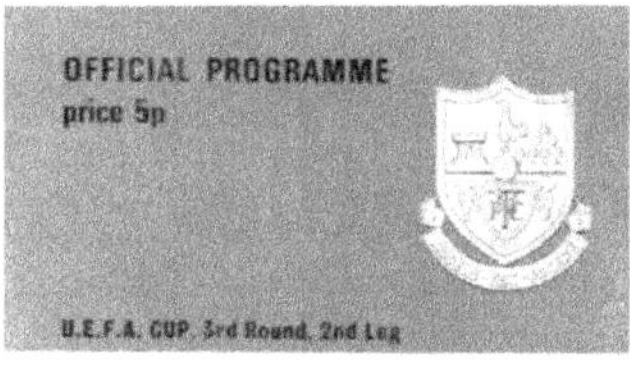

TOTTENHAM HOTSPUR

v

12 December 1973
UEFA Cup – 2nd leg
Dinamo Tbilisi - home

6 March 1974
UEFA Cup – 1st leg
1FC Cologne - away

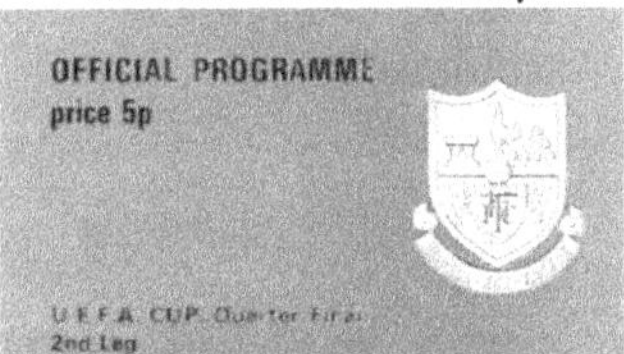

TOTTENHAM HOTSPUR

v

20 March 1974
UEFA Cup – 2nd leg
1FC Cologne - home

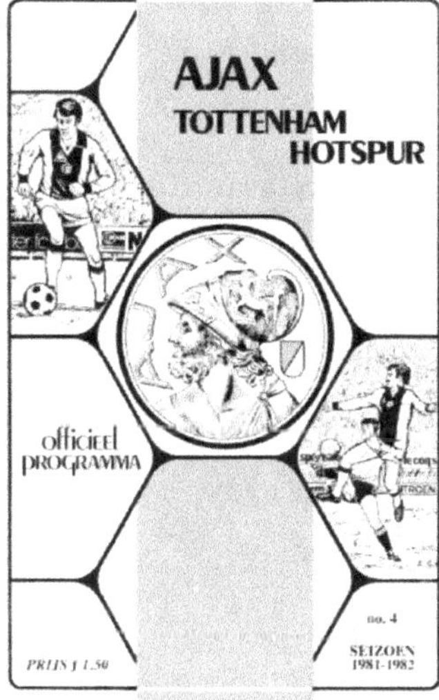

16 September 1981
European Cup-Winners' Cup - 1st leg
Ajax - away

29 September 1981
European Cup-Winners' Cup – 2nd leg
Ajax - home

DUNDALK

TOTTENHAM HOTSPUR

21 October 1981
European Cup-Winners' Cup - 1st leg
Dundalk - away

4 November 1981
European Cup-Winners' Cup – 2nd leg
Dundalk - home

3 March 1982
European Cup-Winners' Cup - 1st leg
Eintracht Frankfurt - home

EUROPEAN MATCHES

17 March 1982
European Cup-Winners' Cup – 2nd leg
Eintracht Frankfurt - away

15 September 1982
European Cup-Winners' Cup – 1st leg
Coleraine - away

28 September 1982
European Cup-Winners' Cup – 2nd leg
Coleraine - home

20 October 1982
European Cup-Winners' Cup – 1st leg
Bayern Munich - home

3 November 1982
European Cup-Winners' Cup – 2nd leg
Bayern Munich - away

14 September 1983
UEFA Cup – 1st leg
Drogheda United - away

28 September 1983
UEFA Cup – 2nd leg
Drogheda United - home

19 October 1983
UEFA Cup – 1st leg
Feyenoord - home

OFFICIEEL WEDSTRIJDPROGRAMMA
FEYENOORD - TOTTENHAM HOTSPUR

2 November 1983
UEFA Cup – 2nd leg
Feyenoord - away

EUROPEAN MATCHES

23 November 1983
UEFA Cup – 1st leg
Bayern Munich - away

23 November 1983
UEFA Cup – 1st leg
Bayern Munich - away - Die Blaue

7 December 1983
UEFA Cup – 2nd leg
Bayern Munich - home

7 March 1984
UEFA Cup – 1st leg
Austria Vienna - home

21 March 1984
UEFA Cup – 2nd leg
Austria Vienna - away

3 October 1984
UEFA Cup – 2nd leg
SC Braga - home

24 October 1984
UEFA Cup – 1st leg
Club Brugge - away

7 November 1984
UEFA Cup – 2nd leg
Club Brugge - home

28 November 1984
UEFA Cup – 1st leg
Bohemians Prague - home

EUROPEAN MATCHES

12 December 1984
UEFA Cup – 2nd leg
Bohemians Prague - away

6 March 1985
UEFA Cup – 1st leg
Real Madrid - home

20 March 1985
UEFA Cup – 2nd leg
Real Madrid - away

21 August 1991
UEFA Cup – 1st leg
Sparkasse Stockerau - away

4 September 1991
UEFA Cup – 2nd leg
Sparkasse Stockerau - home

2 October 1991
UEFA Cup – 1st leg
Hajduk Split - home

23 October 1991
UEFA Cup – 1st leg
Porto - home

7 November 1991
UEFA Cup – 2nd leg
Porto - away - magazine

4 March 1992
UEFA Cup – 1st leg
Feyenoord - away

EUROPEAN MATCHES

18 March 1992
UEFA Cup – 2nd leg
Feyenoord - home

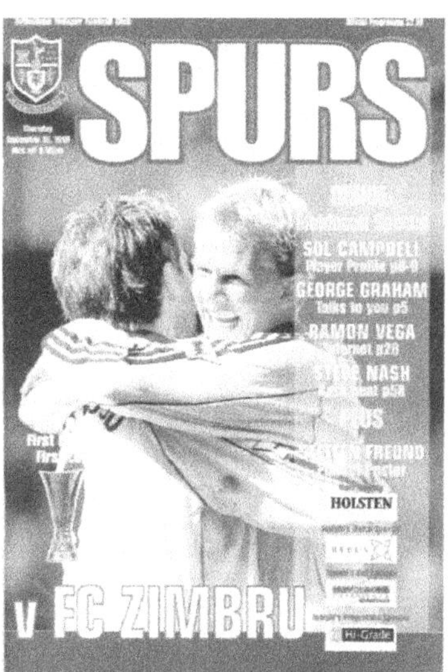

16 September 1999
UEFA Cup – 1st leg
Zimbru Chişinau - home

30 September 1999
UEFA Cup – 2nd leg
Zimbru Chişinau - away

28 October 1999
UEFA Cup – 1st leg
1FC Kaiserlautern - home

4 November 1999
UEFA Cup – 2nd leg
1FC Kaiserlautern - away

14 September 2006
UEFA Cup – 1st leg
Slavia Prague - away

28 September 2006
UEFA Cup – 2nd leg
Slavia Prague - home

2 November 2006
UEFA Cup – group stage
Club Brugge - home

23 November 2006
UEFA Cup – group stage
Bayer Leverkusen - away

EUROPEAN MATCHES

14 December 2006
UEFA Cup – group stage
Dinamo Bucharest - home

14 March 2007
UEFA Cup – 2nd leg
SC Braga - home

12 April 2007
UEFA Cup – 2nd leg
Sevilla - home

20 September 2007
UEFA Cup – 1st leg
Anorthosis Famagusta - home

4 October 2007
UEFA Cup – 2nd leg
Anorthosis Famagusta - away

25 October 2007
UEFA Cup – group stage
Getafe - home

8 November 2007
UEFA Cup – group stage
Hapoel Tel Aviv - away

29 November 2007
UEFA Cup – group stage
Aalborg - home

14 February 2008
UEFA Cup – 1st leg
Slavia Prague - away

EUROPEAN MATCHES

21 Feb 2008
UEFA Cup – 2nd leg
Slavia Prague - home

6 March 2008
UEFA Cup – 1st leg
PSV Eindhoven - home

12 March 2008
UEFA Cup – 2nd leg
PSV Eindhoven - away

18 September 2008
UEFA Cup – 1st leg
Wisła Kraków - home

2 October 2008
UEFA Cup – 2nd leg
Wisła Kraków - away

2008-09
Spartak Moscow
Group Stage programme

23 October 2008
UEFA Cup – group stage
Udinese - away - black issue

23 October 2008
UEFA Cup – group stage
Udinese - away - fold-out

23 October 2008
UEFA Cup – group stage
Udinese - away - newspaper

EUROPEAN MATCHES

6 November 2008
UEFA Cup – group stage
Dinamo Zagreb - home

27 November 2008
UEFA Cup – group stage
NEC Nijmegen - away

18 December 2008
UEFA Cup – group stage
Spartak Moscow - home

19 February 2009
UEFA Cup – 1st leg
Shakhtar Donetsk - away

26 February 2009
UEFA Cup – 2nd leg
Shakhtar Donetsk - home

17 August 2010
Champions League – 1st leg
Young Boys - away

25 August 2010
Champions League – 2nd leg
Young Boys - home

29 September 2010
Champions League – group stage
FC Twente - home

20 October 2010
Champions League – group stage
Internazionale - away - La Interista

EUROPEAN MATCHES

20 October 2010
Champions League – group stage
Internazionale - away - il Calcio Mondiale

2 November 2010
Champions League – group stage
Internazionale - home

24 November 2010
Champions League – group stage
Werder Bremen - home

7 December 2010
Champions League – group stage
FC Twente - away

15 February 2011
Champions League – 1st leg
AC Milan - away - Metro Stadio

15 February 2011
Champions League – 1st leg
AC Milan - away - Il Milanista

9 March 2011
Champions League – 2nd leg
AC Milan - home

5 April 2011
Champions League – 1st leg
Real Madrid - away – Media Punta

13 April 2011
Champions League – 2nd leg
Real Madrid - home

EUROPEAN MATCHES

18 August 2011
Europa League – 1st leg
Heart of Midlothian - away

25 August 2011
Europa League – 2nd leg
Heart of Midlothian - home

29 September 2011
Europa League – group stage
Shamrock Rovers - home

20 October 2011
Europa League – group stage
Rubin Kazan - home

3 November 2011
Europa League – group stage
Rubin Kazan - away

30 November 2011
Europa League – group stage
PAOK - home

15 December 2011
Europa League – group stage
Shamrock Rovers - away

20 September 2012
Europa League – group stage
Lazio - home

25 October 2012
Europa League – group stage
NK Maribor - away

EUROPEAN MATCHES

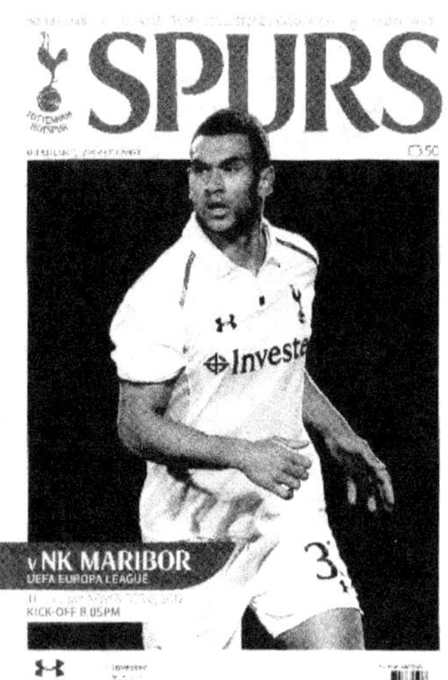

8 November 2012
Europa League – group stage
NK Maribor - home

22 November 2012
Europa League – group stage
Lazio - away - Cittaceleste

6 December 2012
Europa League – group stage
Panathinaikos - home

14 February 2013
Europa League – 1st leg
Olympique Lyonnais - home

21 February 2013
Europa League – 2nd leg
Olympique Lyonnais - away - La Tribune

7 March 2013
Europa League – 1st leg
Internazionale - home

4 April 2013
Europa League – 1st leg
FC Basel 1893 - home

11 April 2013
Europa League – 2nd leg
FC Basel 1893 - away

22 August 2013
Europa League – 1st leg
Dinamo Tbilisi - away

EUROPEAN MATCHES

29 August 2013
Europa League – 2nd leg
Dinamo Tbilisi - home

19 September 2013
Europa League – group stage
Tromsø - home

3 October 2013
Europa League – group stage
Anzhi Makhachkala - away

24 October 2013
Europa League – group stage
FC Sheriff - away

7 November 2013
Europa League – group stage
FC Sheriff - home

28 November 2013
Europa League – group stage
Tromsø - away

12 December 2013
Europa League – group stage
Anzhi Makhachkala - home

20 February 2014
Europa League – 1st leg
Dnipro - away

27 February 2014
Europa League – 2nd leg
Dnipro - home

EUROPEAN MATCHES

13 March 2014
Europa League – 1st leg
Benfica - home

20 March 2014
Europa League – 2nd leg
Benfica - away - O Benfica newspaper

21 August 2014
Europa League – 1st leg
AEL Limassol - away - Goal News

28 August 2014
Europa League – 2nd leg
AEL Limassol - home

18 September 2014
Europa League – group stage
Partizan Belgrade - away

2 October 2014
Europa League – group stage
Besiktas - home

23 October 2014
Europa League – group stage
Asteras Tripolis - home

6 November 2014
Europa League – group stage
Asteras Tripolis - away

27 November 2014
Europa League – group stage
Partizan Belgrade - home

EUROPEAN MATCHES

19 February 2015
Europa League – 1st leg
Fiorentina - home

26 February 2015
Europa League – 2nd leg
Fiorentina - away - tutto-viola

26 February 2015
Europa League – 2nd leg
Fiorentina - away - il Brivido Sportivo

17 September 2015
Europa League – group stage
Qarabag - home

1 October 2015
Europa League – group stage
AS Monaco - away

5 November 2015
Europa League – group stage
Anderlecht - home

26 November 2015
Europa League – group stage
Qarabag - home

10 December 2015
Europa League – group stage
AS Monaco - home

18 February 2016
Europa League – 1st leg
Fiorentina - away - tutto-viola

EUROPEAN MATCHES

25 February 2016
Europa League – 2nd leg
Fiorentina - home

10 March 2016
Europa League – 1st leg
Borussia Dortmund - away

17 March 2016
Europa League – 2nd leg
Borussia Dortmund - home

14 September 2016
Champions League – group stage
AS Monaco - home

27 September 2016
Champions League – group stage
CSKA Moscow - away

18 October 2016
Champions League – group stage
Bayer 04 Leverkusen - away

2 November 2016
Champions League – group stage
Bayer 04 Leverkusen - home

22 November 2016
Champions League – group stage
AS Monaco - away

7 December 2016
Champions League – group stage
CSKA Moscow - home

EUROPEAN MATCHES

16 February 2017
Europa League – 1st leg
KAA Gent - away

23 February 2017
Europa League – 2nd leg
KAA Gent - home

13 September 2017
Champions League – group stage
Borussia Dortmund - home

26 September 2017
Champions League – group stage
APOEL - away

1 November 2017
Champions League – group stage
Real Madrid - home

21 November 2017
Champions League – group stage
Borussia Dortmund - away

6 December 2017
Champions League – group stage
APOEL - home

13 February 2018
Champions League – 1st leg
Juventus - away - Juve Toro

7 March 2018
Champions League – 2nd leg
Juventus - home

EUROPEAN MATCHES

3 October 2018
Champions League – group stage
Barcelona - home

24 October 2018
Champions League – group stage
PSV Eindhoven - away

6 November 2018
Champions League – group stage
PSV Eindhoven - home

28 November 2018
Champions League – group stage
Internazionale - home

13 February 2019
Champions League – 1st leg
Borussia Dortmund - home

5 March 2019
Champions League – 2nd leg
Borussia Dortmund - away

9 April 2019
Champions League – 1st leg
Manchester City - home

17 April 2019
Champions League – 2nd leg
Manchester City - away

18 September 2019
Champions League – group stage
Olympiacos - away

EUROPEAN MATCHES

1 October 2019
Champions League – group stage
Bayern Munich - home

22 October 2019
Champions League – group stage
Red Star Belgrade - home

6 November 2019
Champions League – group stage
Red Star Belgrade - away

26 November 2019
Champions League – group stage
Olympiakos - home

19 February 2020
Champions League – 1st leg
Red Bull Leipzig - home

10 March 2020
Champions League – 2nd leg
Red Bull Leipzig - away

MISCELLANEOUS

12 - 22 May 1970 – Malta tour
Blue Review
Sliema Wanderers magazine

12 - 22 May 1970 – Malta tour
Malta Spurs Supports Club
magazine

6 April 1982
Barcelona – away
Barca magazine

20 March 1985
Real Madrid – away
Real Madrid magazine

23 May 1985
Seiko – away
Seiko Sports magazine

8 August 1989
Viking – away
Viking Magazine

9 August 1990
Viking – away
Viking magazine

2 - 9 June 1991
Kirin Cup - Japan
magazine

29 October 1991
Grimsby Town – away
brochure

MISCELLANEOUS

18 March 1992
Feyenoord – home
ITV magazine

25 July 1993
Lyn Oslo – away
Lyn newspaper

3 & 5 August 2004
Kappa Cup – Seville
newspaper supplement

BILL NICHOLSON OBE
MEMORIAL SERVICE

WHITE HART LANE
SUNDAY, NOVEMBER 7, 2004

7 November 2004
Bill Nicholson Memorial Service
RIP Mr Tottenham

15 September 2011
PAOK – away
group stage magazine

25 October 2012
NK Maribor – away
group stage magazine

14 May 2017
Manchester United – home
Farewell Ceremony

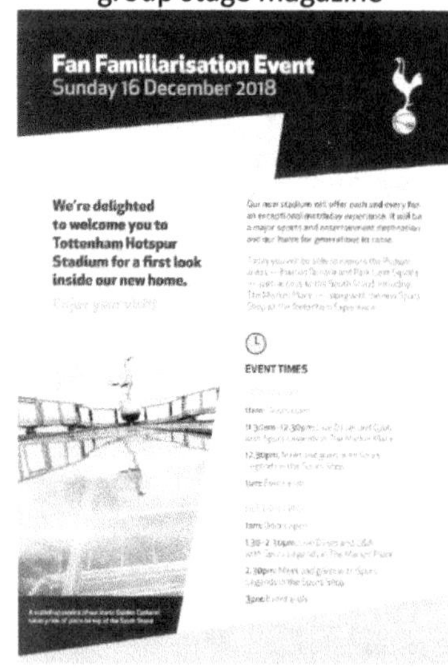

16 December 2018
Fan Familiarisation Event

23 December 2018
Everton – away
boardroom sleeve

PIRATES

Few football fans from the 1960s and 1970s will not have been caught out buying a "souvenir programme" from some non-descript vendor manoeuvring his way among the fans heading for the ground. By the time the purchaser realised all he had acquired was a cover page identifying the teams, with out-of-date line-ups across the middle pages and a list of FA Cup winners on the back, the "pirate" vendor was nowhere to be seen. At least it was pretty obvious that the buyer had been conned and an official programme was readily found.

Pirate programmes are rarely, if ever, seen at domestic matches these days, but they are common for matches abroad, and most of Spurs' European competitive games over the past few years have seen pirate issues, frequently several of them produced. Many foreign clubs have given up producing programmes, relying on the internet or local sports newspapers to communicate with supporters. With the desire of British football fans for a match souvenir well known, the ever-improving capabilities of desktop publishing have seen the gap rapidly filled. Most collectors prefer official publications but there are those who are content to accept an unofficial one if that is all that is available and publishers in countries such as Belarus and Ukraine only too happy to satisfy the market.

It is not always easy identifying pirate programmes. Some of them are so poorly produced as to be obvious, but there are others so well produced that many clubs would be happy to call them their own. Perhaps the only obvious ways to identify pirates is if they are written solely in English so clearly aimed at visiting supporters, or do not contain details of the publishers and/or printers.

Over the following pages are examples of pirate programmes that were available at Spurs' matches. They do not include issues that were only available on ebay, frequently days or weeks before a match and sometimes not produced until it became clear that there was no official publication.

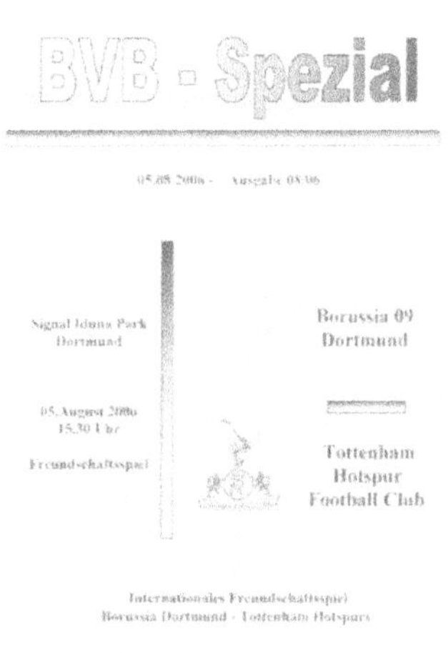

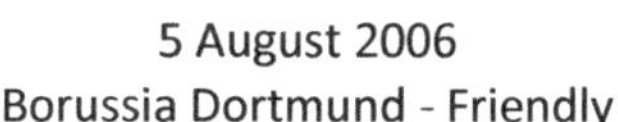

5 August 2006
Borussia Dortmund - Friendly

5 August 2006
Borussia Dortmund - Friendly

14 September 2006
Slavia Prague – UEFA Cup

PIRATES

14 September 2006
Slavia Prague – UEFA Cup

19 October 2006
Besiktas – UEFA Cup

19 October 2006
Besiktas – UEFA Cup

19 October 2006
Besiktas – UEFA Cup

8 March 2007
Braga – UEFA Cup

8 March 2007
Braga – UEFA Cup

5 April 2007
Sevilla – UEFA Cup

6 December 2007
Anderlecht – UEFA Cup

12 March 2008
PSV Eindhoven – UEFA Cup

PIRATES

24 July 2008
Hercules - friendly

14 September 2010
Werder Bremen - Champions League

20 October 2010
Internazionale – Champions League

20 October 2010
Internazionale – Champions League

15 February 2011
AC Milan – Champions League

15 February 2011
AC Milan – Champions League

5 April 2011
Real Madrid – Champions League

5 April 2011
Real Madrid – Champions League

4 October 2012
Panathinaikos - Europa League

PIRATES

4 October 2012
Panathinaikos - Europa League

14 March 2013
Internazionale - Europa League

22 October 2015
Anderlecht – Europa League

16 February 2017
KAA Gent – Europa League

17 October 2017
Real Madrid – Champions League

15 February 2018
Juventus – Champions League

18 September 2018
Internazionale – Champions League

11 December 2018
Barcelona – Champions League

11 December 2019
Bayern Munich – Champions League

TOUR ITINERARIES

Both before and after the Second World War, one of the delights of Spurs' tours was the production of tour itineraries. Initially designed almost exclusively for the members of the touring party and their families, it was not long before they expanded to provide information about the club and were handed out as part of the public relations exercise the club officials were expected to undertake. The obvious difficulties of obtaining programmes for foreign tours, if they even existed, and the limited numbers in which they were produced, have made the booklets, of which the last appeared in 1974, a most popular and unusual collectible.

May 1950
Belgium & Germany

May – June 1952
Canada

May 1955
Austria, Hungary & France

TOTTENHAM HOTSPUR
FOOTBALL CLUB

Tour to
CANADA and
UNITED STATES
May – June, 1957

ITINERARY

May – June 1957
Canada & United States

TOTTENHAM HOTSPUR
FOOTBALL CLUB

Tour to
HOLLAND
May, 1961

ITINERARY

May 1961
Holland

May – June 1966
Bermuda, USA, Canada & Mexico

TOUR ITINERARIES

TOTTENHAM HOTSPUR
FOOTBALL CLUB

Tour to
SWITZERLAND
May 29th to June 8th
1967

ITINERARY

May – June 1967
Switzerland

TOTTENHAM HOTSPUR
FOOTBALL CLUB

Tour to
GREECE & CYPRUS
May 13th to 31st, 1968

ITINERARY

May 1968
Greece & Cyprus

May – June 1969
United States & Canada

May 1970
Malta

May – June 1971
Japan

TOTTENHAM HOTSPUR
FOOTBALL & ATHLETIC CO. LTD.

Tour to
ISRAEL
June 1st to 9th, 1972

ITINERARY

June 1972
Israel

TICKETS

While the general consensus is that ebay has helped collectors acquire seemingly unobtainable programmes at lower prices than used to be the case, the fact is that there are many programmes that remain elusive and thus expensive. Indeed, so elusive that when they do come on the market, fierce competition sees ever-increasing prices.

Many collectors, faced with paying considerable sums, if only rarely, to fill the remaining gaps in collections that were proving increasingly difficult to house because of the never-ending increase in the size of programmes, turned their attentions to ticket stubs, widely available at reasonable prices and taking up minimal space. Thus it was possible to pick up stubs from the 1961 and 1962 FA Cup finals for less than the programme cost, whilst many League and early round cup matches were available for little more than a couple of pounds. In recent years tickets have become increasingly popular and have risen sharply in price, often far exceeding the cost of the corresponding programme. At an auction in August 2020, a collection of 27 stubs from the 1960-61 season (including duplicates and reserve matches) sold for £1,600 plus buyer's commission (taking the total to £2,000!). Similar lots attracted equally substantial bids.

Those who turned to tickets early enough undoubtedly picked up some bargains, especially when you realise that tickets are invariably in shorter supply than programmes. Spurs may have regularly hosted over 50,000 and sometimes over 60,000 fans during the late 1940s, through the 1950s and into the double season, but the ground then was largely standing, with only the upper tiers of the East Stand and the West Stand having seating. With season ticket holders usually using a credit card style ticket or, in later years, voucher book, the number of tickets potentially available for collectors drops dramatically for ordinary matches where paying on the gate was the norm.

Although there are many supporters and collectors who will turn up irrespective of who the opposition is, what the competition may be, or, more importantly, how well or badly Spurs are playing, there are those who are a little more selective. There have therefore been matches where the attendance did not even reach the 10,000 mark (friendlies against Hamburg and Bordeaux, a League Cup tie against Birmingham City), resulting in tickets for those matches being in short supply.

The arrival of all-seater stadia and all-ticket matches in 1989 has increased the chances of picking up a stub from games since then, but it is still the big match tickets that attract the big prices. Over the next few pages we offer illustrations of some of the various designs of home tickets Spurs have used in the years since the War (even those awful tickets from 1989-90, which have all the attraction of a used entry ticket to a bingo hall), together with a selection of away and neutral venue big match tickets and some examples from away friendly matches Spurs have played since "Away The Spurs" was published in 1994.

Of course, there are many other collectables related to collecting match tickets, such as ballot cards, press, lounge, and boardroom passes, invitations, pass out vouchers, etc, and that ignores car park passes. Space does not permit the inclusion of such items in this book.

7 May 1951
FC Austria

7 January 1956
Boston United

19 November 1960
Birmingham City

TICKETS

7 May 1951
FC Austria

7 January 1956
Boston United

19 November 1960
Birmingham City

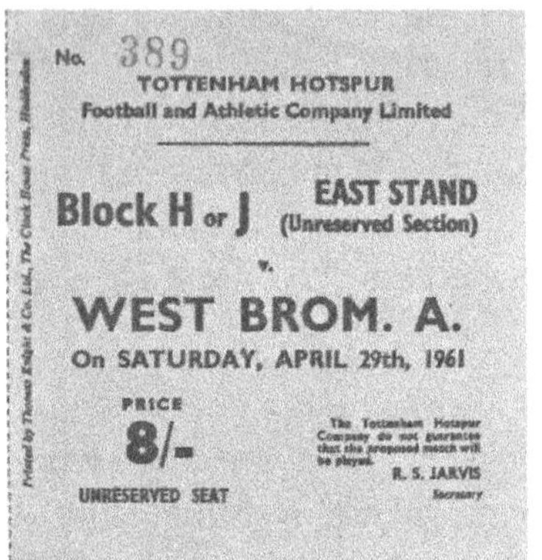

29 April 1961
West Bromwich Albion

12 August 1961
Football Association XI

20 September 1961
Gornik Zabzre

29 September 1962
Nottingham Forest

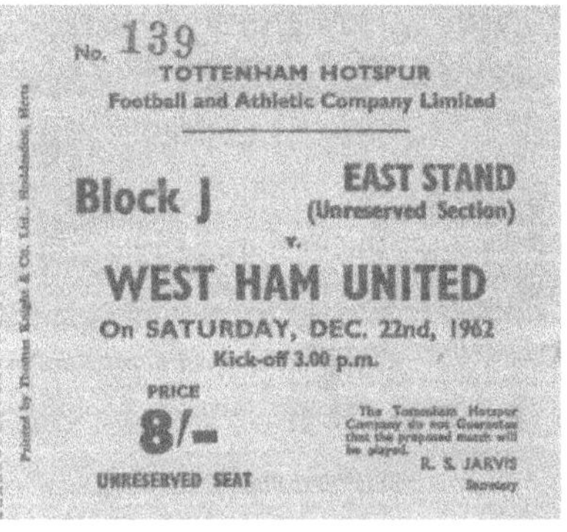

22 December 1962
West Ham United

27 November 1963
Manchester United

10 November 1964
Scotland XI

27 March 1965
Wolverhampton Wanderers

16 April 1965
Blackburn Rovers

TICKETS

9 March 1968
Liverpool

17 October 1972
Feijenoord

26 August 1978
Chelsea

TOTTENHAM HOTSPUR
Football & Athletic Co. Ltd.

13 December 1980
Manchester City

10 February 1982
West Bromwich Albion

24 April 1982
Notts County

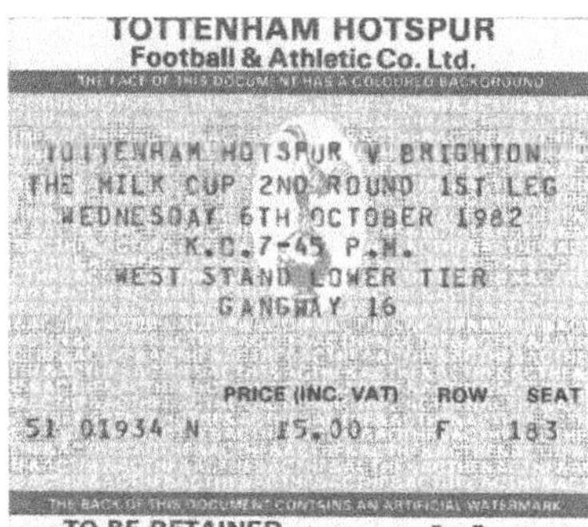

6 October 1982
Brighton & Hove Albion

23 May 1984
Anderlecht

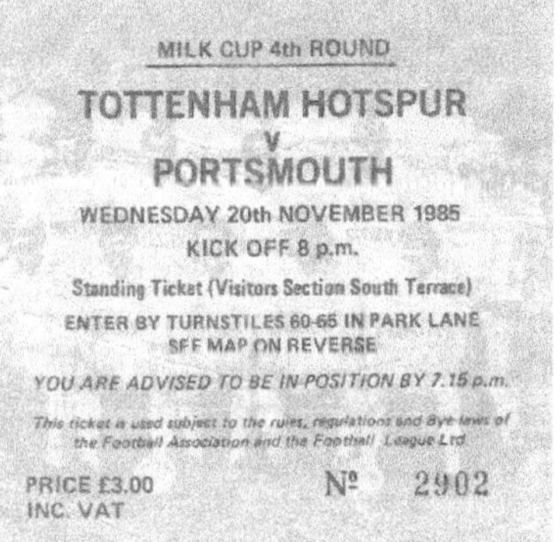

20 November 1985
Portsmouth

17 January 1989
Monaco

26 March 1989
Liverpool

30 December 1989
Nottingham Forest

TICKETS

1 May 1990
Northern Ireland XI

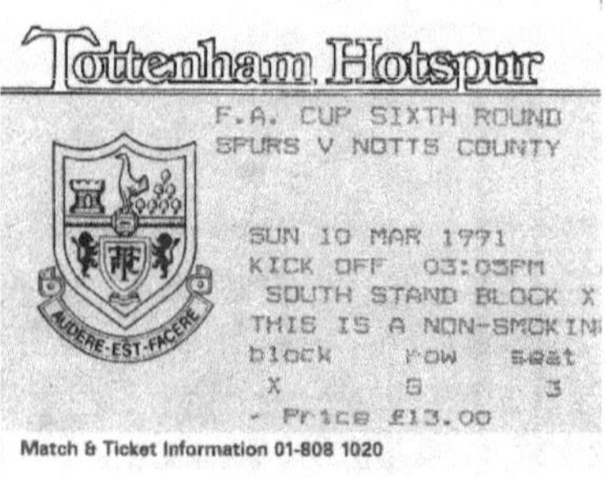

10 March 1991
Notts County

14 September 1991
Queens Park Rangers

5 September 1992
Everton

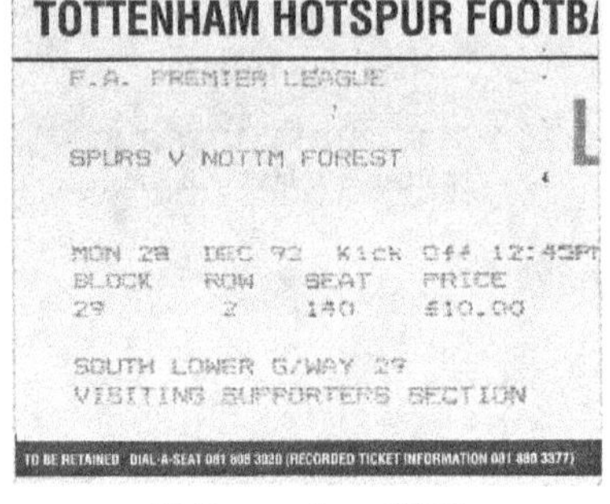

28 December 1992
Nottingham Forest

11 April 1995
Manchester City

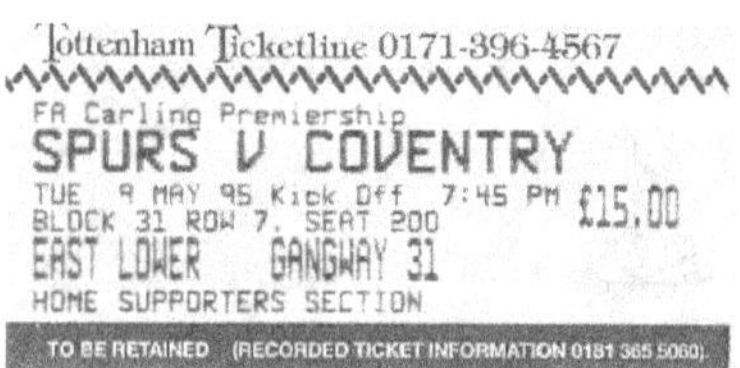

9 May 1995
Coventry City

30 September 1995
Wimbledon

13 January 1996
Manchester City

23 August 1997
Derby County

22 August 1998
Sheffield Wednesday

16 September 1999
Zimbru Chișinău

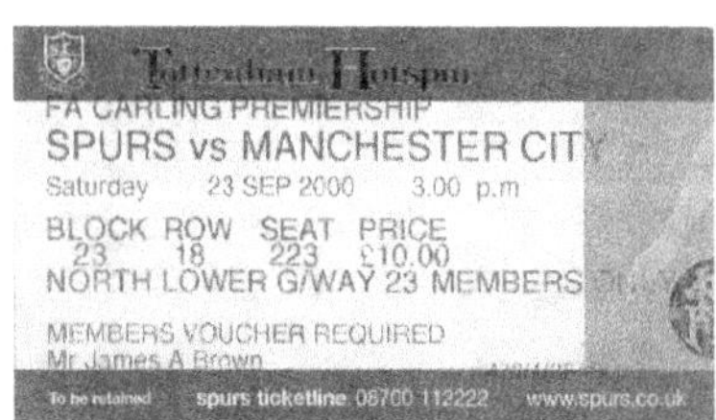

23 September 2000
Manchester City

8 August 2001
Fiorentina

7 August 2002
Celtic

TICKETS

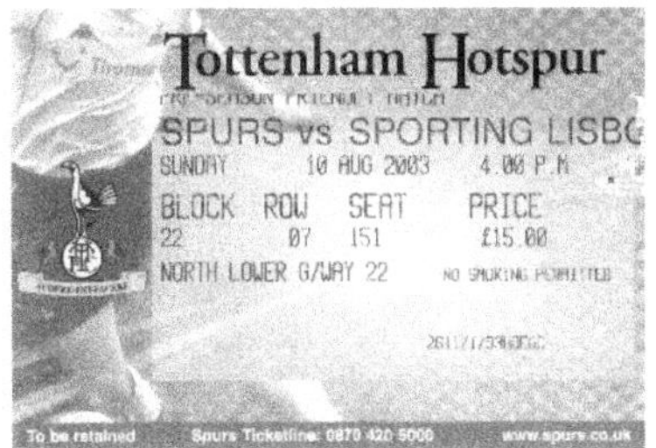

10 August 2003
Sporting Lisbon

7 August 2004
Cagliari

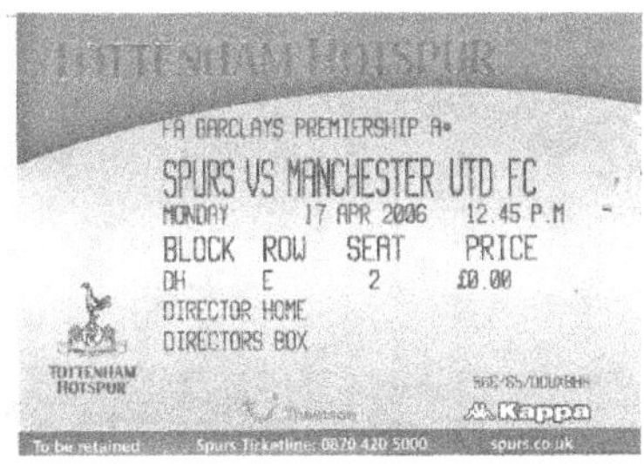

17 April 2006
Manchester United

30 July 2006
Internazionale

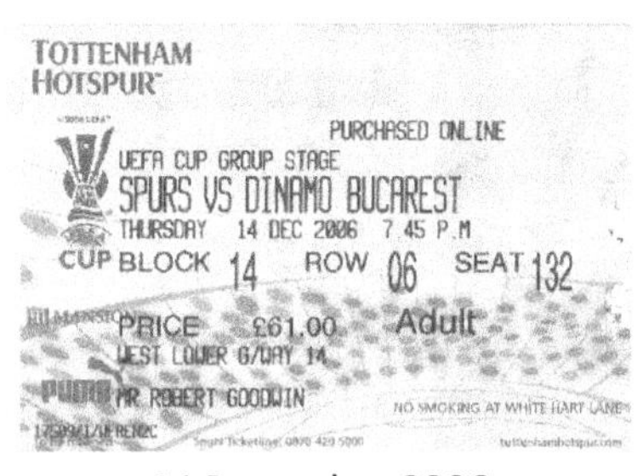

14 December 2006
Dinamo Bucharest

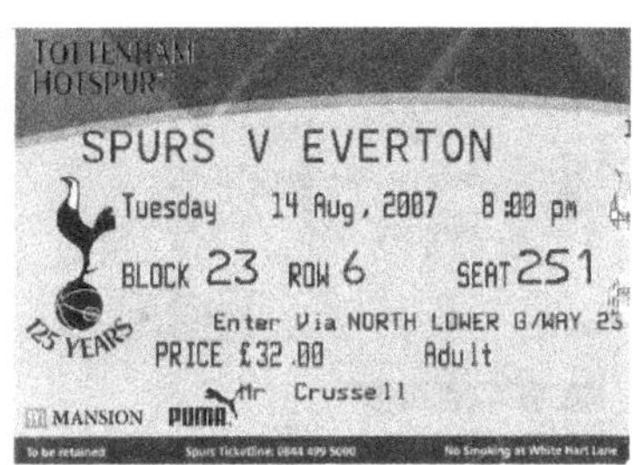

14 August 2007
Everton

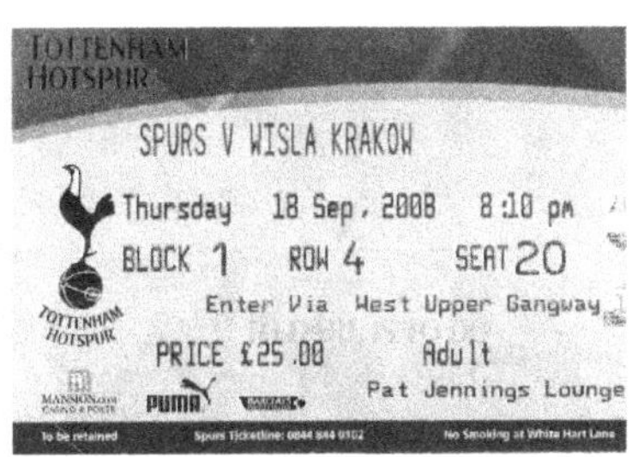

18 September 2008
Wisła Kraków

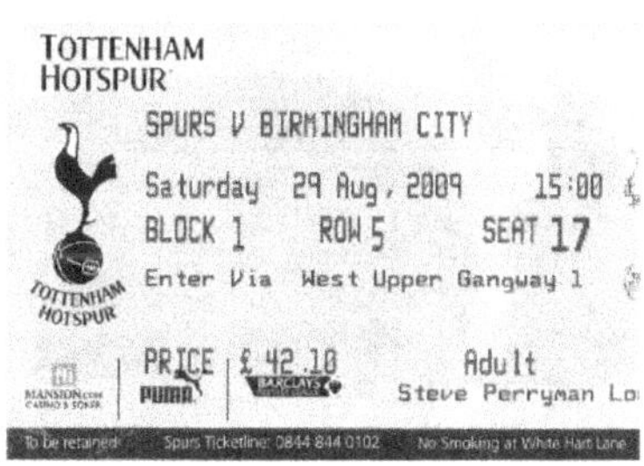

29 April 2009
Birmingham City

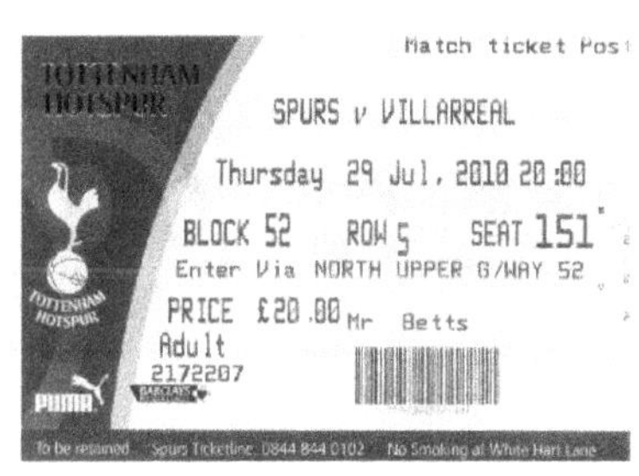

29 July 2010
Villarreal

25 August 2010
Young Boys

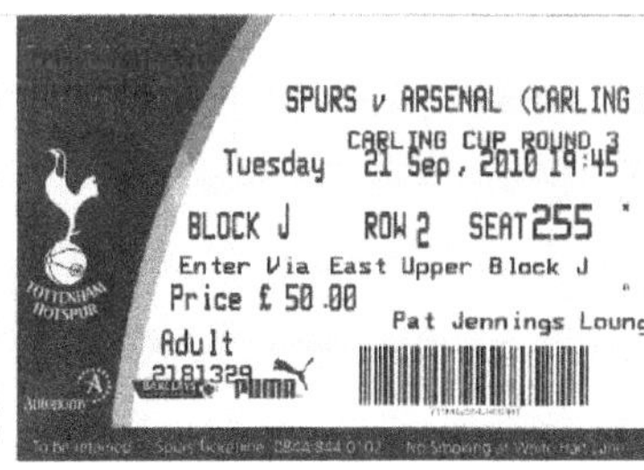

21 September 2010
Arsenal

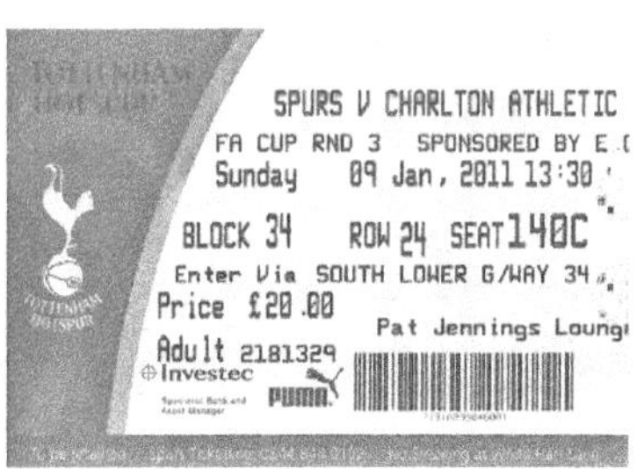

9 January 2011
Charlton Athletic

6 August 2011
Athletic Bilbao

20 October 2011
Rubin Kazan

17 March 2012
Bolton Wanderers

TICKETS

1 September 2012
Norwich City

20 September 2012
Lazio

29 August 2013
Dinamo Tbilisi

21 September 2014
West Bromwich Albion

17 September 2015
Qarabag

20 September 2015
Crystal Palace

14 September 2016
Monaco

14 May 2017
Manchester United

20 August 2017
Chelsea

16 September 2017
Swansea City

18 August 2018
Fulham

26 September 2018
Watford

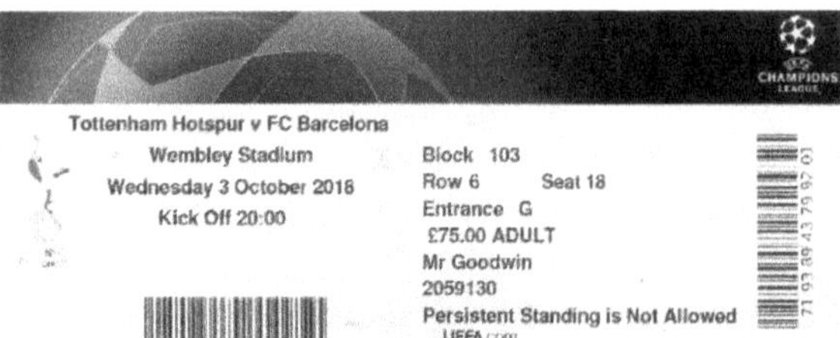

3 October 2018
Barcelona

4 March 2020
Norwich City

TICKETS

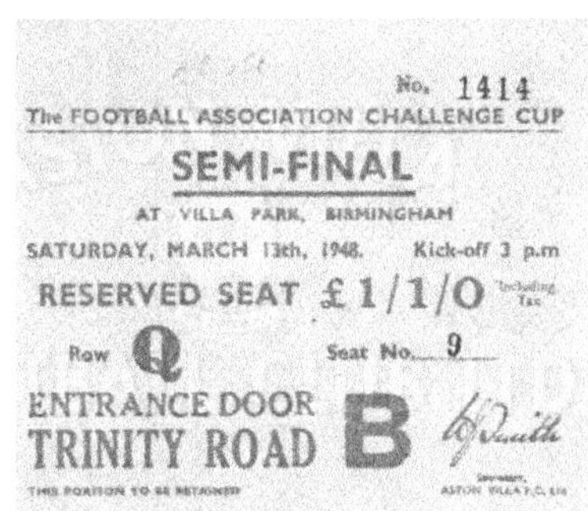

13 March 1948
Blackpool – FA Cup

21 March 1953
Blackpool – FA Cup

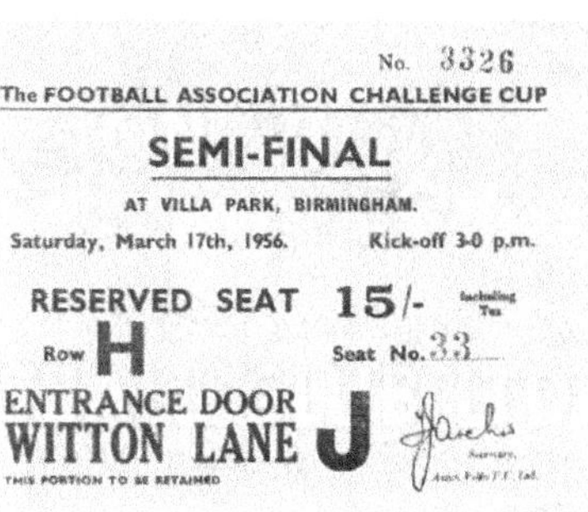

17 March 1956
Manchester City – FA Cup

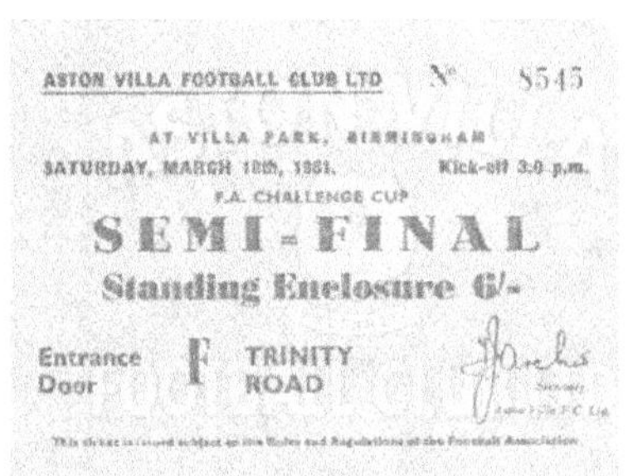

18 March 1961
Burnley – FA Cup

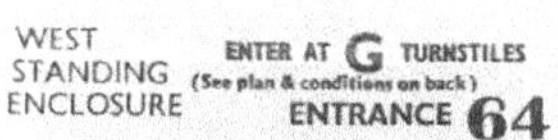

6 May 1961
Leicester City – FA Cup

21 Mar 1962
Benfica – European Champions Cup

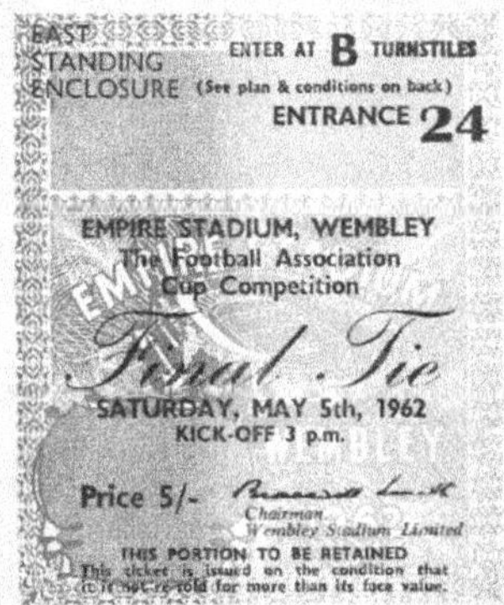

31 Mar 1962
Manchester United – FA Cup

5 May 1962
Burnley – FA Cup

24 April 1963
OFK Belgrade - ECWC

15 May 1963
Atletico Madrid - ECWC

29 April 1967
Nottingham Forest – FA Cup

20 May 1967
Chelsea – FA Cup

TICKETS

12 August 1967
Manchester United – FA Charity Shield

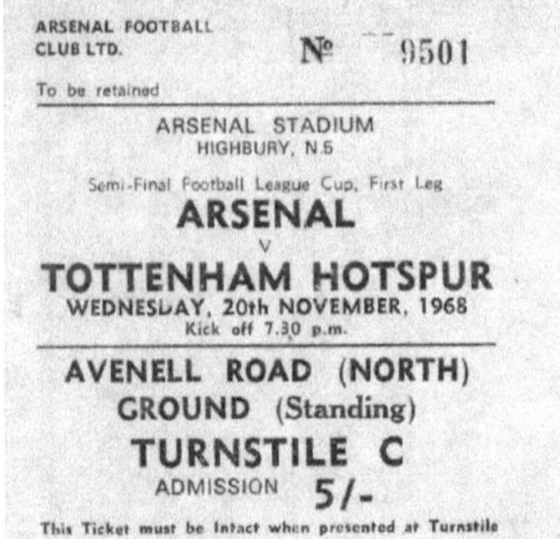

20 November 1968
Arsenal – FL Cup

16 December 1970
Bristol City – FL Cup

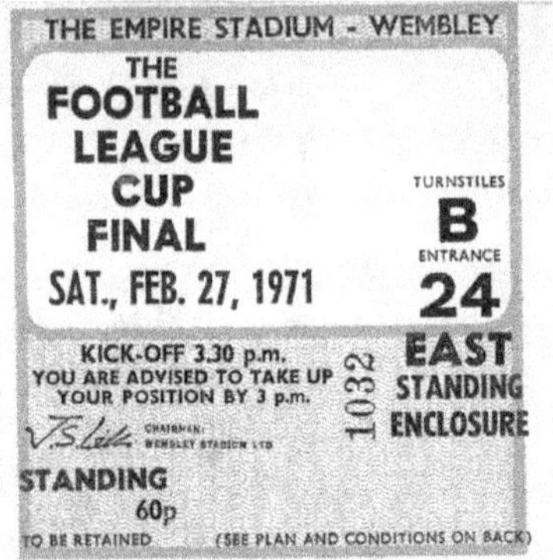

27 February 1971
Aston Villa – FL Cup

22 December 1971
Chelsea – FL Cup

19 April 1972
AC Milan – UEFA Cup

3 May 1972
Wolverhampton Wanderers – UEFA Cup

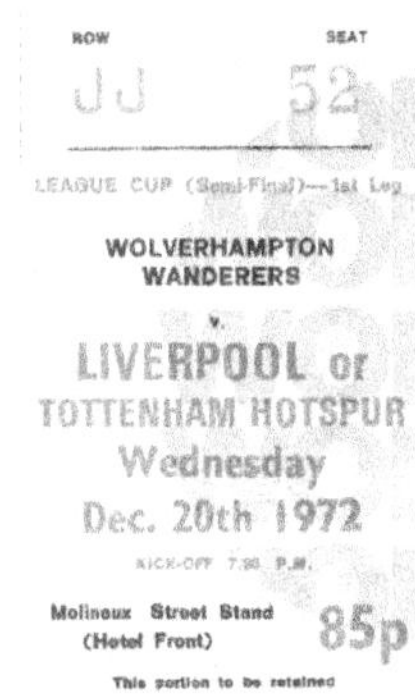

20 December 1972
Wolverhampton Wanderers – FL Cup

THE EMPIRE STADIUM, WEMBLEY
THE
FOOTBALL
LEAGUE
CUP
FINAL
SAT., MARCH 3, 1973
TURNSTILES
G
ENTRANCE
64
KICK-OFF 3.30 p.m.
YOU ARE ADVISED TO TAKE UP YOUR POSITION BY 3 p.m.
1662
WEST
STANDING
ENCLOSURE
No money refunded or tickets exchanged
STANDING
60p
TO BE RETAINED
SEE PLAN AND CONDITIONS ON BACK

3 March 1973
Norwich City FL Cup

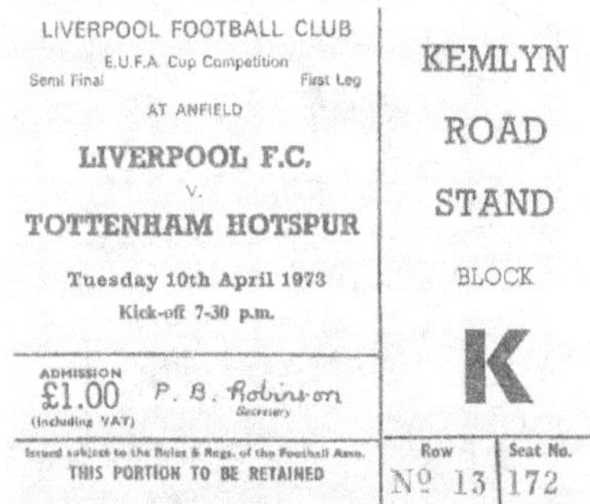

10 April 1973
Liverpool – UEFA Cup

10 April 1974
Lokomotive Leipzig – UEFA Cup

29 May 1974
Feijenoord

TICKETS

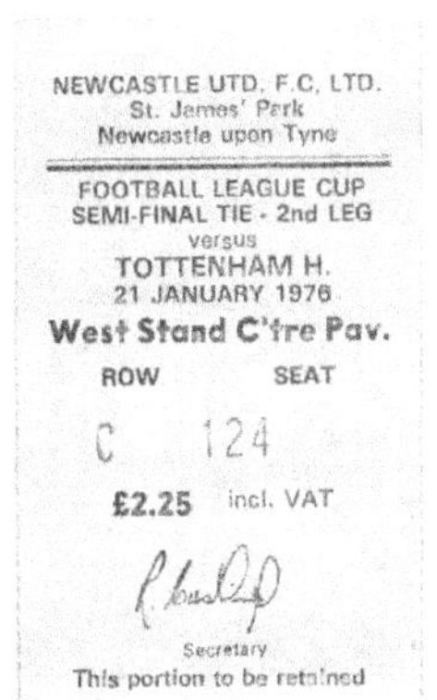

21 January 1976
Newcastle United – FL Cup

11 April 1981
Wolverhampton Wanderers – FA Cup

15 April 1981
Wolverhampton Wanderers – FA Cup

9 May 1981
Manchester City – FA Cup

14 May 1981
Manchester City – FA Cup

WEMBLEY STADIUM
Football Association
F.A. CHARITY SHIELD
SAT., AUGUST 22, 1981
TURNSTILES
H
KICK-OFF 3.00 p.m.
YOU ARE ADVISED TO TAKE UP YOUR POSITION BY 2.30 p.m.
ENTRANCE
58
WEST
UPPER
STANDING
ENCLOSURE
195
STANDING
£3.00
TO BE RETAINED
ISSUED SUBJECT TO THE CONDITIONS ON BACK

22 August 1981
Aston Villa – FA Charity Shield

3 February 1982
West Bromwich Albion – FL Cup

13 March 1982
Liverpool – FL Cup

3 April 1982
Leicester City – FA Cup

21 April 1982
Barcelona - ECWC

22 May 1982
Queens Park Rangers – FA Cup

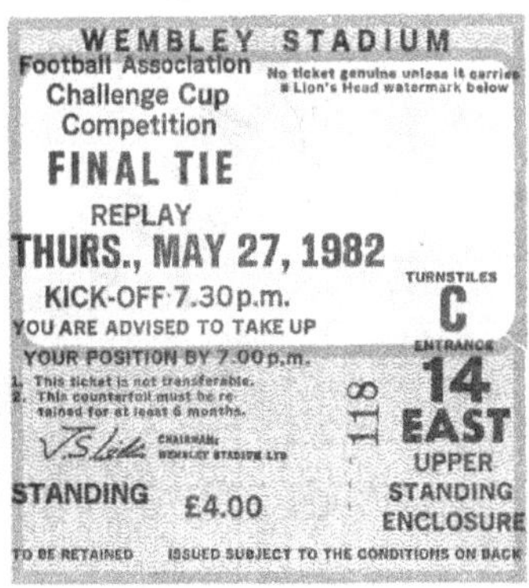

27 May 1982
Queens Park Rangers – FA Cup

TICKETS

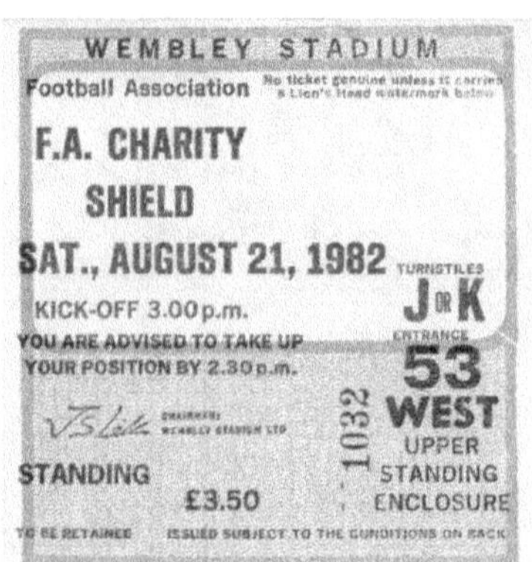

21 August 1982
Liverpool – FA Charity Shield

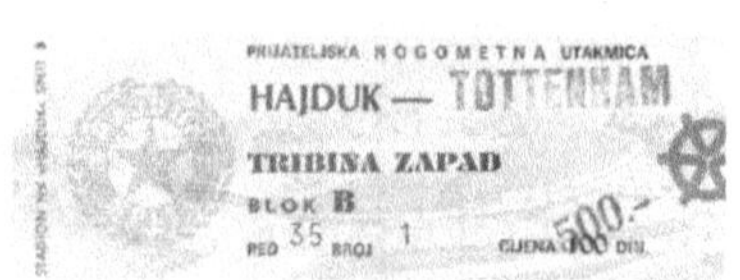

11 April 1984
Hajduk Split – UEFA Cup

9 May 1984
Anderlecht - UEFA Cup

11 February 1986
Everton – Screen Sport Super Cup

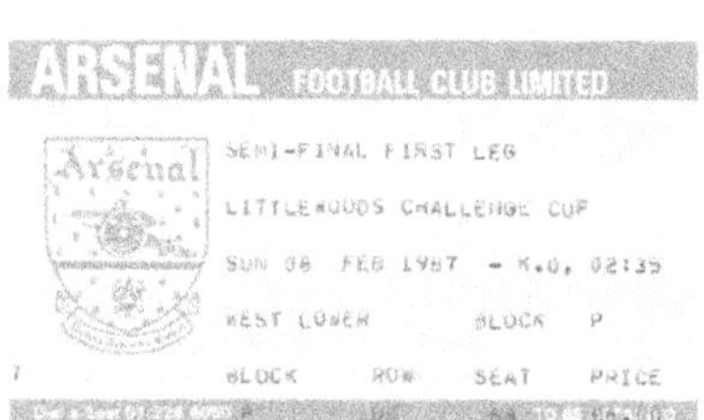

8 February 1987
Arsenal – Littlewoods Cup

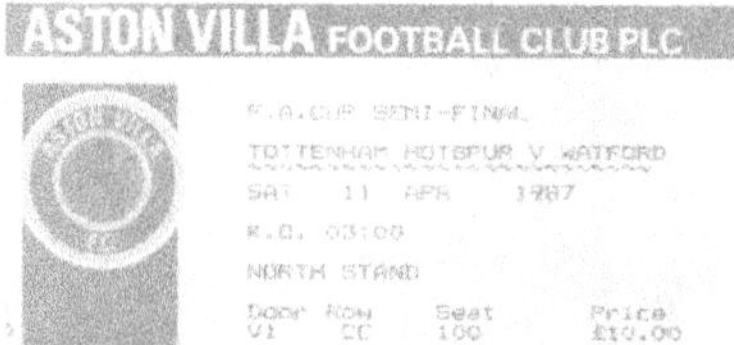

11 April 1987
Watford – FA Cup

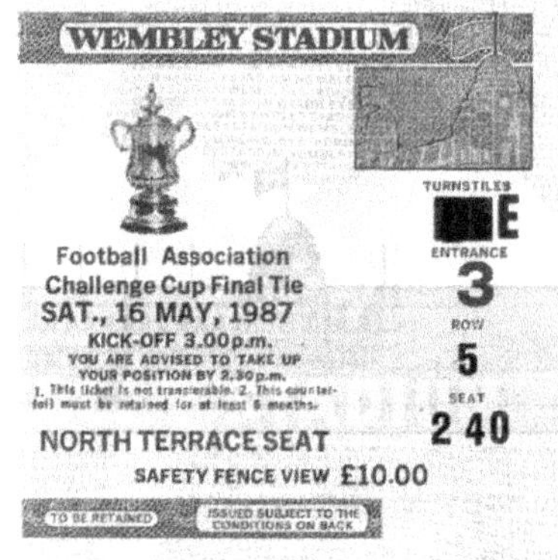

16 May 1987
Coventry City – FA Cup

14 April 1991
Arsenal – FA Cup

18 May 1991
Nottingham Forest – FA Cup

10 August 1991
Arsenal – FA Charity Shield

9 February 1992
Nottingham Forest – Rumbelows Cup

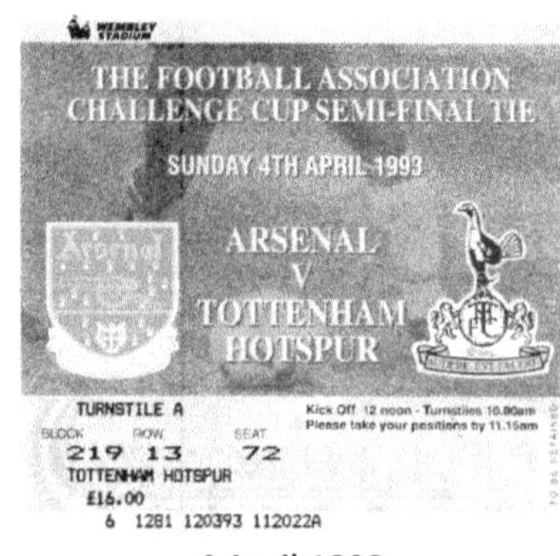

4 April 1993
Arsenal – FA Cup

TICKETS

9 April 1995
Everton – FA Cup

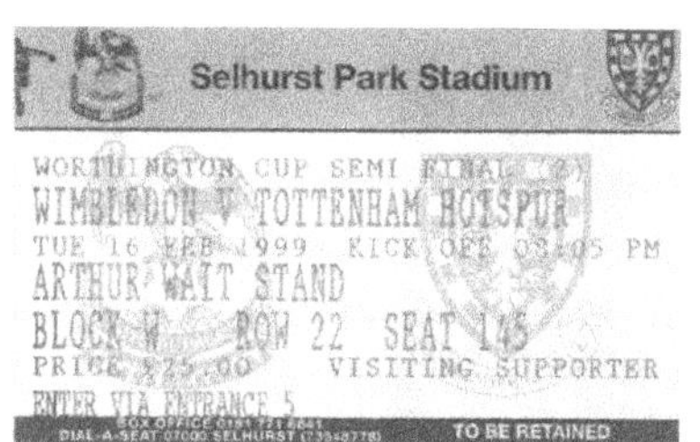

16 February 1999
Wimbledon – Worthington Cup

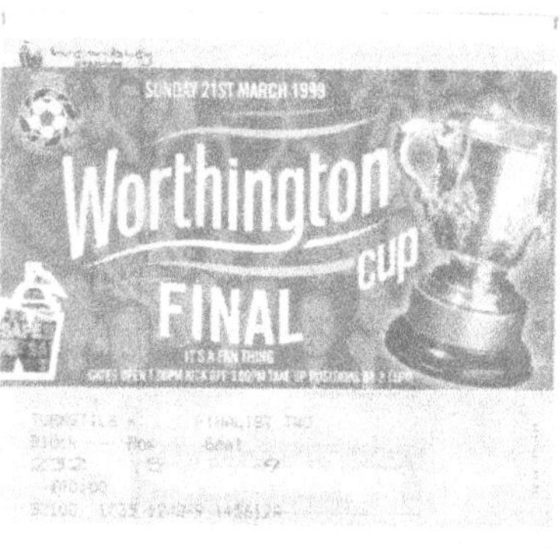

21 March 1999
Leicester City – Worthington Cup

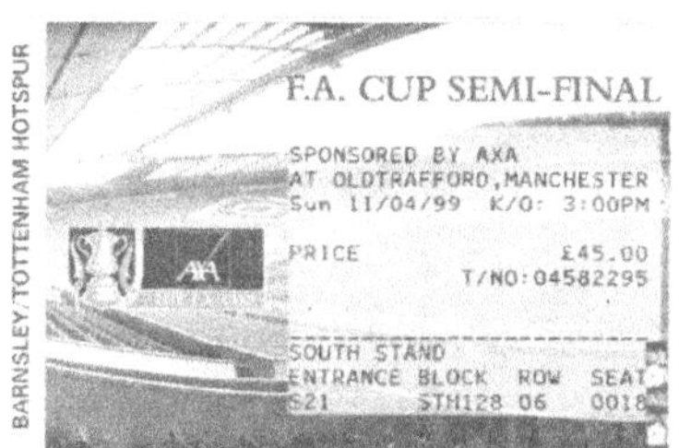

11 April 1999
Newcastle United – FA Cup

8 April 2001
Arsenal – FA Cup

9 January 2002
Chelsea – Worthington Cup

24 February 2002
Blackburn Rovers – Worthington Cup

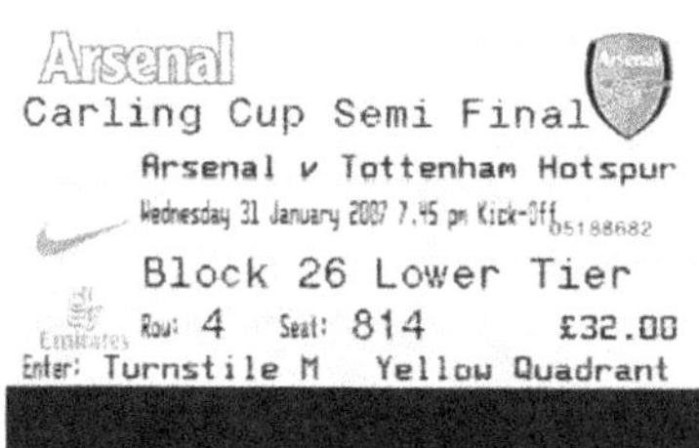

31 January 2007
Arsenal – Carling Cup

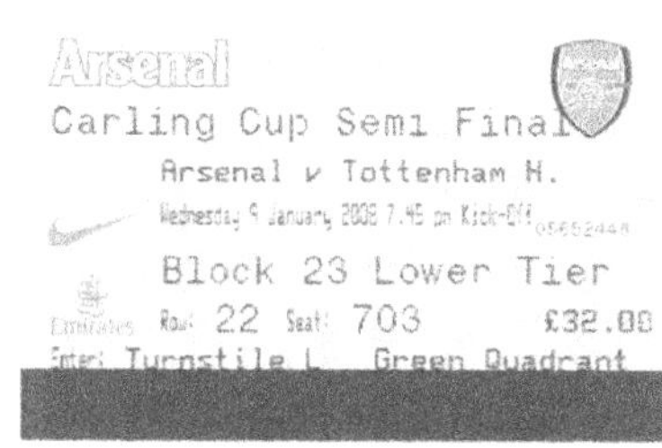

9 January 2008
Arsenal – Carling Cup

24 February 2008
Chelsea – Carling Cup

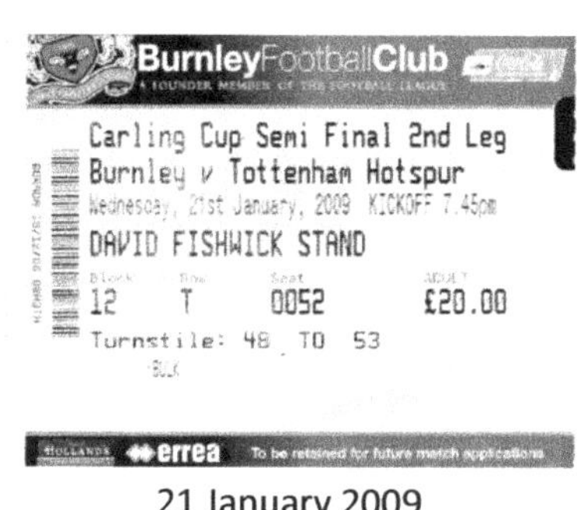

21 January 2009
Burnley – Carling Cup

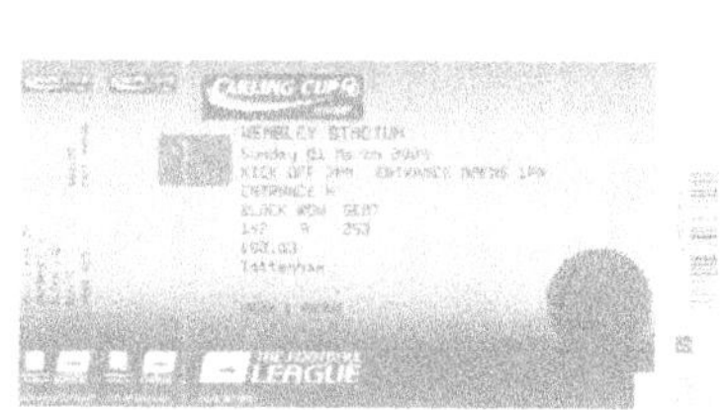

1 March 2009
Manchester United – Carling Cup

TICKETS

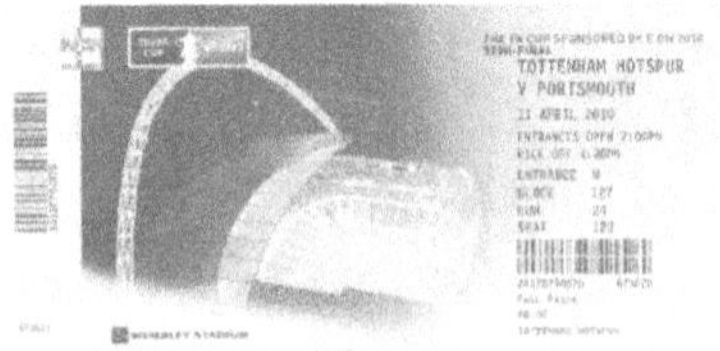

11 April 2010
Portsmouth – FA Cup

15 April 2012
Chelsea – FA Cup

29 January 2015
Sheffield United – Capital One Cup

1 March 2015
Chelsea – Capital One Cup

22 April 2017
Chelsea – FA Cup

21 April 2018
Manchester United – FA Cup

24 January 2019
Chelsea – Carabao Cup

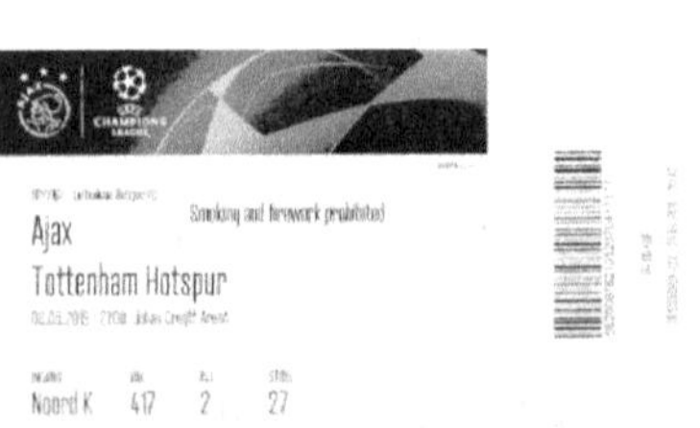

8 May 2019
Ajax – Champions League

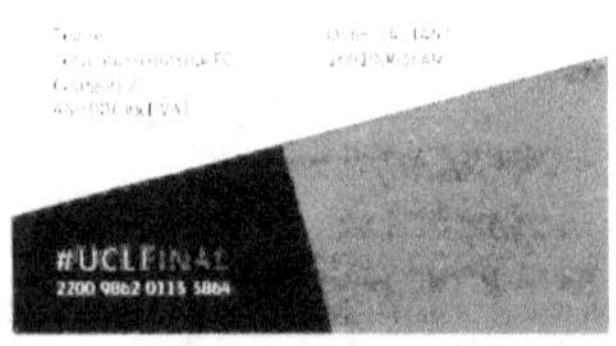

1 June 2019
Liverpool - Champions League

TICKETS

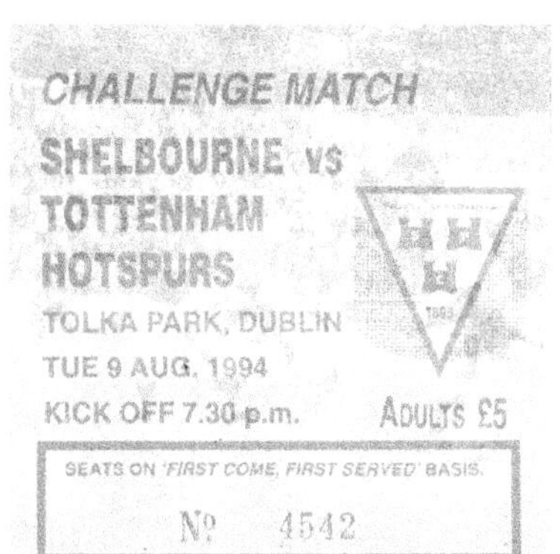

9 August 1994
Shelbourne

21 May 1995
Eastern/Kitchee Select

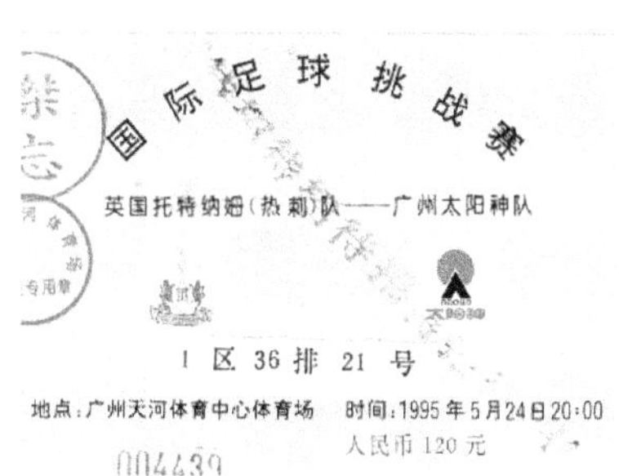

24 May 1995
Guangzhou

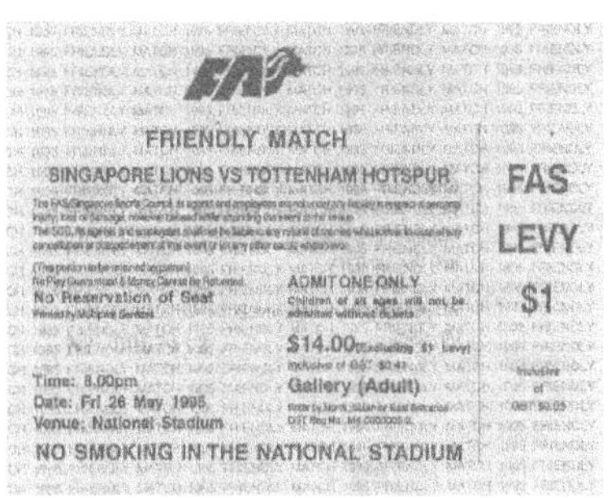

26 May 1995
Singapore Lions

22 July 1995
Silkeborg

24 July 1995
IFK Götebog

29 July 1995
Sampdoria

25 July 1996
Odd Grenland

17 July 1997
Faaberg

10 July 1998
Grasshopper Club

5 August 1998
De Tubanters

15 July 1999
IF Elfsborg

TICKETS

OFFICIAL OPENING OF WOODSIDE PARK
BISHOP'S STORTFORD
V
TOTTENHAM HOTSPUR XI
FRIDAY 3RD SEPTEMBER 1999
KICK-OFF 7.45PM
GROUND ADMISSION
ADULTS £8.00 CONCESSIONS £4.00

3 September 1999
Bishop's Stortford

19 July 2000
Skellefteå AIK

12 August 2001
AEK

4 March 2003
Bohemian

14 May 2003
DC United

26 July 2003
Orlando Pirates

29 July 2003
Kaizer Chiefs

15 July 2004
FC Copenhagen

ESTADIO OLÍMPICO de SEVILLA
Kappa CUP

5 August 2004
Partizan Belgrade

20 May 2005
Club M

16 July 2005
Boca Juniors

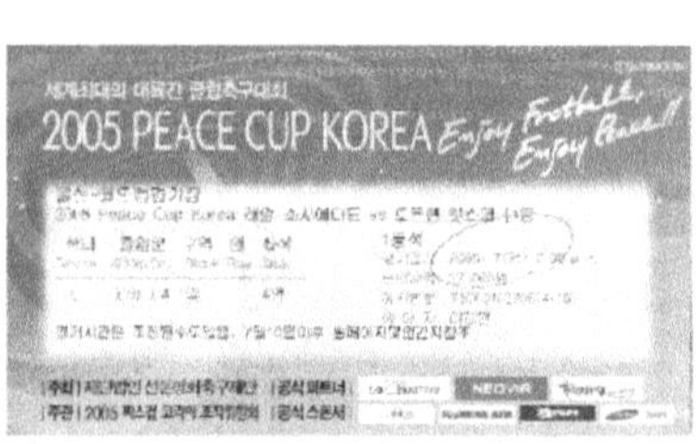

21 July 2005
Real Sociedad

TICKETS

14 July 2006
OGC Nice

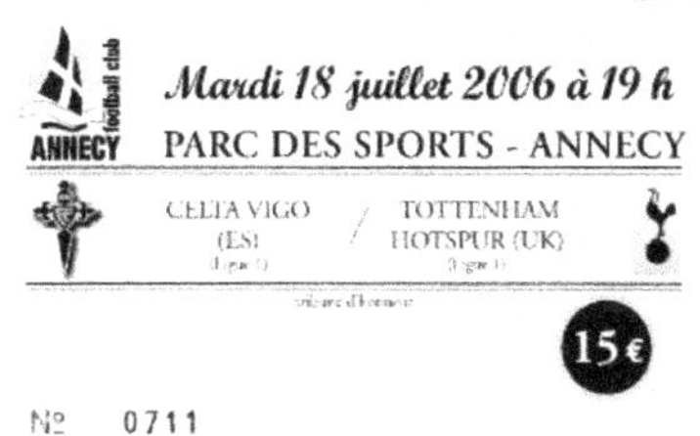

18 July 2006
Celta Vigo

5 August 2006
Borussia Dortmund

12 July 2007
St Patrick's Athletic

28 July 2007
Orlando Pirates

31 July 2009
Hull City

2 August 2009
South China

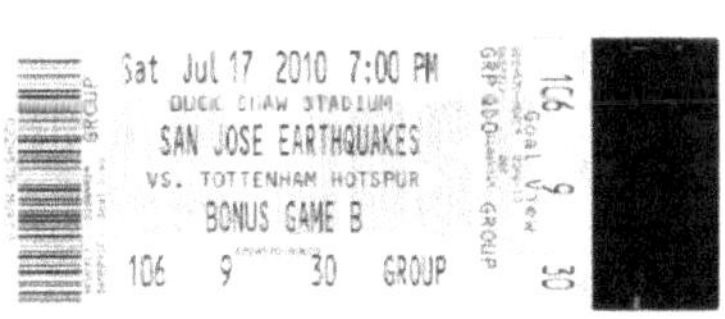

17 July 2010
San Jose Earthquakes

22 July 2010
New York Red Bulls

3 August 2010
Benfica

16 July 2011
Kaizer Chiefs

24 July 2012
LA Galaxy

28 July 2012
Liverpool

9 August 2012
Valencia

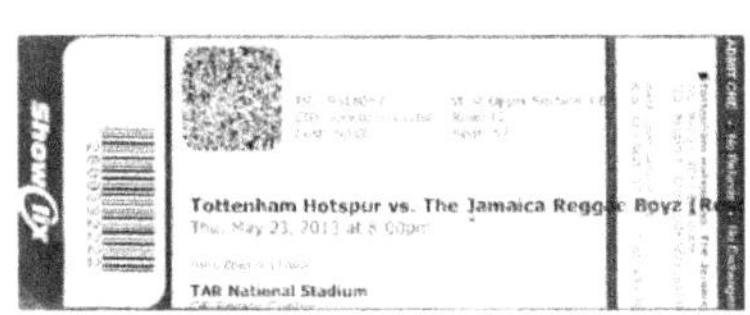

23 May 2013
Jamaica Reggae Boys

TICKETS

27 July 2013
South China

3 August 2013
Monaco

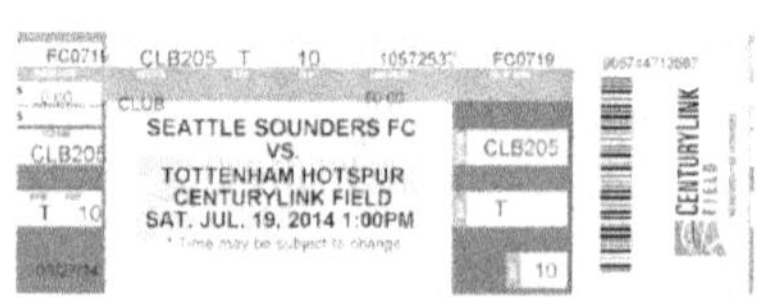

19 July 2014
Seattle Sounders

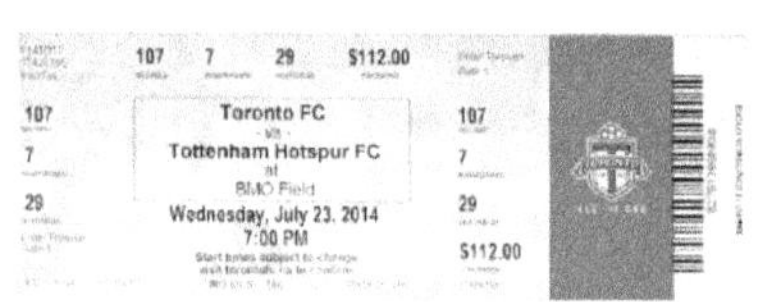

23 July 2014
Toronto

2 August 2014
Celtic

27 May 2015
Malaysia XI

29 July 2105
MLS All Stars

5 August 2015
AC Milan

26 July 2016
Juventus

5 August 2016
Internazionale

26 May 2017
Kitchee

29 July 2017
Manchester City

4 August 2018
Girona

21 July 2019
Juventus

25 July 2019
Manchester United

How The Cup Was Won – 1901

How The Cup Was Won – 1921

and

The Spurs Alphabet

are still available on www.lulu.com

www.ingramcontent.com/pod-product-compliance
Lightning Source LLC
LaVergne TN
LVHW060510100826
845148LV00006B/949

* 9 7 8 0 9 5 4 0 4 3 4 4 5 *